Evolving Spirituality

William J. Hague

Evolving

Spirituality

Department of Educational Psychology
University of Alberta

Cataloguing in Publication

Hague, William J., 1932-
    Evolving spirituality

Includes bibliographical references and index.
ISBN 0-88864-915-0

    1. Psychology, Religous. 2. Moral development. 3.
Psychology and religion. I. University of Alberta. Dept. of
Educational Psychology. II. Title
BL53.H33 1995   200'.1'9   C95-910080-6

Production and Design: Bayard Typesetting & Editing

Cover Design: Ray Au, Graphic Design Services, University of Alberta

Cover Photograph: Ian Edwards

Printed by: Quality Color Press Inc.

Dedication

> *To the three stars of the constellation*
> *Family*
>> *Rose Marie, Carolyn and Daniel,*
>> *risen above my horizon*
>> *not only to grace the time*
>> *but to signify direction for a journey*

Contents

Preface

My story is written on shorelines of Cambrian seas,
Engraved on rocks under ancient ice.
It is vast; I small
Its time endless; mine not so
nevertheless
It is my story.

This is written in the mountains. The stream that rushes past my campsite tumbles to the Pacific. Not too far away, another brook sets out for the Atlantic. This place is called the Great Divide. It has for aeons been a dividing place. It was long ago the shoreline separating land and sea. There was an explosion of living things here in the beginnings of the earth. Five hundred, thirty million years ago, strange creatures slithered and swam, walked and wobbled here in warm, tropical seas. All perished, most leaving no line; some left only delicate impressions of their mysterious presence as fragile bodies in the sand of a collapsing primeval shore. Stopped suddenly in their time, they were somehow cherished by the earth and later lifted up through enormous powers over more aeons to mountain heights far above the old seas. Some of them had primitive backbones—something like the strong, supple ones humans have today.

People live here now in little villages. Trains trundle over the Great Divide with wheat for China and autos from Japan; buses full of tourists pass through the valleys. Some see the mountains only behind glass; others stop to wonder. What are we? Where do we come from? Where are we going? Mystery.

This place is a dividing place;
There is a terrible beauty here.
It is not to be passed over lightly.

This is not a book of paleontology; it is a book of psychology. As such it needs a context, a place both personal and objective. The place of psychology is within the living drama of process, a process of today but rich with the resources of "before" and open to the possibilities of "not yet." A sense of time and place is important in life and in psychology. Where I am is an outcome of where I have been and where I intend to go. It is my continuing story; it is also the story of the cosmos. Recently we have been reminded (sometimes sharply by catastrophes) of our interconnectedness not only with other humans but with our planet earth. Psychology can be enriched by this awareness; morality is full of it, and religion, especially as it reaches out into its spiritual dimensions, can be enlightened by a new parable responding to the ancient question "Who is my neighbor?"

This book is an attempt to describe how humans who reflect on their spiritual breathing, their psyche, can not only exist but participate and contribute to the larger process. This call to be participant in the bettering of evolution is a moral dimension unique (at least in our awareness) to our time. Its urgency challenges religion to ascend to new heights. Religion has sometimes, weighed down by too much baggage, been reluctant to respond. Sometimes, going against its mandate, it is divisive, cutting person from person, community from community, nation from nation. When it does this it is more a cleaver than a "great divide." Our quest in this book is, instead, for the heights of land where clouds and mountains meet in mystery (perhaps even in chaos!). There we search for order, pattern, beauty, meaning, goodness. That it can be found there by religion at its best is the backbone of this book.

This book is intended to replace *New Perspectives on Religious and Moral Development* (Hague, 1986) now out of print. Although in some chapters it incorporates materials from the older book (chapters 2, 3, 4, 6, 7, 9, and 12), these have been expanded and brought up to date, while additional chapters (1 and 14) have been added to provide introductions to the interrelationship of religion, spirituality, and morality (chapter 1) and to take them farther afield in dealing with contemporary appreciations and addressing today's religious and moral challenges. Chapters 10, 11, and 13 celebrate the rebirth of an invigorated understanding of character education, while chapter 13, "Toward a Moral Spirituality for Our Time," seeks answers to how awareness of our human and ecological interconnectedness can develop to the maturity of responsible moral action.

The principal psychological theory behind this book is again Dabrowski's theory of Positive Disintegration, concentrated in a newly written chapter (5) that I hope explains this complex theory as lucidly as possible without shortcutting its depths. If, as research indicates, people who come to high levels of development are clearly aware of the spiritual, then Dabrowski's multilevel approach offers an avenue for study of religious and moral development. When this grand theory of human development at its highest levels is not evident explicitly, with its phoenix mystery it still permeates the whole of this work. The poet Nelly Sachs invites us to participate:

Press, oh press in the day of destruction
The listening ear to the earth.
And you will hear through your sleep
You will hear,
How in death
Life begins.

Kicking Horse Pass, Yoho, July 1994

Introduction

Always the beautiful answer who asks a more beautiful question.
　　　　　　　　　　　　　　　　　　　　—e.e. cummings

After teaching a course in the psychology of religious and moral development for a few years, I had a new insight. It occurred to me one fine spring day, when other things were growing too, that, basic to the content of the course, yet sometimes not expressed or even consciously appreciated by myself or all my students, were certain unspoken themes, a hidden curriculum, behind it all. The "facts" were there in the course outline, but questions lingered like "Why these facts and not others?" "What's there and what's missing?" "What presumptions are behind it all?" These were questions I had not really asked, and students were often too polite to press. So I sat down on that warm spring afternoon to uncover this hidden curriculum.

What came of these ruminations was a list of presuppositions and a record of roads already taken that were now setting the directions of the course. The list initially was short. But over the years, and following many eager class discussions, the items on the list evolved, meshed, merged, and new ones emerged until, on the first day of each new term, I could hand my students a paper revealing what I thought was behind the course outline. The paper came to be entitled "Ten Tenets Tentatively but Tenaciously Tendered." The stunning beauty of this subtle use of alliteration was lost on a few of my students over the years, but the substance of the tenets gave some indication of where I was as we began the course and challenged them to reflect on where they were personally regarding religion and morality. I think I owe you, the readers of this book, a similar manifestation of underlying themes, presumptions, roads taken, and roads not taken before you make the investment of choices and begin to read. I promise (with some small exceptions) to spare you any annoying attempts at alliteration, even though such alternatives may be allowable at all times. I would then, here at the beginning when all is fresh, dig a good bit beneath the topsoil and reveal what lies below the surface. These are some of the major presuppositions of what is to follow.

First, a word about a word. The word *perspective* is, I think, important when trying to understand both religion and morality. Perspective tells us what is near and what is far; it tells us something about proportions, what is important, and what is less important or even trivial. With a sense of proportion we can set our values so they become the stars by which we steer our lives. Religion at its best gives perspective on what is of greatest value. I could go on, but these words clipped from a newspaper tell it much more poignantly:

Cancer death shows need to put life in perspective

On Sept. 22 a young woman passed away suddenly in the night after a brief but valiant struggle with a deadly cancer.

With her hopes and dreams within sight, and the realization and anticipation of the future she had so dearly longed for almost in her grasp, she was taken. The devastating grief of this tragic injustice begs for an answer to "why?" By what cruel fate has a loving compassionate, beautiful mother been claimed?

How can such a rare individual, a model of selflessness, be denied her small dream? These unanswerable questions are asked many thousands of times each day.

There are several observations that can be drawn from this cruel violation of what should have been, but two stand out above the rest. First, this horrible group of diseases called cancer need to be stopped....

Second, and at least as important, is that all of us who are families and friends of the unfortunate victims of this insidious disease need to gain something from the grief we all feel at the human loss.

It is a painful lesson to have to experience this loss in order to realize the importance of doing all we can to stay close to the people we care about. Get rid of the trivial bickering and get life in perspective. Dump the pursuit of material gain at any cost, do away with the greed, the insensitivity, the selfishness. Realize what is of real value.

The people we might take for granted may not be there tomorrow, and unexpected loss of someone you love is an emotionally devastating and brutally painful experience. Love them while you can, and don't stop. I know. The young woman who was so recently and so tragically taken was soon to be my wife. Simon Burns (*Edmonton Journal*, October 1, 1993)

Someone has said, "There are two kinds of people in this world: those who divide everything into two and those who do not." In presenting my approach to the psychology of religious and moral development, I have tried to be one of "those who do not." In other words, I have attempted a holistic approach, taking into account the whole human person in process, trying to avoid as much as possible those dichotomies like body-soul, natural-supernatural, reason-emotion, and even religious-moral. Dichotomies are neat ways we use to try to understand the human psyche. Sometimes they are helpful, but whether they correspond to anything in reality is another question. Sometimes, I think, they are something we force upon reality for our own convenience, but then get caught up in them, and are led to see separation, antagonism, and conflict within the human person that is not really there. I have tried to emphasize the essential unity of human nature, of all nature in fact, seeing it as organic and whole.

One of the themes that flows from this holistic approach and runs through this book is that of convergence. Teilhard de Chardin, if he did not use the exact words, at least expressed the beautiful idea: "All that rises must converge." You will find these words, rich with meaning, sometimes on the surface, sometimes buried deep within this book. Throughout your reading you will find my images (and I hope your own), and the image here is one of ascending spirals merging, flowing together. There is a flowing together in the process of the universe so that all that evolves to higher levels, while becoming more complex within itself, more individually developed, becomes, paradoxically, more at one with others and integrated in itself. True individuality, true diversity, is creative of unity and oneness. This, I propose, is the major thrust of individual religious and moral development. It is anagogic; its aim is to ascend higher. As an individual moves through the ascending spirals of human development, the religion that is part of this development becomes more potent in creating a unity and oneness with other human beings, with all creation, and with God. The same is true of religion as a social phenomenon. Religions may degenerate from the mystic, unitive vision of their founder into power politics. In place of noting similarities and encouraging unity they may emphasize divisions, differences, and distinctions. Their structure is not the ascending circle of the spiral, but a rigid hierarchical triangle. Vital religions, on the other hand, thrive on the flow and process of community, which is their bloodstream.

The same flowing together is evident in another mainstream beneath the surface of this book. It is the convergence in recent years between religion and science, particularly the science of psychology. There never really should have been any enmity between the two of them in the first place. Science truly concerned with whatever is true would see religion as friend and mapmaker, giving the bigger picture, the overall view, perspective on the factual. Religion, playing its role of perspective-giving, and not embroiled in sectarianism, power struggles, and other pursuits more worthy of politics than religion, would have seen science as an ally with something to give to enrich the religious view. It would have been a mutually enriching relationship, for science has often been more in need of support and guidance than condemnation, especially condemnation stemming from ignorance, threat, and fear of the unknown. But it is my contention that both religion and science have grown up, developed over the last few years. And because they have risen to new levels they have converged, and we enter now into an exciting era of cooperation and mutual growth for religion and science, including the science of psychology, of course. As a result we can say: "Good religion is good psychology, and good psychology is good religion."

Obvious by now is the conviction behind all this that the world is not a static place or even some gigantic clock, once set in motion and ticking on now with the precision and predictability of a perfect machine. No, the world is not static, or even machine-like. If it is organic, it is in process. The universe is still being built, and all beings involved in that process are called upon to contribute to it. This book is an attempt to put religion and spirituality in a process context—the vast context of an evolving universe. As part of the organic whole of creation, human beings with their higher levels of consciousness and free will are called to contribute value to the building of the universe. That religion has something to say about the nature of such things is an evident theme by now. That religion has something to say about how we should contribute to that process is an idea that will lead us to understanding how religion and morality flow together.

Before you have read far into this book you will find the word *levels* used frequently and the term *multilevelness* cropping up over and over again. That is because it is my conviction that a multilevel approach to anything (psychology, religion, and morality included) opens up new paradigms for understanding and new skills for diving to great depths within the currents of process. Hopefully, you will find this important concept of multilevelness adequately introduced at the appropriate place.

The multilevel paradigm steers us away from the narrowing approach that says there is only one right way to be religious. On the contrary, this book is about the varieties of religious experience, going a step beyond by maintaining that religion is not something added to human nature as a nice alternative like an optional part that a car buyer may or may not add onto his purchase. Religion in its vast variety of forms is integral to human nature at all levels. All human beings are religious in some sense of the word; they just practice their religion at their level of development. It will be our task to distinguish and explore these levels from the lowest abuses of the word *religion* to the highest levels of its actualization. If we want to know what religion is supposed to be, the best religion, we should look at those persons who have reached the highest levels of human development, for they epitomize the qualities of true religion and true morality.

I do not pretend that what follows in this book is a study of comparative religions. It does not study very many specific sects or religions. This is a limitation, and in some respects a deficiency, for I am sure it would have been a richer study of the varieties of religious experience had its author not been limited in his knowledge of history and comparative religions. Instead it is primarily a psychological study, seeking to find some depth in philosophy and theology, especially Christian theology. Those of you from other religious traditions will, I hope, be gracious enough to accept these limitations.

Certainly this book is not based on the all-too-prevalent idea in some religious circles that human nature is essentially evil; nor is it based on cynicism about humanity or, on the other hand, a naive optimism. It is founded rather on a belief that humans can transcend themselves because there are transcendent dimensions within the human personality, and that it is the primary role of religion and morality to explore and develop these dimensions.

The passages through life toward these higher levels are not spontaneous and easy, demanding no conflict or pain. It seems a basic paradigm of creation that ecstasy comes only with agony, that tears and joy mix, that only effort leads to triumph, that pain and birth are one, that life and death dance together at the stillpoint of the turning earth. My own experiences, my relationships as a counselor with people in distress, have led me to believe that all these paradoxes abound in the human journey. Surrounded by pain and ugliness, and frequently because of pain and ugliness, the will toward health and growth is vibrant in the human heart, and life springs forth out of the most unlikely situations. Religion is there nurturing this life, not by giving reasons, not by always answering the question "Why?" but by helping with the question "How?" And that is how, again, religion flows on into morality, and, lofty as it is, speaks to the most practical of realities.

Another item buried quite deep within the hidden agenda of this book is a tendency to emphasize the role of emotion in human development. This is contrary to mainstream psychology, which has stressed the study of cognition. I emphasize emotion for two reasons: (a) Cognition has had more than its share of attention by psychologists. This is because an ancient philosophical tradition has for centuries given a preeminent place to the controlling powers of intellect, and because cognitive factors have seemed easier for a behavioristic psychology to measure. Psychological literature is full of cognitivistic studies; only recently has emotion begun to capture wide interest and respectability as the proper subject of science. (b) I believe that the aspect of the human psyche that we parcel out and label as emotion, feeling, passion has a large and respectable part to play in human development: large, because feeling is a pervasive thing and a powerful force in human decision making; respectable, because emotions, passions at their higher levels, are as good or better guides to objectivity than cool intellect, which for so long has held the center stage of objectivity and thus respectability.

It is pleasant to go on like this, making dogmatic statements without a shred of evidence. But perhaps it is time to conclude this introduction with a few more personal remarks. Throughout this book you will find many metaphors of mountains, trees, and rivers. That is because I live not far from the Rocky Mountains of Alberta and was fortunate as a child to travel through them in old steam trains that huffed and puffed their way over high mountain passes, and then trundled heavily down to the Pacific. I learned to love and be impressed by the beauty and proportions of those mountains from my parents, particularly my mother who was perhaps the first to put mountains and life in perspective for me. Behind it all was my father whose sensitive nature I have come to realize only now taught me that it is all right for a man to have feelings and to care. In later years I was fortunate too to climb among the crags and to feel a real relationship with the old twisted trees that clung to the windswept mountainsides. They seemed an image of human suffering. But, with their tenacity and vigor, they modeled human endeavor and vitality too. I have seen mountain rivers rushing to the sea and noted the swirling eddies, brief occasions in the process but integral to the system. I have seen shimmering white mountains mirrored in calm blue-green lakes, broken only by the jump of a tiny fish or a squirrel coming for a drink, and that has told me something about the perspective of space and the dimensions of a man within the universe. I have climbed over rocks that were there long before me and will be there long after me, and that has said something about the perspective of time in my brief life. That is why you must forgive me if I bring my friends the mountains into my psychology. They have been good to me. They are beautiful. Perhaps I can acknowledge that beauty and give back to them something of what they have given me.

And now a word about you, the reader. Who do I visualize you to be? An ordinary, everyday human being, probably a university student interested in religion and morality, and bringing to your study all the "baggage" of your past experiences with religion and morality. Some of you will, I know, affirm that you are already devoutly religious and even certain of your own personal salvation. Others, like a Saturday afternoon shopper, will say, "Just looking, thank you," and move on. Still others will deny that you are religious and insist that you gave up all that years ago when you got away from home and finally grew up. Do I see you as a religious and moral person? Yes. But not necessarily in any sense of belonging to some specific religion or being sure of your moral principles. I see you as religious in that, by even opening a book about religion and morality, you have taken some steps in a quest for meaning, perspective, and responsibility in your life.

I hope this book is something with which all of you, male and female, can identify. Authors are currently called upon to write in a nonsexist style. Sometimes this can be done smoothly; sometimes it leads to contortion and clumsiness of language, distracting from the content. If you do not always find male and female acknowledged in the form of this book, I hope you will find both the masculine and feminine experience of religion and morality always acknowledged and frequently celebrated in its content.

Some years ago when I first started teaching, I felt a need, a moral responsibility, to cover everything I could in a course and to give as many answers as I could to important questions. Since then I have met many of my "old" students who greet me with a statement such as: "I always remember what you said about ..." Invariably it is something I don't remember saying (like "Yes, life is messy"), maybe because it did not seem important at the time. But the understanding the student had was what made it important and meaningful to him or her. This is what the great teachers have been telling us all along: Teaching is not transfer of knowledge where everything depends on the teacher. Teaching is exposure to greatness, and the greatness, even if it is not in the teacher, may still be in the questions asked. It is this "meeting over great questions" that makes education great. The questions of religion and morality are great. In the process this meeting is an occasion to which you bring the specialness of yourself and your questions, asked not just of the teacher but of life itself. Perhaps the German poet Rilke is best here:

Toward all that is unsolved in your heart.
Be patient
Try to love the questions.
Do not seek the answers which cannot be given
You would not be able to live them.

Live everything
Live the questions now
You will then gradually without noticing it
Live into the answers
Some distant day.

May this study of religion, spirituality, and morality be an occasion in which you learn to love the questions themselves and sometimes experience the beauty of an answer.

Beyond Study

The utterances of the heart—unlike those of the discriminating intellect—always relate to the whole. The heartstrings sing like an Aeolian harp only to the gentle breath of a premonitory mood, which does not drown the song but listens. What the heart hears are the great things that span our whole lives, the experiences which we do nothing to arrange but which we ourselves open to.
                    —Carl Jung (Psychological Reflections)

At this point, I would like to drop into a deeper, more subjective approach to religion and morality. Most of the above is pretty heady stuff. But religion and morality are matters of the heart too. I invite you now to look into your own feelings, appreciating there the full spectrum of emotional coloring that can enrich our understanding of spirituality and morality

The scene is Venice. Two dauntless shoppers, my daughter Carolyn and I, are wending our way through narrow streets and over arched bridges in search of the perfect Venetian crystal. We are out to buy; the only question is, "Which color?" We had seen thousands of them in the store windows, flashing rainbows at us—each crystal different. After much discussion at a shop window, comparing the merits of radiant red with cool green, we decide on a brilliant blue, merging into violet. We enter the store to claim our prize. I lift the crystal carefully from its place in the window. The blue disappears. The crystal is just clear glass. So are all the other crystals in the store—just clear glass! Our carefully chosen color has gone. But Carolyn, from her vantage point three feet below my eye level, cries out: "Look Dad; hold it up to the light. It's red and orange and yellow and green and blue—all the colors of the rainbow. All the colors are in our crystal!"

Few words are so emotionally loaded as *religion* and *morality*. When you put the two words together, the emotional temperature rises even more. Religion and morality are words laden with a great deal of our emotional baggage. Think of the word *family*. It is not an abstract term for most of us, but a concrete word, loaded with the experiences, the memories, the values—the emotional baggage—that we associate with our own experiences of family. So too religion and morality are words that for most of us symbolize our experiences with religion, our personal conceptions of morality. Because these impressions are concrete, vivid, and emotion-laden, it is difficult to find anyone who can remain truly indifferent when either of these topics crops up. It is still more difficult to imagine why anyone *should* be indifferent.

This makes for great difficulty in talking about religion and morality. Because we often reach into the depths of our subjective selves and come up with impressions and feelings that are deeply personal, we tend to talk to others about our subjective experience, and because we are using the same words as others use, we presume these words mean the same thing to them. But your concept of religion, for example, may date back to your childhood experiences in Sunday school, and you may see religion as an ecclesiastical organization stifling in its dogmatism. I, on the other hand, may see religion as a liberating, purely personal experience gained most easily by a good shot of drugs. Thus we each use the same word but are miles apart in our meanings. We cannot communicate until we come to some sort of mutual understanding, until we free ourselves as much as possible of that personal baggage that prejudices the meanings of these words.

We cannot communicate about religion and morality until we are willing to take up new perspectives. You will notice I have said "new perspectives" and not "definitions." It is tempting when we want to communicate to try to create a definition, but definitions are not the answer here. Definitions are elusive and illusory. They depend on other words that themselves slip and slide about in their meanings. They are illusory because they give us a false sense of security, a sense that, once we have pinned them down with a definition, we can fully understand concepts and experiences with our minds alone. Something perhaps more perfidious about definitions is that they tend to kill their subject. Defining is something like catching and pinning a butterfly to a table, dissecting its parts, classifying them, and then proclaiming an understanding of what a butterfly is. We forget that such a process involves killing the butterfly first. A definition used in this manner leaves out what is most important about a butterfly—that to be a butterfly it must live. Definitions, in their attempt to be precise often leave out the vitality, the complexity, the beauty, the uniqueness of each occasion and the process of each existence.

Should we then give up hope of communicating about anything so individual as the experience of religion, anything so vital and personal as the conduct of morality? Certainly not. If the answer is not to rush into definitions, neither is it to say that one cannot communicate with another on such a subjective topic. The answer lies, I think, in seeing these topics for what they are: immensely complex, multilayered, multifaceted, vital experiences of mankind. The more we appreciate the complexity of concepts, the more we are forced to look at them from various perspectives. Perhaps the word *multifaceted* is the best introduction to a metaphor. Any important concept is multifaceted like a cut diamond or a crystal. Looked at from one angle it flashes red, from another it flashes blue; that is why to get at what a diamond is you turn it round and round, cocking your head from side to side to get new glimpses of the whole spectrum of colors coming through. And you come to realize it is not just red or blue or yellow; it carries all the colors of the spectrum, and yet paradoxically it is none of them for it is perfectly clear. This is an appreciation we would never have had if we had kept our static view, if we had not stretched for new perspectives and thereby appreciated the complexity, the multifacetedness, the changeability of the diamond in new light. Once we see reality as *complex, multileveled,* and *in process,* we know it demands of us an appreciation from more than one perspective.

Part I

Chapter 1

The Way Ahead

At the beginning of a trip, a good guide gives his or her companions a map to describe the country ahead: where they are going, how they will get there, and what to look for along the way. At the beginning of this journey through the psychology of religious and moral development, I owe you a map to outline the route, to assign purpose, and give perspective on what lies ahead.

First, this is a psychology book. Psychology is much more than its stereotypes: the picture of Freud soberly analyzing a neurotic client lying on a couch in a dark room cluttered with strange icons from foreign worlds. Psychology is much more than any kind of mere analysis of people. That is only one small part of it. The whole picture is much more. A good way of getting at the whole picture is to look at the origins of the word *psychology* itself. Interestingly, the word comes from sources rich with an appreciation of the human person as a being replete with many, many aspects. For those of us interested in the psychology of religion, it is doubly interesting that the word psychology has in its origins a spiritual meaning. Scholars in the 18th century made the word up out of two Greek words: *psyche* and *logos*. The *ology* part means a study of something. The psyche part (the Greek word for "breath") indicates that we are interested in something about human beings that cannot be grasped like the physical, but seems no less real. We call it the spiritual. As is so often true with many of our words, it all goes back to the ancient Greeks. Psyche was a character in Greek mythology, often portrayed with butterfly wings to show that her movements were quick and light. She moved like a breath of wind or, better, like a human breath coming from deep within. The Greeks acknowledged that there is more to the human person than just the physical; they saw that, like a breath, the human spirit comes invisibly from the mysterious depths within the person. So they named it psyche or spirit. Psychology is at heart a study of the whole human being, but particularly from the aspect of that which goes beyond and transcends the physical. Physiology takes care of the physical; psychology addresses a something that, although we can know only its effects, like dandelion seeds on the wind, we are convinced is real; not only real but of the essence of being human. In fact, this psyche, although based in blood and brain and nerve, in some ways has the potential to transcend the physical. The psyche is the breath of life that we often call "spiritual."

The particular kind of psychology that this book uses is *developmental* psychology. That means that the approach is especially interested in human beings as they grow and change. Thus it does not specialize in mental illness or statistics or experiments with rats, but in the process of humans unfolding through time and growth into becoming whole, integral beings. Development is the process of becoming fully what one can be. Another word is *integrating*—becoming integral, whole. Developmental psychology is concerned with the process of integrating.

It seems, then, that psychology should be a particularly good way of understanding religion, which is concerned primarily with spiritual matters and ultimately with the whole person. A basic premise on which this book is built is that a psychology of religion must be holistic, not just picking out parts of persons like the body or soul and concentrating on one as if it were everything. Nor does an adequate religious psychology set up rigid dichotomies. Dichotomies tend to get oversimplified into saying, "A is just the opposite of B," and, moreover, "A and B are, by their very nature, at war with each other." Some religious people have done this: setting up a warlike antagonism between body and soul, for example. This dichotomy tends to get oversimplified as one (the soul usually) being good, and the other (the body) bad. A holistic view tends to look at things as coming together when they are healthy to form a whole. The view is one that looks for cooperation and partnership in a beautiful and good system—like a rose with its blossoms and its thorns, each having a role in supporting a good and beautiful totality.

This very idea of partnership in place of opposition between religion and psychology has recently emerged as a contemporary fact. However, as we will see, there hasn't always been a friendly cooperation between psychology and religion, partly because psychology in the last century, emulating the physical sciences, separated from its ancient ally, religion, in an effort to describe behavior purely in materialistic terms. Some religions, on the other hand, denounced this kind of modern psychology as materialistic and Godless. Fortunately, both psychology and religious institutions have come recently to appreciate what each has to offer the other. The social sciences, led by the physical sciences, especially physics, have adopted a less arrogant view of their ability to measure all things, finding for themselves the spiritual dimensions that religion has traditionally pointed to. Religious leaders, holding back on their previous, too quick condemnations, have come to appreciate the potential of psychology to understand religious and spiritual things. As a result, both religion and psychology have been enriched. Thus, in this book, we can celebrate the reconvergence of religion and psychology in their common concern: the human spirit.

This common concern is strengthened by new and deeper understandings of what we mean by religion. Religion is something that most of us have experienced in one way or another—in our home, in our school, in our church or synagogue or temple, or simply in our observations from a

distance of people who call themselves religious. We each have our personal experience of religion that colors our idea of what it is. If you are
talking to ten people and use the word *religion*, you can count on at least ten
different understandings. One will see religion as a source of security and
comfort learned in the home. Another will see it as a kind of threatening
tyranny demanding an awful price in humanness. One will see it as the
assured road to truth; another as the haven of narrow-mindedness and
bigotry. Whatever the view, there is usually emotion involved. Because it
strikes deep into our spiritual being, religion is usually surrounded with
strong feeling. A religious debate heats up quite quickly. This is appropriate,
for to those who take it seriously much is at stake: beliefs, values, family and
cultural traditions, life meaning, even self-esteem.

Travellers usually bring along some baggage. It contains some essentials
and a lot of "stuff." The same is true of those who explore religion and
morality. We all carry a certain load of preconceptions we gathered as we
grew up about the nature of religion, the existence and nature of God, about
morality and how one actually lives a good life. Before travelling it is good
to check through our personal baggage for the essentials. It will help in
understanding not only the topic, but ourselves, and it will help in communicating with others. To facilitate this, the page at the end of this chapter
contains three short work sheets that call you to reflect on your own personal
ideas and feelings about religion, about God, and about morality. They also
invite you to reflect on how you came by these thoughts and feelings.
Because emotions run strong in all three topics, you are asked to reflect not
just on abstract ideas or dogmas, but on the feelings that go along with
them—feelings that may well go back to childhood even before the concepts
were fully understood. The idea is to dig around not just in your head, but in
your soul, and see what's there. You can write notes right in the book if you
wish or on separate pieces of paper, or, preferably, on the first pages of a
small notebook. This could be the beginning of a personal, spiritual journal!

Two Meanings

This book tries to get at the idea of religion by looking at it first from two
possible perspectives. Religion may be understood in one way as something
organizational—belonging to a religious organization, and as such more a
sociological term denoting membership in a group. Membership in a religion
generally includes the three major dimensions of a religious group, the three
C's: Creed—a set of beliefs, Code—an array of moral rules, and Cult—a
collection of ritual practices. When we use the word religion it usually has
this first meaning of belonging to a denomination. Sometimes this is called
organized religion. This does not imply that any other kind of religion is
disorganized, only that it is more individual.

The second meaning of the word religion does not emphasize belonging
to a particular group; it can be understood as a personal search for the

transcendent, for what goes beyond the everyday, short-term, immediate to the experience of living in all the dimensions of being human, transcending the immediate for an appreciation of the larger picture of one's own life—the "more beyond" that usually takes shape in the form of meaning and purpose in life, the great themes of the vast drama in which one is by birth invited to take a role. This broader experience is usually called spirituality—the sense and practice of the numinous, the mysterious, that which is too great to fully comprehend—the transcendent. When we have the vision to look beyond the material, we find the spiritual. This transcendent dimension can be found outside the person or within. It is a sense or awareness of the transcendent in life in both broad and personal dimensions.

Spirituality may find expression in religion; religion at its best will be deeply spiritual, but spirituality is quite distinct from organizational religion. Organizations set boundaries: those who are "in" and those who are "out," the believers and the nonbelievers, the faithful and the heretics, sometimes even going so far as claiming to know who are "the saved" and "the damned." "Spirituality has nothing to do with boundaries. Only the material can be bounded," say Kurtz and Ketcham (1994, p. 24) in a book that reminds us that a spiritual person is not a perfect person. No one is perfect. The spiritual has been used since ancient times in contrast to the material. Because we cannot see or touch or adequately describe the numinous, the mysterious, makes it no less real. We can know more than we can say. The transcendent is simply that which is too great to fully comprehend—but real. This transcendent dimension can be found outside the person or within. It is a *sense* or awareness of the "more" in life in both broad and personal dimensions.

A full spirituality does not stop with cozy, comfortable feelings or mystic, rapturous experiences. It affects our behavior. It is the *practice* of the transcendent insofar as spirituality, like religion, addresses questions of worthwhileness and value. When these values impose a sense of obligation we are into how one ought to behave—morals. Mature spirituality moves one to some kind of action; often this is moral action.

At their best, both religion and spirituality strive to achieve similar goals—an exploration of those dimensions of the human person that are beyond the purely physical, dimensions that are overarching, transcendent, full of meaning and great purpose and direction. Above all, true religion and spirituality, because of their larger view, give perspective to life—a double perspective: not only a distant vision of the "more" beyond, but a relative perspective of the here and now: a sense of proportion, of importance, a sense not only of value, but of relative value, of that which is more worthwhile and perhaps even worthy of being our ultimate concern. This helps us get our priorities right. Spirituality centers on personal experience. Religion, on the other hand, is more organizational, set often in a community of believers who share and organize and explain these experiences (sometimes even decide if they are orthodox or not) and codify appropriate behaviors (rituals and morals) for their faithful.

The list of statements on the following page is not a test, but an opportunity for you to explore what religion and morality mean to you *concretely*. After each statement write an R if you think the statement is religious or about religion, an S if it is spiritual, an O if it seems to be neither religious nor spiritual, but about something else. Try to name that "something else." For best understanding, compare your choices with someone else's.

For most, this sense of the transcendent involves some sort of seeking for and union with a god who is described in ultimate terms. It is a vision of that which is overarching, of vast proportions, larger than life, and yet very relevant to life. In it are wrapped up all our values, and particularly what we value beyond all else—those things we hold to be of greatest value—our ultimate concerns. Everyone has an ultimate concern, some goal or interest that is most absorbing and of the highest value in their eyes. Ultimate concerns range from the trivial to the most meaningful, from collecting what others call junk to making money or achieving fame, from using other people as a ladder to power to caring for the dying. Religion's task is to show us what is truly valuable, valuable enough to be worthy of our ultimate concern. Religion in this sense is a process of being ultimately concerned. We will see more of this when we look at the idea of faith as the process of being "ultimately concerned."

Morality

Religion's landscape is painted on a huge canvas. Such vast proportions yield perspective, on self, on others, on our relationships with others, especially with that God who, we discover, is not only in but is this larger picture.

If one were to take religion as something of such huge proportions, then the task of the religious person is to find one's self in that terrain and map out a route to travel it well. This is where morality comes in: when we concern ourselves with the question: How should I act? we are into the practical— how to live—and this involves values, questions of what is truly worthwhile. What is worth pursuing?

There is a long tradition of religion being involved in moral guidance. Religions have consistently taken it on themselves to teach people how they ought to live. There are great variations on how this relationship of religion and morality is seen. Some people would say, "The relationship is natural. Religion by its very nature has the God-given authority and role of teaching us how we should live." Not all would agree. Some say we can, using our human reason and experience of living together, devise our own moral guidance quite nicely without religion. And besides, religion doesn't have that great a history of being so moral itself. But you have in your hands a book that puts religion and morality together as in some way having something to do with the process of human development. There is a hint here too

Religion-Spirituality Scale

Put the appropriate letter(s) after each statement

R = Religious   S = Spiritual   O = Other

1. "In the beginning was the Word ..."

2. Be good to your Mom and Dad.

3. For the first time in my life I knew the truth of the words: "The heavens proclaim the glory of God."

4. The rain stopped in time for the wedding, Thank God.

5. Love your neighbor as yourself.

6. Love conquers all.

7. Teaching is a sacred trust.

8. The quality of mercy is not strained.

9. There is one God and three divine Persons.

10. The boundary condition of the universe is that it has no boundary.

11. I know that my Redeemer liveth.

12. Happiness is a by-product of the search for meaning.

13. Honor thy Father and thy Mother.

14. God does not play dice.

15. Within chaos one finds strange attractors bringing order out of chaos.

16. The Great Spirit breathes in the four winds.

17. Remember thou keep holy the Sabbath day.

18. Jewish soldiers take their oath of allegiance at Masada.

19. God is dead.

20. The Lord is my shepherd.

21. Do unto others as you would have them do unto you.

22. Do you swear to tell the whole truth, so help you, God?

23. "Father, into your hands I commend my spirit."

24. Holiness is wholeness.

25. The Virgin Mary appeared to some children in Yugoslavia and urged them to pray for peace.

Figure 1.1.

that they have something to do with each other. So one of our first tasks when we move into the section on morality will be to explore the question: What does religion have to do with morality? The answer I propose is that they have very much to do with each other. As we saw above, religion's task is to indicate what is truly valuable and moreover to point out what is of ultimate value. Among these values are moral values. Religion and morality are not the same thing, but they are complementary; at their best they complete each other.

For now there remains the task, while we are discussing the meanings of words, of returning to those two key words, so similar in denotation, but quite different in connotation: religion and spirituality. You may have noticed that I have used *religion* and *spirituality* almost interchangeably in the paragraphs above. And maybe that is not entirely fair since the connotative meanings make a fairly strong distinction between the two. We have distinguished two meanings of *religion* as institutional and as personal experience of the godhead or the numinous. The second meaning starts to merge with spirituality. But perhaps *spirituality* has connotations of a yet more personal and pervasive a way of living than does the term *spiritual experience*. Spirituality definitely connotes that one's religious convictions influence one's actual behavior, maybe even establishing a life theme that one might describe as "deeply religious." Mother Teresa of Calcutta could be described as "deeply religious, a spiritual person." On the other hand, we tend to call people religious even if their religious beliefs are just beliefs and do not affect their way of life. Going a step further, we call people religious even if their religion is fanatical, insane, and even immoral, as in "religious fanatic" or "satanic cultist." *Religious* tends to describe beliefs and perhaps practice, but *spiritual* accentuates a way of life and says something about the life-quality of the person. Often we see the spiritual in terms of having a sense of meaning and purpose in life. Later, we will study Viktor Frankl, who in the concentration camps of World War II discovered that meaning gives a sense of worthwhileness to life and, as a by-product, may bestow happiness. We will see him resisting calling this meaning religious for the same reasons we have outlined here, and preferring instead to call it spiritual.

Beyond spiritual we could go into *mystical* and accentuate the sense of oneness with the universe and God that spirituality may bring at its higher levels.

Before going on, I must note the above use of the word *levels*. It is indeed a signal word throughout the rest of this book for indicating directions and, above all, distinctions along the pathways of development. Like the mountain climber who looks for indications in the rock and vegetation of how high he has climbed, so the developmentalist looks for indications of the level of development. *Higher* usually means more advanced, *better* more desirable. Thus developmental psychologists have had a penchant for breaking down the process of development into stages or levels. The levels are not so much within the person as they are ways psychologists have of describing the gradual process in terms of plateaus arrived at and traversed before ascending to a higher, even better level.

This idea of levels is especially relevant in this book because, as you will see, much of it is formed around Dabrowski's theory of Positive Disintegration, which we will look at in detail later on. Dabrowski, like other developmentalists, used the idea of levels of development, but went beyond to a broader, more elaborate concept he called multilevelness. He saw levels not only in the upward process of development, but in the way we use and understand concepts. We can distinguish within our concepts various levels of meaning. We have already done this somewhat in looking at levels of meaning of the concept of religion. We will do it more elaborately and systematically after we have explored the theory of Positive Disintegration in greater detail.

Always, always there is the cosmos overarching all we know from our limited perceptions; it is there reminding us of the larger scene than the here and now. There is the richness of other people's perspectives on religion, other people's practice of morality. There is the time dimension, begging us to search our roots in the past so we might better imagine what we can be in the future.

On Mount Wapta in Yoho Park there is a shale shoulder that has significance for what we are about. It is called the Burgess shale, and it contains the fossilized remains of creatures that inhabited this region when it was ocean floor 530 million years ago. Harvard paleontologist Stephen Gould (1989) calls these creatures the most important animal fossils we know. They tell us something about animal life long ago. But more importantly, they tell us something about human life right now. They help us put ourselves in a perspective of vast proportions. There are many fossil beds in the world; most give only shadowy images of the life that was once there, but by some geological fluke the Burgess shale has preserved even the three-dimensional shapes of its creatures. And what a variety of shapes lived in the mid-Cambrian period! It is fantastic in the original sense of the word. You can get a sense of how long the road of evolution has been, but above all a sense of the myriad possibilities that lie behind us. There are not just a few animal designs there, variations played on one or two themes. Rather, the Burgess shale lures paleontologists on to discover more and more varieties of creatures that inhabited the earth in these very early times. Fantastic as the variety of forms is in our oceans today, they are probably not as numerous as 530 million years ago. There were not as many species of aquatic life as we have today, but there were more body plans—a vast, exotic profligacy of wild designs. Some are no doubt ancestors of later animals, including humans. Most of these animals with their whimsical shapes have no descendants we can recognize. They lived and perished, probably, like the dinosaurs, victims of their circumstances. Nature embellished life not by directing it into logical categories (it leaves these classifications for humans to do), but by trying out an astounding variety of more and more complex designs.

The Burgess shale tells us that evolution is not the same thing as survival of the fittest; instead, it appears that the fullness and richness of life is part of the interplay of chaos in its effort to create what is new and better. The mystery that the divine revelation of creation presents us with is that development does not come, it seems, from some kind of power contest, but from the sheer lavishness of creation, recklessly trying out myriad possibilities thrown into the boiling cauldron of chaos. From our human point of view, nature squanders much, but that is her way. Creation was and still is lavish with possibilities

We will see (chapter 5) that an ancient paradox of life and death is expressed in modern terms by Positive Disintegration theory: There is another paradox concealed here—*chaos*. The term *chaos* until a very few years ago had only a pejorative meaning; its origins are in the Greek word for abyss, chasm, with all the appropriate gloomy and threatening connotations. In English its traditional meanings have concentrated on a state of utter confusion, a disorganized state of things, a heterogeneous agglomeration, a mess giving a sense that all is left to mere chance. Chaos is real; we know that only too well when tragic accidents happen. But recent mathematical and scientific research points to the possibility that the problem is not in chaos but in our limited appreciation of it. Though we may have considered it a meaningless, orderless mess, happily chaos does not seem to conform to our preconceptions. It invites us to delve into complexity. There is more and more evidence that order is at work, an immensely complex order that we are only beginning to appreciate. A powerful principle of order, too large for our poor minds, seems to be at work. We are only beginning to see it; only beginning to perhaps find God not outside chaos, wrestling to control it, but *within* chaos as a creative, healing force.

With these things in mind, I would like now to approach that enigmatic vital thing we call religion in its spiritual setting with some appreciation of its multidimensionality. We will leave the term *morality* for the second half of the book. Religion will be quite enough of a challenge for us now.

My image of God

As a Child	Now
My image(s) of God then	My image(s) of God now
The pictures I drew of God then	The pictures I would draw now
Names I gave God	Names I give God
How I came to have a God image then	How I came to have my present image
How I felt about God then	How I feel about God now
What I did about it then	What I do about it now
Draw a picture of God	

My Idea of Religion

As a Child	Now
How I got it then	How I came to it now
Where it came from then	Where it comes from now
How I felt about it then	How I feel about religion now

My Idea of Morality

As a Child	Now
My ideas then	My ideas now
How I got a sense of right and wrong then	How I came to what I think now
How I felt about it then	How I feel about morality now

Figure 1.2.

Chapter 2
What is Religion?
The Dimensions of Religion

A god comprehended is no God.

I don't know Who—or what—put the question. I don't know when it was put. I don't even remember answering. But at some moment I did answer Yes to Someone—or Something—and from that hour I was certain that existence is meaningful and that therefore, my life, in self surrender, had a goal.
  —Dag Hammarskjöld (1964, Markings, Whitsunday 1961)

In chapter one we looked, by way of an overview, at some understandings of religion. Essentially we saw that religion has two basic meanings: *institutional* religion and *personal* religion. We saw that there are many grey shadings around these words, one merging into the other so that neat definitions are impossible. We saw too that the word *religion* shades off into spirituality. To add to the confusion we noted (promising to come back to it later) that religion is sometimes identified with morality. The issue becomes complex—and fascinating. Only complex things hold our attention very long. Maybe that's partly why religion and morality are such attention-getters. Sometimes it is good to know that we are not alone in our confusion. To bring you this solace as you start this exploration, I would like to review what some scholars, the "experts," have said about religion. You will find no great consensus among them either—only different perspectives.

You will find the phrase "religion at its best" or "true religion" scattered throughout the following pages. Religion (or what we call religion) has many manifestations. Some of them are degenerate parodies of religion; some are religion gone awry; some are religion shot through with greed and power politics or simply watered down by weak people who drag religion down with them. There are many levels of religion, as we will see. Much of what I have to say is about religion as it can and should be. Obviously lived "religion" doesn't always measure up.

First, we should get some of the cases of abuse of the word religion out of the way. Some of these abuses are cults that put themselves under the religious rubric to gain some respectability or tax advantages. Some "religions" are simply madness masquerading behind the name. Take, for example, the story coming out of Manila that appeared in the *Edmonton Journal*, December 29, 1992.

> "Religious cultists convinced that flat tires are the key to salvation created major traffic jams by deflating tires on scores of buses and cars." When culprits were asked why they did it, they replied that their leader said it was God's will, "Air is from God. This is the solution to the crisis of our country."

We can chuckle at this simple, naive faith, but we stand in horror at "religious" cultists who sexually abuse, mutilate, and murder in the name of God. Strange insanities, dark perversions, and the fascinations of magic weave themselves into the fabric of religion. It is sometimes impossible to separate the threads.

True religion is complex enough without going more into its aberrations. The facets of religion have been described by the scholars in many different ways. Later we will look in more depth at the varieties of religious experience as William James described them over a century ago.

One more recent multidimensional approach is that taken by Glock and Stark (1965). In an attempt to measure religion, Glock and Stark looked at it from five dimensions: ideological, ritualistic, experiential, intellectual, and consequential. The ideological dimension includes religious activities such as prayer and worship. The ritualistic refers to church attendance. The experiential dimension encompasses intense religious experiences like conversion, mystical experiences, visions, prophecy, and speaking in tongues. The intellectual dimension is meant to include knowledge of religious dogmas and practices, whereas the consequential dimension deals with the flow of religion outward into behavior in other spheres of life.

The Glock and Stark (1965) approach has been most useful to psychometricians interested in measuring religion for research purposes, and their inventory has been used extensively in examining those dimensions of religion such as frequency of church attendance that can be reported in numerical terms.

Perhaps for our purposes a more useful way of getting various perspectives on religion is the approach taken by Michael Argyle and Benjamin Beit-Hallahmi of Oxford University (1975, pp. 178-207). They chose to look at theories of religious behavior from the perspectives of the *origin* of religion, the *maintenance* of religion, and the *consequences* of religion. The origin theories attempt to explain religion from the perspective of how it arose. Maintenance theories attempt to explain why individuals or societies hold certain belief systems. Consequence theories deal with the effects of religious behavior on either individuals or groups. This approach will serve as a general framework here for looking at some of the many facets of religion.

Theories of the Origin of Religion

A way of handling the forces of nature. Religion arose as a way for primitive man to explain and control as much as he could the forces of nature. Storms, fires, floods, and earthquakes are devastating forces that humans must come to terms with. To personify them into a god who could be placated, manipulated into changing things for the better, appeased by sacrifice, and then worshipped and thanked when salvation came, was and still is a primitive urge. James Michener expressed it in a fictional yet realistic way in *The Source*, describing a rainstorm experienced by cavemen.

> In these critical moments, when the fall of rain was greatest, obscuring even the mouth of the cave, Ur saw his wife standing in the storm, her tired face uplifted, crying, "Storm, go back! Go back and leave our fields!" And whether the spirit of the storm heard or not, no one could later say but it abated and the waters receded.

> When the storm was gone Ur sat bewildered on a rock, marveling at how close the flood had come to destroying his home.... Then out of the corner of his eye, he saw his wife doing a most perplexing thing. "Wife," he shouted, "what are you doing?" And as she threw handfuls of wheat into the swirling waters she explained in a low voice, "If the storm has left us our wheat, the least we can do is offer him some in thanks." (1966, p. 104)

It was probably in just such stressful situations that men (and perhaps even more so, women) saw "god" as a human-like deity that could be argued with, bargained with, propitiated, and thanked.

This approach to God and the religious experience is not one of merely antique, historical interest. Pushed to their limits by any kind of adversity, a man or woman today will discover and begin to bargain with a personal god he or she was unaware of in normal times. Catastrophe, private or public, sends one searching for a higher power to control it all and make it "go right" for us.

Family projection. Freud considered God as only a father projection stating that (1973, p. 244) "God, at bottom, is nothing but an exalted Father." This may well be Freud's own projection of his image of the 19th-century Germanic family with its solid patriarchal structure, but apart from Freud's narrow vision we still can see that religion is full of familial images: "God the Father," "Holy Mother Church," "Christ our Brother," and the saints as dutiful "Children of God." Those who maintain that this approach explains religion base it on two assumptions: (a) Belief systems are not original creations of each individual as he or she grows up, but are transmitted from generation to generation; and (b) Belief systems endure because the private fantasies and images of individuals correspond to these cultural traditions (Spiro & D'Andrade, 1958). Whether one takes the limited orthodox Freudian view of God as a father projection or the more contemporary approach supported by research (Argyle & Beit-Hallahmi, 1975, p. 185) that it is possible that culture conveys the paternal image of God, while the affective attitude toward God is derived from relations with parents, it is impossible to deny a psychological link between a child's conception of God and her relationship with her parents. In point of fact, religious education must take this dynamic into account.

Conscience projections. This Freudian-based theory of the origin of religion touches on the moral aspects of religion (Flugel, 1945). It is based on the idea that when the child is punished by his parents he feels anxiety. To overcome this, the child identifies with the parents and wishes to be like them, conforming to their demands. Parental demands are internalized in this way, and the child becomes conditioned to feel guilty even when the parents are not around. This is the Freudian "superego." The superego or conscience projection hypothesis states, "There is a being, God, and an institution, religion, that serve the adult as magnified parents who enter the conscience and punish or reward, helping to maintain the adult's typical balance between desire, morality and action" (Ostow & Sharfstein, 1954, p. 76). When the superego comes into conflict with instinctive desires, this conflict is relieved by projection of the superego that now appears as God. The repressive demands of the superego can then be seen as prohibitions of some outside person. Often this person is God the all-knowing one, the heavenly bookkeeper who records rights and wrongs, who never forgets, and punishes eternally. According to this theory, God arises from the guilty individual's need for the complete and total conscience.

The need to explain. Human beings need belief systems to provide themselves with a coherent, subjectively rational account of their behavior and the apparently irrational world around them. Research has shown that individuals feel pressured to have a set of beliefs compatible with one another (e.g., Asch, 1958) and compatible with the individual's experiences (Festinger, Riecken, & Schacter, 1956). One remarkable thing about belief systems is that they are most acceptable when shared with members of some social group such as a church. In fact, Festinger et al. (p. 40) showed that when the evidence for religious beliefs fails to materialize or is contradicted by other evidence, church members become even more fervently entrenched in their beliefs. Frequently religious sects predict the end of the world for a specific day. When it does not happen the lack of proof does not weaken their belief, but induces followers to increase their church membership by trying to convert others. There may well be, in fact, an inverse relationship between the security with which persons hold their religious beliefs and the ardor of their attempts to convert others to them. If deep inside I feel shaky about my beliefs, it is reassuring to me to see others being "converted" to them.

Belief systems cluster around two main centers—my experience of myself and my experience of my world. Some belief systems help me explain myself to myself. They form my identity and purpose in that they tell me who I am and where I am going. My sense of identity needs to be fortified with some assurance that what I am is valuable. Religion, as we shall see when we look at Erik Erikson, often provides this feeling of personal worthwhileness. Religion provides too a sense of personal life meaning. "Man's search for meaning" has been thoroughly and graphically documented by Viktor Frankl (1959, 1965, 1967, 1969, 1978). He prefers to have his psychology identified as "spiritual" rather than "religious" but is perhaps reacting to the baggage of sectarianism that the word religious usually carries with it. Here we are trying to preserve the word religion from being associated only with religious sects and seek to look at it in a broader sense. In that sense religion does have as its purpose to give meaning to life, to draw the big picture, "to paint life in broad strokes."

Not only does religion have a function of explaining oneself to oneself and giving personal meaning to life, it has a more general, abstract, "philosophical" function of explaining some of the great questions of life that revolve around the agonies of pain, suffering, death, and injustice. The biblical Book of Job is an attempt to answer "Why should the just man suffer?" And although it finds its "answer" in the inscrutable mind of an all-powerful God, it is a theological treatise with intense psychological themes.

Later we will see that William James wrote about the "twice-born man" who agonizes over questions of ultimate meaning: Why live? Why be moral? Is there any hope for a just world, or is justice an illusion? These are the kinds of questions firmly in the domain of the religious.

One important advantage that religion has over philosophy in considering questions of meaning and identity and making them relevant to the individual is the diversity and richness of the language of religion. Philosophy is largely limited to words and logic and all that is intellectual and verbal, whereas religion goes beyond words into the language of symbols in poetry, art, ritual, and myth. Because, as Susanne Langer says (1951, p. 127), the human mind is "profoundly symbolific," we should not be surprised to find the human mind working with "symbols far below the level of speech." Words often fail to fully express religious ideas. Nonverbal expressions such as art, ritual, and music often convey more surely than words what religion has to say to each individual about his or her own identity in the community, the directions of society, and the ultimate meanings of life. For example, the stained glass windows of Europe's medieval cathedrals were specific teaching devices for simple, nonliterate people. The rich collection of symbols in art, ritual, and myth that religions of all kinds have drawn us to are witnesses to our need to express the inexpressible, to answer the unanswerable, to grasp the individual with a sense of life meaning. Joseph Campbell (as we will see later) has recently made us more aware of the power of myth and symbol to explain life meaning to us in metaphorical terms that penetrate to the core of our beings. Rollo May (1991), an existentialist philosopher and psychotherapist, has heard the cry for meaning in his clients and indicated the power of myth to convey that meaning.

We have the myths and legends of ancient people that tell us what their belief systems were. We can recreate the Gregorian chant of a medieval monastery. We can interpret the stone carvings of Mayan civilization to learn about their belief in human sacrifice and the need to constantly rebuild their pyramid temples to appease their gods. We can explore the astronomy of the Mayans and find as they did that their enthusiasm for building observatories and plotting the course of the stars was not purely scientific; the measure of the stars and Venus had practical, agricultural, and economic implications. With such import it is easy to see this could take on religious implications. It is easy to see why their leaders were not just politicians, but scientists and priests who probed the heavens for the meaningful. We have a parallel today when the formerly "materialistic and atheistic" sciences now speak in theistic terms about the nature and origins of the cosmos. Physics, astronomy, and biology have much that is worthy of consideration for those concerned about ultimate meaning.

One outstanding benefit of climbing medieval cathedral church towers up never-ending spirals of stairs is to get a sense of the power of belief systems. There at the top of the tower, hundreds of feet above the ground and perhaps tucked away in some corner of the roof, stands a stone angel or a saint carved with exquisite care. As it is far from the busy market square below, very few may ever have seen it, still fewer breathless tourists would have stopped to admire it. But it has stood there for 500 years as symbolic testimony to the art and loving concern of some craftsman whose whole life meaning may have been taken up in carving just such statues "for the glory of God" and not for the eyes of man. Over the countless years, how many lives have found meaning, and expressed this meaning, in the creation of religious symbols that still communicate beliefs to us?

Theories of Maintenance

Social learning. Argyle and Beit-Hallahmi (1975, p. 189) describe social learning theory in this context as a statement that religious behavior, beliefs, and experiences are simply part of the culture, transmitted from generation to generation like any other set of customs. This theory hardly needs any proof. It is quite evident that individuals are reinforced for maintaining the religious practices of their forebears and their society. Catholics encourage Catholicity, Jews Judaism, and so on. One of the great limitations of this theory is that it cannot account for variations in religious activity. Left to itself it would postulate a never-changing religious tradition, making no room for Christ to rise up out of a Judaic tradition or Luther to come forth out of Roman Catholic Europe. This theory does not readily account for individual motivational forces and how religion fails to satisfy individual human needs, thereby calling forth new religious expressions as a means of satisfying those needs.

Some features are common to nearly all religions, such as envisioning God as a personified (usually male) presence and recognizing the existence of good and evil forces. One could attribute the universality of these and other concepts to social learning, or explain them as something innate in human nature, as we shall see later in the Jungian idea of the collective unconscious.

Deprivation and compensation. Some have epitomized this view in the statement "The greater a man's disappointment in this life, the greater his faith in the next." Marx formulated it in an often-quoted sentence: "Religion is the opium of the people." Religion is said to have a drug-like effect. Glock (1964) distinguishes five kinds of deprivation that may give rise to religious reactions: economic, social, organismic, ethical, and psychic. Religious activities are a kind of compensation for the deprivations of poverty, social class, ill health, old age, perceived immorality in the world around, or personal feelings of inferiority. Rachel, in Margaret Laurence's *A Jest of God*, with all her self-consciousness, nervousness, and feelings of inferiority is open to the intensely emotional religious experience of a prayer meeting. Religion provides a ready rationalization for "the evils of this world" and a promise of happiness in the next when "the humble shall be exalted and the mighty brought low." Not only does God keep account of suffering and deprivation in this world, but He will set things straight in the next when justice shall be done. This kind of thinking has two effects: one to give some sort of rational meaning to suffering and loss, the other to sometimes excuse oneself from the obligation of eliminating deprivation because this life is only a temporary sojourn in this mortal body, and the prelude to real life, which is eternal and blissful for those who have suffered on earth. "There's pie in the sky when you die." This rationalization is particularly appealing to some religious leaders who use it to demand more sacrifice, more alms, and more submission from their church members. These leaders avoid responsibility for delivering any kind of compensation for such sacrifices beyond the promise that "God will reward you in the next life." We need not go back to the selling of indulgences in medieval times for examples; "religious hucksters" are doing the same thing on television today.

Argyle and Beit-Hallahmi (1975, p. 194) indicate an interesting offshoot of the deprivation theory: "The greater level of church membership and church attendance among those in higher socioeconomic status in both the USA and Great Britain has been used as an argument against the validity of deprivation theories of religiosity." They counter this argument on two grounds: the nature of middle-class religious activity, and the possibility that church attendance may well be a response to a kind of middle-class deprivation. They quote Goode (1966) as suggesting that church attendance should not be used as a measure of religious behavior because it has become a secular activity, a tendency of the middle class to be involved in socially acceptable volunteer organizations. The church then becomes a source of complacent satisfaction for middle-class social needs. "The comfortable pew" has replaced the austere prie-dieu.

Relief of guilt. Guilt relief as a motivation for being religious is founded in psychoanalytic theory, one prediction being that people with guilt feelings should be attracted toward any religion that has as its doctrine either the forgiveness of sin and salvation or some sort of self-punishing rite that may compensate for the feeling of guilt.

Douziech (1981) makes some important distinctions about different kinds of guilt, expanding the concept beyond personal guilt to existential guilt feelings and thus broadening the role that religion plays in relieving guilt. Contrary to some of the mainstreams of psychology (especially those of Freud and Albert Ellis) that see guilt as just another neurotic symptom to be cured, Douziech recognizes a constructive, even growthful kind of guilt. He distinguishes subjective guilt into neurotic and real or true guilt. Neurotic guilt is a distorted experience marked by fear and psychological paralysis that centers around real or imagined moral failures. True or real guilt, on the other hand, can be of three kinds: constructive, existential, or collective. Collective guilt is a failure through omission to take appropriate action when political authorities violate human rights. It is a communal sharing of the guilt of inaction. "For evil to persist, it is not so much necessary that bad men have their way, as it is that good men remain silent." Existential guilt is an awareness of the disparities that exist in the world, and feeling in some way responsible especially by inaction. Constructive guilt or value guilt is a sense of wrongdoing arising out of real, unnecessary failure toward the moral order or objectively valid social contravention's, or one's own principles of conduct. This kind of guilt, far from being "sick," is a real and objectively based sense of the disparity between what one is and what one ought to be. This contradiction in one's life, this gap, this disparity can be a healthy motivator toward change and improvement. Religion, then, has a powerful and positive role to play in the relief of guilt, pointing out the disparity between what is and what ought to be, and closing the gap between the two by positing ways of behaving that are both objectively moral and growthful for the individual and healing for the community.

Fear of death. We saw when considering theories of the origin of religion that seeking answers to the meaning of life and the question of death was a way of answering cognitive needs. Here we consider death from a more emotional, personal point of view in which religion becomes a solace, a comforter, and in some cases a guarantee of immortality, assuaging the individual's fears about the afterlife.

As we would expect, people become progressively more religious as they get older. From the age of 60 onward there is an increasing amount of religious concern and an increasing belief in an afterlife (Argyle & Beit-Hallahmi, 1975, pp. 68ff). The most avid and participant followers of religious television are older people seeking comfort and reassurance of immortality.

Some existential writers (Tennensen, 1966) go so far as to state that religion is a death-denying institution, an ontological hebetant. At first glance it is difficult to agree that the institutional religions deny death. Death is a recurring theme of religious writings, religious art, and liturgy. Some sects center their whole cult around a kind of worship of death. Yet in a certain sense religion is death-denying because its theme so often is that death is not the end of life but the beginning of a new and better life. "Vita mutatur non tollitur," said the preface from the Requiem Mass. "Life is changed, not taken away ... and when this earthly dwelling falls apart, a new and glorious eternal dwelling place is prepared in heaven."

To an existentialist of the most gloomy ilk this kind of thinking is religion at its worst—rationalizing window dressing, covering up the harsh reality that death is *it*—the cold and bitter end. With the sweet picture of something better to go to, the chilly fear of that "undiscovered country from whose bourne no traveller returns" (*Hamlet*) is warmed considerably. Between the two extremes of absolute death denial and the acceptance of the "fact" that there is nothing more beyond lies the role of religion in meeting the individual's cognitive and affective needs for an understanding and personal acceptance of what death means. The individual, faced with the anticipation or the looming fact of one's own death, can turn to religion with its potentially broader perspective to give some kind of death acceptance and reconciliation.

Ingmar Bergman has given us many an example of institutional religion failing in this role of successfully interpreting death, notably in his film *Cries and Whispers*. In this film, centering around the death of a young woman, a minister is called in to pray at the deathbed. He begins a long and solemn prayer, but a prayer riddled with the word *if* that resonates with all his personal doubts and faith ambiguities. Ironically, the traditional comforting, perspective-giving role of religion in facing death is more than negated by the minister's own doubts: "If there is a God; if he is just; if he rewards the good; if one actually does any good in life." With all these theological preconditions the resolution of the prayer is null, and nothing is left but the void.

Sexual motivation. One need not adhere to the Freudian approach to see sexuality as something closely linked with, and motivating, religious behavior. Religion and fertility have been closely intertwined through history and prehistory. Some religious rites as an expression of man's oneness with nature have shown overt sexuality through rituals of sacred prostitution and other forms of sexual activity (Delisle, 1976). Archeologists have found innumerable nude female statues with exaggerated sexual features. Originally these were called "Venuses" and were presumed to be the "playboy centerfolds" for ancient men. However, a new appreciation shows them as goddess figures celebrating the fertility of woman and the fertility of the earth in one symbol. Far from pornographic, they are deeply religious, reminding us of our unity with and dependence on Mother Earth.

Subtle but explicit expressions of sexuality are contained in sacred literature such as the biblical Song of Songs.

His left hand is beneath my head,
While his right embraces me.
I adjure you, O daughters of Jerusalem
... That you disturb not, nor interrupt our love,
Until it is satiated. (2:6-7; Gordis, 1974, p. 51)

The mystics have expressed their experiences with God in terms loaded with sexual symbolism. "By Command of the Bridegroom when He intends ravishing the soul," says St. Teresa, "the doors of the mansions and even those of the Keep and the whole castle are closed; for he takes away even the power of speech" (Underhill, 1961, p. 377).

The Tantrics of northern India symbolize the union of consciousness and energy by statues and paintings depicting the sexual embrace of Shiva and Shakti. They seek to experience the state of cosmic oneness implied by such symbolism through Yogic breathing and visualization exercises combined with ritualistic sexual practices.

Obsessive-compulsive behavior. Religion in some form provides a legitimate outlet for some obsessive-compulsive behavior. Frequently recurring thoughts that one cannot rid oneself of are often laden with religious and moral content. Reik (1951) has elaborated on this theme. The recurring thoughts of the chanting Hare Krishna member, the repetitions involved in brainwashing a religious cult convert are techniques used by so-called religious sects to employ the power of repetitiousness on the mind to induce a "religious" obsession. For some obsessive neurotics, their repetitive thoughts take the form of religious symbolism and ideas. Religious rites also provide a mode of expression for compulsive behavior. There are rituals that one *must* perform to satisfy some inner need, allay some guilt feeling, or avert a calamity. "Step on a crack, you break your mother's back," sing the children as they dance down the sidewalk in a kind of game that becomes all too serious for the compulsive neurotic who cannot step on a crack for fear of dire consequences. Compulsive handwashing is another ritual that not only finds itself reflecting the dramatic actions of Pontius Pilate, but the handwashing rituals of religion. The Catholic Rosary, with its repetition of "Hail Mary" through five or even 15 decades of the beads, is another example of repetitious ritual, as is the bowing of Jewish pilgrims as they pray at the Western Wall in Jerusalem. And, as if God were sometimes not paying sufficient attention, one must speed up the rocking motion to intensify the urgency of the prayer. Thus religious ritual can provide a socially acceptable outlet for existing neurotic compulsions, but it can also become a form of compulsive behavior in itself.

To say that all this is "simply neurotic" is to misread what religion does. Life and nature are full of cycles and repetitions just as music has rhythm and beat. It gives a reassuring sameness that bespeaks stability. Children love to have the same story read to them over and over again. Religious ritual is also a means of focusing the mind so as to exclude mental and sensory distractions, and thereby precipitate into consciousness the various forms of religious experience. Its deliberateness and conscious intentionality distinguish it from the rituals of the obsessive-compulsive neurotic who performs them as a defence that prevents certain dangerous, anxiety-provoking thoughts from entering the conscious mind. If religious ritual and ideas strongly appeal to obsessive-compulsive neurotics with a pathological need for security, this does not denigrate religion. It shows that religion, which speaks so deeply to the basic needs of mankind, is sometimes used to truly answer those needs and is sometimes abused in the service of neurotic pathology.

Theories of Consequence

For society. We have seen how religion may well arise from the need of a society to find some sort of identity and integration of its belief systems. Sociologists from Durkheim's time (1915) have explained religion's function as that of providing legitimation for social arrangements. When customs or laws such as obedience to authority or prohibition of incest work well for the good of society, they come to be sanctioned by religious norms, rewarded by religion's promises, or punished by religion's threats. According to this view, the socially acceptable and workable comes to be the norm that religion sanctions. Religion then becomes a great integrating force in society, as it did, for example, in medieval times in Europe. It has the power to reward the believer with membership in the group and thereby satisfy some needs for safety and belonging. Religion can also threaten to punish the intransigent with shunning, excommunication, death, or eternal damnation. The intertwining of religion and politics throughout history bears witness to the elements of truth in this view that religious behavior becomes meaningful in the context of the consequences of the interaction of religion and society.

For individuals. Religion has consequences for the individual too, consequences that go beyond the mere explanation of myself to myself as we saw in the origin theories of religion. Personal integration is one such consequence. Personal integration can be taken in two senses: a sense of wholeness within myself, and a sense of connectedness with other people, with other things, and with God, whatever that "god" might be. Another consequence is that religion can give meaning to life, paint life in broad strokes. This is where religion excels at putting our individuality and fragile uniqueness in perspective. Religion helps "figure to emerge from ground" in the gestalt of our lives. When figure emerges from ground, it is something like an object hidden in a painting gradually taking shape before our eyes and then popping into full view. The object may be oneself. The self comes into view, but not a self in isolation; there is about the self a larger scene, a ground, a context of time and place that gives proportion and leads to value. Two things happen: I emerge from context as an individual, and at the same time I find myself in relationship.

Religion brings out the true value dimensions of the things of this world, the worthwhileness of ourselves, and reveals our individual place in the cosmos thereby causing it to shine forth. We will work this out more fully later on; let us just say for now that one of the great consequences of religion is perspective—perspective of myself against the background of the universe.

It is here in this last dimension of religion that we find its most valuable contribution and come closest to understanding what religion is—not defining but understanding. We come closest to understanding because with this concept of religion as *that which gives perspective to life*, the possibility of experiencing the integrating power of religion is unlocked. It is experience rather than definitions that leads to understanding.

A relatively simple but helpful way of looking at religion is that proposed by Daniel Batson and his associates (Batson, Schoenade, & Ventis, 1993). Batson is known in social-psychological contexts for his research into three religious orientations. Two are described by Allport: *extrinsic* (religion as something to be used) *intrinsic* (religion as something to be lived). Batson himself contributed a *quest* orientation to address some of the many questions left over from a simple bipolar approach. Gordon Allport (about whom we will see more later) observed the ways people practiced their religion; some just used religion as a means to some other goal like power, wealth, or fame. Others seemed literally to take it to heart to the extent that it became not only intrinsic but an end in itself. Batson, in turn, from his research added a third way of describing religious people: he called it the *quest* orientation. It describes those who see religion not as a possession, something one *has*, but as the search for something of supreme worth, something not finished and therefore not to be clung to, nor something to be used as a means to something else, but as the highest pursuit and motif of one's existence. This quest orientation resembles the spirituality of the classic mystics such as Teresa of Avila and John of the Cross who expressed their search in anagogic terms of the ascent of a mountain or the staircases of a castle. Viktor Frankl describes a similar spirituality for "modern man in search of a soul" as a quest for meaning.

What, Then, is Religion in the "Definitions"?

We have eschewed definitions of religion as being too limiting and destructive in themselves of the elements that are vital for the individual experience of religion. We have seen that experience is the only way of fully understanding. Despite their drawbacks, however, definitions are useful to the act of verbally communicating to others those aspects of our understanding of religion not destroyed by the confining limits of those definitions. To communicate the theme on which the remainder of this book is based, and explore the roots of that sense, we should now pursue directly some meanings of the word religion.

Paradoxically, the most direct route would be what seems to be the most indirect route. If the so-called exact sciences fail to be exact in "measurable" areas like physics (compare Capra, *The Tao of Physics*; Zukav, *The Dancing Wu-Li Masters*; Hawking, *A Brief History of Time*), how much more so psychology in the realm of religion—a notoriously inexact science dealing with the most mercurial of concepts.

Argyle and Beit-Hallahmi (1975) adopt a straightforward, everyday, limited definition of religion as "a system of beliefs in a divine or superhuman power, and practices of worship or other rituals directed toward such a power" (p. 1). The limitations of this definition will become apparent as we go along. Other attempts (Spinks, 1963) at defining religion do shed new light on the idea from various angles. Sir James Frazer (*The Golden Bough*, 1911, VI, p. 222) defined religion as the "propitiation or conciliation of powers superior to man which are believed to direct or control the course of nature and of human life." Frazer's definition brings out two aspects of religion: the theoretical and the practical. The theoretical may be called *theology*, whereas the practical finds expression in two forms: worship, which is an attempt to propitiate the gods by rituals and prayer, and morals, which are the attempt to propitiate the gods by good conduct.

Definitions themselves have followed two mainstreams, one emphasizing the *communal* aspects of religion, the other the *individual's psychic life*. Emil Durkheim (1915, p. 50) emphasizes the aspect of religion that attracts social scientists, because it is eminently measurable—participation in a religious community. It is relatively easy to measure some aspect of religion by the frequency of church attendance. Although this measure falls far short of the full meaning of religion, it is tempting for social scientists to measure the quantity of church attendance and believe this to be an accurate measure of religion. Participation in a religious group is a measure of one aspect of the communal component of religion but neglects to differentiate individual experience from mere custom or social conformity.

Durkheim (1915) saw religion as a "unified system of beliefs and practices relative to sacred things, that is to say, things set apart and forbidden: beliefs and practices that unite into one single moral community called a Church, all those who adhere to them." For Durkheim the idea of religion is inseparable from church. Faith then becomes the acceptance of a set of dogmas and moral norms. By accepting, believing, and doing as the church requires, one becomes part of the "in" group and the potential recipient of whatever social, spiritual, and eternal benefits are promised to that "in" group. By rejecting the teachings of the church, either by not being converted to it or, once converted, rejecting the teachings of the community, and thus being "excommunicated," one is susceptible to the social consequences and threats of temporal or eternal punishment that the church decrees for nonbelievers. By this definition, creed (a set of "truths" to be believed) and code (a set of moral norms to be followed) form the core of religion, and faith is the acceptance of these. This is a concept of religion to which Jung and many others reacted strongly. It is perhaps the stereotypical definition of religion that most hold, particularly those who have rejected religion for whatever personal reasons they may have. Remarkably, many who adamantly state, "No, I am *not* religious," have strong beliefs and values that guide them in good lives. Perhaps their denial of being religious says more about the image organized religion has created for itself than it does about "the lack of faith and morality in our society today."

A definition that emphasizes the communal aspects of religion to the exclusion of the individual's psychic life is deficient. Some scholars, taking the opposite tack, have emphasized religion as an individual's faith in a power beyond oneself, an attempt to gain stability and emotional security in life. God in this context gives the individual some sort of security in life in the face of life's limitations and manifold threats. Worship and serving a god offer appeasement to that god and guarantee as much as possible the surety the individual seeks, whether it be tomorrow's sunrise, a good harvest, or eternal salvation. This individual approach can be called the religion of *self-conservation*.

Another approach to individual religion, coming to it from the opposite (yet, paradoxically, complementary) direction, is the religion of *self-transcendence*. This view of the religious person sends him or her off on a quest, emphasizing the courage to go beyond the stability of mere self-conservation to higher levels of consciousness. Paradoxically, this is the ultimate in self-conservation, for religion has always presented the paradox that to find oneself one must lose oneself. Because self is inextricably bound up in relationships with others, self-transcendence is the ultimate self-discovery. In transcending oneself one finds oneself; in finding oneself one finds others; in finding others one finds oneself, reflecting in others through the medium of relationship. Such paradox upon paradox is the beauty of religion.

You will find these themes recurring throughout this book, for they are some of the facets of religion that reveal themselves when we make the effort to examine religion from various perspectives. For now, in an attempt to get something of common understanding of the concept of religion, a statement follows under the title "What is Religion?" It is, of course, not *the* statement; it is *a* statement. It is not proven, nor are all its points systematically developed to a final conclusion, for our notion of religion is in process. This statement, besides providing a common ground for discussion, is a preview of what is to come and what will be developed more in subsequent pages. But, incomplete as it is, the time is ripe to present it so we can go on.

What is Religion as the Word is Used Here?

It is important first to say what religion is *not*. That can clear the air of much confusion.

Much madness, unhappily, goes on under the name of religion. Much politics wears the cloak of religion. Much moneymaking is done in accounting systems that confuse the spiritual with material loss and gains. Whether it be ritual murders or a suicidal "religious" sect or abusive, dominative, "religious" relationships, or politically expedient "religious" conversions, or the selling of "religious" salvation, it is all phoney, a false front, a ploy hiding what is really going on. The perpetrators themselves may not always be fully conscious of the ploy. There is much confusion and self-deceit in this madness. But it is important for us to understand that because something or somebody carries the title "religious," this does not make it so. We must first clear out all those forms of madness and exploitation that take on religious words to play their charade.

On a more positive note: Religion as we have seen is often identified with membership in or attendance at a church (a handy measure for sociologists). Attendance at a church may be an outcome of religion, and indeed religious teachers have usually drawn around them a group of followers who have organized a "church" with certain dogmas as criteria for membership and certain rituals (liturgy) as a type of community interaction and worship. This liturgy is better than the creed in taking us back to the essence of religion, which is awareness (consciousness) of one's true complexity and multilevelness as a human being and the relationships that flow therefrom.

An evolving world is continuously involved in the activity of organization because this is a basic characteristic of mass/energy. Each person is a manifestation of that same activity like an eddy in a flowing river. What organizes the system is awareness (consciousness), awareness of ourselves as part of this great organization of both persons and things. Religion, then, is nothing less than cosmic consciousness—with certain personal limitations.

We can let a limited personal awareness blind our view of our part in the total complexity; or limited awareness may even seem to be membership in the total organization. This may happen in two ways: religion in the narrow sense may show itself as isolationism, insularity, pietism, the "Jesus and I" phenomenon. Or we may have exclusivism in the dogmatic sense of the "in" people and the "out," the saved and the damned. This may be based on "orthodoxy": adherence to a set of dogmas, or legalism, where conformity to a set of religion-based laws is the criterion of membership. This type of religiosity often manifests itself in crusader-like attempts to convert others to *our* way (which of course is the only "right way"). History is strewn with plentiful examples, many of them bloody, of religious bigotry and zeal for this great rationalization called "God." Often the ardor of attempts to convert others is in direct proportion to the narrow insularity and gnawing insecurity of the religious person. Religious zeal can be a compensation for deep feelings of insecurity, a compensation for the security that should come from establishing one's identity rooted in relationships with other persons both human and divine.

Human beings seek the security of an identity rooted in relationships; these are founded in the earliest years of childhood and continue throughout a lifetime, becoming successively more integrated.

To the extent that we separate ourselves conceptually from others, we form a barrier to oneness with others. Caught in this separateness that we can help create ourselves, we behave in a way that brings suffering to ourselves and others. This is hell. Hell truly is "other people" (Sartre, 1956) if we really believe it to be so.

Truly religious people, especially the mystics, by exemplifying its peaks have shown us what religion really can be. Rooted in a secure sense of personal identity from which they can dare to launch out, to risk loving (to transcend themselves), and passing through the disintegrative crises of life in a positive, growthful way, these people find the delimiting barriers crumbling. There is union with others based on consciousness of what I am—a person who by nature *must* be in relationship with others or I am no person at all.

My more or less consciousness of this (to a degree that wavers from time to time) is my ordinary experience of religion. When the barriers between myself and others fall totally in those rare and precious moments of full awareness of who I am, these are mystical religious experiences. Heaven would be the perfect and continual possession of this experience, which is at one and the same time both transpersonal and perfectly personal fulfilling— the ultimate, what Teilhard de Chardin (1973) called the omega point.

This striving for full consciousness we call "religion." Its rejection we call "hell." Its temporary attainment is the mystical, fleeting experience of ecstasy in which we stand outside ourselves, distance ourselves from ourselves and thus obtain objectivity, putting ourselves in the right relationship of tiny figure against vast background, seeking and finding objective truth in the abstract and objective moral truth. This is love: universal love. Its idealization we call "God," who is love in action and who is for many personal, since God is the ideal of interpersonal and transpersonal union, calling for respect and awe at the distance between the human and the divine, and yet luring into the intimacy of friendship between persons (Armstrong 1993, McFague 1982).

The whole idea of "God as person" seems to fit quite comfortably for some, whereas for others it is awkward and uncomfortable, something outgrown in the passage beyond the remembrances of a childhood, filled with anthropomorphic images of God as an old man seated on the clouds of heaven. Some, consequently, throw out the whole idea of a personal God as something psychologically immature and theologically unsatisfactory. Because we get confused and even clash over our images of God doesn't mean we have to throw out our notions of God or deny God's existence. Religion is simply looking for a bigger picture than the limited one our own individual life may provide. In that bigger picture, God can be "in heaven." God can be "in the trees of the forest." God can be "in people." Evidently (whatever God is) God is there, in existence. God has "spoken" to men and women for through the ages, communicating through many masks.

It is relevant to note that classical Greek actors held masks in front of their faces not to deceive the audience, but to reveal their role in the drama. They spoke their part through the masks (per-sona) The multitude of personas we have created to relate to God testify not only to the fertile imaginations of humans, but to the riches of God "Himself." We live in a chaotic world, yet there are moments, as when watching a glorious sunset, meeting a good friend, or when the obstetrician says, "Yes, your baby is perfectly healthy," that a sense of order, beauty, and rightness comes to rest on us. These moments give God voice, and if we wish therefore to visualize a divine person behind that voice, then it is our choice. Sometimes we create our own individual persona for God: the mask through which God the mystery enters by word and spirit-breath into our lives.

For many too the image of God as "He," with all its masculine connotations, is enough to make the picture truncated and disturbing. The feminist movement has done more than resurrect the goddess concept and, it is hoped, will lead us beyond simply calling God "She." Riane Eisler (1987) has from the position of an anthropologist warned about the danger of setting up the competition that may come by simply replacing a patriarchal with a matriarchal society. It could lead to the same evils of a domination model that the male image of God has been a part of for ages. To get involved in simplistic divisions and dichotomies is not in the best interests of a mature theology. Instead, Sallie McFague (1987) (for one) has given an array of models of God from which to choose that are relevant in an age of nuclear threat and ecological concern.

At heart, the problem lies not with a personal God, but with our limited concept of person. If we continue to identify person with physical body, then the anthropomorphisms ("the eye of God," "the right hand of God," "a wrathful God") are in control, limiting instead of aiding in the forming of a relationship worthy of persons. When we love, when we care, when we pray, when we worship, we enter into a personal relationship. Some day, when psychology and theology have communicated long and deeply, we may have a more adequate, broader concept of what a person is. We will have returned to the core message of the ancient religious myth of divine incarnation—God becoming human to show humankind what personhood might be. If God is not the exception to metaphysical principles but their chief exemplification (Whitehead), may He not also be the chief exemplification of personhood? May "He" as total person, not only exemplify what we have come to know as masculinity, but also encompass femininity as well?

The problem is not with God, but with our language, our customs, and ultimately our limited comprehension of what it is to be a person. Perhaps at death, when the occasion that is each person perishes, each individual passes over into an interpersonal relationship the dimensions of which were incomprehensible throughout the passages of life. In the meantime, developing persons can have a truly interpersonal relationship with God expressed in terms meaningful to their level of development and comprehensive of their notions of gender. The concepts *person* and *God* are vast enough to encompass many interpretations and meet the relationship needs of a wide variety of human beings, male and female, and at every level of development. This power of religion to lure the individual into personal relationships both human and divine heightens the basic paradox that the person as religious, though at heart solitary in the quest for meaning, is drawn inevitably and happily into community of persons.

We have seen that the two mainstreams of definitions of religion tend to follow either the courses of community involvement or personal, individual experience. Somehow, this dichotomy must be resolved and a blending of "the one" and "the many" form a holistic concept of religion that is itself supposed to be a unifier. Later we will look at the ideas of Alfred North Whitehead more thoroughly, but for now let me pull out from *Religion in the Making* (1973) one of his "definitions" of religion. It is both scientific and poetic. It will serve us well here: "Religion is what the individual does with his own solitariness" (p. 16).

Some background will help in understanding this enigmatic statement. In a sense the distinction we have made between religion as institutional belonging and religion as the experience of personal relationship with the divine is contained in this brief definition. Religion is not sheer solitariness—the individual in eremitic isolation. Religion is *what one does* with one's own solitariness—the actions that flow from solitariness. Solitariness ensues when one comes face to face with the great mysteries of life: death, suffering, evil. Faced with these mysteries, not only in contemplation, but sharpened to a razor's edge when real life makes the questions no longer hypothetical but practical, one can feel an overwhelming solitariness. Then what do we do with this solitariness? We turn to religion for some understanding of these mysteries that overwhelm. Usually the question first asked is "Why," as if some reason must be behind it all. When rationality fails, usually the question resolves into "How?" as we seek some way to take the mystery into our lives. Religion's role, at its essence, is to give some answers to these questions, setting them in broader significant perspectives that point out meaning.

The lower levels of religion, according to Whitehead, are essentially sociable, conforming (religion as a means). The highest level of religion he entitles "rationalism"; rational religion is religion the beliefs and rituals of which have been reorganized with the aim of making it the central element in a coherent ordering of life (religion as an end). This ordering of life affects not only thought (dogma), but behavior (morals). This final, highest phase (the quest orientation) introduces the note of solitariness, and with it religion moves away from the psychology of the herd and toward the intuitions of the few. Martyrdom becomes possible when one can and must stand up for one's beliefs. Because rational religion is universal it introduces the note of solitariness. The reason for this connection between universality and solitariness is that universality is a disconnection from immediate surroundings. It is an endeavor to find something permanent and intelligible by which to interpret the confusion of immediate detail. It is like stepping back to get perspective, especially when the picture is too huge and too close to be fully comprehended.

A Note on Prayer and Ritual

If religion is both solitary and communal, do these two dimensions ever merge? Or is there at least some bridge that may cross the chasm between the two? The chasm is spanned by prayer and ritual. For most people the solitariness of their religious quest becomes too much to bear. They yearn to fuse their religious insights and aspirations with those of others in a common set of symbols. These are the great religious symbols of art, of the coming together in community ritual, and the going apart in private prayer. The coming together seems obviously enough a fusing of community, but what of the going apart?

Christ in the garden of Gethsemane, the night before He died, withdrew a few steps away from His best friends to communicate in solitude with His Father. His prayer on that occasion was a model of solitary, mature prayer; solitary because that is the lot of the man as he confronts death; mature because His prayer was shaped by the qualities of the integrated human being He was. Above all, His prayer was not manipulative. It was conformation to something much larger than Himself. Often prayer is taken as a device to manipulate God, to make him change the world to suit our individual wants, our narrow perspective. This is the "God, don't let it rain on my picnic" phenomenon. Freud was probably right when he concluded that some religious people are caught in a permanently childish dependence on God as an all-powerful Father who can be manipulated, cajoled, appeased, and even bribed into running the world the way they want it to be run. My son Daniel at the age of five said, "I'm going to blast off to God in a rocket ship and tell Him that I want to live forever." I was more impressed by Daniel at that age reflecting on his own mortality than by the means he took to do something about it, asking God to change things to suit him. But this was appropriate to his age. Perhaps we can all be impressed too by the modern means of transportation he chose to communicate with God. For many of us the single-seater rocket ship is the individual prayer of manipulation.

However, to induce God to change the course of the universe is much less the psychological function of prayer than to induce *within ourselves* a change of heart, of mind, of perspective, of need, of wants. Doing this makes prayer no less a religious act nor less powerful; it simply switches the agents of change from being totally in the hands of a "sugar daddy" in heaven to being, at least to some extent, in one's own hands. It is a matter of taking personal responsibility. Prayer then becomes reflective, all-things-considered time for turning from the egocentrism of the individual's part alone, to the perspective of the individual who emerges, figure against ground, and begins to grasp the whole scene. Whitehead said, "Religion is world loyalty." Maybe we are beginning to get closer to what he means. Prayer in this sense is perspective-giving. That is why it is essential to religion.

"Prayer is religion in act," says William James (1958, p. 352). Prayer distinguishes religion from moralizing or from the aesthetic sentiment, or from mere philosophy, no matter how comprehensive or perspective-giving that philosophy may be. Real prayer is not mere repetitious ritual, the vain exercise of words, like the empty-hearted turning of a prayer wheel or vacant fingering of a rosary, but a movement into personal relationship with the mysterious power we recognize as divine. James (1958) puts it succinctly:

> Wherever ... this prayer rises and stirs the soul, even in the absence
> of forms or of doctrines, we have living religion. One sees from this
> why "natural religion," so called, is not properly a religion. It cuts
> man off from prayer. It leaves him and God in mutual remoteness,
> with no intimate commerce, no interior dialogue, no interchange,
> no action of God in man, no return of man to God. (p. 352)

It remains only a step beyond what William James is saying here about prayer being communication between the human and the divine to conclude that religion is a personal relationship between divine and human persons. That is a mystery beyond psychology. Some day we may know enough of what a person is to know in what way God is the chief exemplification of personhood. In the meantime, we will continue to relate to God according to our insights, and according to our individual levels of development, ranging from childish attempts at manipulation to the highest levels of unity and oneness of persons both human and divine: a oneness found above all in union of wills with the divine. "Father, if it is possible ... But not my will but yours be done."

This union of wills, this interpersonal communication (that consists more of listening than of talking), this mature relationship of human and divine persons is eloquently expressed by the theologian William Marrevee in his Sunday missal commentary on the Roman Catholic liturgy:

> What may we expect from prayer? That we get God interested in us,
> in our concerns?

What we may expect from prayer above all is that it brings home to us God's gracious presence to our life. Our day to day life has its pain and joy, its cracks and holes, its shattering and exciting experiences, and we wonder ... does it really matter, is there any sense to it all?

In prayer we bring all of life with its broken and incomplete features before God. Not everything will become clear; but what prayer can do in us is to make us grow in the awareness that all the things that make up our everyday life, our concern for daily bread, our disappointments and joys are not indifferent to God, but matter to Him.

That is expressed in the underlying theme of the Our Father: confidence and trust. The end result of prayer is not that we change God's mind, but that we perceive life differently. Prayer does not change God; it changes and renews us. Without taking the threatening and chaotic features away from our life, it sets us free from a paralyzing anxiety. It makes an element of peace and confidence enter our life; an awareness that in the final analysis we are cared for. It may help us to get on with life. Difficulty and pain will not suddenly disappear, but when honestly placed before God they may become the fertile soil from which confidence and trust are born.

God's most sought-for gift of prayer enables us to approach God as a Father who cares, a Father in whom we can trust despite and in the midst of at times seemingly contrary evidence.

Religion and Faith

The words *faith* and *religion* are sometimes used interchangeably. It is just as easy to talk about "faith development" as "religious development" and suppose we are meaning the same thing. However, I think it is important to distinguish the two. So, while we are about the task of clarifying how we shall use certain terms, we should turn our attention to what we mean by faith and religion.

First, perhaps I should speak to the point of why I am using the word religion at all, with all its connotations of sectarianism and group membership. Why not, some of my students have objected over the years, use the word *spirituality* or even *consciousness* and get rid once and for all of the need to make all these distinctions? "After all," they say, "the way you are using the word *religious* certainly emphasizes the levels of personal experience that are spiritual." My main reason for hanging onto the word religious is to help save the word religion from being limited to its powerful connotation, organizational religion. Right now the word religion, although weighed down as it is with sectarian connotations, still contains the concept of the individual in a relationship of love. I think we should use the word religion despite the difficulties, to keep it a rich and growing term expressive of both the individual and collective facets. Perhaps we can even add to the richness of the word religion. Let us attempt to do that now by comparing it with faith.

The great Protestant theologian Paul Tillich gave one of the most meaningful definitions of faith (1958, p. 1) when he said: "Faith is the state of being ultimately concerned." Perhaps we could better call it the *process* of being ultimately concerned. However, Tillich is trying to tell us that people have many concerns ranging from bare subsistence needs like food and shelter, to spiritual concerns: cognitive, aesthetic, social, political. There are levels of concern, and at whatever level a person fixes his or her ultimate concern that is where the person establishes his or her faith. If the ultimate concern is in enjoying oneself, then hedonism is one's faith. If one's ultimate concern is in making money or gaining power, then materialism or control is one's faith. If one's ultimate concern is the love of God and fellow man then one's faith is religious in the highest sense. Faith is an act of the total personality, including all the elements of personality and giving a centering force to the dynamics of personal life. As ultimate concern, faith involves choice, belief, and commitment to whatever we have chosen as being worthy of ultimate concern (Tillich, 1967, 1974).

This is where religion can come in as something quite distinct but a partner and a guide to faith. If faith is the state of being ultimately concerned and religion is what gives perspective to life, then religion tells us what is worthy of our ultimate concern.

Religion tells us what is truly valuable.

Religion is that consciousness, at whatever level, that gives perspective to the lives of individuals and shared meaning to the community. If the religious consciousness of an individual or a community is at a high level, it tells us by experience, by example, by teaching, by tradition what is truly worthy of ultimate concern. Religion at its best thus confirms true faith, integrating the whole personality, because, as we have seen, faith is an act of the whole personal life. In other words, because religion gives perspective to life, if it is true religion, it gives true perspective, grounding our faith in what is truly worthwhile, truly worthy of ultimate concern. If it is of lesser caliber or false, religion yields idolatry, for it sets up gods that are not worthy of worship and goals that are not deserving of pursuit.

We will see more about the psychological process of faith development and its interplay with religious development later. But perhaps it would be helpful now, while we are still concentrating on faith-religion relatedness, to attend to a distinction that Peter Berger makes in his book *A Rumor of Angels, Modern Society and the Rediscovery of the Supernatural* (1970). Berger distinguishes inductive and deductive faith and thereby clarifies two rather distinct ways of coming at faith via religion. He says:

> I use induction to mean any process of thought that begins with experience. Deduction is the reverse process; it begins with ideas that precede experience. By "inductive faith," then, I mean a religious

process of thought that begins with facts of human experience; conversely, "deductive faith" begins with certain assumptions (notably assumptions about divine revelation) that cannot be tested by experience. Put simply, inductive faith moves from human experience to statements about God, deductive faith from statements about God to interpretations of human experience. (p. 57)

What Berger is saying has important implications for how we approach our own religious identity and how we approach the education of others in our faith. If we limit our view of religion to it being largely an institutional phenomenon, an organization clustered around a set of beliefs, doctrines, dogmas, and traditions passed down from generation to generation, then the main task of the religious person is to learn these beliefs that his religion passes on, accept them "in faith" (which often means *blind* faith), and live by them. A grade 3 student I once encountered expressed this attitude very well: "Religion is fairy stories," she said, "except in religion, you have to *believe* them." Perhaps we had the makings of a religious conformist there, perhaps a religious cynic. Whatever the case may be, she expressed the results of a kind of deductive approach to religious education very well: religion as a set of dogmas, and faith as the passive acceptance of those dogmas no matter how incredible they might be. The *inductive* approach gives faith an entirely different role, that of a search for personal meaning stemming from one's own experience of life. This quest is urged and guided by religion, which is there to call the person to seek answers and help find personal answers in the tradition of wisdom it passes on. Religion in this setting has the consciousness-enriching role of giving perspective to individuals and shared meaning to the community. Nel Noddings (1993), in a brilliant book, writes about *Educating for Intelligent Belief or Unbelief.*

Life Meaning: Victor Frankl

What is transitory is only our opportunities.
The past is the safest form of being; we have eternalized everything.
*—Viktor Frankl (*Man Alive *interview)*

Our discussion of religion and faith as the search for meaning would not be complete without including the man whose ideas and whose personal presence have centered on the problem of finding meaning in the contemporary situation. Viktor Frankl, an existential psychologist, has spoken directly to the problem of the need for meaning and presented practical means of achieving that meaning (1959, 1978). What Frankl has to say about the search for meaning is productive in our discussion of religion. He is so brilliantly clear and relevant to our times that he can enrich our study of the development of religion and faith in today's world.

Frankl certainly came to his theory inductively from his own experience of life, torn open for observation in the rawest of situations, the concentration camps of Nazi Germany. Born of Jewish parents in 1905, he became a physician and taught at the University of Vienna Medical School as a neuropsychiatrist. During World War II, he and his family were taken off to the concentration camps. There, in the ugliest and potentially most dehumanizing situations, he saw that some prisoners were reduced to the level of animals, while others rose to new heights of humanness, not despite the situation, but, it seemed to him, because of the situation. What made the difference, Frankl concluded, was that some prisoners had a sense of purpose in their lives, or even discovered a sense of meaning there in the death camps. What is needed to survive or even develop in the most inhuman of situations is the conviction that life always has a meaning and a purpose. Frankl (1959, p. 121) recalled the words of Nietszche, "He who has a why to live for can bear with almost any how." The role of each individual is to actively discover and live that meaning. After the war Frankl formalized his reflections into a theory that he called *logotherapy* and published it in a book entitled initially *From Death Camp to Existentialism* and later *Man's Search for Meaning* (1959). This book is the absorbing account of his sufferings and searchings and the sufferings and searchings of others in the concentration camps, and the belief that grew out of that experience, a deep conviction of the importance of searching for meaning in life, not just in the threat of death camps, but in the stresses of the everyday life all of us live. Nothing, he maintained, is without meaning if we can only understand that meaning is there to be found in every life, and every situation.

Frankl believed, as an existentialist, in the freedom of the will. "Man," he said, "is free to rise above the somatic and psychic determinants of his existence" (1969, p. 3). From this basic assumption he moved on to his concept of the will to meaning. Man reaches out for meanings to fulfill; he is responsible for the specific meanings of his life.

Frankl outlined three ways in which meaning can be discovered: by pursuing some task, some work, some cause; by being involved in relationships to others; sometimes by accepting unavoidable suffering.

In advocating a search for meaning, Frankl is attempting to heal what he calls the collective neurosis of our time (Hague, 1978). In this task he is in the tradition of existentialist philosophers, theologians, and psychologists such as Kirkegaard, Tillich, Rollo May, Karl Jaspers, and Martin Buber. Rollo May in particular (1953) attacks Freud's tenet that sexual repression is the common ailment of our time. True as that may have been in Freud's Victorian Vienna, sexual repression is not today's most common ailment. The collective neurosis of our time is emptiness, alienation, separation, loneliness, boredom, aimlessness, and existential frustration. The answer, Frankl and others maintain, to this noogenic neurosis is the search for meaning.

Basic, of course, to Frankl's theory is his conviction that life is not meaningless or totally absurd as some other existentialist philosophers and artists have maintained. Instead, Frankl is a leader in that branch of existentialism that is convinced that life does have meaning. This meaning is available to everyone, and the meaning is there to be found under any condition. As an existentialist, Frankl believes that each life situation is unique, as is the meaning of each particular situation. Thus individual meaning cannot be wholly transmitted through tradition. The task of tradition, rather, is to pass on universal meanings and values. Against this background of universal meanings, the human person emerges as an individual, figure against ground, discovering his own personal meanings. In finding his own personal meaning, an individual uncovers the spiritual significance of his or her life. Transcending the here and now, I can grasp the greater picture of life, finding myself in that larger context, putting my life, my task, my suffering in the perspective of the transcendent. This idea, as we shall see, flows beautifully into Whitehead's philosophy of process and illumines the place of the individual within the whole. It flows beautifully too into our theme of religion as perspective-taking.

Frankl maintains that religious people *may* have an advantage in finding meaning in life, but he also wants to clearly insist that mere membership in a religious organization does not bring meaning. He (as we have done) goes to some pains to distinguish religion from spirituality, finding the German words for the two remarkably similar but clearly distinct. Frankl maintains that his psychology has to do with the spiritual (*geistig*) rather than the religious (*geistlig*). He is anxious to maintain that meaning is available to all regardless of religious affiliation. I think the broader notion of religion that we have adopted avoids this difficulty; in fact it emphasizes the relevance of logotherapy for understanding religion and faith. If we take what Tillich and others are saying about faith involving ultimate concern, we see a remarkable convergence among psychologists, philosophers, and theologians on the theme of the search for meaning in life. Faith is the process of the search for meaning. Institutional religion has no monopoly on providing the terms of this meaning; it can be found, as Frankl himself exemplifies, in the most secular of situations. However, religion can provide meaning, and religiousness at the higher levels is best at pointing toward meaning in life. Religion can be the guide and friend to the questing individual who seeks to discover what it is that will give ultimate meaning to life. It gives ultimate meaning because that task, that relationship, that suffering, that value is truly worthy of his or her ultimate concern.

In his later years Frankl was fond of challenging (rather impishly) the wording of the American Constitution, which speaks of the "pursuit of happiness." Happiness, he insisted, cannot be *pursued*; it slips away like quicksilver between your fingers when you try to grab it. Happiness *ensues*; it follows from the search for meaning.

Religion's Demand to Be Participant

Yalom (1980) proposes that finding meaning is not necessarily synonymous with having found ultimate or cosmic answers. It is an ongoing spiritual quest. The demand of that quest is *engagement,* a heartfelt commitment to be involved in a struggle with all aspects of existence. Like the hero's journey, life demands involvement. Involvement entails awareness of the situation and commitment to it. The situation may be the call of human relationships, the commitments of a task, or the acceptance of an inevitable suffering. The picture, though, is not all grey and bleak; there is joy in engagement as one actualizes one's potential. Again, the Greeks had a word for it, *agonia:* pain but not passive pain; rather the agony of the runner in the race, feeling the pain, knowing it is the result of his striving, but striding on because the goal is worthy. This is the *quest* religious mentality that Batson (1993) describes.

This is one of those elusive but insistent and annoyingly true concepts of the existentialist philosophers. It goes back to Heidegger (1962) who deplored an inauthentic "forgetfulness of being" when one is immersed in everyday diversions. He pointed instead to an authentic "mindfulness of being" where one is reflective, thoughtful, often wondering, and, above all, actively engaged and participant in life. There is a vast difference between the Beatles' "Father Mackenzie writing the sermons that no one will hear" and Mother Teresa of Calcutta, or Bishop Romero martyred for his commitment to the poor. Later in this book we will see Gordon Allport listing "the capacity to lose oneself in one's work" as a characteristic of the mature person. Freud, Maslow, and many others have recognized this too. Yalom (1980) has sharpened the focus of "meaning in life" as spiritual commitment by insisting on engagement.

This has been a long and rather complex chapter. It is an important one, however, and its main themes are the foundation of much that is to come, Oversimplified, they are:

Faith is the process of being ultimately concerned—whatever that concern may be.

Religion, at its best, helps us to discover in our lives what is truly worthy of our ultimate concern.

Religion's role is to give perspective on value, meaning both personal and universal, and to call one to engagement in the world.

Chapter 3

Psychology and Religion: An Historical Overview

In order to be at peace, it is necessary to feel a sense of history—that you are both a part of what has come before and part of what is yet to come. Being thus surrounded, you are not alone; and the sense of urgency that pervades the present is put in perspective.

—Elisabeth Kubler-Ross

To put the relationship between religion and psychology into perspective, we should look briefly at the recent history of that relationship. It will also give us a chance to review some of the most significant authors and see what they have to say about religion from a psychological point of view. We will begin with Freud and move up to significant contemporary authors. If there is any trend in this history it is one of convergence, with Freud creating great distance between religion and psychology, followed by others representing a gradual but sure movement of the two camps closer together. This convergence is characterized by diminishing mutual mistrust and increasing appreciation of what religion and psychology have to offer each other.

Sigmund Freud

Freud lived in the late 19th and early 20th centuries. We begin with him, not because he was the originator of a psychology of religion (we can, as we have seen, trace western psychology and its interest in the spirit, the human psyche, back to the Greeks), but because the psychology of religion as a separate discipline really emerges only in 19th-century studies in social psychology. As the father of modern clinical psychology in that century, Freud made an immense contribution to the development of the psychology of religious and moral development.

It is important to recall the social setting in which Freud practiced clinical psychology. Seated in his famous office at number 19 Bergstrasse in Vienna, Freud saw a constant stream of neurotic people who seemed to him to represent the problems of his time. It was the Victorian era, when sex was something not to be talked about, and the established religions strongly encouraged what to Freud was profound sexual repression. One cornerstone of Freud's theory of psychopathology was that sexual repression was the wellspring of neurosis. Religion was constantly there in the lives of his patients playing its part in the neurosis. Religion either helped generate or helped express neurosis through the acceptable religious symbols that were conscious statements of unconscious repressions.

Freud was a product of 19th-century materialism. As a scientist of his time he could not affirm faith or values. It was thought at that time that a truly value-free science was not only possible, but necessary if psychology was to attain "scientific objectivity." A scientist could not speak of faith and values and still maintain his credibility in the scientific community. Empirical knowledge, not divine authority, was the cornerstone of this science. In the moral realm, the intricate psychological workings of conscience were to be explored, and value issues were to be scorned as mere subjectivity, unworthy of hard-nosed science.

Freud was, of course, interested in morals, particularly as these were expressed in the working of the conscience. He devised a schema of the human psyche giving an important place to conscience, which is part of what he referred to as the *superego*. A homely analogy to Freud's concept of the structure of the psyche would be that of the structure of an egg. The yolk represents the core of the psyche, which Freud called the *id*. Surrounding this is the white of the egg, representing the *ego*. All of this is encompassed and held in by the shell, the *superego*. The id at the core of the person is a boiling, seething mass of libidinal, sexual energy, seeking expression in the outside world. If the ego is strong and well developed it can control and direct the sexual urges of the id. For most people, however, the controlling structure that holds in the sexual drives is that hard, resistant shell on the outside, the superego. The conscience is part of the superego, and according to Freud it is something the individual acquires as an infant when he learns the prohibitions and taboos of the society around him. Parents in particular are the source of these prohibitions as they tell the child in a God-like way what is right and wrong. They punish him or her for wrongdoing, especially by inducing feelings of shame and guilt. Shame and guilt, then, caused largely by Mom and Dad as they teach the prohibitions of society to their children, form the dynamics of a repressive conscience, a conscience largely concerned with holding in unacceptable sexual urges.

Freud was also influenced by the anthropology of his time. In 1913 he published *Totem and Taboo* in which he attempted to apply new psychological concepts to primitive cultures. Freud presented the idea that there was a psychological connection between the religious practices of primitive man and the neurotic behavior of contemporary men and women. Behind *Totem and Taboo* was the Freudian notion that the mythologies of world religions show that religion is nothing more than the projection of psychological processes onto the outside world much as a movie projector throws images on a screen.

He attributed the origin not only of religion, but of all civilization, culture, morality, and law to the psychological connection between the Oedipus complex and totemism that existed in primitive societies. Freud had given the name Oedipus complex to the situation where the son hates and even kills his father because of his own desire to possess his mother. In *Totem and Taboo* Freud made a psychological connection between this situation that he thought he saw in his Viennese clients and the findings of anthropologists that a totem animal must not be killed except communally, and that members of the same totemic group were not permitted to have sexual relations with women of the same tribe. From this psychological association Freud concluded that God was merely the projection of the father figure, and that guilt, the standards of sexual morality, and the practice of sacrifice were derived from patriarchal totemism. In *Totem and Taboo* Freud says: "The individual conception of God is in every case modeled on the father. God is at bottom nothing but an exalted father" (Argyle & Beit-Hallahmi, 1975, pp. 183-184).

In *The Future of an Illusion* Freud defined religion as consisting of "certain dogmas, assertions about facts and conditions of external (or internal) reality, which tell one something that one has not discovered oneself and which claim that we should give them credence" (1928, p. 43). Here we see Freud as a scientist of his time, scorning faith because one has not discovered it himself, and visualizing religion solely as a set of dogmas and practices without considering religion as an individual and communal experience of real dimensions of the person.

The word *illusion*, as Freud uses it to describe religion, is worthy of comment. Freud carefully points out that, "an illusion is not the same as an error, it is indeed not necessarily an error.... It is characteristic of an illusion that it is derived from men's wishes. Thus we call a belief an illusion when wish-fulfillment is a prominent factor in its motivation, while disregarding its relation to reality, just as the illusion itself does" (1928, pp. 53-54).

According to Freud, religion is nothing more than an expression of wishful thinking: a desire to escape from the hard, cold facts of reality. This desire stems from the psychological factors of a small child's relationship to the father, a relationship strengthened by the child's all too vivid awareness of helplessness in the face of the realities of an unknown world which is a terrifying void of darkness.

Religion was something early man sought as a comfort and protection against this threat. The need, Freud contended, continued up to contemporary times. You can find it today expressed in the films of Ingmar Bergman, who was heavily influenced by Freud. In Bergman's early films we see, set against the grey background of a bleak Scandinavian landscape, the man or woman trying to find the comfort of a father with whom he or she could never communicate as a child. Usually the need for communication and comfort is projected onto God, who fails to speak, and the film ends as bleakly as it began in a black void of faith. This is especially true of *Winter Light,* in which the main character is a Christian minister without faith or ability to be a father to his parishioners who look to him for the comforts and reassurance of religion. At the end of the film, one is left with the enigma: Have events changed him? Has he heard the voice of God in the people around him? Or does he just go on as he began, hearing neither God nor his parishioners and with nothing to give them?

In *The Future of an Illusion* Freud indicated a number of resemblances between religious observances and the behavior of obsessive-compulsive neurotics. He found that a substantial part of religious law and ritual is concerned with feelings of guilt, a strong desire to control "evil" instincts, and scrupulous attention to detail. Freud saw religion as a universal obsessional neurosis.

Although psychoanalysis is anachronistic, and rests largely on idiosyncratic assumptions and tenuous conclusions derived by Freud from the limited scope of his clinical practice, Freudian psychology has continued to have a profound influence on psychology in general and religious psychology in particular. Much of the reaction to Freudian psychology has been negative condemnation: for example, papal statements have denounced psychoanalysis as materialistic, atheistic, and pansexual. Freud, like the rest of us, brought to his understanding of religion his own personal background and the attitudes of his time. As we have seen, Freud conceived of religion as merely a set of dogmas and not as a personal experience. He never considered that man might be by nature a "religious animal."

Some of Freud's followers had the courage to step outside Freud's limited concept of religion, and Jung in particular had a vision of humans as essentially religious beings. Some of those who stayed within the realm of Freudian orthodoxy, and transcended their "Father" by seeing new and more contemporaneous repercussions of the theory, made valuable contributions to the psychology of religion and morals. Some of these neo-Freudians, particularly Karen Horney, Eric Fromm, and Erik Erikson, are outstanding.

What positive things did Freud give the psychology of religious and moral development? First and foremost, he planted firmly in our vocabulary the word *unconscious.* To acknowledge that not all of the psyche is out in the open, to recognize that dynamics of which we are not aware are acting upon us, is a valuable concept for all psychologists to have. He shook moral decision making out of the purely rational flowerpot in which it had been growing since Greco-Roman times and planted it in the more realistic, if stormier, garden of unconscious, biological needs (a more holistic view of mankind). He acknowledged the dynamic forces of emotionality as shapers of moral decisions, rather than enlightened reason, which had become enshrined in scholastic theology and canon law. He saw moral thinking as developmental, something that went through unfolding stages of development, and not something that arrived in full bloom at the age of 12 as Roman (and subsequently Church) law had decreed.

Freud saw the human psyche, including the religious sentiment, as biologically based, which insight helped religious psychology to avoid two errors: (a) confusion of the biological with the spiritual, and the resultant well-meaning but misdirected attempts to control the biological solely with spiritual means; and (b) the tendency to moralize, to immediately consider the client as "bad" instead of perhaps ill.

It is interesting to note that in some ways we have come almost full circle. Today's emphasis in psychology on the ability of the human psyche to control physiological functioning, even to counteract pain by producing pain-controlling dopamines, brings us back to the more "primitive" attempts to affect the physiological by spiritual means. In the past and in contemporary primitive societies the very real connection between the spiritual and the biological was explained in terms of miracles and direct divine intervention. Today we know something more of the chemistry of the body and how subject it is to hypnosis, relaxation, sensory deprivation, ritual, and even good old-fashioned determination and will power.

The ascending spiral of psychology has come full circle also in the realm of morality. Today we no longer burn witches or put to death a Joan of Arc because she hears voices. Mental illness, partly thanks to Freud, does not carry with it a moral condemnation. The alcoholic is considered ill and not depraved or simply lacking in will power. But is there not too a reaction against the "bleeding heart" liberal syndrome that would explain away morally wrong behavior in terms of "bad" environment or defective genes? Philosophers and psychologists of the most humane and humanistic persuasion are reminding us that "we are our choices." We are perhaps less likely to simplistically explain evil in terms of illness, crime in terms of an unhappy childhood, drug addiction in terms of helplessness. As we will see, Dabrowski's "third factor" in the theory of Positive Disintegration clearly puts responsibility for personal development and the moral direction of that development in the hands of the individual.

If Freud were alive today, even given the limitations of his personal background, he would certainly not construct the same psychology as he did. He was too much aware of his times for that to happen. Freud would see that today, for instance, men and women are not guilt-ridden over repressed sexuality, but rather quite the opposite. He would discover with other great psychologists such as Viktor Frankl and Rollo May that the pervading neurosis of our time is emptiness, meaninglessness, and loneliness. He would discover that the neurosis of our time is not repressed sexuality, but a pervading lack of direction, purpose, and meaning in practically everything—including sexuality. Given the development in religious thinking (due partly to his goading), he would probably see more readily the positive contributions religion has to offer in resolving the neuroses of our time.

Carl Jung: The Self as Soul

Carl Jung was a contemporary of Freud's and indeed in the beginning a disciple. He separated from Freud over some fundamental issues, many of which touched on religion. Jung concentrated on the unconscious as did Freud, but diverged from him by not centering on lower instinctual levels, but on higher spiritual levels. Freud had seen religion as symptomatic of illness; for Jung the absence of religion was the chief cause of psychological disorders. For Freud, God was nothing more than a projection of the father image; for Jung the human father took on a God-like image, not the other way around. Freud, as a rational scientist, looked for the day when psychology would succeed in explaining away religion, as an analyst would explain a patient's dreams. This would dispel the illusion, curing the fundamental neurosis of mankind. Jung, on the other hand, saw religion as an essential activity of humans; rather than explaining it away, psychology had the exciting role of throwing more light on religion so that one could explore not only what is fundamental in human nature, but what is indicative too of its higher reaches.

It is important to know, first, what Jung meant by "religion." He outlines this most succinctly in his *Psychology and Religion* (1938), "I want to make it clear that by the term 'religion' I do not mean creed.... Creeds are dogmatized forms of original religious experience. The contents of the experience have become sanctified and usually congealed in a rigid, often elaborate structure" (p. 6). Clearing the table of what he does *not* mean by religion allows him to state what he *does* mean by the term, "Religion is the careful and scrupulous observation of the experience of the numinosum: a quality of a visible object or the influence of an invisible presence that causes a peculiar, involuntary alteration of consciousness" (p. 4). From these statements it is clear that Jung was concerned with the human, psychological experience of religion rather than its content. Religion was not a belief system coming from outside the individual, nor was it a set of behaviors that helped one fit in with the expectations of a religious group. Rather, it was something intensely personal, something mysterious and literally wonder-full, something mystical. What was the source of this experience of the cloudy but awesome realms of the human psyche? It was the human psyche itself. It was the individual psyche imposing some order, searching for some understanding of the outpourings of the unconscious as they flowed into the realm of consciousness. We should look at this idea of the unconscious as Jung elaborated it in a spiritual, mystical context, because for him the unconscious is the dynamic center of religious activity. After exploring the dynamics in the Jungian view of religion, we will then go on to look at the developmental process toward what Jung called *individuation*.

The Inner World of the Unconscious

Basic to Jung's psychology is the idea that the psyche is not identical to consciousness and its contents. The psyche is much more. The unconscious is a world vast and rich with colorful characters and mysterious symbols. Only when our dreams let these characters and symbols escape into consciousness do most of us become aware of this active and ancient part of us that we share with other humans. Dreams were important to Jung. We all experience them and sometimes dismiss them as silly and meaningless. Jung was not so quick. He saw real meaning in dreams, often symbolic meaning, and encouraged us to explore our dreams to get to know ourselves and our religious experience better. He has shown us that exploring our dreams to reach the depths of our unconscious gives us a wider religious community than just the members of our church; it opens the heritage of centuries of humans looking for the face of God in a truly mundane world.

"Man has developed consciousness slowly and laboriously, in a process that took untold ages to reach the civilized state ... And this evolution is far from complete, for large areas of the human mind are still shrouded in darkness" (Jung, *Man and his Symbols,* 1928, p. 6). Jung called these unknown areas of the psyche the unconscious. According to Julian Jaynes (1976), anthropological evidence suggests that consciousness is a fairly recent acquisition of human nature. In the total perspective of human evolution it is still fragile, menaced, and something mankind is still "experimenting" with. For many psychologists consciousness is quite enough to deal with; for Jung, however, there is no understanding the whole person without taking into account the unconscious, which is real and active. He spent his life exploring it and found the unconscious to be peopled with myriad symbols that affect daily living but escape into consciousness usually only through dreams and symbols. Jungian symbols can be as abstract as mandalas—circular geometric designs such as spirals—or as concrete as symbolic animals or humans. From the "Lion of Judah" in Biblical times to the "Lions Football Team" of our own time, we use symbols that convey a message about what to expect in the conscious affairs of life from the symbolization of the animals we choose to represent us. Similarly, Jung would say that many of the people who occupy our dreams are symbolic of roles being played out in our conscious lives: the wise old man, the trickster, the virgin-mother. These and many other symbols appear again and again in the chronicles and monuments of history all over the world, and in our present-day art, literature, religious teachings, and ritual. Jung called them "archetypes of the collective unconscious," finding them something we all share (some more consciously than others), but buried deep in the unconscious of all human beings. According to Jung, our psyche is not isolated. It is bathed in a sea called the *collective unconscious.* In Jung's words (1966, p. 169), the collective unconscious is "the precondition of each individual psyche, just as the sea is the carrier of the individual wave."

The unconscious can bring into consciousness aspects of the self that one has for various reasons preferred not to look at closely. Jung called this critical role of the unconscious the *shadow* because it personifies the dark side of human nature. The shadow represents unknown or little known attributes of the ego. When one senses the presence of one's own, one becomes aware of (and often ashamed of) characteristics and impulses previously unknown or denied. Frequently the pitfalls and little sins the unconscious digs up in the self are the very faults that one has so plainly seen in others. Perhaps one tells oneself, "It's nothing; it doesn't matter; nobody will notice because everybody's doing it." The shadow, however, quietly but persistently continues to whisper, "This is not just other people; this is the other side of you."

In dreams and myths the shadow may appear as a person of the same sex as that of the dreamer or the hero, who feels an uneasiness with the archetypal person. But often another inner figure emerges. If the dreamer is a man, he will discover a female personification of his unconscious (the anima); in the case of a woman, the personification will be a man (the animus). The anima or animus turns up in the depths of the shadow, bringing up new problems but also new possibilities. Von Franz (1978) described the anima as:

> a personification of all feminine psychological tendencies in a
> man's psyche, such as vague feelings and moods, prophetic
> hunches, receptiveness to the irrational, capacity for personal love,
> feeling for nature, and—last but not least—his relation to the uncon-
> scious. It is no mere chance that in olden times priestesses (like the
> Greek Sibyl) were used to fathom the divine will and to make con-
> nection with the gods. (p. 186)

It is no mere chance either, and fascinating, that men of classical Greece who so prided themselves on their rationality should seek guidance from the Delphian Sibyl, not only a female, but one who, under the influence of drugs, uttered incoherent prophecies. Great decisions of fortune and of war were made on rather tenuous interpretations of murky words. Something deep and powerful was at work.

The dangerous aspects of the anima appear too in literature as the *femme fatale,* the Greek Sirens or the Lorelei of the Rhine who lured men to their destruction. The Slavic countries had their myths too of the spirits of drowned girls (the Rusalka, the Willies) who bewitched and drowned men.

The positive, enriching aspects of the anima appear in the goddesses of fertility, the wise women (witches), and as *Hagia Sophia,* Holy Wisdom, in the feminine personification of wisdom venerated in the great basilica of Constantinople. The anima takes on the role of guide or mediator to the world within and to the self. The anima, personified in Dante's Beatrice, puts a man's mind in tune with right inner values, opening the way to more profound inner depths he may not reach on his own.

The proper, positive role of the anima is to serve as mediator between the ego and the self. Jung felt that the self normally expresses itself in some kind of fourfold structure, and he outlined four stages of development of the self (the parallel with Dabrowski's levels and overexcitabilities that we will see later is noteworthy). The first stage is instinctual and biological, symbolized by the figure of Eve. The second is romantic and aesthetic, but still characterized by sexual elements, personified by Faust's Helen. The third level raises *Eros* to the heights of spirituality, personified in the virgin-mother, a mythic image that comes down from ancient Egypt to its Christian personification in Mary. The fourth and highest level is the most holy and the most pure, symbolized by the *Hagia Sophia,* Holy Wisdom, or the Shulamite in the Song of Solomon. Sometimes the images get transposed and confused. Just outside ancient Ephesus in Turkey and near the site of the temple of the goddess Artemis, known to the Romans as Diana, the goddess of the moon, there is today a Christian shrine that is claimed to be the last home of the Blessed Virgin Mary. It is interesting that the Christian "Virgin-Mother" should be associated in men's minds with a pagan goddess to the extent that the early Church Fathers chose Ephesus as the site for the Council that defined doctrines on the "Mother of God." There is, of course, today, for the convenience of Christian tourists in this Moslem land, a religious goods store on the site. One glass display case, when I was there, contained rows and rows of statues of Mary for sale. It was all very Christian. But, mixed in among the images of Mary the "Mother of God" were statues of the goddess Artemis! The anima takes many forms.

Out of the deepest shadow of a woman's psyche, Jung says, emerges the animus, not so often in the form of an erotic fantasy or mood, but the personification of a conviction that the woman sees as sacred. It may take the form of an obstinate, inexorable, even cold "male" power. Like the anima in the man, it may be a negative force. This is the "Bluebeard" image. There is too the theme and thrust of "Beauty and the Beast" where the animus remains in the shadows, an unknown, pitiable one. Only by blindly trusting and loving him will the woman be able to redeem him. One could try to write this all off as 19th-century romanticism; Jung would insist that it goes much deeper than that.

The animus may appear as a group of men. It then represents a collective rather than a personal element. According to Jungian psychology, when a collective element is speaking through women, they habitually refer to an indefinite "one" or "they" or "everybody," and the words *always* and *should* and *ought* frequently occur.

Jung maintained that the animus, like the anima, goes through four stages of development: He appears first as a personification of mere physical power, a "Rambo" type person or an athlete. At the next higher level he possesses a capacity for initiative or planned action exemplified by Shelley, the romantic, or Ernest Hemingway, the man of action, or perhaps the

Marlboro man, blissfully smoking his cigarette at the summit of the mountain he has "conquered." At the third stage the animus becomes "the Word made Flesh" personified by the professor or clergyman or the great political orator. At the fourth and highest level the animus is the incarnation of meaning: the wise guide to spiritual truth. Like Gandhi he is the mediator of religious experience by which life takes on new meaning. The animus can connect a woman's mind with the *Zeitgeist* of her times, making her more receptive than a man to new creative ideas. As a man of his day, Jung needed to look back to examples of ancient seers to exemplify woman's creative spiritual role; men today need only look at some of the women of their own time who lead the way in a creative, life-giving revolution.

Both the anima and the animus are celebrated in symbolism from ancient sacred traditions that mark the shadowland passages of life from initiation to old age. The basic goal of initiation, for example, is taming the wildness of the juvenile Trickster and setting him on a course for release from—or transcendence of—the confines of immaturity. The Trickster in turn becomes the Wise Old Man or Woman. The child begins to pass from an immature, unrealistic sense of completeness when ego consciousness starts to emerge. For the adult a sense of completeness is achieved through a union of consciousness and the unconscious. Out of this union arises what Jung called "the transcendent function of the psyche." By means of this a person can attain the highest goals: the full realization of the potential of his or her individual self. We will see more of this when we look at what Jung called *individuation*.

Archetypes of the Collective Unconscious

Jung spoke of "archetypes of the collective unconscious," the themes of dreams and works of art since the dawn of mankind. Some of these archetypes are mandalas, generally circular, somewhat abstract figures that keep recurring in art (e.g., the Aztec sun calendar). That things go in circles or cycles is not just incidental to human nature; it is in the nature of the cosmos in which human nature participates, as the child in the womb participates in the life of the mother. The theme of "earth mother" or "wise old man" are not mere coincidences as they appear over and over, particularly in religious contexts. They are the fruits of the collective unconscious. The great myths of mankind follow symbolic themes; it is not coincidental that Jonah spent three days in the belly of the whale and Christ three days in the darkness of the tomb. Mystical numbers appear again and again, with three and seven recurring most frequently in religious traditions. It is not just coincidental that there are three persons in the Trinity, seven branches on the Jewish menorah, and seven sacraments in the Catholic Church.

Myths encompass the crossing of the sacred and the profane in symbols that have meaning on many levels. I wondered when I saw the film *The Deerhunter* why the sight of a deer with a magnificent rack of antlers staring calmly at its hunter had a special power for me, why it seemed to have a strength beyond other images. Then I remembered my father's gold watch chain. I went back to it, finding it stored away in a treasure chest of precious family keepsakes. On the watch fob was the image of a deerhunter and a deer with two great antlers, between them a shining cross. My father had explained to me when I was a little boy that this was the story of St. Hubert, patron of his parish church back in Lancashire, England. St. Hubert, so the legend goes, had been a hunter and an evil man. One day he confronted a deer in the forest with a cross shining in its antlers. He saw it as Christ, saw how he had been persecuting Christ, not only in animals but in other human beings, and was converted to a good life. I recalled the same story told to us by a German guide as we toured the Black Forest, but this time the saint had a German name. And so on and so on back to St. Paul on a sandier, sunnier road to Damascus, falling from his horse in a sudden realization of what he was doing to Christ in other people. From St. Paul through St. Hubert to the war in Viet Nam, the symbol of the deerhunter, Jung would say, is not coincidental. It is an archetype of the collective unconscious.

Where has the centripetal pull of Tolkein's *Hobbit* or C.S. Lewis's *The Lion, the Witch, and the Wardrobe* come from for very young children who have little conscious experience of life, but find powerful strange attractors in such images? The film *Shadowlands* depicts the spiritual journey of the great English religious writer C.S. Lewis, reflected in the experiences of a boy growing up. It explores images of passage from here to there, from reality to fantasy, from the outer world to the inner world, from life to death, from bliss to suffering and back again. The mysterious wardrobe in the film and in Lewis's children's story *The Lion, the Witch and the Wardrobe* is a strong image of passage. An archetype explains the self to the self. An archetype can inform a child of the inevitable passages in his or her life when they are most sensitive to hear, and before a cacophony of adult voices can confuse them.

Through dreams and fantasies the psyche expresses itself in symbolic language, and this expression, though intensely personal, is not totally unique. In fact the symbols of the psyche are shared by countless numbers of humankind, and have been shared over the ages in symbols that go back into the farthest reaches of human existence. It was as if by being human one participated in a legacy of symbols and unconscious stirrings that had significance and signification far beyond the individual, for they were born of participation in humanness. These symbols or dreams, art forms (even doodles), paintings, dances, and literature are not similar from being to being by mere chance. They are similar because they share in the *collective* unconscious.

Many archetypes come from the ancient mythical past as expressions of how humans experience natural things such as day and night, birth and death, summer and winter, male and female. Archetypes transcend peoples and ages. They seem somehow to be present in our very "bones" or, better, "hard-wired" into our nervous systems as some vestigial remains of our ancient and communal origins. For those readers who look for the physiological roots of this transition I refer you to Joseph Pearce's remarkable book *Evolution's End* (1992). Pearce does not address the question of archetypes directly, but his description of the evolution of the human brain suggests neurological possibilities for explaining the collective unconscious.

The world is alive with symbols if we stop to reflect. Let's look at one common symbol: fire. Brian Swimme and Thomas Berry, in *The Universe Story* (1992), argue for the power of fire as a symbol passed down through the ages of mankind.

> The controlled use of fire is the first extensive control of the human over a powerful natural force with almost unlimited possibilities that would be associated with human development over the centuries.... Beyond its use for warmth and possibly for food preparation, a psychic advance accompanied the physical skill, since fire makes a unique impress in human consciousness. Control of fire gave to the human a sense of power as well as an increased sense of human identity in distinction from other living beings. With the fire in the hearth a communing with mythic powers takes place, social unity is experienced, a context for reflection on the awesome aspects of existence is established. The hearth becomes the place where the basic social unities, he family, the band, the clan, the tribe, all achieve the intimacy needed for effective social cooperation. Around the hearth is security from possible predators as well as the assurance that comes from community bonding. (p. 152)

We need not go back to prehistoric times for rites and rituals of fire. We can see them in our own times. Matching the image of primitive man hunched around his cave-entrance fire, gnawing on a bone and enjoying the companionship and security of his fellows, we can ourselves experience primal fire.

> It is Friday evening in summer; the highway out of the city is clogged with the cars and campers of urbanites who, forsaking their comfortable homes and *Jenn Airs*, are in search of "wilderness." Once they are in the campground, inevitably they will collect wood and light a fire they can gather round, sharing the food, the conversation, the security of the lighted circle in the dark forest and the mystery of the consuming flames. The fire is at very least a communal gathering point. Those who reflect on fire and friends may find the consuming flames, the ascending smoke a spiritual experience.

Sometimes it is confused by 35-foot luxury campers complete with microwaves and TVs that are called "Wilderness," but our desire "to get back to nature" runs deep. It helps us in an artificial world to get in touch with the participation mystique of so-called "primitive man" who does not build a wall between himself and his environment and therefore experiences what happens without as happening within, and vice versa. In this holistic and unitive view human consciousness is free to participate in the consciousness of the world around. Religion is full of rich archetypes: life blossoming from death, light shining out of darkness, strength coming from weakness, salvation from the most humble and unlikely of sources. At its best religion takes us back to what is deep within us.

Individuation

If full spiritual development is to occur, one must move beyond collective archetypes toward the *real* archetypes, the transpersonal archetypes. Jung called this process of realization of potential *individuation*. Ken Wilber (1993) maintains that Jung himself did not fully express the difference between collective and transpersonal archetypes: those that go with higher mysticism. One moves into a realm where the central archetype is the self. But this self is not that of lower levels of development, formed in contrast and sometimes in opposition to the other. Dualities subside and oneness with all that is marks the individuated person. The transcendent function is a process that "furthers the course of individuation by providing personal lines of development that cannot be reached by adhering to collective norms" (Ewen, 1980, p. 80).

Individuation is "the unfolding of one's inherent and unique personality aided by the *transcendent function* and leading to the differentiation of the self." This is "a lifelong task that is rarely if ever completed" (Ewen, 1980, p. 80). Individuation is a stage beyond "mere health" and usually occurs in the second half of life when new meaning is sought and one strives to live up to one's potentialities. It is a process of increasing complexity of the psyche, but with greater and greater integration. Through the process of individuation one becomes a full member of the human community. For Jung the fully developed, self-actualized human being would by definition be a religious person because religion involves actualization of the highest potentialities. Without this high level actualization, any person would be a truncated specimen of humanity, cut off from full development, and possibly pretending that such potential for meta-levels did not exist in him or her. For Jung *the transcendent function* is a process that joins various opposing forces into a coherent middle ground and furthers the course of individuation, which must be personal.

Jacobi describes Jung's thinking about a pivotal aspect of Eastern culture, the Tao, in these terms:

> Unfortunately ... our Western mind, lacking all culture in this respect, has never yet devised a concept, not even a name, for *the union of opposites through the middle path*, that most fundamental item of inward experience which could respectably be set against the Chinese concept of *Tao*. In terms of Jungian psychology this con-

cept might roughly be defined as "revolving around oneself" in which all sides of the personality are drawn into the movement. The circular movement, which from a psychological point of view may be compared with the consciously experienced individuation process, is never "made" but is "passively" experienced. In other words it is an autonomous movement of the psyche. Thus the circular movement has all the moral significance of activating all the light and dark forces of human nature, and with them all the psychological opposites of whatever kind they may be. (1970, p. 140)

Postscript

The ripeness of Jung's psychology for understanding the development of a mature, soulful religion is evident. His view on personal religion has an immediate appeal for those who come to the notion of religion as the experience of a relationship with God as something not abstract, but a mysterious (and personal) presence to which one can feel related in a dynamic tension. Jung emphasized individual experience but viewed it in expansive dimensions that take it out of sheer egocentric narcissism. In fact, this personal religion draws one into relationships beyond the immediate in the vast context of one's place in all of creation. A few pages ahead, we will see Whitehead describing religion as "what an individual does with his own solitariness"—not that religion *is* solitariness as such but what one *does* with one's place in a vast, incomprehensible universe.

Writers continue to find depths of spirituality relevant to our time in Jung's thoughts. Thomas Moore, for example, in his book *Care of the Soul: A Guide for Cultivating Depth and Sacredness in Everyday Life* (1992) follows an ancient model of spiritual counseling, using Jungian psychology and myths to help his clients (and his readers) understand their emotional problems and be sensitive to the sacredness of the ordinary moments of everyday life.

Jung was not perturbed by accusations that "You can't prove all this is real." As for the realness of the spiritual, Jung makes a strong statement, again from the pages of *Psychology and Religion* (1938):

It is an almost ridiculous prejudice to assume that existence can only be physical. As a matter of fact the only form of existence we know of immediately is psychic. We might well say on the contrary that physical existence is merely an inference, since we know of matter only insofar as we perceive psychic images transmitted by the senses. (p. 11)

Given Jung's view that the psychic is essentially spiritual, one can argue that, for him, the spiritual is much more "real" than the material; there are no fallible intermediaries between oneself and one's own internal experiences.

A paradox emerges for us if we follow Jung through this way of thinking: the more one delves into self, searching one's own unconscious and interpreting self to self, the more one discovers others within oneself. Something is discovered within that is highly personal and yet communal, highly individual, but not isolationist, intensely experienced, and yet sharing of a common experience because it is part of the collective unconscious. In finding the self one finds that others are already there within. Paradoxically, by withdrawing into self, one participates in the world outside. By individuation he or she becomes even more a part of the whole. These are the kinds of experiences the mystics tell us they have known. It is difficult to deny that what Jung is talking about is truly religion.

Jung's psychology places the individual within the vast schemata of time and place, giving us a multileveled, complex maze of consciousness. Lest we get lost in the maze, though, he spins out a thread of Ariadne to guide us to the highest levels of consciousness and the greatest possibilities of participation in the interrelatedness of the universe. This is what religion is about and why it is central in Jung's psychology. With his emphasis on consciousness, it is clear that Jung was interested in the human *psychological experience* of religion rather than its social structures or content. It was for him something deeply personal, mysterious, and mystical, at the very heart of being human, and intending toward the apex of being human. Religion in Jung's view should be eminently humanizing. It should make men and women "holy," that is, whole, healthy, and in right relationship with one another.

Long before it was faddish to delve into mysticism, Jung, and later Joseph Campbell, explored its themes to get deeper into the universal experience of spirituality. Perhaps after reading this section, you have been impressed by Jung's religious insights; perhaps you have found it all simply confusing, a jumble of strange ideas too exotic to believe. Whatever your first impressions, I encourage you to give Jung and Campbell a chance in helping to understand religion in a nontraditional way. Jung has become popular at the present time for his insights into religion as a profound human experience of what is quintessential in humankind's relationships. That tells us something about the quest for spirituality in our time.

A Hero's Journey: Joseph Campbell

Joseph Campbell has brought home to us in the 20th century today the psychology of Jung. He deepens and extends it for 21st-century relevance. For many perhaps Carl Jung's spirituality is fascinating, but seems to be something "out there" in a few mystics or at least in dreamers who remember their dreams vividly. But Jung claimed that the collective unconscious is part of the universal human condition. It has taken Campbell's lifelong research in mythology to bring it down from dusty attics, making it real and relevant to us today. He insists that myths are not just fantasies of the past, but the realities we deal with today. Understanding myths can only enrich our lives in the 21st century. I find it intriguing that, although Campbell is dead, as I write these words I use present and future tense. His enthusiasm and his ideas are very much alive today. His writings and his interview videos with Bill Moyer made millions of people more aware of the depths within themselves individually and what they share with other humans around the globe today and back through ages of time. Campbell explored the many metaphors as images and myths that humans have used to describe the experience of being human when they transcend their merely reptilian brains into realms of the spiritual.

Myths

With the name of Campbell, the word *myth* has slipped into this account. Myths are usually stories peopled with characters and events that are real, not necessarily in their historical veracity, but in the way they tell us something about the human condition. When challenged by sheer rationality they fall apart, but when explored in their depths by someone not looking for literal consistency but for higher, transcendent truths, they have a power to bring home those truths as no history or linear argument could. Rollo May (1991, p. 37) asserts that a lack of appreciation of myth is a kind of "poverty" in our lives. We are goods-rich, but symbols-blind and consequently meaning-poor. Insofar as we ignore the place of myth in our lives, we exclude a dimension of our religiosity. Jung and Campbell too have told us this.

Perhaps the central, classic myth is that of the hero's journey. It's themes are woven through art, history, and the daily experience of living. The mythical hero (unlike Arnold Schwarzenegger) usually appears quite inept and comes from humble beginnings that make him ill prepared, it seems (like the biblical David), for the mighty task he is given to perform (perhaps to slay a dragon or a giant). But, despite his fears and the fragility of his weapons, he ventures with trepidation into the jaws of death (the darkness of the dragon's den perhaps) and conquers the evil one. Perhaps in this victory his own life is lost, but somehow he is resurrected, honored, and even glorified as a hero. It is the classic theme of the most unlikely succeeding because his heart is pure, his mind clear, and his trust is in a power outside himself. Toward the end of his life, Campbell was fond of pointing out that this ancient tale endures in modern mythologies such as Star Wars. Luke Skywalker rises from humble beginnings, under the tutelage of a wise old man, to save his people from the enemy. He does this by abandoning the modern faith in technology, and trusts himself. In a dramatic climax, he "saves the world" by transcending faith in technology and employing "the Force" within him. Hollywood also celebrated the myth of a very different hero, *Forrest Gump*. In this film, simplicity and moral integrity ultimately conquer mere sophistication.

"Heroes" continue to journey today. Campbell quietly challenged us to participate in an ancient human drama by finding and pursuing the "heroic" in our lives. He brings spirituality as a real possibility into our lives by pointing out that everyone is called into a spiritual journey by virtue of being human. It is in some degree a hero's journey, since all are drawn by some goal and consequently faced with some challenge, including the challenge of our own perceived ineptitude. How that goal is conceived and how that challenge is accepted and overcome are the mythic (but no less real) dimensions of life.

The journey for both Jung and Campbell is essentially a spiritual journey: what Campbell (1988) has called *The Inner Reaches of Outer Space*. In his book by that name he says:

> The universally distinguishing characteristic of mythological thought and communications is an implicit connotation through all its metaphorical imagery of a sense of identity of some kind, transcendent of appearances, which unites behind the scenes the opposed actors on the world stage. Schopenhauer ... takes up the idea, remarking that in the later years of a lifetime, looking back over the course of one's days and noticing how encounters and events that appeared at the time to be accidental became the crucial structuring features of an unintended life story through which the potentialities of one's character were fostered to fulfillment, one may find it difficult to resist the notion of the course of one's biography as comparable to that of a constructed novel, wondering who the author of the surprising plot can have been; considering further, that as the shaping of one's own life was largely an effect of personalities accidentally encountered, so, too, one must oneself have worked effects upon others. The whole content of world history, in fact, is of destinies unfolding through time as a vast net of reciprocal influences of this kind, which not only are of people upon people, but involve also the natural world with its creatures and accidents of all kinds. (p. 110)

The work of Joseph Campbell cannot be neatly summarized in a couple of paragraphs, but Campbell, in the style of Marshall McLuhan, frequently presents his thought in aphorisms that sum up a lifetime of scholarship and reflection. He says, for example:

> Eternity is a dimension of here and now...
> The divine lives within you...
> Awe is what moves us forward. (Osbon, 1991, 2-25)

> The purpose of the journey is compassion.
> When you have come past the pairs of opposite you have reached compassion.

Each of these statements is an invitation, a lure not to pass them by, but to dig deep within the self for what they may mean to you. One way of doing this is to read something from Campbell's many fascinating publications where he explains the ancient myths, inviting the reader to see their significance in life.

William James

No look at the giants of the psychology of religion would be complete without paying sufficient respect to William James, a man of universal genius whose insights in the field of religion are largely represented by a single book, the *Varieties of Religious Experience* (1958). *Varieties* is old; it is the publication of the Gifford lectures delivered in Edinburgh in the period 1901-1902, but its value is such that it remains a classic.

William James was a philosopher trained in chemistry and medicine who majored in psychology. He wrote as a scientist of his time but without the arrogance of a scientist attempting to explain away religious phenomena as "nothing but" in the tradition of the behaviorists that was so fashionable at the time. Rather, he speaks of "man's religious constitution." In this book he marvels at the varieties of ways humans express and experience that religious constitution. Just as the book is usually famous for its small print, so is it equally famous for its intriguing footnotes and the marvelous collection of case studies James uses to illustrate the varieties of religious experience.

The fact that William James could speak to his audience of academics about religion and that his *Varieties of Religious Experience* would still be a classic in psychology almost a century later is due to a basic premise on which he builds his presentation. James does not see religion as something apart from other psychic phenomena, something quite other and belonging in a separate compartment. He holds that religious phenomena are continuous with other psychic phenomena:

> There is religious fear, religious love, religious awe, religious joy, and so forth. But religious love is only man's natural emotion of love directed to a religious object; religious fear is only ... the common quaking of the human breast, insofar as the notion of divine retribution may arouse it; religious awe is the same organic thrill which we feel in a forest at twilight, or in a mountain gorge; only this time it comes over us at the thought of our supernatural relations. (1958, p. 40)

James does not pretend to cover the whole of religion. Early in the book he distinguishes institutional religion from personal religion and says he will confine himself to personal religion. This brings him abruptly to the question we have already faced: that of defining what he means by religion. For his purposes James defines religion as "The feelings, acts, and experiences of individual men in their solitude, so far as they apprehend themselves to stand in relation to whatever they may consider the divine" (1958, p. 42).

Later James says, "Religion, whatever it is, is a man's total reaction upon life" (1958, p. 45). He does not, however, hold that *any* total reaction upon life is religion. He does not maintain that *any* understanding, broad and encompassing as it might be, of the nature of the universe deserves the name of religion in the strict sense because a concept of the universe may not include a solemn experience of the divine.

James takes this concept of the solemn experience of the divine and develops the distinctions that are subtle yet important to his idea of religion. "When," he says, "we compare these intenser experiences (of the religious person) with the experiences of tamer minds, so cool and reasonable that we are tempted to call them philosophical rather than religious, we find a character that is perfectly distinct" (1958, p. 52). The stoic, the mere moralist, the man who is limited to philosophy lacks something that the religious person (and, par excellence, the mystic and ascetic saint) has in abundance. That quality that distinguishes the religious person from the stoic who can only grit his teeth in the face of adversity is a state of mind in which "the will to assert ourselves and hold our own has been displaced by a willingness to close our mouths and be as nothing in the floods and waterspouts of God" (p. 53). James goes on to describe this state of mind as one that banishes fear in a state of trust in the divine:

> What we most dreaded has become the habitation of our safety, and the hour of our moral death has turned into our spiritual birthday. The time for tension in our soul is over, and that of happy relaxation, of calm deep breathing, of an eternal present with no discordant future to be anxious about has arrived. Fear is not held in abeyance as it is by mere morality, it is positively expunged and washed away. (p. 53)

In this passage James is describing not only the experiences of the religious mystics at their loftier heights, but a state of mind that can be had to some degree by all who experience religion at their own level of development. It is significant that this rhapsodic account of the heights of religious mysticism is a picture too of the very young child who has developed a basic sense of trust. We will see more of this when we explore the developmental stages proposed by Erik Erikson.

William James is careful not to give the impression that religion is escapism, a getting away from evil or pain. Mature religion no longer cares to escape; it consents to the evil outwardly, while inwardly it knows pain and evil have been overcome. How this experience, happiness despite suffering, comes about James admits he cannot understand since it is in the domain of higher mysticism. But he does draw an analogy from a painting by Guido Reni in the Louvre showing St. Michael with his foot on Satan's neck. The allegory, he points out, is that "the world is all the richer for having a devil in it, so long as we keep our foot upon his neck" (1958, p. 55). In the religious consciousness that is the position in which the fiend, the negative or tragic principle, is found; for that reason the religious consciousness is so rich in emotion. The colorful picture William James paints of religious experience depicts two main images: the ordinary experience of religion, and the extraordinary, conversion or mystical experiences. James considers these two states as different approaches to what he calls, "the more."

On this topic of mysticism, James addresses himself to an aspect that has widespread relevance for our time. James did not have the variety of drugs available to him, nor such a widespread usage as we are familiar with now, but he does consider the relationship between intoxicants and drugs and "mysticism" (1958, p. 297ff). He speaks to the issue of mystical experience as a deliberately self-induced state and not as an integral part of an individual's religious quest. James tends to see drug-induced "higher" consciousness experiences as multifarious manifestations of mystical experiences separated from each other by the most diaphanous of veils. At this point I would like to depart briefly from my current task of "objectively reporting" what James said, to express an opinion that may well be in opposition to James's personal experience and convictions. However, it is an attempt to look at religious and particularly mystical experiences from a multilevel point of view. It is based on the conviction that truly religious experience at a high level is a *metanoia*, a lasting conversion of the whole person, and not just a passing consciousness-raising experience, beautiful and even profound as that may be. We will see more of this in the concluding chapter on levels of spirituality and what distinguishes them.

The question arises in our culture where hallucinogenic drugs are so readily available whether there are "shortcuts" to higher levels of consciousness and ecstatic experiences that do not involve the pain and suffering and long years of discipline of the mystics. Can one, simply by taking a drug, or having his or her brain chemistry naturally go awry as in schizophrenia, suddenly come to a deep experience of consciousness that is truly mystical, or "over-belief" in James's sense? The final research data is not in yet, but I think that before arriving at any conclusions one must distinguish between the authentic mystical experience and transient chemical change. Mystical experience is the fruit of one's life intention and one's suffering, and flows over into lasting, loving, compassionate action. The quick turn-on, however, is an experience that does not come from the depths of a personality, but only from a transient chemical change, and does not subsequently flow into a style of life that puts into action the ideas of "love" and "peace" and "brotherhood" that were supposedly experienced while in ecstasy. We know that the great mystics such as Teresa of Avila, John of the Cross, and Francis of Assisi used (perhaps intuitively) techniques such as sensory deprivation, spending long hours alone in prayer, perhaps transfixed before a crucifix in a secluded room. Recent experimentation has shown that when the mind is deprived of outside sensations, it tends to produce its own stimuli in the form of hallucinations. Though we can now perhaps better understand the neurological sources of "visions," we can also appreciate that the actions of the great mystics were part of their lifestyle, and the visions did flow out into a relationship with others that put into practice what they had experienced.

They did not just narcissistically experience loving union; they practiced it in their lives. Essentially, the classical mystics went the route of agony before they reached their ecstasy. Quite literally they experienced the loneliness (and discipline) of the long-distance runner. As usual, the Greeks had a word for this: *Agonia,* a pain taken on voluntarily for the joy of running the race and the goal that lay ahead.

James sees religion as "belief in an unseen order, and that our supreme good lies in harmoniously adjusting ourselves thereto" (1958, p. 58). He says that life is lived by millions of people as if there were "something more" than mere sense data. He believes that "the more" exists objectively and that we seek union with it, but does not identify the more with any particular deity. He discerns in the more a "hither side" and a "farther side." The more in religious experience with which we feel ourselves connected is on its hither side, and is the subconscious continuation of our conscious life. Because the near side of the more is a subconscious continuation of our very selves, this subconscious self forms a bridge between ourselves and the more and forms the basis for communication between theology and science.

But what about the mysterious farther side of the more? Can we come into contact with that? James says we can pass over to the farther side and calls this *over-belief* (1958, pp. 386-387), the state of those who have had a conversion experience or a mystical experience. They report to us what the more is like on the farther side. They tell us (as best they can for their experiences are literally beyond words) of their experience of beauty, completion, total self-awareness, and, at the same time, awareness of others in a new realization of their oneness with all. They may describe their experience in traditional religious terms as oneness with God. The great mystics have given us many expressions of this; the footnotes throughout James' book are full of such accounts.

William James makes an interesting and illuminating distinction, one with much promise for new understanding of the religious person, and one that is echoed in the theory of Positive Disintegration. In *Varieties of Religious Experience,* he distinguishes between the "once-born" and the "twice-born." The once-born see God not as a strict judge or a glorious, demanding king, but as the animating spirit of what is to them a beautiful, harmonious, unperturbed world. The once-born are not deeply reflective, nor are they particularly distressed by their own imperfections. They read the character of God not in the disordered world of man, but in a romantic and harmonious world of their own making. Life is a self-centered fairy tale complete with its reassurances that "everything will come out all right in the end." This religion, which is blind to the evils of the world, is what James calls the religion of "healthy-mindedness." He cites Walt Whitman as an example of this, as one who could write: "I celebrate myself, and sing myself."

This is the kind of healthy-minded religiosity that seems to permeate religious card and gift shops where pretty posters extol the glories of God's love, and cards ringed around with flowers carry sweet verses about the comforts of the Lord. If there is a crucifix, the wounds and suffering have been subdued in favor of ornamentation, gold filigree, or even glow-in-the-dark paint. It goes beyond bad taste; it is a whole approach to life that sees it as a pampered rose garden and God the gentle keeper of us flowers.

James contrasts this healthy-mindedness with the state of the "sick soul" who must be twice-born in order to be happy. The sick soul is not blind to the evils of the world; he is very much aware of the injustices around him and of the evils and injustices within him. He reflects deeply on the human condition and agonizes over the evil that men create for their fellow men. He "hungers and thirsts" after justice. The sick soul is not morbid, perpetually depressed, or obsessed with the existence of sin, but he is aware of evil, feels sadness that it exists, and experiences a torment and turmoil within himself that the world and man are not perfect. He is troubled that he has a hand in that imperfection, even if by way of default. Far from pessimistic, he knows the great mystery that agony and death lead to resurrection and life, that death is necessary for life, that joy is the by-product of suffering. Unlike the cultivated rose garden of the once-born whose flowers are shaped to spell out immediately the words *joy, peace, happiness* without suffering, life is more like an old limber pine tree on the windswept side of a mountain, its roots clinging desperately to the little soil that is there, its trunk rotten, old, and dead-like, its branches twisted by the wind into grotesque contortions. But somewhere, through it all, there is an irresistible force that is budding forth into a new green sprig of life. The sick soul sees that this image of life is more realistic, and when he is twice-born he comes to realize that it is more beautiful too in its stark realism.

An interesting piece of religious prose was popular a while ago. It is called "Footprints" and perhaps it epitomizes the once-born soul that James talks about. It goes like this:

Footprints

One night a man had a dream. He dreamed he was walking along the beach with the LORD. Across the sky flashed scenes from his life. For each scene, he noticed two sets of footprints in the sand; one belonging to him, and the other to the LORD.

When the last scene of his life flashed before him, he looked back at the footprints in the sand. He noticed that many times along the path of his life there was only one set of footprints. He also noticed that it happened at the very lowest and saddest times in his life.

This really bothered him and he questioned the LORD about it. "LORD, you said that once I decided to follow you, you'd walk with me all the way. But I have noticed that during the most troublesome times in my life, there is only one set of footprints. I don't understand why when I needed you most you would leave me."

The LORD replied, "My precious, precious child, I love you and I would never leave you. During your times of trial and suffering, when you see only one set of footprints, it was then that I carried you."

This is a comforting piece, envisioning God as one who rescues a precious child. But the child is merely passive, being carried. For an adult and responsible contrast to this "healthy-mindedness" try making a substitution for the last line. For example, "During the times of trial and suffering, when you see only one set of footprints, it was then that you were walking in *my* steps." For a Christian this says more about the real nature and message of Christ's life and death. For any believer it changes the whole sense of one's relationship with God and the place of suffering and the nature of religion. It is the insight and conviction of the twice-born.

Dag Hammarskjöld was such a man. His diary, called *Markings,* is an expression of the uneasiness of the twice-born, the sick soul. "Bless your uneasiness," he says, "as a sign that there is still life in you" (1964, p. 119). The beauty and tension of the sick soul he expresses in "Single Form":

The breaking wave
And the muscle as it contracts
Obey the same law.

An austere line
Gathers the body's play of strength
In a bold balance.
Shall my soul meet
This curve, as a bend in the road
On her way to form?
(p. 145)

Besides exploring the vast varieties of religious experience, James has reminded us that people do not simply *have* a god, but they *use* their god. To understand what he means I think we have to distinguish several meanings of the word *use.*

1. *Use* can be taken in a very negative sense as exploiting God, in a kind of I-it relationship that seeks to fill up the deficiency needs of the human being. "God" has been used politically by "religious" leaders to exploit and murder people. Take, for example, the Crusades, the Inquisition, the Wars of Religion, the Spanish conquest of the Indian peoples of America, and, more recently and closer to home, the abuse of our Native peoples in the name of religion.

2. *Use* can be taken in another pejorative but not quite so negative sense as "depending upon" out of weakness. We use someone in this sense when we lean on them passively for support either physically or mentally. Perhaps a good example of this is one woman's "proof" for

the existence of God. She expressed it to me in these terms, "I know God exists because I *need* him."

Even if it is something to react against and something whose existence we resoundingly deny, we use this God as a rebellious teenager uses parents.

By contrast we can "use" someone (God included) positively in an "I-thou" relationship when we utilize that person and our relationship for our mutual growth and development. When James says we do not simply have a god, but we use our god, I think he means that it is very difficult to put the concept of God on a shelf and forget it. The concept of a deity is so much a part of our human makeup that we use it to explain the mysteries of life, in some way to find order in the chaos, to give hope. Karen Armstrong (1993), in her *History of God,* explores how God has been sought (and used) for 4,000 years by Christianity, Judaism, and Islam.

Summary

James himself (1958, p. 367) sums up his *Varieties of Religious Experience* in five brief points:

1. That the visible world is part of a more spiritual universe from which it draws its significance and meaning.

2. That union or relationship with that higher universe is our true goal.

3. That prayer and contemplation and inner communion with the spirit (whatever that might be for the individual) is the real activity of life, the process whereby spiritual energy produces real effects in the world as we know it.

Religion also includes the two following psychological characteristics:

4. A new zest for life, showing itself in "lyrical enchantment" or the driving forces of earnestness and heroism.

5. Feelings of safety, security, peace, and warm relating of self to others.

Alfred North Whitehead

In the absence of perspective there is triviality.
—*Whitehead* (Modes of Thought)

I am including Whitehead because there is need of a grand design into which we can place our ideas of religion and God, and ourselves. Whitehead gives a sweeping, cosmic vision. In life, details pile up and block our view of the whole; we must find something organizing and intelligible to sort out the confusion and restore a broader horizon. Whitehead does this. Unfortunately, great thinkers of grand schemes are not always capable of plain talk. Whitehead does set your imagination going though. Having ploughed through original works that both frustrated me with their esoteric language, and drew me in at the same time with the grandness of their vision, I must here settle for an all-too-brief snapshot of a vast and beautiful landscape. There is little room for detail, only highlights significant for our present study. I have tried in the following section to be as true as possible to what he said, while still capturing the creative power of his thought. I hope those two things come through.

The ideas of Whitehead deserve a special introduction for several reasons. First, he is not a psychologist, but a philosopher who describes a vast scenario in which to appreciate the full dimensions of religion and morality; he offers an approach to religion and morality that is refreshingly different, and, because the view is large and new, his words come in unfamiliar language, offering ideas that challenge some of our most fundamental assumptions. When your vision goes beyond the descriptors of your language, you must invent new words or use old ones with new meaning. This is what Whitehead does. When your ideas stretch the borders of accepted theology, you challenge not only the intelligence of your readers, but their imagination and courage. Studying Whitehead demands a certain "tolerance of ambiguity," a willingness to keep our minds open, to be patient with the language, and secure with the challenges.

Whitehead would be the last to say that his ideas are "the truth"; he had too much appreciation of the fact that our understanding of creation and its creator is still developing itself in process. His cosmic vision will urge us to expand our views by putting them in a larger context.

Alfred North Whitehead, the mathematician-philosopher-theologian, born and educated in England, who died in 1947 after a long teaching career in the United States, is the father of "process thought" in modern times. Whitehead was influenced by existentialism and employed its resources to analyze the human condition, proposing a faith answer to some of the questions existential philosophy raises. Whitehead was also influenced by the biblical work of Bultmann for whom revelation was not a dogma, not a message, but an event, an existential encounter, a continuing personal meeting of God and mankind. Gestalt psychology (in its original European sense) influenced Whitehead too, leading him toward an organismic view of things. Whitehead insisted we must look at experiences as a whole; especially we must see humans as organic with nature. Humans are one with nature, distinguished from it mainly by higher levels of consciousness and the ability to be purposive beings. Experiences are above all to be "felt," by all creation, but most intensely by human beings. Enjoyment is not something automatic, given, ready-made; it is to be achieved through discovering the "aim" of creation and joining in with it. The degree of joining in varies with the level of consciousness of the being and its intentionally directed striving.

Lest all of this seem too heady and abstract (which is a tendency of process thinkers), I recommend a practical book on religious education by Mary Elizabeth Mullino Moore (1991) titled *Teaching from the Heart: Theol-*

ogy and Educational Method. In an enthusiastic and concrete style she builds a method of religious education based on process, presenting at the same time an understanding of process thought much more simply and perhaps more lucidly than many of Whitehead's disciples. The fact that she encourages "heart" in teaching stands to her credit too.

Process

When the Greek philosopher Heraclitus stated that one could never step into the same flowing river twice, he proclaimed that the basis of reality is change and flow—the "becomingness" of things is their essence.

Whitehead used the word *occasion* in a special sense, different from our usual meaning when we say, "On the occasion of your graduation." When you see, as Whitehead did, that the very essence of everything is process, and open yourself to a grand view of the flow of the process of all that is, you see everything in it (yourself included) as a tiny occasion in that dynamic flow. It brings home that each entity, each thing is part of that process, coming into being as an occasion and ultimately perishing. This "going-on" of creation is purposive, and each participant, each actual occasion is called upon to be creative in this dynamic process. By using the term *actual occasion*, Whitehead avoids the static concept of the atom or molecule or even *entity* or *being*. All is in process, and to express it one must grasp this central notion of actual occasion. Actual occasions or "drops of experience" are the final real things of which the world is made; there is no going beyond them to find anything more real. All of reality from God downward is explainable only in terms of actual entities. There is a "perishing of occasions" as the old reaches its fulfillment, and in its particular configuration passes away. But this is the cyclical death and resurrection theme of nature (and of religion) where the perishing of summer into autumn becomes the opportunity for the blossoming of springtime. The new emerges from the old, like the tiny green redwoods sprouting from the rotting hulk of a hoary old tree that has died, fallen to the ground, and is perishing in its present form, to appear again as a new occasion, a new life. Though occasions may perish, one thing that is never lost is their *value*, the genuine abiding contribution made by that which perishes. George Eliot recognized this in the concluding lines of *Middlemarch*:

> But the effect of her being on those around her was incalculably dif-
> fusive; for the growing good of the world is partly dependent on un-
> historic acts; and that things are not so ill with you and me as they
> might have been is half owing to the number who lived faithfully a
> hidden life and rest in unvisited tombs. (1986, p. 825)

In Whitehead's sweeping view, each occasion contributes in its own degree, varying from individual to individual according to its level of conscious participation, in the building of the universe. Value abides because it is cherished by God, taken up into His nature, used, and made contributory to that which continues.

The basis of experience is emotional, and "living emotion" is given a central place in Whitehead's thought. We grasp and are grasped by experiences. This is "prehension" in Whitehead's terminology, not just apprehension that implies mere understanding; prehension is relatedness. Because the world is a society of mutually prehending occasions, Whitehead called it "organismic"—interrelated and developing, not disparate and static. Deep ecologists such as Thomas Berry (1990) have a keen awareness of this relatedness, this interconnectedness. Although we may be mostly given seemingly minor roles to play, we are all part of a great story, a valued occasion in a grander process that asks us to be not just a spectator, but participant.

Relatedness

The sources of this dynamic interrelatedness, at least at its highest levels characterized by consciousness, are rooted in intuition, a profound awareness deeply felt of something under consideration. Intuition may operate in different realms: the artist's intuitive sense of the "rightness" of a work of art, the moral sense of "rightness" that individuals at the higher levels of development feel, the religious perception based on intuition that there is, despite setbacks, a persisting stream of goodness and love in a world in process. Sallie McFague (1987) exemplifies this most succinctly in *Models of God* when she says, "Christian Faith is most basically a claim that the universe is neither indifferent nor malevolent, but that there is a power (and a personal power at that) which is on the side of life and fulfillment" (p. x).

Rightness and quality are characteristics one intuitively knows; they can't be attained by reason alone. For Whitehead, *tenderness* and *persuasion* are important words. They speak of that attractive dynamic of the universe that we call love. It is the attractiveness of beauty that draws. No occurrence or occasion is identical to another, nor are they all on the same level of significance. Some things are recognizable as important because of their aesthetic quality, their beauty, which attracts us. *Aesthetic* here does not mean solely artistic creations, although it certainly does include them; the word points to the deep feelings a particular occasion arouses. Language, as we use it, portrays this powerful force of feeling, for we say that something "appeals to us," "strikes us"; in other words, it has the capacity to impel us to say, "Yes, that's it; that's right!"

Ethics

This idea of mankind being lured intuitively toward the rightness of beauty has implications for Whiteheadian concepts of morality and ethics. The impetus toward morality, according to Whitehead, does not rule out power and coercion, but it is persuasion, not force, that is basic. Love is the major motif. Whitehead has little use for moralism. Aesthetics are more important than ethics. God is no ruthless moralist, and humans are to be "lured," not driven, to fulfillment. An actual occasion is ultimately shaped by selection among various possibilities, by limitation. An infant is a bundle of huge potential. But choices are made and directions chosen for the infant and later by the child. When a choice is A or B and you choose A, B is lost and that is a limitation, but "Value," says Whitehead (1925, p. 94), "is the outcome of limitation." A new concrete occasion comes into existence as a result of how it prehends its relevant past and gives it new focus. Value is the intrinsic reality of the occasion, unique and with impact on further process. Value, therefore, is always concrete and realized only in individual actual occasions. When greatness of experience is contributed to the process, greatness of value is achieved. Whitehead's thinking envisioned grand perspectives.

Process thought goes beyond humanistic ethics in its concern for the unity of mankind and the integration of all reality. The concern of a true morality goes beyond mankind alone to mankind as organic with the universe. Whitehead was ahead of his time when he stated that it is the survival of the universe and not just humans that is his ultimate and grand vision of morality. The transcendent moral vision of today's ecologists is something Whitehead took for granted decades ago before we were so aware of the threat to our planet and ourselves.

People have a special place in furthering the process of the universe by virtue of their high level of consciousness and free will. This leaves the way open for great possibilities and terrible deficiencies. A person can strive toward his or her aims, rejecting what does not seem to contribute or, alternatively, cut off valuable possibilities by one's own decision or lack of decision and so fail to accomplish the achievement of enduring good. One might call this "sin." The possibility of participating in the process at a higher level of consciousness is the responsibility of each person who has his or her own identity and of each community that likewise has its own identity. Morality, done in isolation from the rest of reality, is never a private affair; every moral decision has some impact on the whole and bears the weight of that responsibility. Individual interests must be harmonized with the more general interests. Whitehead suggests that the aims of a civilized society are "fineness of feeling" and "generality of understanding." The first aim of morality is the continuance of process in its maximal effect at both the level of the individual and of society. Each individual human occasion contributes his or her fineness of feeling, and the whole process achieves a generality of understanding.

Qualities of Process

In *Adventures of Ideas* (1967) Whitehead suggests some qualities that ought to be furthered by process. These qualities are truth, beauty, adventure, art, and peace. *Good* and *right* are not included in this list because they are, to him, overused words with imprecise meanings. These five qualities he lists do give sufficient clarity to symbolize what humans actually find valuable in process.

Truth is the conformation of appearance to reality. Sense perception is the primary way of attaining truth, because despite some failures it is our usual way of discerning the authentic nature of things. The things we perceive provide steady values, incorporated into the subjective form of the prehending occasion, becoming part of the data out of which new occasions emerge.

Beauty goes beyond truth in the spontaneous adaptations of some of the factors prehended by an occasion. These adaptations occur as the occasion pursues a certain aim in which intensity of feeling and conformity to a common pattern combine for the attainment of harmony. Beauty is thus wider and more fundamental than truth, because it deals not only with the conformation of appearance to reality, but also with the perfection of the subjective forms that are shaped by their interrelation.

Adventure must be part of anything so fluid as process. The vitality of thought is in adventure. "Ideas won't keep," says Whitehead. "Something must be done about them. The idea must constantly be seen in some new aspect. Some element of novelty must be brought into it from time to time; and when that stops, it does. The meaning of life is adventure" (Price, 1954, p. 254).

Art is the purposeful adaptation of appearance to reality. Art depends on how mankind has been shaped by beauty toward perfection. But perfection is not a static concept; it must always promote novelty and originality. Thus Whitehead includes adventure as a necessary quality, lest inspiration yield to mere repetition.

Finally, peace calls the individual beyond self without denying self toward the integration of order and love. This sounds to me something like what we call integration in psychology, and describes in process terms what the theory of Positive Disintegration calls its highest level, Secondary Integration. It also sets the scene for our descriptors of the highest levels of spirituality in the last chapter of this book.

God: the Chief Exemplar

Whitehead's concept of God is complex. It is disconcerting for some, because it eschews all static concepts of perfection and moves instead to dynamic process in harmony with the rest of his thought. So many other theologies have defined God as the *exception* to all we know: that one whom we can begin to understand only by denying him the characteristics we know of ordinary things. Traditional theology has described "God the ineffable" as "unchanging," "limitless," "timeless," "immovable." We have thus defined God by saying what he is *not*. Whitehead takes a new and refreshing approach. He says that God is dynamic, changing with creation, temporal; time is as real for God as for creation. Not only does He affect creation, He is affected by it. God's perfection is not a frozen state, but is found in His capacity for and actualization of His relationships with all that is not Himself. God, then, is not a self-contained being requiring nothing but Himself, but a richly related being, participating and sharing. Relationship characterizes deity. Because love is relationship sharing, and caring, God is love. God, for Whitehead, is not the exception to all metaphysical principles, but their chief exemplification. Because He is supreme and unsurpassable by all that is not Himself, He is not to be treated as only an exemplification of all metaphysical principles. He is their *chief* exemplification, and therefore He is worshipful. God is that process by which we are made new, strengthened, directed, comforted, forgiven, "saved" in the fullest sense of the word. The process that is God lures us by its beauty into feelings of wonder, awe, and reverence.

Only God may surpass Himself, moving on from a present stage to the fuller realization of His possibilities. The divine self-identity is shown by His exemplification in an eminent fashion of that which constitutes all self-identity (including our own identity): faithfulness or self-consistency; awareness and use of the past; capacity for relating oneself without any loss; inexhaustible reserves of strength in love; and purpose or subjective aim. These words have the ring of a list of qualities of an ideal human being; they are preeminently in Whitehead's God. All of these qualities are continually being enriched in God as He realizes fuller and fuller relationships. Thus God is both eternally loving, faithful, and perfect in relationships and yet active in enriching these relationships. God acts in the world by providing the "lure" that evokes self-decision in respect to His purpose of love. He gives each entity its initial aim for self-realization, but does not coerce that entity to fulfill that aim. He provides occasions and opportunities for entities to realize themselves as co-creators, opportunities that they may choose not to use, but once chosen they are the stuff of real religion and true human union with the divine.

Religion

Whitehead's notion of religion again is complex but in harmony with the rest of process thought. He has expressed it best in one of his books that is, fortunately, one of the easiest to read: *Religion in the Making* (1973). Early in that book he gives one of his many "definitions" of religion: "Religion is the art and the theory of the internal life of man, so far as it depends on the man himself and what is permanent in the nature of things" (p. 16). Perhaps better remembered, although more easily misunderstood, is his famous more poetic "definition" of religion: "Religion is what the individual does with his own solitariness" (p. 16). We have already explored this definition somewhat when discussing the nature of religion in general. Whitehead's idea of religion may begin in solitariness, but it peaks in community (Pittenger, 1981).

Religion, whether we take it as institutional or personal-experiential, is a multileveled thing, the levels being also a kind of recapitulation of the stages in the historical development of mankind's religiosity. At its most primitive level, religion is *mere ritual*, which Whitehead (1973) defines as "the habitual performance of definite actions that have no direct relevance to the preservation of the physical organism of the actors" (p. 20). Rituals are not workaday routines meant to put bread and butter on the table. They are, in the immediate practical realm, superfluous but essential in the *elan vital*. Animals perform rituals, and rituals with humans go back beyond the dawn of history. Ritual is the primitive outcome of superfluous energy and leisure. The actions involved in everyday pursuits such as hunting and fishing are repeated for their own sakes in ritualistic actions such as dances. Their repetition repeats the joy of exercise and the emotion of success. Gradually, ritual is repeated and elaborated for the sake of its emotions, and this emotion is the second level. Whitehead claims that religion and play have the same origin in ritual, because ritual is the stimulus of emotion, and, according to the quality of the emotion elicited, a habitual ritual may diverge into religion or play. The Olympic Games of ancient Greece, for example, were tinged with religion. Sports fans today have their rituals that border on the religious, from the singing of the national anthem through the ritual chants and "the wave" and to the communal consumption of beer and hot dogs.

The third belief stage emerges because mere ritual and emotion move on to a more intellectual level, usually expressed in myths. Myths explain the purpose of ritual and emotion. If the hero of the myth, Campbell says, is a thing we call it "magic"; there is special power in the thing. If the hero is a person, we call the ritual with its myth "religion." The Jewish Passover supper is a good example, involving the retelling of a story involving heroes of the past, the ritual standing to express haste, the ritual food, and the ritual questions: Why is this night different from every other night? In religion, Whitehead says, we induce, and this can be progressive. In magic we compel, and this, as we know from Whitehead's philosophy, is unprogressive. "Though religion can be a source of progress," Whitehead explains, "it need not be so, especially when its dominant feature is the stage of uncriticized belief" (1973, p. 27). And here we see Whitehead coming back to the theme of so many others, that religion reduced to a set of stagnant dogmas is a stultifying situation and not religion as it is meant to be and can be, a transcendent and transpersonal experience. Whitehead continues:

> It is easy for a tribe to stabilize its ritual and its myths, and there
> need be no external spur to progress. In fact, this is the stage of relig-
> ious evolution in which the masses of semicivilized humanity have
> halted the stage of satisfactory ritual and of satisfied belief without

impulse toward higher things. Such religion satisfies the pragmatic
test: It works, and thereby claims that it be awarded the prize for
truth. (p. 27)

"The age of martyrs," Whitehead springs on us (1973, p. 28), "dawns with
the coming of rationalism." It is important to understand that by *rationalism*
Whitehead does not mean reason, intellect, or cognition as opposed to
feeling and emotion. It is more like "intelligence" as Pearce (1992) uses the
word to contrast with mere "intellect." Whitehead sees rationalism as more
of an ordering of things and rational religion is religion where beliefs and
rituals have been reorganized with the aim of making it the central element
in a coherent ordering of life. This ordering of life affects not only thought
(dogma), but behavior (morals). Religion in this sense is that painting of life
in big strokes, seeing the big picture, figure emerging from ground: what is
important, what is of ultimate concern, clearly emerging from the secondary,
the background, the peripheral. Rationalism in religion is putting things in
perspective. "In the absence of perspective there is triviality," Whitehead
says.

The earlier phases of religion, according to Whitehead, were essentially
sociable. "Many were called and *all* were chosen" (1973, p. 28). This final,
highest phase introduces the note of solitariness, and with it religion moves
away from the psychology of the herd and toward the intuitions of the few.
Because rational religion is universal it introduces the note of solitariness.
"Religion," said Whitehead, "is what the individual does with his own
solitariness" (p. 16). The reason for this connection between universality and
solitariness is that universality is a disconnection from immediate surroundings. "It is an endeavor to find something permanent and intelligible by
which to interpret the confusion of immediate detail" (pp. 47-48). When
religion matures, it becomes something more than merely social, tribal—the
blind following of dogmas—but something intensely individual (preserving
at the same time an individual's relationships with society). The appeal of
religion moves from the tribal custom to direct, individual intuitions—ethical, metaphysical, or logical (p. 35), as the individual attempts to get distance from religion as social custom, to interpret for himself the meaning of
his existence, the problems of good and evil, the reasons for being moral, the
purpose of living itself. This history of rational religion is full of tales of
disengagement from the immediate social routine. Christ had to withdraw
from the customs of the Pharisees, who in the name of religion had become
something less than the high level of religiosity toward which He was
leading His followers. But even though religion is what one does with one's
solitariness, it is not antisocial or even nonsocial. Precisely because it is the
individual's withdrawal to a higher level, he or she becomes capable of
being engaged in society even more deeply. "Religion is world loyalty,"
Whitehead says (p. 59), and his image of the religious person is one deeply
in touch with his or her own intuitions rather than blindly adhering to a set

of dogmas. It is one of deep social engagement too. Religious education should give a sense of sharing in a growing culture. It should, as Whitehead (1950) describes it in *Aims of Education,* be "exposure to greatness" and a moving on from the past into the future with zest.

Immortality. What does Whitehead have to say of immortality, life after death? The *traditional* concept of "soul" finds no place in Whitehead's thought, and there is no automatic presumption of such a soul continuing on after the individual's bodily death. Instead, Whitehead proposes what has been called *objective immortality.* All actual entities, he says, have two qualities, factuality and value. In their factuality all occasions perish as they achieve their ultimate completion. In their value they are taken by God into his consequent nature and forever are known to Him, treasured by Him, and employed by Him in His further agency in the world to bring about increasing possibilities of good and increasing actualizations of these possibilities. Southwell expressed it "Not where I breathe but where I love I live." It was even better put by Whitehead himself who spoke the following recorded words near the end of his own life, surely the result not just of impersonal philosophy, but deep personal reflection:

> It was a mistake, as the Hebrews tried, to conceive of God as creating the world from the outside at one go. An all-foreseeing Creator who would have made the world as we find it now—what could we think of such a being? Foreseeing everything and yet putting into it all sorts of imperfections to redeem which it was necessary to send his only son into the world to suffer torture and hideous death; outrageous ideas. The Hellenic religion was a better approach; the Greeks conceived of creation as going on everywhere all the time *within* the universe; and I also think they were happier in their conception of supernatural beings impersonating those various forces, some good others bad; for both sorts of forces *are* present, whether we assign personality to them or not. There is a general tendency in the universe to produce worthwhile things and moments come when we can work with it and it can work through us. But that tendency in the universe to produce worthwhile things is by no means omnipotent. Other forces work against it. God is *in* the world, or nowhere, creating continually in us and around us. This creative principle is everywhere, in animate and so-called inanimate matter, in the ether, water, earth, human hearts. But this creation is a continuing process, and the process is itself the actuality, since no sooner do you arrive than you start on a fresh journey. Insofar as man partakes in this creative process does he partake of the divine, of God, and that participation is his immortality, reducing the question of whether his individuality survives death of the body to the estate of an irrelevancy. His true destiny as cocreator in the universe is his dignity and his grandeur. (Price, 1954, pp. 370-371)

Process thinking is central to the story of creation and our human role in it. Whitehead's philosophy anticipated chaos theory by several decades. If chance and emerging novelty are operating principles of the universe, and if human freedom is a critical factor (Birch, 1991), we have the core tenets of current science and ecology. If he were alive today, I am sure he would be aware of recent scientific findings (Barlow, 1994; Briggs & Peat, 1990; Capra & Stendl-Rast, 1992; Gleick, 1988; Hawking, 1988; Pickover, 1990; Stewart, 1990; Stewart & Golubitsky, 1993) and intensely involved in questions of complexity, order, beauty, and value. He would envision anew the role of God and see a powerful concrescence in it all.

Whitehead's Stages of Religious Development

Whitehead slips into his discussion of religion (1973, p. 16), a tiny system of stages of religious development. In the whole context of his work, it is certainly not very important, but it is interesting for our purposes here and does throw light on what he means by religion as solitariness. Whitehead says that religion runs through three stages if it evolves to its final satisfaction. "It is the transition from God the void, to God the enemy, and from God the enemy to God the companion. Thus," he goes on, "religion is solitariness; and if you are never solitary you are never religious." For a man who grew up in an English parsonage, taught mathematics most of his life in Cambridge, and then, toward the end of his life after having read through the theology books he collected, called a book dealer in and sold "the whole lot" to him, this is an interesting stage theory, worthy of some further psychological development.

I see Whitehead's religion of rationalism as something akin to James's sick soul, the individual who can no longer accept the placebo effect religion so often has when it remains primarily a consoling social function. For religion to go on to its "final satisfaction," to reach maturity or better, "integrity," the individual must face up to questions of life meaning: the existence of God and what kind of being He is, what purpose one has, and ultimately one's own death. This is not done on one's own, alone. But one must do it for oneself. To reach Whitehead's first level of "God the void," the individual must be able to untrammel him or herself from much of the religious baggage acquired as a child: the presumptions, the myths, the father images, the superstitions, the fears, and, above all, the childish way of dealing with God: "If I am good, You will reward me with good things in this life and salvation after it." To renounce all such comfort may well leave the individual searching for God and finding nothing but a dark void. This is frightening. But even more frightening is the second level of "God the enemy," when the "hound of heaven" comes charging out of the darkness.

Francis Thompson (1922) expressed this fearful pursuit in the "Hound of Heaven."

I fled Him, down the nights and down the days;
I fled Him, down the arches of the years;
I fled Him, down the labyrinthine ways
Of my own mind; and in the mist of tears
I hid from him: and under running laughter.
Up vistaed hopes I sped;
And shot, precipitated,
Down Titanic glooms of chasmed fears,
From those strong Feet that followed, followed after
But with unhurrying chase,
And unperturbed pace,
Deliberate speed, majestic instancy,
They beat—and a Voice beat
More instant than the Feet
"All things betray thee, who betrayest me." (p. 45)

God at this stage becomes an enemy, a persistent pursuer who calls me to something I dread. I am pursued by him "down the labyrinthine ways of my own mind." This is not pressure from outside, from others; this is of my own mind, of my solitariness. The dread of the demands this pursuer makes are resolved only when the solitary one at last turns and responds to the pursuer's request, "Rise, clasp my hand and come!" The resolution is Whitehead's ultimate stage, "God the companion," when solitariness is resolved (but not taken away) in a union of persons, human and divine.

Chapter 4

Religion as Development: The Contributions of Allport, Maslow, Erikson, and Fowler

All rising to great places is by a winding stair.

—Francis Bacon

Implicit behind much of what has been said in previous chapters is the idea that the religious experience is something that develops. This idea has not always been accepted and appreciated. In previous centuries a static notion of creation held sway in philosophy and theology. Faith and religious experience were looked on as essentially adult phenomena, and any study of religion would see faith and religion as a *thing* adults *have*. Studying religion from that static point of view, one would do a cross-sectional analysis of what adult faith is, extrapolating from that to the "deficiencies" of the child's religious experience, and, perhaps for legalistic purposes, assigning a somewhat arbitrary age when the child would pass from childhood into the "age of reason," responsibility, and adult maturity.

Today we have a much different view of religion, a more organic, holistic, evolving view of faith, or rather "faithing," as a process (Fowler, 1986). In this view religion is not something that comes ready-made, to be put on like a cap at a certain age. It grows rather like a seed; and a pine tree is as much a pine tree whether it is pushing a few green tufts up just above the brown grass or towering hundreds of feet over the tops of the other trees; it is just at different stages in the process of its individual development. The individual practices religion at his or her level of development, and religion takes many forms. Thus there are, as William James pointed out, "varieties of religious experience," and they vary not only from individual to individual, but within the individual person as his or her life process unfolds.

We owe this insight into religion as a process to philosophers, theologians, and psychologists. Because our present concern is essentially to study the psychology of development, I would like to turn our attention now to some fundamentals of developmental psychology in general, thereby laying the foundation for an exploration of the ideas of several psychologists who, I think, have especially contributed to our understanding of religion as developmental process. The four I have selected for fairly extensive consideration are Gordon Allport, Abraham Maslow, Erik Erikson, and James Fowler. Because these psychologists look at development from somewhat divergent perspectives, it is important for us first to consider the variety of possible approaches to human development. This will involve a brief glance at theoretical roads that, though interesting, we will not take, and description of the roads that form the principal route of our present study.

Theories of Development

Theories of development fit into three main categories: psychoanalytic, behavioristic, and what for want of a better, all-inclusive word we can call *organic*. Psychoanalytic theories of development were reviewed when we looked at Freud's psychology; we will return to them again when we study Erik Erikson, who is a neo-Freudian, and later look at psychoanalytic methods as one of several "ways" of moral education.

The behavioristic approach really denies that there is such a thing as development in the way we are using the term. The core of this theory is a passive model of the human person that maintains that the individual is shaped by environment. The philosopher Locke maintained that the mind is an empty slate (tabula rasa) until sensory impressions make their mark on it. Simple ideas are impressed on the mind, adding to those already there and forming complex ideas through association. Growth of the mind from this point of view is an adding on, quantitative process, an accumulation of elements supplied by the environment.

The emphasis of this approach is on behavioral reactions that an individual can be observed to make in response to environmental stimulation. The focus is not so much on the impressions themselves within the individual as on the external behavior that is observable and thereby measurable. This approach has an appeal to scientists who look for behaviors that they can measure. There is little room in this approach for words such as *faith, love, values,* even *religion,* for these things are unknown quantities except insofar as they can be measured through observing the behavior that goes under the name of faith or love or religion. It is a limiting, reductionistic, quantitative approach to the topic of our study, religion. But it does have great appeal for some psychologists who are interested in moral behavior. For such scientists it has the benefit of giving them something concrete to work with—actual behavior that can be judged and measured rather than nonquantitative internal thoughts, judgments, attitudes, principles, and stages of development. We will come back to behaviorism in the final stages of our study when we will look at it as one of the "Ways of Moral Education."

Organic Theories

The organic theories picture the human being as an active agent in his or her development. Development then is a self-constructive process. What a person develops to be is the result one's own actions. The philosopher Kant, in contrast with Locke, saw the human person as a self-organizing, self-moving, self-formative being and not a passive slate to be written on by the environment. Organic theories are of two major types:

1. Piaget (1967) emphasizes equilibration in the developmental process. For Piaget and others who follow him, development proceeds from relative disequilibrium to increasing equilibrium. If imbalance is created within the individual due to interaction with some sort of external perturbation, the individual will operate to regain equilibrium. Consequently, according to this approach, the individual changes herself and develops in a never-ending response to the disturbances that upset her equilibrium. A simple thing like curiosity is a good example. An infant resting peacefully in a crib hears a sound, let us say her father's voice. At first the baby may react only by showing diffuse excitement, flailing her arms and legs about. But with maturation and learning she reacts to the perturbation of her equilibrium by doing something that helps decrease the disequilibrium; she turns her head and satisfies her curiosity by looking at the source of the sound.

2. The other branch of organic theories (Werner, 1948) characterizes development as an orthogenetic process. "Ortho" means orderly, organized in proper relationship to each other. (An orthodontist "organizes" your teeth.) The central idea is that the individual initially is a rather general, global diffused being; he or she is composed of functional structures that are structurally undifferentiated and functionally unrelated. Like an infant trying to walk or pick up a penny off the floor, things like legs and fingers just don't work smoothly together at first. The orthogenetic process is directed toward increasing differentiation, centralization, and hierarchic integration of the individual's personality organization. In other words, as the person develops he or she become more complex, but all the "parts" learn to work together under the direction, for example, of the nervous system that takes control. It's like a mother coming home to a messy house.

We just passed by a key word; it deserves to be plucked out and given special recognition, for it will wend its way through pages to come, particularly those about Positive Disintegration theory and about values and morals. It is the word *hierarchical.*

A hierarchy is an ordering of things according to their place as higher or lower. A hierarchy is built on the principle that better things belong higher on the hierarchy. "Better" means we are into judgments of value, desirability. You could construct a hierarchy of ice cream flavors. At its top would be the flavor you like best; at its base would be one or many flavors you can't stand. In a hierarchy, "higher" means "better." Hierarchies go beyond flavors of ice cream to such things as prestige, power, wealth, fame, beauty, health, strength of character, goodness, holiness, honesty, and love. Alert readers will have noticed that we can place this long list of things on a hierarchy and give them a place, high or low; all have one thing in common: they all have value; all are in some way desirable. Super alert readers will have noticed that I have placed them in an order which may say something about my values! Super, super alert readers will want to add: "I can't put them into any place on a hierarchy really until I know how all these values relate to each other." But that, I think, would take us out of hierarchies and into heterarchies. We'll save that for the section on values later in the second half.

Suffice it to say for now that when we talk about development in the sense of organic theories, we are not just concerned with *more of,* but our intention is to describe human development as going on to *better than.* We make a value judgment when we say, as most developmentalists do, that a higher stage is a better stage and to move on "up" the stages or levels of development to increasing complexity, yet organization of that complexity according to certain hierarchic norms. The word *higher* has in this context the connotation of *better.* That is why the metaphor of some developmental psychologists as topographical mapmakers, cartographers, describing the pathways of life's journey is apt. The invitation is not only to go forward but to go up. We'll come back to this especially when we look at the valuing process.

Developmentally, human beings are actors who operate to keep themselves adaptively interacting with their environment. In this way they conserve their own organization at the same time as they transform it. A new stage of development unfolds when a new or transformed system becomes dominant and subordinates or incorporates previously existing systems. This way an individual maintains continuity, identity, even though passing through stages that are themselves discontinuous. Werner and Kaplan (1963) describe development as a synthetic process, intertwining two antithetical organismic tendencies: the tendency to maintain continuity in order to conserve one's identity, and to elaborate discontinuity in order to move on in development. We will study Erik Erikson's developmental theory, centering on identity formation, as an illustration of this theoretical orientation. In general Werner and Kaplan see development as an evolutionary process from passive, conforming reactions to external stimuli to interpretive actions, personal constructions of oneself, one's experiences, and one's environment. In other words, the developing human being moves from being the passive pawn of his environment to being a self-controlled, self-directed, autonomous individual who actively constructs his environment instead of merely reacting to it.

Werner (1948) adapted the biological principle of orthogenesis and used it to describe the process that characterizes human development. For Werner the direction of development is toward (a) increasing differentiation of primitive systems that initially are fused with each other into one global organization, causing (b) the emergence of novel and increasingly discrete systems that are, though more discrete, also increasingly integrated within themselves, so that (c) the most advanced (i.e., differentiated, specialized, and internally integrated) systems have the power to integrate into a hierarchy (i.e., functionally subordinate and regulate) less developed systems. Thus, in the course of development, the human's systems unfold organically into a complex of multiple and varied forms—but an organized, hierarchical complex controlled by the most highly developed systems. These orthogenetic principles will have special relevance when we come to consider in some detail Dabrowski's theory of Positive Disintegration, which elaborates these principles and brings them to fruition in a comprehensive theory of human development.

Let's take a step back and try to summarize and put into perspective some of the main things we have been saying about human development. We have seen that developmental psychology can be looked at in three different ways according to whether you take a psychoanalytic approach, a behavioristic approach, or an organic approach. But whatever the basic philosophical orientation, developmental psychologists of all brands are interested in the same thing—change within the person. So change, in a way, is what developmental psychology is all about; but only in a way, because if the process were *all* change, if by developing I became *totally* different, then tomorrow I would not be the same person I am today. Development, besides moving on to something different, must also involve a certain element of sameness. If there is to be discontinuity, there must also be some continuity. If there is to be a newly developed me, there must also be a continuing me that supports my sense of continuity. Although I am somewhat different, I am convinced that it is the same *I* today who was yesterday. When I awake on a bright fresh morning, I may feel like a new person, but never a *totally* new person, and I know that the *I* who studies for an exam today will be the same (though much wiser!) *I* who some day will go up on the stage at convocation to receive my diploma. What will have changed is the complexity, the personal richness, the qualities of my personality. And that is the twofold thrust of developmental psychology—increasing complexity without losing unity. Or, on the other side of the coin, an enduring sense of one's personal integration that is strong enough to maintain one's identity through the myriad changes that must come about in the process of differentiation.

Psychologists are divided on what brings about these changes, but a common theme that seems to run through many theories is that change is brought about through some sort of disturbance of the status quo, some sort of disequilibrium, perturbation, crisis, or disintegration that provokes growth. How does disturbance promote growth? Theorists are divided in their explanation into two main camps: ontogenetic and evolutionary. (We will see examples of each when we come to study the individual developmental psychologists in detail.) Some, such as Erik Erikson, maintain that a crisis flowing from the events of a biological and social conflict attuned to a certain period in the life cycle brings on the need to move from a lower level of development to a higher. If the individual successfully resolves the conflicts inherent in the lower level, he builds a higher level of development on the foundation of the successfully completed lower level. Building higher levels of development depends on the successful resolution of the lower level that serves as a foundation. Thus the individual moves from stage to stage, his qualities as a person being those at and below the rung of the psychological ladder to which he has at that stage climbed. One can, according to the individual's age and social environment, set criteria that should be met at each stage of development.

A second major approach to the developmental process (which we will later see exemplified at length in Dabrowski's Positive Disintegration theory) also maintains that development comes about through some sort of crisis, disturbance, or disintegration, but the development, instead of building on lower levels, causes the disintegration of lower, more primitive levels of development and replaces them with a higher level of development. This higher level of development is more complex, more discrete, but also more integrated, so that the most advanced levels of development have the power to integrate into a hierarchy the more primitive, automatic, and less-reflective systems.

We have spoken here about stages and levels of development, and almost any developmental psychologist has his or her own set of stages or levels that describe some part or the whole life span of human development. The question is: Do they correspond to anything "out there" in reality? Do real children and adults actually go through stages? Grandmothers in their wisdom describe children as "just going through a stage," so I guess we must accept the existence of stages in a certain sense. But the diversity of stages and levels that scholars (and even grandmothers) assign to human beings makes one wonder how they can all be reconciled with each other. Perhaps it is better to consider all the stages and levels and charts and tables that we have as the various ways in which certain scholars (and grandmothers) have interpreted reality from their own observations. Each reflects an expert but subjective interpretation of reality seen from a different point of view. Each has its own value, but none is *the* way human beings develop. There is no need, then, to try to reconcile all the stage theories or try to force-fit them together; no need, above all, to try to force-fit ourselves, our friends, or our children into the too-tight pigeonhole of a stage, a level. Stages help us describe and understand, but they don't make watertight compartments.

Far from being a series of watertight compartments, a cluster of pigeonholes, or even a ladder reaching to the upper floors of some psychological skyscraper, the image of human development is something quite other. The visual image that is most meaningful for me is the spiral. The spiral grows out of itself, each loop overlapping, growing out of the lower level loop yet surpassing the lower level in its breadth and comprehension. The spiral illustrates the fact that a human never remains in a state of stable equilibrium, but is in constant flux between one stage of disequilibrium and another. The mutually controlling and impelling dynamisms of development at the same time demand upward movement, not through chaos, but through controlled process like the hands of a potter that draw out and up but do not scatter. The loops of the spiral overlap and grow out of each other, illustrating continuity within the developmental process. But each loop is progressively higher and distinct both quantitatively and qualitatively from other loops in the spiral, indicating developmental discontinuity. The spiral is an ancient mystical symbol and in all its beauty is illustrative of a profound paradox of development—that in order to go forward it is necessary in some way to go backward. The process of progress involves regression insofar as one moves on from what has been to what might be; one is called to reflect on what has been, what is, and what might be. The very process of dissatisfaction with what is, given the right conditions, impels the movement toward what ought to be. For example, one twist of the spiral, and thus a movement upward may be incited by a twinge of dissatisfaction with one's egocentrism, one's limited vision, and a consequent endeavor to take the perspective of others in a situation. If the whole thrust of human development is a movement away from the egocentrism of childhood toward the broader vision and broader caring of maturity, then the spiral with its movement from a tight-knotted core outward, always encompassing more, is an apt image of development as process.

The Optimal Person

The spiral forms an apt image also to take us to a consideration of another aspect of human development that will be particularly important when we want to cross over from talking about development in general to the study of religious development. It is the whole question of what is the ultimate goal of human development. It is sometimes put in terms of: What is the best kind of person? What is the optimal person? What is the mature person like? The spiral is an apt image of our answer because the spiral has no top, no capital, no ending point; instead it spins off into infinity.

We are going to see Gordon Allport's description of the mature person, and we will look at Maslow's criteria for the self-actualizing person. Because both these men believe that development is a qualitative process, their notions of "best" are not static, but continuously open to growth.

Developmental psychology has frequently used the term *mature* to describe the optimal person, but it can be a misleading word. Mature is a concept borrowed from physiology. It means ripening without learning. If we carry over all the physiological (and therefore quantitative) meanings and connotations of the word, we limit our meaning to the notion of reaching a plateau, an end point, beyond which there is no going. Physiologically, when a person has reached his or her mature height, for example, that person will not grow any taller. Carried over too literally into psychology, the word *maturity* may lead us to conclude that there is a terminus of human development, a state of perfection, which is the ultimate and dreadfully static goal.

Integration

A word that some psychologists use to describe the higher levels of development is *integrated*, or perhaps better *integrating*. This is a more dynamic, holistic concept, and better expresses the qualitative nature of human development with its limitless possibilities. We are already familiar with integration as the dynamic force in the developmental process that retains the unity of the individual throughout the process of differentiation. An integrated person is a unified being. Though composed of different parts, he or she is an operational, unified entity. We can describe a person at almost any level of development as being integrated in this sense unless the personality has undergone a massive breakdown with little hope of reintegration on a higher level. In this sense, the person, if developing, is differentiating and integrating throughout a lifetime. As we will see later when we look at Dabrowski's theory, an individual may form a unity, a functioning unit, at any level of development; he or she may even form a unit impervious to the forces of change in life and remain integrated at a low level of development (primary integration). On the other hand, a person may undergo disintegrating processes that make personality more complex, but still have personal unity.

There is another sense in which *integrated* is used, and that is in the sense of "integral," "whole"—having all those qualities present that *should* be present in a human being. In this sense an integrated person is not just a unity, but a whole. All those qualities are there that we agree make up the ideal human being. The criteria for what these qualities should be precisely will vary from culture to culture, and from psychologist to psychologist, and we are about to examine in detail the criteria some have set out. But one theme runs clear: these qualities are not stagnant, a formed picture; they are in process of development. Thus the integrated person, the best of humanness, is not perfect, but in process. We have already seen that Whitehead proclaimed process as the very stuff of the universe and did not exempt God from being in process. One of the themes of this book is to look especially at the high end of human development and there find religion at its best; a subtheme is to proclaim that even there, at the highest levels of development, nothing is finished, perfect.

Now that we have reviewed some of the basic questions any developmental psychologist must deal with, we can go on to look at the contributions of some outstanding recent and contemporary psychologists to our understanding of religious development. Only one of these, James Fowler, has totally dedicated his study to religious or faith development; the other three are, ex professio, what we might call "secular" psychologists. Two of them, Allport and Maslow, have written quite extensively on the psychology of religion. All of them have at some time addressed the topic of the psychology of religion, and each has a unique contribution to make that is worthy of our consideration. One stands out as an almost archetypal grand-father figure in contemporary psychology. That person is Gordon Allport, who was once voted by members of the American Psychological Association as the second most influential theorist (after Freud) in their day-to-day clinical work. It is due in large part to Allport's insights, his vision, and his daring to propose ideas about the psychology of religion to a scientific world that was not always convinced of the legitimacy of the study of religion, that the ice jam between was broken, and a mainstream of psychology's and religion's mutual interests joined. It is to Gordon Allport, then, that we will first turn our attention.

Gordon Allport

Gordon Allport combined scholarship and integrity as a scientist, earning him respect in the scientific community, with a personal depth and broad-ness of vision, giving him insight and boldness to explore the religious dimensions of humankind at a time when behaviorism and reductionistic views were sending psychology in a quite opposite direction.

Allport's interests and scholarship spanned a broad range of personality and developmental psychology. Among his many publications the most relevant to our present topic are: *The Nature of Prejudice* (1954, 1958), *Becoming: Basic Considerations for a Psychology of Personality* (1955), *The Allport-Vernon-Lindzey Study of Values*, a personality test based on Spranger's value types, and *The Individual and His Religion* (1950, 1960), which we will later look at in greater detail. Foundational among his many writings in the area of general personality psychology is a major work entitled *Pattern and Growth in Personality* (1937, 1961). In this work Allport presents an overview of developmental psychology that elaborates and illustrates some of the general principles of development we discussed earlier in this chapter. But what Allport does in this book that is unique and helpful to us here is devote a whole chapter to a description of what he calls "The Mature Personality." Considering the stature of the man, the compre-hensiveness of the survey, the creativity of his criteria, and their relevance to our study, his description of the mature person deserves a summary. It is important to note that Allport uses the word *mature* even though the concept it represents is one of personality *integration*.

After reviewing various descriptions of the mature or "sound" personality, including a summary of Maslow's 14 criteria for the self-actualizing person, Allport (1961) goes on to present his own criteria, which number six. He prefaces his list with two admonitions: (a) Healthy persons are not always as happy and as free from conflict as some might imagine; "Suffering cleaves two ways: sometimes it seems to break and sometimes to make, personality" (p. 282). (b) All the criteria point to an ideal seldom if ever achieved; "The sturdiest of personalities have their foibles and their regressive moments; and to a large extent they depend on environmental supports for their maturity" (pp. 282-283). The six criteria for maturity Allport lists are as follows.

Allport's Criteria for Maturity

Extension of the sense of self. The "mature" person has strong interests outside himself; he is truly participant in the world around him. This is different from being merely active in the world. Many people are intensely active; they are task-involved, but the mature person is ego-involved. He is not like an automaton, the passive reactor to what happens to him. Rather he sees himself as part of the whole, and is interested in participating by getting himself involved. Allport (1961) says, "Unless our work, our study, our families, hobbies, politics or religious quest become significantly appropriate, we cannot possibly qualify as mature personalities" (p. 285).

Allport (1961) says, "True participation gives direction to life. Maturity advances in proportion as lives are decentered from the clamorous immediacy of the body and egocenteredness ... Everyone has self-love, but only self-extension is the earmark of maturity" (p. 285).

Warm relating of self to others. The mature person is characterized by two quite different kinds of warmth—intimacy and compassion. He can be deeply involved with people, and on the other hand has a certain detachment that makes him respectful and appreciative of the rights of others. This respect for others is achieved through an imaginative extension of one's own experiences of life. Here we meet tolerance and the "democratic character structure" that others such as Maslow list as desirable qualities. By contrast the immature person feels that only he himself has the distinctively human experiences of passion, fear, preference, and even salvation. "His church, his lodge, his family, and his nation make a safe unit, but all else is alien, dangerous, to be excluded from his petty formula for survival" (1961, p. 286).

Maslow (1962, pp. 39-40) spoke about "B" or "Being" love and "D" or "Deficiency" love, and that is what Allport is contrasting here; the love that sincerely wants the welfare or becoming of the other with no strings attached, and the "love" that is given in a kind of marketplace mentality where it is literally traded off for something else—usually the filling of some deficiency in oneself: "I love you for yourself" versus "I love you strictly because I need you to fill up a deficiency in me." Allport (1961) says, "A possessive, crippling love—such as some parents burden their children with—is common enough but unwholesome for both giver and receiver" (p. 286). Kahlil Gibran's Prophet describes the ideal of intimacy without possession when he speaks of children:

Your children are not your children.
They are the sons and daughters of Life's longing for itself.

Emotional security (self-acceptance). This facet of maturity includes the ability to avoid inappropriate reactions to partial features of oneself. Allport takes the example of sexuality, and indicates that the self-accepting person accepts his sex drive without resorting to the salacious and the scatological, nor to the prudish and the repressed. Frustration tolerance is especially important. The mature person puts up with frustration, biding his time, circumventing the obstacle, or if necessary resigning himself to the inevitable. "It is definitely not true," Allport (1961) says, "that the mature person is always calm and serene, nor is he always cheerful ... but he has learned to live with his emotional states in such a way that they do not betray him into impulsive acts nor interfere with the well-being of others" (p. 288). This self-acceptance (not to be confused with self-satisfaction) is founded on a sense of security—the kind of basic trust that we will see Erik Erikson describing as the task of the newborn infant and the foundation of all future securities, and indeed (according to Erikson) of all future development. Allport says:

> The sense of security is by no means absolute. No one has control
> of time, tide, taxes, death or disaster. As the sense of self expands,
> one takes on new risks and new chances of failure. But these insecu-
> rities are somehow held with a sense of proportion.... Self-control is
> a reflection of a sense of proportion ... [that] is not an isolated attrib-
> ute in personality. It comes about because one's outlook is generally
> of a realistic order, and because one possesses integrative values
> that control and gate the flow of emotional impulse. (p. 288)

These words concluding this quotation from Allport are themselves particularly integrative of our present study. We have already touched on the controlling role of higher-level functions, and here is an example of higher-level sense of proportion gating the flow of lower level impulses. It is noteworthy, too, that when Allport talks about a "sense of proportion" (a term that, by the way, belongs in aesthetics too), he comes easily to a mention of values. In the second half of this book, we will find ourselves following much the same path as we search for the ways in which moral values are chosen and subsequently direct our lives.

Realistic perception, skills, and assignments. Thought and feeling are, according to Allport, the warp and woof of the fabric of life. The mature person is realistic; he does not bend reality to fit his own needs and fantasies. Not only are perceptions mostly realistic and accurate, but the individual has the appropriate skills for solving problems and doing tasks. Along with veridicality and skill, Allport lists the capacity to lose oneself in one's work, pointing out that Freud, Maslow, and other scholars have made the same claim. *Age quod agis,* says the old Latin motto: Do what you are doing; give yourself to the task and not to self-preoccupation. Mature people are problem-centered, not self-centered. Something worth doing is worth giving yourself to, and some things are worthy of intensive dedication; in fact, as we have seen with Frankl, some tasks can give life meaning.

Self-objectification: Insight and humor. Allport (1961) quotes the famous saying of Socrates: "Know thyself." He then goes on to comment on how rarely this rule is really followed on account of the peculiar difficulty of getting an objective picture of oneself. There are two selves, the self I really am (real self) and the self I think I am (self-concept). The more these concepts overlap, the more they share in common, the more objective the person is, "for what a man thinks he is in relation to what he really is provides a perfect definition and index of his insight" (p. 291).

Allport (1961) goes on to relate a sense of humor to insight, making the relationship clear. Quoting the novelist Meredith, Allport says that humor is "the ability to laugh at the things one loves (including, of course, oneself and all that pertains to oneself) and still to love them" (p. 292). The real humorist sees the sometimes cosmic contradictions behind the scenes of life—often with himself in the starring and pretentious role. Humor is to be sharply distinguished from the cruder sense of the comic. Most people have a sense of the comic, a laughing reaction to absurdities and horse play—pie-in-the-face kind of humor. Primarily the mere comic consists in the degradation of another human being, with aggression not far below the surface. "Related to aggressive wit," says Allport (p. 293), "is laughter at the risqué, which seems due to the release of suppression. Aggression and sex are at the basis of much that we call comic." Allport probably did not have the plethora of sitcoms on television that we have today, but if you watch them critically you will see that much of what they call comedy is aimed at the release of repressed aggression and sexuality.

Allport (1961) makes a further interesting observation:

> A young child has a keen sense of the comic, but seldom if ever laughs at himself. Even during adolescence the youth is more likely to view his failing with acute suffering than with laughter. There is evidence that people who are less intelligent, who have low esthetic and theoretical values, prefer the comic and lack a sense of humor based on real relationships in life. (p. 293)

Insight and humor go hand in hand because they are at bottom a single phenomenon—self-objectification. "The man who has the most complete sense of proportion concerning his own qualities and cherished values is able to perceive their incongruities and absurdities in certain settings" (1961, p. 293). Once again, the phrase "sense of proportion" comes into Allport's description of the mature person.

The unifying philosophy of life. "Maturity requires, in addition to humor, a clear comprehension of life's purpose in terms of an intelligible theory"

(Allport, 1961, p. 294). It is not enough, says Allport, to have a sense of humor. An exclusively humorous philosophy would lead to cynicism, and the cynic is a lonely soul for he lacks the companionship of a life-goal. The mature person possesses a unifying philosophy of life, which gives directedness. Here we come back again to Frankl's theme that a sense of purpose is essential for mental health in general and certainly for the higher levels of development. The child lacks long-term objectives, which become only vaguely defined in adolescence. But a lack of a sense of purpose or confusion over it is not restricted to teenagers. Lack of purpose is, as many commentators (e.g., May, 1953) have pointed out, perhaps the chronic illness of our time, and strikes at any stage of the life cycle, including old age.

Allport gives much emphasis to value orientations as an important part of a unifying philosophy of life. He outlines the six major value types that Spranger used to describe the configuration of values that people hold. The six values are: Theoretical, Economic, Esthetic, Social, Political, and Religious. According to Allport, any individual holds these values in a configuration of various proportions. Those that are predominant give thrust to the life of the individual. For example, the highest value for the religious person is unity. He or she seeks to comprehend the universe as a whole and find his or her own relationship to it. Some people of this type are *immanent mystics*, finding their religious experience in the affirmation of life and participating in it as fully as possible; others are *transcendental mystics*, seeking union with a higher reality by withdrawing from life.

Allport's discussion of the importance of a guiding philosophy of life and the values accompanying it flows naturally into an examination of what he calls "the religious sentiment." We will discuss this more thoroughly when we explore his book *The Individual and His Religion* in some detail. It is enough to say for now that Allport saw religion as an integral part of the mature person. Religion may be merely extrinsic in the sense that a person may find it useful in serving his immediate ends such as infantile self-assurance, exclusion of others, or feelings of superiority. It is no coincidence that studies (Allport, 1958) show prejudice is more common among churchgoers than nonchurchgoers. But religion is capable of giving the individual that sense of proportion that, as we have seen, is a pervading theme of Allport's descriptors of the mature person. "In fact," he says, "a case might be made for the superior sense of humor of the religious person who has settled once and for all what things are sacred and of ultimate value, for nothing else in the world then needs to be taken seriously" (p. 301). It is interesting when religious people, especially the caricatures of religious people we sometimes meet, feel they have to make the point that "Even religious people can have a sense of humor," as though there were some intrinsic contradiction between religion and humor, admitting of only rare exceptions. In fact the opposite is true; if one truly has the sense of security that comes from knowing what is really of worth and what matters, then one can laugh at what remains; it no longer needs to be taken seriously. Religiosity with all its pretensions and pomposity is the perfect set-up for a joke. Religion with all its perspective and proportion is the haven and the heaven of humor.

For mature persons religion serves the function of telling them what is important, giving them a sense of proportion, giving them perspective on life that is objective. They know what is of value and what is not. This is Allport's description of human persons at their best; it is also, interestingly, a description of religion at its best. The rising spirals of development we spoke of earlier are beginning to intermesh. All that rises must converge.

The Individual and His Religion

We noted previously that among the many writings of Allport one stands out as most relevant to our study of the psychology of religion. It is *The Individual and His Religion* (1960), and as a landmark publication in the psychology of religion it deserves a fairly extensive review here. Following quite naturally from Allport's description of the mature person as someone who has a guiding philosophy of life, the theme of this book is that religion can give meaning to life. Unlike Frankl, Allport does not hesitate to call the search for meaning a religious quest. Formal, institutional religion has the potential to awaken and develop the transcendent dimensions within the individual. But it is on religion as a personal, individual phenomenon that the author concentrates his attention. Allport claims early in the book (p. 3), "the subjective (personal) religious sentiments of mankind—whatever the fate of institutional religion may be—are very much alive and will perhaps always remain alive as their roots are many and deep." To find one's personal niche in creation as best one can is the right of each individual as a religious person.

Allport says that most people have a dual set of expressions; one deals with factors within comprehension and control, the other with factors beyond comprehension and control. The latter is the realm of religion. Whereas science deals with problems of empirical causation, religion deals with problems of meaning. At the more highly developed levels of development, religion has, according to Allport, the following attributes:

1. A variety of higher-level, psychogenic interests that concern themselves with ideals and values beyond the range of viscerogenic desire. Unless the individual transcends the lower levels of immediate biological impulses, his life is stunted and infantile.

2. The ability to objectify oneself, to be reflective and insightful about one's own life, to see oneself as others do, and, at least from time to time, to sense one's place in a cosmic perspective.

3. The possession of some unifying philosophy of life that will provide direction and coherence and a pattern for integration. Later, we will see

these same three themes reemerge in Dabrowski's Positive Disintegration theory as:

a. The process of moving beyond lower level, impulsive behavior, through its disintegration and replacement by higher level, more reflective functioning;

b. The dynamism of "Subject-Object in Oneself," providing at one and the same time, self-objectivity and the ability to identify with others;

4. A hierarchy of values and a hierarchy of aims, leading to an ego ideal.

The Mature Religious Sentiment

Allport (1960) goes to great lengths in *The Individual and His Religion* to describe what he calls "the mature religious sentiment." It is:

> The disposition built up through experience to respond favorably and in certain habitual ways to conceptual objects and principles that the individual regards as of ultimate importance in his own life and having to do with what he regards as permanent or central in the nature of things. (p. 56)

This is a definition worthy of reflection, and Allport helps us to appreciate the many facets of the mature religious sentiment by outlining its attributes.

Well-differentiated. Mature religion is well differentiated to a complex structure, but ordered in its complexity like any other well-developed system.

Dynamic. The mature religious sentiment provides its own driving force. Unlike immature religion or religiosity that is motivated by pressure from the outside, the mature religious sentiment is autonomous—not only autonomous in not being blindly conformist to outside persuasions, but "functionally autonomous" in that special sense that Allport developed. Allport rejected Freud's determinism that traces adult behavior directly back to events of childhood. Freud claimed to explain the *why* of adult behavior by finding some event, some trauma, some unresolved crisis that had occurred in childhood and was now causing certain neurotic behaviors in the adult. Just as smoking, fingernail biting, chewing the end of one's pencil could be traced by Freud back to some unresolved oral fixation created by weaning, so religious feelings and behavior could be traced back to unresolved problems with the father, who had, in the adult's eyes, become the "Heavenly Father." Allport had no patience with this Freudian determinism that made adults slaves of what had happened to them in childhood. Instead, he proposed that motives are "functionally autonomous"; what one does is done for motives that, by and large, are here and now. Allport says:

> A religious sentiment that has become largely independent of its origins, functionally autonomous, cannot be regarded as a servant of other desires, even though its initial function may have been in this

order. It behaves no longer like iron filings, twisting to follow the magnet of self-centered motives; it behaves rather as a master-motive, a magnet in its own right by which other cravings are bidden to order their course. (p. 64)

Productive of a consistent morality. It was clear to Allport that the development of true religion included moral development, for morality was that dimension of religion in which the values intrinsic to religion flowed into judgment and action. The mature religious sentiment constructs a personal value hierarchy directive of moral standards and creative in character development. We will see this theme coming out again when we explore Maslow's psychology and study Dabrowski's theory in detail.

Comprehensive. The mature religious sentiment is a comprehensive system. It calls for a broad philosophy of life that asks important questions and paints life on a broad canvas. Allport says, "The hurly burly of the world must be brought into some kind of order, and the facts calling for order are not only material; they include emotions, values and man's strange propensity to seek his own perfection" (pp. 67-78). The order in which the individual places the colors on the broad canvas is not just any order; it is the order of perspective guided by a personal hierarchy of values. As a quality of religion at its best, comprehensiveness makes for tolerance. In a broad perspective, one knows that one's own life alone does not contain all values or all facets of meaning. Others have truth too. Mature religion is open to the truth of others. It is said that Albert Einstein, with all his intelligence, was not in the habit of contradicting his opponents. Instead, he would listen to what they had to say, thanking them, if their objections brought new light to his own understanding. Religious people and religious sects would have fared much better over the years if they had been so open to new understandings, new contributions to their own process of development.

Integrating. If the mature religious sentiment mixes colors together on the broad canvas of life, it does not do so helter-skelter. Values dictate that there must be perspective—an order of what is first and foremost, an appreciation that some things deserve more and some things less of our concern. Religion has the power to integrate.

One major task of religion is to integrate into our understanding and acceptance of life the understanding and acceptance of death and, more broadly, the problem of evil. For the religious person who relates to a personal deity, the abstract question of why there is evil in the world if God is good becomes concretized when facing the death of a loved one, the suffering of children, the starvation of some accompanied by the gluttony of others, the pain of the innocent while the guilty thrive. Reconciling evil with a good creator has been a task religion has attempted for centuries dating back to the Book of Job, translated into a modern idiom in Archibald MacLeish's play *J.B.,* and expressed in personal terms by Rabbi Harold Kushner who watched his son dying and wrote of the experience and problem in a book entitled *When Bad Things Happen to Good People* (1981). Religion can be there, helping one to integrate the evil, whether it be the evil of a great injustice or the pain of an opportunity lost and a love not known. This is expressed poignantly, I think, by a poem written by a graduate student, Gregg Janz (1983), during his counseling internship at the Cross Cancer Institute in Edmonton:

On life and limitations

long dangling translucent cords of precious oxygen
running frantically from the wall, your needed breath of life
lightly casting webs of shadow on your fragile face and arms
your silver ghostly hair delicately crushed by weight of head
you never looked or knew, but I was there

silently looking lost in my thoughts of how we shall meet
who was this person behind the tired face and soft closed eyes
while still the grim seeds of death grew rapidly in your breast
so powerless against that inner roaring and devouring monster
you never felt my helplessness, but it was there

your thin white fragile arms bruised from needles and life
I sense your fear and pain through your deep wall of sleep
did you sense my growing impatience, frustration and doubt?
the paradoxical helplessness of the helper, a thinly worn veil
you never felt my fear, but it was there

your inevitable final days mirroring the fragility of my own
too hurried, too tired just too many things between you and I
one more day Mrs. B now is that really too much to ask?
but it was an eternity between you and I, being more than you
could give you never felt my anger and sadness, but it was there

I'll always remember walking into your room and finding you gone
it was finished the final chapter closed, the pages forever locked
away the emptiness of the room echoed your loss and my deep felt
guilt
a humble and precious reminder of the limitations of my fleeting art
you never felt my caring, but it was there

Always, as this poem exemplifies, real religion is there in times of profound feelings and great questions, helping to resolve, if not the question "Why?" as though there must always be a reason, at least the question "How?" for there can always be a way. It can be a way not just to adapt, not just to cope, but a way to contribute to our growth, our personal process, and the process of the building of creation. Religion, the great integrator, takes up feelings of pain, questions of meaning and purpose, integrating them into our own "How" of how one may go on, not despite the questions and pain, but because of them. "Unless the grain of wheat falls into the ground and dies ..."

Fundamentally heuristic. A heuristic belief is one that is held tentatively until it can be confirmed or until it helps us discover a more valid belief (Allport, 1960, p. 72). A mature religious person can act wholeheartedly without having or pretending absolute certainty. As we saw in the first chapter of this book, religious dogma can be a haven of security for some, and the degree of certainty with which it is held, including the impossibility of any change, can be in direct proportion to the need for personal assurance, and the deficiency needs that assurance seeks to fulfill. Psychology speaks of "tolerance of ambiguity" as a desirable quality in human beings. It involves the ability to maintain security, and subsequently courage, in the face of the unknown and the unsure. If psychology calls it "tolerance of ambiguity," religion calls it "faith."

This brief treatment falls far short of doing justice to *The Individual and His Religion* and falls much shorter of doing justice to the author, Gordon Allport. But perhaps this treatment, deficient as it is, can be best integrated with our main themes by quoting the words of Allport (1960) at the conclusion of this book:

> My theme has been the diversity of form that subjective religion assumes. Many different desires may initiate the religious quest, desires as contrasting as fear and curiosity, gratitude and confirmity. Men show a varying capacity to outgrow their childhood religion, and to evolve a well-differentiated, mature religious sentiment. There are many degrees in the comprehensiveness of this sentiment and in its power to integrate life. There are different styles of doubting, different apperceptions of symbols, contrasting types of content that vary both with the culture and with the temperament and capacity of the believers. There are innumerable types of specific religious intentions. How the individual justifies his faith is a variable matter, and the certitude he achieves is his alone.
>
> From its early beginnings to the end of the road, the religious quest of the individual is solitary. Though he is socially interdependent with others in a thousand ways, yet no one else is able to provide him with that faith he evolves, nor prescribe for him his pact with the cosmos.
>
> Often the religious sentiment is merely rudimentary in the personality, but often too it is a pervasive structure marked by the deepest sincerity. It is the portion of personality that arises at the core of life and is directed toward the infinite. It is the region of mental life that has the longest-range intentions, and for this reason is capable of conferring marked integration on personality, engendering meaning and pace in the face of the tragedy and confusion of life.
>
> A man's religion is the audacious bid he makes to bind himself to creation and the Creator. It is his ultimate attempt to enlarge and to

complete his own personality by finding the supreme context in which he rightly belongs. (pp. 141-142)

Abraham Maslow

Allport's concluding words, quoted above, form a natural transition to the ideas of Maslow, for he too saw religion as occupying "the farther reaches of human nature." Maslow as a young psychologist freed himself from the two psychological mainstreams of his student days, Freudianism and behaviorism, and became an eminent exponent of what came to be known as Third Force or humanistic psychology, with its roots in existentialism and its concern for the holistic. Maslow was especially interested in the high end of human development, and is subsequently best known as the father of *self-actualization*, a term that has enjoyed much popularity and widespread interest, as well as some regrettable abuse, at the hands of those who have oversimplified, not appreciating the full developmental context Maslow (1954, 1959, 1962, 1966, 1967, 1971, 1973, 1977) created.

Almost any introductory psychology text presents Maslow's famous hierarchy of needs, usually illustrated with a diagram showing how one moves as if ascending a staircase from low-level physiological needs through various intermediate needs up to the highest level need—self-actualization. Self-actualization is to be what one can be, to take the potentials in one's life and actually realize their fulfillment. The idea of self-actualization has an immediate appeal for most people. It grabs them. "Yes," they say, "that's what I want—to be what I can be!" It is tempting to begin the quest without further ado, attacking this psychological Everest without the proper equipment. But Maslow has provided the equipment and the maps, or, better still, has described the kind of person who successfully makes the ascent. Maslow (1973) described the qualities of self-actualizing persons, those special people he knew who were striving for and some of whom had reached the heights of human development; he called them the "growing tip" of the human race, few in number like the sparse needles at the top of a spruce tree, but leading the rest of the tree to new heights of development. Maslow (pp. 178-196) saw the self-actualizing subjects of his research as having these characteristics:

1. More efficient perception of reality and more comfortable relations with it;

2. Acceptance of self, others and nature;

3. Spontaneity;

4. Problem-centering;

5. Detachment and the need for privacy;

6. Autonomy: independence of culture and environment;

7. Continued freshness of appreciation;

8. The "Mystic Experience," the "Oceanic Feeling";

9. Social feeling;

10. Deep but selective social relationships;

11. Democratic character structure;

12. Ethical certainty;

13. Philosophical, unhostile sense of humor;

14. Creativeness.

Maslow sketched a picture of a strong and attractive personality, someone all would like to know and most would like to be. The similarity of these criteria with Allport's mature person is quite striking, as is the crossover of characteristics that we have come to recognize as those of the higher levels of religious development, especially concern for ultimate meaning and contact in some way with it in mystical or oceanic experiences. Of special interest to our study too is Maslow's (1973) statement about the quality he calls "ethical certainty": "I have found none of my subjects to be chronically unsure about the difference between right and wrong in his actual living ... they rarely showed in their day-to-day living the chaos, the confusion, the inconsistency, or the conflict that is so common in the average person's ethical dealings" (p. 194). "Needless to say," Maslow reports, "their notions of right and wrong are often not the conventional ones." Maslow goes on to say that he could describe all of his subjects as "godly men" although none of them were orthodoxly religious, and one called himself an atheist. Whether or not, then, Maslow concludes, one could call them religious depends entirely on the concept of religion that we choose to use. To that topic of how Maslow defines religion we should turn our attention now. To do this, we will pass from 1950, when he made the major presentation of his early research findings on self-actualizing persons, to 1970 when he wrote a revised, and somewhat more mature and reflected-on, edition of *Religions, Values and Peak Experiences.*

There he lays the foundation of his psychological study of religion by lamenting the dichotomization of both science and religion.

> It is because both science and religion have been too narrowly conceived, and have been too exclusively dichotomized and separated from each other, that they have been seen to be two mutually exclusive worlds. (1977, p. 11)

Historically, science was once a part of the body of organized religion. It broke away from religion in the Enlightenment, and Maslow fears that the same thing may now be happening with problems of values, ethics, spirituality, and morals. Some humanistic scientists seem bent on denying the claim of the established religions to be the sole arbiters of questions of faith and morals; some established religions want to maintain their say in what is scientific truth. Maslow feels strongly that this paralyzing dichotomy need not be. Words that until recently had been thought to be the exclusive territory of organized religion are, he comments, now open to scientific investigation. Maslow goes on to describe the dichotomies he discerns between organized religion and personal religion, between the legalistic ecclesiastic and the prophet, between what he calls religious "peakers" and religious "organization men." To understand the rather black and white dichotomies into which Maslow puts organized religion and personal religion, one must see personal religion from Maslow's own point of view, centered around "peak experiences."

Peak Experiences

Maslow was captivated by the mystical, oceanic experiences that his self-actualizing people reported as part of their lives; he saw these peak experiences as the quintessence of personal religion. These experiences are special moments, rare in some lives, frequent in others, in which the person experiences feelings, understandings, attitudes, perceptions, integrations that are above and beyond ordinary humdrum life. According to Maslow, peak experiences, naturalistic as they are, closely resemble the religious experiences the mystics have described. Peak experiences are characterized by:

1. Perceiving the universe as an integrated and unified whole;
2. Tremendous concentration of a kind that does not normally occur;
3. Detachment from concentration on the self as subject, and greater objectivity;
4. Egolessness, unselfishness;
5. The experience itself is self-validating and an end in itself;
6. Disorientation in time and space;
7. Experience of the world as good and worthwhile;
8. An appreciation of the intrinsic values of Being;
9. Emotions of wonder, awe, reverence, humility, surrender, and worship;
10. Dichotomies, polarities and conflicts of life are resolved;
11. Fear disappears;
12. Sometimes there is the after-effect of action, love, or even conversion;
13. A feeling of being graced by the experience;
14. A sense of the sacred, glimpsed through the momentary, the secular.

This listing hardly does justice to the breadth and depth of Maslow's description of peak experiences. One can find them more fully described in Maslow's writings (1977, pp. 59-68), but for me a concrete example is more illuminating than extending the list of descriptors. A friend described an experience she had in the midst of a period of anxiety and depression. She was walking alone. The place was a scene of vast, sweeping dimensions at that spot on the prairie landscape where the Smoky River converges with the Peace. It was autumn; the high banks of the rivers were covered with yellowed grass, and a cloudless blue sky arched overhead. Lost in thought about herself, the direction her life was going, and a creeping sense of isolation she felt within her, she fell into the yellow grass, and gazed up at the blue sky. Suddenly an ecstatic sense of oneness overwhelmed her, a unity with all that she felt, a sense of oneness with others, with God, with the cosmos. Later, words could express the experience only as: "I felt at one with the blue and the yellow, because, for the first time in my life, I really knew what blueness and yellowness are!" Knowing what blueness and yellowness are doesn't make much sense. But they were the best words the woman could find to express her ecstatic feeling of unity at that instant of peak experiencing. It went beyond the experience of color to the integration of a life.

Maslow would call this experience religious even though the setting was "secular." In fact, if I may put words in his mouth, he could call it religious because it was *not* in a traditional, churchy setting. Throughout much of Maslow's writings he depicts organized religion as more likely to quash true religious experience than nurture it. He does this because he sees religion largely as a personal, solitary experience, and there is much in the annals of history and the research of psychology to support the fact that organized religions, in the interests of self-conservation, have persecuted their prophets who have been forced to step out of the organizational circle in order to be truly religious.

The danger in what Maslow is saying is that he does exactly what he deplores: create a new dichotomy, a dichotomy between being a member of a religious organization and being authentically religious. In his lifetime Maslow did not deny the possibility of being authentically and personally religious in a religious organization, but the battles he was fighting in his time led him to create in the minds of some readers an impression that religious organizations and true religiousness were totally mutually exclusive. Part of the blame for this unnecessary dichotomy rests with Maslow's fascination with the peak experiences his self-actualizing people reported and his tendency to equate the mystical, experiential with "religion." This Eastern, mystical emphasis seems to ignore the broader social dimensions of religion that Western civilization has championed. The New Testament gives a succinct and less experiential definition of religion: "What God the Father considers to be pure and genuine religion is this: to take care of orphans and widows in their suffering and to keep oneself from being corrupted by the world" (James 1:27). Western mysticism has always balanced inner personal experience with the social, compassionate aspects of religion. Maslow noted that his self-actualizing subjects had great social feeling, which must, if it was authentic, have flowed into action, but he was not inclined to incorporate this dimension into the concept of religion that he championed, at least initially.

In his Preface to *Religions, Values and Peak Experiences*, written in May 1970 (1977, pp. vii-xvii) Maslow seeks to right some of the imbalance he perceives in his former work. These second thoughts deserve highlighting here. Regarding the possibility of a self-actualizing person being a member of a religious sect, he says that the profoundly and authentically religious person does integrate the legalistic and organizational trends of religion "easily and automatically."

> The forms, rituals, ceremonials, and verbal formulae in which he
> was reared remain for him experientially rooted, symbolically mean-
> ingful, archetypal, unitive. Such a person may go through the same
> motions and behaviors as his more numerous co-religionists, but he
> is never *reduced* to the behavioral as most of them are. (p. vii)

Later (1977, p. xvi) Maslow summarizes his views on religion and peak experiences in a way that ties him in unmistakably with our major theme: "Man has a higher and transcendent nature and this is part of his essence."

Values

We have touched a little on Maslow's concern with values, but not enough to convey a sense of the important role he saw them playing in the human psyche. In a sense self-actualization was what he set out as the ultimate goal of human development, but he proposed no simplistic concept of actualiz-ing, just any tendency, any inclination, any possibility in the human person or society in general. Instead he pointed to something beyond self-actualiza-tion, the guides toward what should be actualized, what was worthy and moral and truly humanizing. These guides, he said, are values—values set the directions of development. In Maslow's terminology, they tell us what is worthy of actualization, what is intermediate, and what is ultimate; what is only a means and what is an end.

Maslow (1962, 1977) addressed himself to the psychological function of values and to the place of values in education, stripping away the pretense of his time that society could have a value-free science, value-free psycho-therapy, and value-free education. It is commonplace today to accept the role of values in science, psychotherapy, and education, but it is so because people like Maslow were willing to look behind the façade and tell the world that all aspects of human development are permeated with values.

Let me narrow down the many things Maslow said about values and put them into a context directly relevant to our themes. If one sees oneself as a person essentially in relationships with other persons both human and divine, one will seek to actualize those relationships with other humans and with God. The religious person is actualizing some of his or her highest level potentials. The self-actualizing person described by Maslow bears a remarkable resemblance to the higher-level human beings described by Dabrowski. Dabrowski and Piechowski (1977) subtitled the second volume of their major work *From Primary Integration to Self-Actualization*. Michael Piechowski (1982) has continued to explore and develop the concept of self-actualization in such eminent people as Eleanor Roosevelt. The descriptors of the higher levels of self-actualization are very much in concurrence with Positive Disintegration theory, which, as we will see, forms the core of our present study.

Synergy

Following our style of picking out from the psychologists we are surveying those points that are most relevant to our study, I would like to touch on a topic that, though not originated by Maslow, was something he researched and popularized. Synergy is a concept that, I think, has great relevance for religious and moral development. This idea of synergy originated with anthropologist Ruth Benedict. While comparing various cultures, she began to see two major themes emerging: that some cultures encouraged cooperation, shared ownership, and mutual help, whereas others encouraged competition, exclusive ownership, and exploitation. The former she called high synergy societies, the latter low synergy societies. It seemed that in a high synergy society the pervading motto was, "My good must be your good or it is no good at all," whereas in the low synergy groups the motto seemed to be, "My gain must be your loss, and too bad about you." High synergy groups shared property in common; wealth was something to be given away; power was something to be shared. In low synergy groups the right to exclusive use of private property was jealously guarded; those who had money could make more money; those who had power could use it to accrete more power to themselves. Maslow researched the concept of synergy and found it present to a high degree, particularly in some of the Native North American societies that shared their meager goods in common, while not far away other tribes in more opulent surroundings exploited each other with high interest rates and competed in the destruction of goods in Potlatch ceremonies. Maslow took his findings and applied them to how we might manage our society in a more mutually beneficial, "Eupsychian" way.

The concept of synergy is particularly relevant to the religious scene. Religious communities, at least in the first ardor of their beginnings, seem to be high synergy societies. The Acts of the Apostles (2:44) describes a community where "All the believers continued together in close fellowship, and shared their belongings with one another." They sold their property and shared with all according to each their needs. Regrettably, religious groups seem to run out of synergy as they age and become more highly institutionalized. The institution tends to congeal into a rigid, pyramidal hierarchy, with power and sometimes wealth concentrated at its summit. Wealth and power are not to be distributed, but coveted. Politics takes over from real religion. Newness, freshness of ideas are discouraged if not actually perse-cuted under the watchful eyes of censorship, trials and inquisitions con-ducted by those who, though they may have little of the spirit of the religion, have in their hands the power of what can so easily be a total institution. Always present for the use of this power is the convenient rationalization that one is "guarding morals" or "preserving the faith."

Regrettably too some so-called religious sects are, at least on the surface, high synergy societies, to which high-minded and dedicated neophytes give themselves and their work, while some "religious founder" lives opulently off the profits of his organization. The word *religion* has been greatly abused; but it serves the organization well when recruiting novices or getting around the law. It is remarkable that "religion" has maintained as much sparkle and attractiveness as it has when so many over the centuries have blackened its name by using it for just another low synergy organization.

All in all, Maslow has contributed much to our appreciation of what it is to be a religious person both within and without a religious organization. He has reminded the scientific and psychological world of the inevitable and important role of values in human development, and encouraged the conflu-ence of religion and psychology.

Erik Erikson

Erik Erikson has been an immensely popular and influential developmental psychologist. Though coming from a Freudian tradition, he has introduced a dimension of sociocultural factors that have taken him well beyond Freud. Erikson incorporates into his description of the individual's passages through the life cycle the need that arises at each stage to resolve certain crises that spring both biologically and socially from the challenges of each passage. Erikson (1963) has described the task of each stage as the resolution of a conflict created by both biological development and social expectations. On at least one notable occasion, when being interviewed by Richard Evans (1967) for his book *Dialogue with Erik Erikson,* he assigned to each stage in the life cycle a certain "virtue" that was needed for the successful resolution of the conflict. Erikson was quick to clarify that he did not mean virtue in the traditional religious or moralistic sense, but was getting more at the root of the word in the original Latin, *virtus* meaning strength (pp. 16-17).

Although Erikson has been interested in religious development, and wrote brilliantly on it in his study of Martin Luther (1959), we do not find a ready-made, complete system of religious development in his writings. Instead, our task here will be to discover some of the insights that Erikson contributes to our appreciation of religious development. To do this we will go to Erikson for the basic framework, constructing some new dimensions with the help of other sources.

Thomas Droege (1972) presents some insights and the beginnings of just such a framework that we can build on. Starting with the premise that faith, as described by Paul Tillich (presented in chapter one), is an act of the whole personality, we can see that faith and religion are not separate elements of life, like add-on options for a new car. Faith includes all those elements psychologists think of as factors of personality—knowledge, emotion, will. Faith is an act of the whole personality in self-surrender, obedience, and assent. Because personality and faith are so intertwined, a process theory of faith is needed to match a process theory of personality development. Erikson steps in here to shed light on the dynamisms of this process and on some of its specific stages.

Basic Trust

Erikson says that the first stage of a child's development centers around establishing a "basic trust." By basic trust Erikson means the realization "that there is some correspondence between your needs and your world" (Evans, 1967, p. 15). A child is not born with trust; it is something given. By giving the child in his or her first year of life a sense that somebody is there who cares, somebody is there to tell you that "all is in order," the mother or father or some reassuring person enables the child to resolve the basic conflict of the first year of life—trust versus mistrust. The successful resolution of this conflict is accompanied by the "virtue" of hope.

Corroboration and a faith setting for the fact of this most fundamental of all tasks comes to us from an interesting and perhaps unlikely source. Peter Berger (1970) describes what he calls "Signals of Transcendence"—prototypical human gestures and words that are within the domain of our "natural" reality, but point to something beyond that reality. One such signal of transcendence is based on the human need for a sense of order. With echoes still in our minds of Erikson's claim that the child needs a foundation of trust, we can turn to Berger's own illustration of a signal of transcendence.

> A child wakes up in the night, perhaps from a bad dream, and finds himself surrounded by darkness, alone, beset by nameless threats. At such a moment the contours of trusted reality are blurred or invisible, and in this terror of incipient chaos the child cries out for his mother. It is hardly an exaggeration to say that at this moment the mother is being invoked as the high priestess of protective order. It is she (and in many cases she alone) who has the power to banish the chaos and restore the benign shape of the world. And, of course, any good mother will do just that. She will take the child and cradle him in the timeless gesture of the Magna Mater who became our Madonna. She will turn on a lamp perhaps that will encircle the scene with a warm glow of reassuring light. She will speak or sing to the child, and the content of this communication will invariably be the same—"Don't be afraid—everything is in order, everything is all right." If all goes well, the child will be reassured, his trust in reality recovered, and in this trust will return to sleep. (pp. 54-55)

Beautiful as it is, this is a fairly routine episode, and most parents who have risen to meet a child's needs in the middle of the night would not see it as a particularly religious act. But if the mother is honest, if she truly means that "everything is all right," her statement transcends the immediate situation of two persons on one particular night in one particular home making a statement about reality as such. Instead it points to a basic trust in the order and meanings of things. It conveys a sense of trust and hope. It puts things in perspective, and that is religious.

But formal religion too, as a community affair, uses gestures and words to convey a sense of trust. Droege (1972) links this first stage of the child's development to formal religion by introducing the rite of baptism as a communal act of conferring trust:

> Meanings are often conveyed more richly in action than in words. Faith, in baptism, is the gift of God through the community, even as trust is the gift of the mother to the child. Through baptism ... the child will realize the gift that is already his if the community really means this baptism. He is literally called into being by this community of concerned people.... The language of the community, which is the language of faith, becomes familiar and understandable to him because he has grown up as a trusting member of the community. (p. 322)

Droege goes on to comment on the symbolic communication of trust by the community as it is presented in terms bespeaking a personal God:

> No other symbol for God other than the personal is adequate for the foundational stage of faith known as trust. One may cringe before the "terrifying and fascinating power" of the holy, or be grasped by an ultimate concern, but one trusts a person ... personal symbols remain the foundation on which all other symbols are built, even as trust is the foundational element of faith on which all others are built. (p. 323)

This brings us back to an important question we considered briefly in the first chapter—the image we have of God as a person—allowing us to reconsider that image now in a developmental context. The inclination might be, following the point that Droege has just made that the personal concept of God is the only one adequate for the very young child, to agree with him, and to rejoice moreover that some people do outgrow this God-as-a-person idea and mature to something more abstract, and consequently more mature. Indeed, Erich Fromm, in *The Art of Loving* (1956, pp. 63-82), does construct a stepladder of one's relationship to God with its lower levels mired down in deep Freudian attachments to protecting mothers and stern, punishing fathers, and its upper rungs in the lofty clouds of abstraction where God, now freed of all human images, is looked on as the great exception to everything we know. But is it really so childish to see God as a person? It need not be. It is true that many who came through some sort of religious education as a child developed an image of God as an old man with a long white beard in a white robe, or at least some variation on that theme. After some mature consideration, most concluded that image simply would not do; it is both psychologically and theologically unsatisfactory. Some, consequently, threw out the whole idea of a personal God. But the problem lies not with a personal God, but with our limited concept of person. If we continue to identify person with physical body, then the anthropomorphisms, the images we have of God as an old man, are controlling us, limiting us, instead of aiding us to form a relationship worthy of persons. A broader, more comprehensive concept of person is called for, not only in the developing individual, but in society at large. What is needed, Sallie McFague (1982) maintains in *Metaphorical Theology: Models of God in Religious Language*, is a model for interpreting our relationship with God that is consonant with postmodern sensibilities that include "a sense of the displacement of the white, Western male and the rise of the dispossessed due to gender, race or class" (pp. x-xi). God as "the great white Father" carries a load of heavy baggage, not least of which is the clutter of presumptions that go with our conception of what it is to be masculine and not feminine. Some Eastern religions have been better than Christianity in giving an image of God that incorporates both masculine and feminine principles. McFague proposes the idea of God as friend as a metaphor that is neither racial, classist, nor sexist and still preserves the concept of God as person, someone with whom one can have a long, profitable, and developing relationship.

Autonomy

The child who has resolved the conflict of trust versus mistrust can pass on to the second major developmental task that is, according to Erikson, the development of autonomy. Most of us have at some time encountered (and I mean that word quite literally) the typical two-year-old whose most used word is "No." The-two-year old says "No" even when it deprives him or her of something he or she would enjoy, like an ice cream cone. But the two-year-old is caught up with the task of gaining his or her independence and being able to assert the new-found ability to choose. Being able to take the opposite direction from all-powerful adults, no matter how small the step, is often more delicious than any ice cream.

Erikson has penetrated this well-known period of child development, known as "the age of opposition," and centered it on the child's quest for autonomy, with the development of the child's will power as the happy outcome of the resolution of this period. The trust that was established in the first year of life becomes the foundation on which this further development involving autonomy and will power must be built. However, the contrast between the two stages is quite sharp. Trust was the response of reliance, of dependence; autonomy is the response of self-direction, of independence. But the child chooses the targets of his rebellion carefully; those against whom he asserts his new-found will must be safe, and yet they must be worth rebelling against. Those rebelled against must be reliable, trustworthy, and strong enough to stand for something of significance to the child. Given these two elements, trustworthiness and a stance against which the child can push, he goes to work to resolve the autonomy crisis of this period.

The conflict is often one of obedience, and thus it becomes a potential ground for faith development. Obedience is a lifelong element of faith, rooted in trust and growing out of it. If ever there was an example of being "rooted in the resources, yet open to the possibilities" it is the child, adolescent, and adult going through Erikson's stages. The human person's faith response to God is not an unmoved, unquestioning, blind submission in which "the will of God" (however that might be interpreted) is to be submitted to without any question. A personal relationship with God precludes that. Outside of a warm, positive, trusting relationship, the will of a father or mother becomes what Carl Rogers calls "a condition of worth": "I will love you *if*..." "You are a worthwhile person only *if*..." This can be one's view of the will of the "Heavenly Father." If the ground of trust has not been laid between child and God, then the "will of God" becomes a threat based on estrangement, and obedience to it is the guilt-ridden burden of a lifetime. But if faith is rootedness, the image of healthy religious development is more like that of a tree, rooted in the ground of personal trust in God, and thus free to choose the possibilities of further growth. Hope can grow from this faith. Security then is not something to be clung to desperately, but something to be grown on, to be the nourishment of that adventure, questioning, and daring that is growth. "To venture causes anxiety, but not to venture is to lose oneself" (Kirkegaard).

Identity

This theme of needing to risk in order to develop, and being able to risk because of the firm securities already established is central to Erikson's entire developmental schema. It appears again at the next important stage of the life cycle—adolescence. Erikson points to identity formation as the theme of adolescence. The major task of the adolescent is to resolve a personal identity crisis, to answer in some way the questions: Who am I? Am I worthwhile? and Where am I going? Adolescence brings rapid change from the relative stability and security of late childhood. Biologically, the adolescent senses major changes within his or her own body. Socially, the adolescent is in a kind of no man's land between childhood and adulthood. The image that best illustrates the dilemma of adolescence for me is that of a tightrope walker over Niagara Falls. As he moves out along his rope, the tightrope walker can glance over his shoulder at the riverbank from which he came. It looks very solid and secure; it was a safe place to be. He can look expectantly ahead to the bank he is approaching; it too looks solid, secure, and invitingly safe. In the meantime he is suspended in space by an all too slender rope, and below it is the chasm. He is in a very insecure position. So the adolescent: he or she can look back, remembering the security of childhood when relatively little was expected, and identity quite easy to grasp. Ahead is the adult world, imagined as a state of establishment, promising the possibility of committed companionship, job, driver's license, material possessions, and freedom from Mom and Dad. There was security in childhood; there is the promise of some security in adult life. In the meantime there is the insecurity of feeling you don't belong in either world. Like the chasm below the tightrope walker, that is extremely threatening. No wonder sociologists and anthropologists have discovered that adolescents in our society and our age have formed a teenage subculture among themselves, with all the danger of it being a camaraderie of individuals driven together by shared feelings of insecurity and alienation.

The resolution of the adolescent identity crisis, according to Erikson, the safe passage between the two worlds of childhood and adulthood, is based on the successful resolution of all previous stages of development. Identity builds on the trust, the autonomy, the initiative, the industry that have come out of the more or less successful resolution of previous conflicts, and the measure to which these positive shaping forces have prevailed. Erikson (1964) uses the image of a trapeze artist in the middle of a swing to illustrate the passage of adolescence. The trapeze artist has to let go of the security of the bar he has been clinging to and reach out for the other bar that is swinging his way, trusting that its timing is right and its strength sufficient to sustain his weight. But in that breathless moment, suspended in space between the two securities, he has nothing to depend on but himself. Trusting in what his past has made him, and what he has made of his past, he reaches for what the future promises to be. Suspended between childhood and adulthood, one grasps and evaluates what has been and what is yet to be in a way unique to this time. Above all, the adolescent searches for values, for what is worthwhile, and in some cases for what is worthy of ultimate concern.

Fortunately, this identity crisis does not take place in a vacuum. Identity formation is not only a sense of inner continuity; it encompasses relationships—one's continuity and meaning for others. The adolescent may progress by inner struggles, but inevitably these struggles are related to the demands of others and, fortunately, aided by the support of others in his community. This is true of the religious community. If Whitehead is right in saying that religion is what an individual does with his solitariness, adolescence is a period ripe for intense religious experience. What the adolescent can do with his solitariness is turn to his religious community, the community of his origins and the community of his aspirations, and there seek confirmation.

It is noteworthy that the word *confirmation* a word encrusted with many "churchy" connotations fits so well here as a psychological need of adolescence. Interestingly, Christian churche̶ used some form of confirmation as the sacrament o̶f as the Bar Mitzvah is the religious rite o̶f ... the young ... the Jewish faith. If the religious com... truly aware ... he adolescen ... ...ament, and not merely going ... you ... ... identity, reco ... the fru ... ...m the youth, encouraging th... ...t search, and accepting the ad...

But ...rmation must ...wo ways: it is a mutua... ...ct of confirming. Not only do... ... community confirm the youth, giving ...m or her a role in it, but the y... ...h must confirm the community, telling i... community whether what it is ...ng about life has personal meaning, and ...finding for oneself a role to p... ...in that religious community, and in soci... ...t large. The virtue that Eriks̶o ...associate... with the successful resolutio... ...f the adolescent identity cri... ...s fidelity. The adolescent, searching f... ...alues worthy of dedicating a ...y must ask the question ... ...t is worth being faithful to? If ...resolves th... ...ne way, he comes to answers that encompa... ..., to others (God included), and to values. Adolescence i... ...me for questioning values and, hopefully, the time of discovering values so that one can be faithful. By deciding for oneself, with the guidance of others, what is value-able, one chooses the concerns, including the ultimate concerns, that may last a lifetime. It is clearly a faith experience. The role of the faith community is to be present to guide, but not enforce these choices. These roles of mutual concern that the faith community and the adolescent play opposite each other are delicate. The community points to what is worthy of being valued, and the adolescent chooses by assent and subsequent fidelity. Teilhard de Chardin expressed the depths of this relationship in these words: "Faith consecrates the world; fidelity communicates with it."

Erikson's life cycle structure goes on to describe the rest of the life span: intimacy in the young adult years, generativity and caring in later adulthood, and integrity marked by wisdom in the mature years, when one must face the ultimate prospect: "To be through having been; to face not being." As we saw in the first chapter, the resolution of this conflict is a religious question of profound proportions.

These stages and their psychosocial dynamics have been thoroughly explored in many other contexts. Here I have attempted to highlight some of the potential within this vast schema for the study of religious and moral development. Some emerging themes particularly important to our present study are:

1. The role of crisis in human development. Across the life span stress and crises are not obstacles but initiators, necessary for development.

2. Human development, including religious development, is a gradual unfolding, and, if we follow Erikson's ontogenetic philosophy of development, one stage builds on the successful completion of a previous stage like a tower of blocks. Some other theories of development do not follow this ontogenetic, stage-on-stage approach. Dabrowski's Positive Disintegration Theory, for example, takes an evolutionary approach to development, maintaining that lower levels that are more primitive and are abandoned by the developing individual in favor of higher, more satisfactory levels.

3. Although Freudian in his origins, Erikson goes beyond Freud, contributing something to the Freudian tradition that broadens its scope and makes it more feasible as a mode of understanding religious and moral development. Erikson puts development in a broader, psychosocial context, depending much less on the determining powers of early childhood experiences with parents and more on broad social forces that affect the whole of the life cycle. This interplay between the developing individual and the societal forces around him or her is a theme that enriches Erikson's explanation of the life cycle, making it fertile ground for understanding religious and moral development.

James Fowler

In recent years the name James Fowler has become almost synonymous with faith development, and Fowler's stages of faith development have influenced religious education methods (Groome, 1980). Fowler is a professor of human development and theology in the Candler School of Theology at Emory University in Atlanta, Georgia. While involved in work at a Methodist summer conference center, he listened to the life stories of hundreds of people who attended interfaith seminars. Fowler began to sense common patterns in their spiritual journeys and similarities in the forces shaping them. Influenced initially by the psychology of Erik Erikson and the theology of H. Richard Niebuhr, he began to systematize his perceptions into a theory of faith development. Eventually, under the influence of Lawrence Kohlberg at Harvard, Fowler adopted the formal, structural-developmental model proposed by Piaget and elaborated by Kohlberg in the construction of his theory of moral development. Although Fowler has modeled his stages of faith development on Kohlberg, and adopted much of the structural-developmental approach, he has preserved more emphasis than Kohlberg on the role of emotions and imagination. This reflects perhaps the importance Fowler (1979) has assigned to the many personal, individual stories of faith journeys that he has used as data for his research and evidence for his "life maps."

Central to Fowler's theory is the conviction that faith is not a static thing, but a process. He insists that we have for too long limited the word *faith* to the role of a noun—a thing; in reality faith is a process, and faith may be used as a verb—an action word. In the tradition of Tillich and Niebuhr, Fowler sees faith as not limited to a traditional religious context; he sees faith or "faithing" as a process of making some sense out of life, a search for meaning. Since the Enlightenment, he maintains, many have found meaning in life outside of religious traditions and religious communities. (Victor Frankl, as we have seen, insists that the search for meaning is not necessarily "religious" but "spiritual.") Faith can be religious, Fowler maintains, but it can also center on such mundane factors as a job, an institution, money, power, even on oneself: it can also center on relationships to other people and to nature. One is reminded here of the kind of life meaning a person like Thoreau found at Walden, or the deeply reflective faithing that was done by Ralph Waldo Emerson who resigned his Unitarian ministry because he felt that the rituals of organized religion tended to ossify the individual's direct contact with the Universe. One is reminded too of the number of contemporary individuals who have found life meaning, based on a sense of oneness with all creation, in a dedicated effort to bring mankind back from its destructive tendency to dominate and exploit the universe. Faith is broader than institutionalized religion.

If faith, as Fowler sees it, is a process, the way people make meaning of their lives, then the content of that faith, "the articles of faith" (to use an old ecclesiastical term) become much less important than the quality of the process and the success of the quest. Ultimately, the search for meaning that is faith is a process of clarifying values. "What values direct my life?" "What do I think is worthwhile?" "What truly is worthwhile?" Faith is a process of bringing into consciousness the values that direct one's life and making a judgment about whether they are worthy of being kept or not. Faith is the process of rising above the blind following of values not reflected on, and moving in directions not really chosen, in favor of choice of values and a sense of perspective and direction.

This sort of movement is precipitated by some critical incident leading to reflection and disembedding of old values, replacing them with better ones. When Fowler speaks of critical incidents as the catalyst of movement from one stage to another, he draws on a philosophical and psychological tradition. Piaget maintains that cognitive development comes about through the creation of disequilibrium in the learner. Erikson, as we have seen, holds that individuals progress through the stages of development as the result of conflict resolution. Kohlberg found that moral development comes about through the conflict created by exposure to higher-level reasoning. The idea that crisis, far from hindering, is actually necessary for development is emerging more and more in contemporary psychology. It is, as we will see, the major theme of Positive Disintegration theory and integral to our concept of religious and moral development.

Stages of Faith Development

Fowler has presented his stages of faith development in several places, but perhaps most thoroughly in his 1981 book *Stages of Faith: The Psychology of Human Development and the Quest for Meaning.* Here he not only explains his stages at length, but draws parallels between them and the stages proposed by Piaget, Kohlberg, and Erikson. A summary should suffice here:

First there is, in the infant period, a pre-stage of undifferentiated faith where the seeds of trust, hope, and love are fused primarily in relationship to parents. Following Erikson's description of the first year of life, Fowler hypothesizes a theme of trust versus mistrust as the basic conflict of this period. The child who emerges from this crisis successfully has built up a fund of basic trust and the relational experience of mutuality with those who love and care for him. Faith encompasses and builds on this kind of trust.

Intuitive-projective faith. Based on the previous pre-stage of trust and undifferentiated faith, the young child builds a bank of images that represent both the protective and the threatening powers around him. These images come from imagination, stimulated by stories and symbols not yet controlled by logic, but shot through with powerful feelings.

Mythic-literal faith. Stage two occurs in late childhood when the individual begins to take on beliefs, observances, and stories that symbolize belonging to one's community. Beliefs and moral rules are appropriated with literal interpretation. The developing ability to think logically helps one to order the world into categories of space, time, and causality. One can now begin to take the perspectives of others and identify with them. Life meanings begin to emerge from faith traditions, particularly stories.

Synthetic-conventional faith. Adolescence brings with it new cognitive abilities. Mutual perspective taking becomes possible, and the adolescent searches for mirrors to reflect self back to self in order to integrate diverse self images into a coherent identity. Values take on new importance, but at this stage they are largely a synthesis of beliefs and values of others, put together to support an identity and to unite one in emotional solidarity with others; they are not reflected on at the depth that comes with further development.

Individuative-reflective faith. Young adulthood offers the possibility (but not the guarantee) of moving on to critical reflection on one's beliefs and values. One can now choose to become part of a social system and to take on the responsibilities for making choices of ideology and lifestyle. Now one can commit oneself to the fidelity of relationships and to life vocation.

Conjunctive faith. If the adult in mid-life and beyond can move past the former stages of faith, a time comes when faith resolves seeming contradictions, when paradox becomes an accepted element of life, when one can embrace the polarities of life (life-death, joy-pain, love-hate) and see life not as monolithic, but multifaceted, or, better still, organic. Fowler (1981) says, "Conjunctive faith suspects that things are organically related to each other; it attends to the pattern of interrelatedness in things, trying to avoid force-fitting to its own prior mind set" (p. 185). There is at this stage an enriched appreciation of symbol and story, metaphor and myth, as vehicles for grasping truth.

Universalizing faith. Fowler's ultimate stage is an integration. Beyond polarities that divide and paradoxes that help explain, persons in this stage, which may have its beginnings in mid-life, are grounded in a oneness with being. Fowler (1981) describes the highest levels of faith development in these terms:

> Persons best described by Stage 6 typically exhibit qualities that shake our usual criteria for normalcy. Their heedlessness of self pres- ervation and the vividness of their taste and feel for transcendent moral and religious actuality give their actions and words an extraor- dinary and often unpredictable quality. In their devotion to univer- salizing compassion they may offend our parochial perceptions of justice. In their penetration through the obsession with survival, se- curity and significance they threaten our measured standards of righteousness, goodness and prudence. Their enlarged visions of uni- versal community disclose the partialness of our tribes and pseudo- species. And their leadership initiatives, often involving strategies of nonviolent suffering and ultimate respect for being, constitute af- fronts to our usual notions of relevance. It is little wonder that per- sons best described by Stage 6 so frequently become martyrs for the visions they incarnate. (p. 200)

Stage 6 people have generated a faith that is inclusive of all being. They incarnate and actualize the spirit of a truly fulfilled human community. They are not numerous. Asked to name representatives of conjunctive faith, Fowler (1981, p. 201) lists Gandhi, Martin Luther King, Jr., Mother Teresa of Calcutta, Dag Hammarskjöld, Dietrich Bonhoeffer, Abraham Heschel, and Thomas Merton. Their highly developed vision, faith, and commitment free them for a passionate yet detached spending of self in love. They have penetrated to the elusive inner core of being and found there a unity and meaning that they feel morally compelled to share with humankind even at great loss to themselves. Loss *to* themselves, but not loss *of* themselves.

Fowler's approach to faith as process clearly puts faith or "faithing" in a developmental context. It is a process. Faith as he understands it is broader than conventional religion; it is a search for meaning and at heart a search for values, some of them ultimate values. Each person has an "ultimate environment," the farthest horizons of one's personal world in which and in relation to which one makes meaning out of life. But life reflected on is of vast circumference, and could for many be empty and confusing like the horizon viewed by a lone sailor in the middle of the ocean, if it were not marked by certain islands. These islands are centers of value, guides in navigation through life. Islands of value set in a landscape of ultimate horizons guide one in the faith process. According to Fowler, this process seems to go through a set of stages. Faith, then, is not monolithic but multilevel. Religion, whether solitary or communal, is likewise a process of multilevel development with its search of ultimate horizons, for islands of value that may give direction perspective and ultimate meaning to life.

Conclusion

The thoughtful reader of this chapter will have noted that our review of developmental psychology, far from covering the whole gamut of theories, has restricted itself to those theories that could best be described as organic, or Third Force, almost completely neglecting the Freudian and behavioristic approaches. This is not denial of the value of these approaches to understanding religious psychology, but it is an acknowledgment that the foundational psychologies most promising for a psychology of religious development lie in what we call broadly the humanistic tradition with its roots in existential philosophy. Psychologists in the humanistic tradition are comfortable with words like *faith, love, religion,* and *values.* In fact, values, as we have seen, are at the heart of humanistic psychology even when dealing with what is usually considered secular or nonreligious. It is obvious too that several contemporary theories of human development feel quite comfortable with acknowledging the fact that humans are religious animals and that religion can be present at varying levels in varying stages of the life cycle.

The thoughtful reader of this chapter will also have noted that it is not unprejudiced. It is not an "objective" view of all sorts of psychologists who have something to say about human development. The psychologists presented here have been chosen carefully to illustrate the underlying themes of this book. Indeed, ideas have been plucked out of their theories to support our themes—without, I hope, destroying the meanings of the original authors. The whole work is, I trust, still true to its sources, presenting them for what they are. Otherwise our principal theme of the convergence of religion and psychology would not be adequately served.

Lest we conclude this chapter leaving the impression that stages of development are something psychologists in our own day have originated, let it be known that the very concept of stages is an ancient religious tradition. It is at least as old as the mystics who saw the development of the soul's relationship to God in terms of stages. Perhaps most famous among these stages, at least in the Western, Christian tradition, are the "Seven Mansions" of Teresa of Avila (1515-1582) and "The Ascent of Mt. Carmel" described by John of the Cross. Somehow it seems natural to see human development and religious development unfolding in a series of stages. The stages described by the classical religious mystics exemplify a tradition of religion as developing; it is a tradition older and more universal than any concept of faith as some static thing that one "gets" almost instantaneously, "clings to" blindly, or "loses" by a single act. The mystics have told us that faith is not something to be "had" like a marble statue but, like a rose, to be allowed to unfold. Fowler (1984) puts the role of developmental psychology in an even broader context, reaching back beyond the mysticism of the last few centuries into deeper and more primitive levels of human nature as a whole. He says:

> Theorists of adult development have begun to play the role in our society that storytellers and mythmakers once played in primitive and classical cultures. They have taken on many of the functions that philosophers and theologians performed in the twelfth through the nineteenth centuries. In our time of fractured images of the human vocation and of fragmented experiences of connectedness to religious and cultural symbols of wholeness, a group of philosophical psychologists are helping us to gain a holistic grasp on the course of human life. Using the organic root metaphor of development in a variety of ways, their research and theories aim to provide empirically grounded chartings of predictable patterns and turnings in human life cycles. (p. 15)

Fowler goes on to suggest that it may not be an exaggeration to say that philosophical theorists of developmental psychology are offering in formalistic and mainly secular terms a "way of salvation" as described by earlier theologians. This parallel, he reminds us, is not so extraordinary if we remember that the Latin root word of salvation *salus* means "healthiness," "wholeness." We are back, it seems, to our familiar concept *integration* and our old theme of human development as a process of movement toward integration or wholeness. "Holiness is wholeness" is an old religious dictum, and St. Irenaeus has been often quoted for his saying "The glory of God is man fully alive."

Process has been the main theme of our survey of religious development. The psychologists we have studied have not been so concerned with content as with process. They do not ask the question: What does faith know? so much as How does faith know it? This psychology does not exclude the matter of religious content, whether it be the beliefs of an individual or the dogmas of a religious sect, but focuses on how content is apprehended. That process, as we have seen, is one of movement from relative simplicity to greater complexity, from almost monolithic integration to the complex system of integration that is necessary to retain the identity and continuity of a human being in the process of becoming much more complex.

I have used the image of the spiral and touted it as the best symbolic representation of the process of development because it incorporates the elements of ascending by regressing back over old pathways, but at a higher level. I also touted it as the best image of the highest levels of human development because the spiral, like the human in process, has no set limits, going off instead into infinite risings. This is poetically beautiful and poetically and psychologically true. But "all analogies limp," says an old philosophical dictum, which, interestingly, is an analogy in itself. All analogies are true in some sense and not true in another. The analogy, the image of the spiral, is true of human development, and I still stand by it, but as an image of process it may imply an ongoing, continuous differentiation alone as the coils of the spiral grow wider and wider apart. The description we have seen of human development at its highest levels tells us that something besides (not *in place of* but *besides*) differentiation is taking place. It is a process of integration, and at the highest levels it is a process of integration in universality. Fowler's stage six is certainly an integration in universality, a special coming together; Erikson's mature adult has integrated values that yield peace; Maslow's self-actualizers at the highest levels feel and act on a oneness with the whole of the cosmos; Allport says that the mature person has an integrating philosophy of life. Whitehead points toward a perfection, not static of course, but leading to a peace that calls the individual beyond himself, without denying himself, toward the integration of order and love. There must be something in this idea that the highest levels of human development offer a new coming together.

The human developmental process seems to begin and end with integration. The child is integrated in his simplicity; the developing adult loses that childish simplicity, and, with luck and good management, achieves an appreciation of his increasing complexity (while still preserving his sense of identity); those few who pass on to the heights of human development seem capable of incorporating an expansive sense of universality that becomes blended within their own personal integration. It is as though the spiral of development ever expands to greater and greater circumferences, but ever swirls inward too, toward greater integration and the peace that, they say, always dwells at the eye of the cyclone. These are paradoxes, and maybe that is where we should leave it. The spiral diverges and the spiral converges at the same time. Maybe it is we who have the problem and not spirals or life (or even psychology). Maybe our long years of dichotomizing, of opposing love and hate, suffering and joy, life and death have made us create too many contradictions that are not really there. Maybe spirals can diverge and converge at the same time and human beings can go from the integration of simplicity, the placid child, to the integration of complexity, the person of peace, through a process of development that is itself disintegration. We have found religion there, vital to all levels of the spiral—at the very eye of conscrescence.

Chapter 5

A Theory for Understanding Religious and Moral Development: An Introduction to Positive Disintegration

Maybe relieving the pain will prevent the formation of a pearl.
—*Carl Whitaker*

Because religion is not only theological but also psychological—a developing aspect of the personality—we need a comprehensive or "grand" psychological theory to explain how religious development comes about and how we might encourage it toward the higher reaches of human nature. Clearly the traditional psychoanalytic and behavioristic theories are not suitable, nor are theories built primarily on cognitive themes of an organism merely seeking equilibrium; they would hardly reflect religion's dynamic movement toward that which is higher; or morality's ever-questing urge toward that which is better. These theories are not holistic, and, as Pearce says (1992, p. 221), "To become whole all parts must be left behind, for a whole is not the sum of its parts, but a different state entirely." Religion at its best is a search for wholeness, a quest for ultimates, the ineffable, the transpersonal, and the highest of moral endeavors. Only a holistic theory with a sense of this quest for the highest of human endeavors has within itself the measure of these goals and the potential to draw a life map for the pilgrim. On the moral side, only a theory with a strong sense of values can direct the quester to what is truly worthwhile. Only a theory with a realistic sense of the difficulties of the journey—the painful, the tragic—can promise hope to find some order in the sometimes painful chaos of individual development. These characteristics, I contend, are found, at least potentially, in the theory of Positive Disintegration proposed by Kazimierz Dabrowski (1967, 1970, 1972, 1973), Dabrowski, Kawczak, and Piechowski (1970), and by his daughter (Dabrowski, 1993).

Up to this point we have examined the ideas and shared the experiences of eminent theologians, philosophers, psychologists, and scientists as they explored the development of religion and morality within the individual and within society. Some are philosophical speculations with implications for developmental psychology; some are psychological theories with developmental aspects; some are theories of developmental psychology with implications for religious and moral development. It is to this latter category we return now: a developmental psychology theory, which although not explicitly a theory of religious and moral development has profound and far-reaching implications for the holistic development of persons.

The theory we turn to now is known as Positive Disintegration. It is a developmental theory particularly relevant to religious and moral development. The Theory of Positive Disintegration (TPD) is a grand, or all-encompassing, theory of how humans develop. I consider it a grand theory not only because Dabrowski was concerned with the whole person, but because its foundational philosophy is clearly stated, its image of full humanness worked out, and its appreciation of health and sickness plainly explicated so that one can see the values on which it is built. Its scope is so vast, its depths so profound, its implications so telling for our present topics that we will spend considerable time in exploring it in depth, looking first at the theory in general as proposed by its author, Kazimierz Dabrowski, and then at the specific implications of the theory for religious and moral development and ultimately for religious and moral education. Because so much of theory, particularly psychological theory, comes not just from the head but from the heart of its author, I am convinced that a theory is best appreciated by those who have first an image of the kind of person who conceived it.

Kazimierz Dabrowski and His Developmental Theory

Kazimierz Dabrowski was born in Poland in 1902, studied in Europe, and suffered through the atrocities of two World Wars. It was this combination of high academic scholarship and deep personal participation in the realities of the world at some of its ugliest moments that brought him the understanding and sensibilities to build a profound and meaningful theory of human development.

Professor Dabrowski studied both medicine and education before receiving his MD at the University of Geneva. In 1931 he received his PhD in psychology at Poznan University, a certificate of psychoanalytic studies at Vienna (under Wilhelm Stekel), and a certificate of the School of Public Health at Harvard in 1934. He studied under Claparede and Jean Piaget and established an institute of mental hygiene at Warsaw in 1935. After World War II and his imprisonment during the Nazi occupation of Poland, he was awarded a "habilitation in psychiatry" at the University of Wroclaw. He was professor of experimental psychology at Warsaw in 1956 and at the Polish Academy of Sciences until 1958. From 1964 until 1979 he was a professor and Director of Clinical Research and Internship at the University of Alberta in Canada, and from 1968 a visiting professor at Laval University, Quebec. In 1979 he returned to Poland and died there in 1980. In his lifetime he wrote more than 38 books and 253 other publications, in English, Polish, and French. Centers for the study of his theory are located throughout Canada, the United States, South America, and Europe. Those of us who were fortunate enough to meet Dr. Dabrowski, first as his students and then as his colleagues in developing the theory, were impressed by the quiet humility of the man, his scholarship and hard work, and above all the depths of feeling that made possible a theory of psychological development that speaks so well to the human condition.

My own memories of Kazimierz Dabrowski are not confined to the innumerable pages of handouts in purple mimeograph ink we shared in each weekly seminar where we explored new aspects of his theory as he developed them in his senior years. My personal memories are of a gentlemanly scholar not given to small talk, not lapsing into personal narrative, but flowing from a wellspring of thought and life experience that gave rise to a mystique of reticence. There was always another depth to be explored. He was single-minded and consumed with the development of "the theory." My memories too are of the "taste-full" evenings at the Dabrowski home, talking, of course, about *the* theory as we devoured elaborate Polish dishes graciously presented by his wife and daughters.

The Theory

Let us begin the study where religion, morality, and the individual intersect: in mystery. It is, after all, at the heart of this psychology. First, the title of the theory—Positive Disintegration—is somewhat baffling. It is more mystical than simply mysterious. Like so many terms Dabrowski used, it contains within it a delightful paradox, a seeming contradiction. *Positive* Disintegration? How can falling apart be positive? Disintegration surely is a negative thing, simply a breakdown as in a "mental breakdown." How can a breakdown, especially a mental breakdown, be something positive?

There is no denying the painfulness of *all* disintegration. Whatever its name, it hurts; sometimes it crushes. But Dabrowski says it can be positive when it leads to growth. If the outcome of the falling apart is a putting together as something better, then even the pain of disintegration takes on a positive aspect. Disintegration, he says, is an opportunity, an open doorway toward growth. Even more, it is a precondition for growth; it is, in fact, necessary or there will be no growth, just stagnation. Disintegration is not something we grow *in spite of*; it is something we grow *because of*. It is a profound fact of the human condition.

We can go back far beyond Dabrowski to the experience of mankind through the ages to find an appreciation of this mystery. We find the wellsprings of understanding the mystery of disintegration in mankind's most primitive and highest experiences of the cosmos. A pervading theme of philosophy, myth, literature, and religion has been the birth of life from death, of growth from decay, of joy from pain. People saw this in nature as winter yielded to spring in the cycle of the seasons, as children were born in pain, as food was consumed to give life, as wheat sprang from the fertile soil.

Ancient peoples, aware of the mysteries of death and resurrection, celebrated it in their religious rites and depicted it in their arts. They vivified it in the myth of the Phoenix, a great, beautiful bird. When it felt its death impending it collected aromatic plants and made a nest. Then it set fire to the nest, and a new Phoenix arose from the ashes. They humanized it in the fertility cults of Catal Huyuk, and the prehistoric goddesses who united not only divinity and humanity, but life and death. The goddess was a projection of mankind's wonder in the midst of the unfolding of nature's cycles and human cycles within them. The ancient Egyptians looked up into their blue desert sky, and seeing the sun dominating all, worshipped it. In this mighty presence they saw the power of the mystery of life and death. They chose to live on the east bank of the Nile where the sun rose. They carried their dead across in boats to the west and buried them where the sun set. The pyramids stand on the west bank as enduring monuments to mankind's aspirations to some kind of afterlife.

The Book of Job is a classic exploration of the mystery of suffering and evil. In the New Testament Jesus drew from an ancient wisdom when he said (John 12:24), "In all truth I tell you, unless a wheat grain falls into the earth and dies, it remains only a single grain; but if it dies it yields a rich harvest." Paul repeated the theme in 1 Corinthians 15:36: "What you sow must die before it is given new life." Life comes not *despite* but *through* death; growth comes not despite disintegration but through disintegration. Order comes not despite chaos, but *out of* chaos.

Just as our ancestors found mystery in the natural things of their day, we find it in nature. Lodgepole pine seeds germinate only after the conflagration of a forest fire has released them to be nurtured by the ashes of the old forest. Tiny, green, fragile sprouts, destined to be giant redwoods, grow from rotting trunks of dead trees. It seems that life and death are not opposite poles, miles apart at the extremes of some dichotomy, but rather partners, dancing an eternal cyclical dance together in a dance called the process of the world, the ongoingness of the universe.

It is a mystery full of hope for what ultimately may be, but on the dark side pointing to the necessity of pain now. Religion at its best addresses mystery not by rationalizing it away, but by giving perspective, perceiving the basic paradox—the seeming absurdity that reveals a deeper truth. In the mystery of death, pain, and suffering the paradox is that the power to give life is found, surprisingly, not outside but within the mystery of death itself. Life constantly surprises us by appearing in the most unlikely places.

In sum, the transcendent paradox of paradoxes running as a theme through the great mysteries is that "opposites" are not opposites at all, but partners. The mystery of death is entwined with the mystery of life, its origins and growth. Life and death dance together at the stillpoint of the turning earth. Suffering, disintegration, death, in and through their lethal powers, have paradoxically a higher power—the power to give life.

Disintegration in Life

The evidence is present not only in nature. The realities of disintegration and rebirth are there in the experience of some men and women. Most of these are themselves "sick souls" in James's sense, not satisfied with trite or reassuring explanations of the world around them that eliminate the pain or wipe it away in a rationalization. Some labor with the mystery of suffering and find it something not to be fled from, but embraced because it is the stuff of creativity and growth and life itself. One of these suffering souls was Kazimierz Dabrowski, surveying the dead and maimed and dying on the battlefields of Europe, experiencing the inhumanity of man toward man in concentration camps, and sensitive to his own inner hurts, but conscious of the need of others. He translated his life experience and learning into a theory that has profound implications for understanding the human condition and drawing from it an optimum of growth and an optimum of human consciousness.

By pointing out that the actions we perform, the attitudes we have, and the words we use to describe them have many levels, Dabrowski opened up a new way of looking at the psychology of human development. As a practicing physician Dabrowski saw something many others still do not see: he saw growth sometimes coming out of the turmoil others called psychoneurosis. He became convinced that psychoneurosis is not an illness, but an opportunity for development. I have found in my work as a counseling psychologist that when people, particularly those who experience pain in their lives, hear of the theory, their response is a strong "Yes" of recognition. "Yes, that makes so much sense to me." "Yes, that's the story of *my* life." "Yes, that gives me some hope that the hell I'm going through right now might turn out to be positive in some way after all." Dabrowski's ideas are something many people can translate into the terms of their own lives.

Dabrowski was well aware that not all disintegrations are positive, not all breakdowns act in the service of increased psychological development. In contrast to positive disintegration where developmental dynamisms (which we shall look at later) are active, negative disintegration is characterized by the lack of such dynamisms. In other words, some people have within themselves the potential to turn a disintegration into a positive growth experience; other people do not have such a potential and may well be slow, paralyzingly hesitant, fearful, or so unaware that they remain even static, lacking in development. Drawing on his own personal experiences and his practice as a clinician over many years, Dabrowski noted that there seemed to be striking differences in the way individuals reacted to the various events of their lives. Some, he noted, experienced the death of someone close in a bland, concrete, and literal way; others tended to take the experience of the death of a loved one and transform it, deepening the experience, plumbing its depths, developing it into a complex significant, intense, and yet enhancing experience. Some people just seemed to be more sensitive to their experiences and more able and willing to have the experiences reach the depths of their psyche and stir them up. Out of these observations grew the concept of "overexcitability"—another Dabrowskian concept we shall see more of later on.

We may trace back Dabrowski's appreciation of the necessity of crisis in life not only to his personal experiences, but also to his European origins. Although Dabrowski reacted strongly to Freud's reductionistic psychology, he carried over into TPD a tragic sense of conflict that was central to Freud. Many North American psychologies, although they have roots in Freud, have parceled out this role of conflict in development, preferring instead the doctrine of the more romantic Human Potential movements, which often promise development without pain.

Physician though he was, he had a vision over and beyond the traditional medical paradigm in which health and disease vie for dominance; where health is stability and the absence of crisis, and disease is instability and the presence of crisis. Dabrowski's paradigm, on the other hand, envisions health as the fluid ability to alternate between psychological stability and crisis, while disease is being locked in chronic crisis or a stuckness at the lowest levels of development.

Put simply, then, development accompanies disintegration that is *positive*; on the other hand, dissolution of mental functions accompanies *negative* disintegration. Both are a falling apart. For the latter the dissolution is chronic, unproductive, and never-ending; for the former a breakdown is an opportunity, a new beginning. An opportunity can be lost, discarded in a dump where it perishes, or grasped, used to realize the better and to create the new and the not-yet-imagined.

Multilevelness

Developmental psychologists are like mapmakers; they picture the layout of the land and describe the routes one may take in traversing it. Their maps are three-dimensional, topographical, because they usually describe the process of development in terms of moving *upward* through stages or levels. Most stage theories are ontological; they emphasize normal growth and development over time. One can expect a child of a certain age to have developed to a point in common with other children of his or her own age in similar circumstances. These are the stages of *normal* development that all parents watch for in their offspring, and that doting parents seem to discover earlier in their own children than they do in other people's.

Dabrowski uses levels in this sense of progression over time; but he uses it in another important sense of levels of quality or value. He points out the higher value of some levels over others without stressing so much the factor of time as the fact that the higher level is in itself *better*. He stresses development upward through higher and better values. Dabrowski's levels are based not just on an ordinal scale of "later," but on a value scale of "better." If we stress the betterness of the higher level without tying it so closely to time, we step beyond stages and chronology. This allows us to apply the idea of levels not only to stage development, but to describing human behavior and organizations. We take the very ideas we have about the qualities we see in humans and distinguish *levels of behavior* within a single concept. Ideas, thoughts, human behaviors themselves have levels. They are so rich with values that we can call them multileveled. Take a word such as *love*. At lower levels sexual energy, sometimes going under the name of love, is simply given a physical outlet without consideration for the other. In fact, the only "personal" relationship involved may be the exploitation of power over the more vulnerable one treated as an object. Sexuality at higher levels is enriched by care, concern, responsibility, and respect in a manner that is truly interpersonal. The personal relationship in turn is enriched in the form of a lasting relationship. There is a vast difference in the meaning given to the word love when we use it to describe an exploitative "one-night stand" and the deep, caring relationship of a couple that has grown over 50 years. One can take many other words and find multiple levels of meaning within them. Dabrowski and Piechowski (1977) describe a number of functions, outlining the levels that exist in them when seen through the eyes of multilevelness. One example is levels of smiling. There is a vast difference, obviously, between the smile of a villain and the smile of a loving grandparent. Dabrowski makes even more subtle distinctions of levels of smiling, moving from the cynical and threatening to the empathic and caring the smile that says: "I am one with you."

Behavior (and consequently the organizations shaped by behavior) are no longer seen as simply unilevel, like a carton of milk—homogeneous throughout. We can look at concepts such as health, happiness, and love, and see they are not monolithic, uniform throughout, but that there are various levels within each of them according to the higher level of values a particular behavior represents. TPD gives us the criteria to distinguish these value shades of meaning by indicating new facets. It is like the experience of a gem cutter who takes a large, rather dull-looking stone, strikes it with precisely calculated blows, and releases the glorious variety of a million new, sparkling facets. Ideas, like diamonds, must be looked at and admired from many perspectives. Ideas thus take on new dimensions of meaning. Behaviors take on new subtleties. Psychological nuances abound. Institutions like the family, education, health care, and religion can be more fully understood. Multilevelness as a value-differentiating concept is an exciting paradigm, naming criteria by which to measure a number of concepts by exploring the levels within them. Problems of semantics yield when we sharpen terms with the tool of multilevelness. Our everyday vocabulary and grasp of what is going on in life at myriad levels are expanded by a multilevel appreciation. The introduction of more precise criteria makes more meaningful research possible. Piechowski says:

> It now becomes less meaningful to consider for instance aggression, inferiority, empathy, or sexual behavior as unitary phenomena, but it becomes more meaningful to examine different levels of these behaviors. Through this approach we may discover that there is less difference between the phenomenon of love and the phenomenon of aggression at the lowest level of development than there is between the lowest and highest levels of love and the lowest and highest levels of aggression. (1977, p. 12)

Let's explore the roots of this cardinal idea, multilevelness, for much does hinge on it. Multilevelness has its foundation in biology. Late 19th-century findings in neurology demonstrated a biological hierarchy in the nervous system, suggesting that evolution is a passage from the most simple to the more complex, from the most automatic to the more voluntary. From this Dabrowski articulated a hierarchical classification of the levels of mental organization. Each level represents a distinct constellation of intrapsychic processes. This gives us an opportunity to peel away the skin of mere "stages" of development and of seemingly univocal concepts and explore the dynamics operating within.

As development proceeds, developmental structures at the lower levels become progressively subordinate to and integrated by higher-level structures. This process by which more simple, reflexive, unconscious, and automatic lower functions become subordinate to and integrated by more complex, inhibiting, conscious, and voluntary higher functions is a biological facet of the term *multilevelness*. Its levels range beyond the biological and encompass the inner conflicts that one feels on a subjective, personal level between what one is and what one ought to be. Behind it all is the valuing process embodied in a dynamism (which we will see later) called *hierarchization*, the construction of priorities in one's life and the active pursuit of them.

Multilevelness is a concept that does not exist in other theories of development, at least not as elaborately developed as in TPD. Most other theories recognize that development goes through a process of ascending levels, but to appreciate that those things that make up the psychological, moral, religious, personal, social, political world as we know it are describable as having levels within them from "lower" to "higher" is a special contribution. It is a matter of seeing behaviors no longer as monoliths, but as complex structures patterned with subtly different levels. Ideas become beautifully complex, behaviors immensely rich. When you examine them closely they yield a plethora of various meanings, and these meanings are not haphazard, but arrange themselves, like ice crystals on a window pane, into a pattern. The pattern is orchestrated by values. The pattern in turn displays the values.

Seen from a distance, the pyramids of Egypt look like three great triangular monoliths; but closer up one can appreciate the row on row of ascending levels that make up their design and direction, telling us much about the people who built them.

The Role of Conflict

Crises—The Play between Continuity and Discontinuity—Integration and Disintegration

Implicit in what we have just looked at is the idea that development does not come without a price. If there are levels in development, there must be some forces that move us from lower to higher. Some are external, in the environment; some are within.

Certainly growing as a human being can be deeply joyous and rewarding, but never effortless. Sometimes it is hard to let go of the old and comfortable and to risk the new and unfamiliar even if we know it is in itself better. If there is to be progress in development through levels, there is bound to be conflict—between the old and the new, between the inferior and the better—if a new integration is to come from disintegration. We can now approach closer to an exploration of Dabrowski's actual levels of development by seeing the process of multilevel development as an interplay, a dance, of disintegration and integration. Some definition of terms would help.

Integration is the continuing articulation of more and more complex organization. TPD distinguishes two levels of integration: They occupy extreme ends of the levels of development: the lowest, *primary integration*, and the highest, *secondary integration*. Both are characterized by feelings of well-being, contentment, and absence of conflict. But what differences between the two! The first is marked by rigidity; the second by integrity. Primary integration has a rock-like quality: unperturbed, unmoving complacency with the way things are, egocentrism that little gets through to disturb. The wholeness of secondary integration, on the other hand, is not egocentric but a profound and peaceful appreciation of all that is, realizing full well that all is not as it should be, but knowing that what ought to be has been realized in some way in one's life.

Disintegration. Traditionally, the term *disintegration* implies abnormality, even pathology. Out of conflict comes disequilibrium. Instead of seeing the disturbance as bad, TPD presents it as an opportunity. The breakdown of a previous lower level, is the necessary precondition for reorganization at a higher level. This disintegration is *positive* if it is directed by developmental dynamisms and serves development, leading to freedom, creativity, and the ability to turn outward. Disintegration is *negative* if it is diffusive of the person. Negative disintegration is limiting of relationships and productivity, involving impoverishment of emotional and intellectual functioning and the fearful avoidance of risks because the individual is preoccupied with self-survival.

Often these challenges of what is higher to what is lower take place in a crisis situation. A crisis must be understood as a developmental situation. It is true that crisis often means a catastrophe ending in disaster, but Dabrowski's view is much broader, seeing a crisis as a turning point, a life passage great or small, where the person is vulnerable it is true, where the risk of catastrophe is there to some degree, but above all where the psychic structures of the person are loosened, pulled apart, with the potential for putting them back together again at a higher level. It seems to me that these crises are of two main kinds: developmental and accidental. By developmental I mean crises that occur as part of the human process of growing up and are tied largely to biological development. For example, Dabrowski points out these are the crisis of the age of opposition of the two-year-old, the crisis of adolescence, and of menopause. About the age of two the child begins to assert his autonomy in a special way. It usually comes out in using the word *No* over and over again. By saying "No" the child asserts that he can go a direction other than that asked of him. By doing this he asserts his independence and develops his budding autonomy. It is a "crisis" period because the child must find his autonomy, his self in relationship to someone who will at one and the same time offer a stable platform against which to react negatively. It is also a crisis for adults who are called on to give a warm, loving acceptance to the little person who tests their patience by rebelling in this way.

Adolescence is a crisis period brought on by biological and social maturation, and, as Erik Erikson points out, it is a crisis of identity—discovering who I am now that my body has changed so much, where have I come from and where am I going. Menopause is also a biologically induced crisis brought on by aging. It again is a crisis of generativity, not just in the sexual sense, but in the whole sense of where do I belong in a world where I have for so long been able to keep pace as a producer, and in a world that idolizes youth and demands productivity in a materialistic sense?

The second major category of crises that Dabrowski includes as opportunities for positive disintegration are not necessarily connected with biological turning points in life. They are crises that occur to some and not to others: the death of a loved one, personal illness, moving to a new city, going into a new job, falling in love, getting married, having a baby, failing an exam. I have deliberately mixed together positive and negative examples of crisis to bring out the point that a crisis is not just a negative affair. It is any turning point in life that stimulates a pulling apart of what we have been and opens the door to being something new and better. A crisis need not be of major proportions either. The death of a child may shatter one's world and bring one into questions of the meaning of life that run deep and hurt bitterly. But being asked by a hobo on the street for a dollar "for a cup of coffee" can also be a mild challenge to one's principles and how one relates to people and their needs. Even a small moment that interrupts the way we have put our lives or our day together and demands some sort of restructuring is a challenge to reintegrate on a higher level.

It should be clear from what has been said thus far that Positive Disintegration is a theory that presents development as a continuous evolution, a process ever going onward. It is not a theory that proposes some sort of state of "perfection" as the ultimate goal of development, nor does it strive for an ultimate maturity. *Maturity* is a term borrowed from physiology. A person grows to his "mature height" and then stops growing. But Dabrowski does not use the word maturity; instead, he talks of integration, of which we will see more later on.

What Makes TPD Different? A Comparison with Other Theories

TPD is not an easy theory to grasp; it is complex; it is also unique, quite different from many other theories. It would be good now to look at some things which make it singular.

The promise of possibilities. Most theories of how humans develop are traditional, ontogenetic, a way of explaining the normal life process of the majority of individuals as physical growth and psychological maturation unfold. They chart the course the majority of individuals in a particular culture go through. Progress is usually measured in stages: infancy, childhood, adolescence, adulthood, and so on. Dabrowski's theory is not like this.

If Dabrowski's developmental sequence is not traditional ontogenesis, what is it? It is an *evolutionary* theory about possibilities—human possibilities—how they come around, how they are created, how they are selected, and the further possibilities that come from choosing initial opportunities. It describes possible paths life can take and it maps responses to them. It especially emphasizes paths toward the ideal. They are like routes up a mountain, some to sheltered alpine meadows filled with frail flowers, others to craggy, windswept heights far above the treeline. There are possibilities of moving on up; possibilities of getting stuck; the possibility of not even starting the climb or starting and then turning back. Above all, this theory describes the prospect at the summit of the mountain. It uses the words and reports the experiences of the eminent men and women who have been there to describe not only the vista, but the journey to get to it. It maps the actual ascent in terms of five levels. During his or her lifetime, a given individual may pass through none or only part of the theory's developmental sequence. In fact, the theory says there may be little or no movement at all; the lowest level of development is characterized by stagnation, complacency, lack of movement. Some are, it seems, satisfied with that. Others may begin to develop, find it too threatening or too painful, and lapse back into something more comfortable. But the upward routes have been mapped by Dabrowski and they are challenges. That is what a good theory, like a good map, should do, entice one to go onward in the journey with some challenging anticipation of what may lie ahead.

The moving on is not without its demands. Dabrowski's theory is distinguished among psychological theories by its call to high standards. It stands out too by its acknowledgment of the tragic sense of crisis in life. It describes a course of action with increasingly higher standards as one progresses. The psychological rites of passage are crises. Crises are breakdowns and undeniably painful, but they create room for heroism, high virtue, and high purpose in life. High ideals make strong demands. All this in the name of achieving higher goals that may be recognized as spiritual—goals that many other psychologies may ignore or, if they reference them at all, it is by way of pointing to their unreality in an effort to pull us back to the "realities" of utilitarianism. An "easy" way is advertised. Some charlatans even promise that all can be done in the course of one "intensive" weekend workshop.

William James (1958), in his *Varieties of Religious Experience*, had an appreciation of how tempting the easy way is. He made his famous distinction between the "healthy-minded" and the "sick-souled." The healthy-minded, "who live habitually on the sunny side of the misery line" while the sick-souled "live beyond it in darkness and apprehension ... born close to the pain threshold which the slightest irritants fatally send them over."

Our reaction to James' distinction may well be a spontaneous urge to choose, if we could, the religion of the "healthy-minded." It sounds more positive and certainly more pleasant. But James is using "sick" in a different way that puts "sickness" of this sort in a much more positive light. He contrasts the two approaches another way, giving each a second name. The healthy soul is the "once-born," the sick soul is the "twice-born." The once-born are not deeply reflective, nor are they particularly distressed by their own imperfections. They read the character of God not in the disordered world of mankind, but in the romantic and harmonious world of nature as they see it. But the sick soul is discontented and must be born again in order to be fulfilled. Not blind, like the once-born to the evils of the world, the sick soul is very aware of the injustices around and within him or her. Deep reflection on the human condition brings anguish over the evils humans create for one another and for their planet. This is not mere morbidity, perpetual depression, or obsession with sin; rather, it is vivid awareness of evil and injustice, and inner turmoil and profound regret that the world is not a perfect place. The hand he or she has had, even by default, in this imperfection troubles the sick soul. Melancholy and a self-critical condition motivate him or her to undergo a search for self-transformation. It is a trouble that does not simply feed on its own gloom, but aspires to something better, some ideal state, and goes beyond mere aspirations to vigorous striving for the ideal. For the twice-born life is struggle, but this is the more productive way because, as James says, it is "based on the persuasion that the evil aspects of our life are of its very essence, and that the world's meaning most comes home to us when we lay them most to heart." Somewhere the sick soul discovers that the pain itself has promise, that agony and death are necessary for resurrection, that joy is the by-product of meaning found in suffering, that there is life and a terrible beauty even in deformity.

Charles Taylor (1989), criticizing some current psychologies that make the cardinal mistake of believing that a good is invalidated if it leads to suffering, says:

> Prudence constantly advises us to scale down our hopes and circum-scribe our vision. But we deceive ourselves if we pretend that noth-ing is denied thereby of our humanity ... Do we have to choose between various kinds of spiritual lobotomy and self-inflicted wounds? Perhaps. Certainly most of the outlooks which promise us that we will be spared these choices are based on selective blind-ness. (p. 520)

The mills of the gods grind slowly, and the gods have their demands.

The movement is evolutionary. Human development is a process in which homeostasis and equilibrium are only temporary interstices in a larger process that has all the dynamism of evolution. Personal development is participation in the evolution of the cosmos itself. Our earth has gone through an evolution involving the upheaval of continents, the slow emer-gence of life that moved from simple living things to more and more complex life, and then through a development of human knowledge and under-standing that has itself become more differentiated, more complex, and yet more articulated and organized. The same evolutionary principles apply to the process of human individual development, beginning in relative simplic-ity and moving on to complexity, organized by systems of values.

Quality is the measure. Many developmental theories are organized into systems, but they are based on *quantity.* When you get to a higher stage you have "more of" something: more muscle power, more information. That quantitative increase is *part* of development. But the other aspect is an improvement in *quality:* better coordination, improved learning skills, for example. When you talk about quality you are into values, judgments about desirability and worthwhileness. Quality statements don't ask simply "Is it bigger?" They ask, and try to find the answer, "Is it *better?*" Positive Disinte-gration is a quality-based theory; it asks questions about worthwhileness; it measures development with the yardstick of value; it has, unlike quantitative theories such as Behaviorism, no difficulty proposing that a "higher" level is a "better" level.

Higher is better, not just later. There is a hint in the vertical metaphor of climbing that I have used of something so basic to the theory of Positive

Disintegration that it may be passed over without being noticed. Like other developmentalists, Dabrowski constantly referred to higher and lower levels, the higher, of course, being the better ones. Some theories work on a presumption that later is better for the simple reason that it is more mature. This notion of maturity is all right when you are talking about physical growth; people grow to a mature height and then don't grow any more. But the plateau of maturity fails to describe the infinite possibilities of human development in which the process never stops. TPD does not use the term *maturity* because it connotes growing to a certain level and then staying there, like someone settling in on a plateau. TPD describes, instead, a process toward integration. Thus Dabrowski's levels, as we will see, are higher levels not simply because they are later, but because they are in themselves better—clarified by the values they represent. The higher levels are more worthwhile because they express higher-level values. To put it another way: A higher stage is not a higher stage simply because it comes later; Dabrowski's later levels come only later because they are higher in terms of values.

Self-actualization. Dabrowski reacted to truncated behavioristic and psychoanalytic theories limited to lower-level instinctive and defense needs; instead, he emphasized actualization needs and constructed actualization hierarchies. In this his ideas converge with Abraham Maslow's, but in a deeper understanding of self-actualization within a value hierarchy. Dabrowski emphasized the role of value hierarchies in organizing development. The term *hierarchy*, however, can carry with it connotations of rigidity, a rule from the top down in the rigid sense that values could be set once and for all into some unchangeable order. The theory of Positive Disintegration does not insist on hierarchies of values as rigid rank orders. Values are in dynamic tension with each other and with the life situation in which they are called on to play their discriminating role. Rigid hierarchies tend to be domination hierarchies. Partnership values, on the other hand, explore their fullest potential to be in hierarchical, actualization partnership and, with this, explore and expand the human actualization partnership potential.

Emotion has a valued place. While we are looking at basic themes of TPD and comparing it with other well-known theories of development, we should check first the place Dabrowski gave to the emotions. The titles of many of his papers and books emphasize *emotional* functioning, emotional development. This is in contrast to major cognitive theories such as those of Piaget and Kohlberg. It is comparatively easy to measure cognitive development using standardized measures such as IQ tests. But Dabrowski, convinced of the central role of emotion in human development, took the more difficult, riskier, and I think more telling route of giving prime place to the emotions. But for him it was not an either-or proposition, throwing out the rational in order to put all emphasis on feeling. Dabrowski appreciated the power of emotions, acknowledging the possibility of guidance coming from higher-level emotions. He emphasized that to be authentic, to be a guide, emotion must work in "equipotential collaboration" with cognition. Emotion is the most rational form of energy.

Autonomy. There is in TPD a strong stream of emphasis on autonomy, not in the sense of isolation from others, but as the acceptance of responsibility, not only for one's immediate actions, but (and this distinguishes TPD from many other theories) also for one's development. This "autonomous factor" does not leave one the helpless victim of the circumstances of heredity and environment. Besides these two classical factors, there is what Dabrowski called the Third Factor. There is a large (but not total) element, choice, determining how one may develop and how high one may climb through levels. We are responsible; this responsibility is twofold: for our actions and ultimately for the direction, and in some degree for the extent of our development. "We are our choices," say the existentialists. "You are responsible for the directions of your development," says Dabrowski.

Positive Disintegration and women's experience. Many theories of development have been conceived with men in mind; some, such as Kohlberg's, were based entirely on research with a male population. The theory of Positive Disintegration favors neither sex. In its effort to describe the higher levels of human development it concentrates on those characteristics that mark the best human beings; both men and women belong to this group. Consequently, I believe it is one of the few theories of development that is especially sensitive to the female experience of life. If you look at the values of Positive Disintegration theory, if you explore its dynamisms, you will find that the goals and dynamisms that carry one upward are the values of a rich experience of not only what it is to receive life, but what it is to have the power to give it. Three value streams easily identified with women's experience are present:

1. *A respect for life as holistic.* Once you see yourself in holistic terms—integral within oneself and integral within relationships—your attitude to self-development changes. If one's concern is to be whole, then the criteria of personal worthwhileness one has constructed are different from those of simply playing a role (especially a dominating role) or, on the other hand, passively pleasing others. The measure of worthwhileness has been chosen and it is within. It is the ideal of the personal best.

2. *An emphasis on the interpersonal.* If human relationships are primary, then "things" take their appropriate place.

3. *A penchant not just for knowing the good, but for actually doing it.* If relationships take precedence, then synergistic morality guides behavior. There is nothing of aggression or competition with others in this theory, nothing of getting ahead in the world at all costs to others. There is, instead, a vibrant theme of the strength of a life lived in consonance with high values. Autonomy is linked with authenticity so

that becoming independent of social influences is not understood as putting down other people. It is rather a joining at a deeper level.

TPD does not identify with the woman, but gives value to her natural attributes of nurture, tenderness, and relational importance, instead of viewing them as weaknesses.

The basic values of TPD are, I think, attractive to both men and women. But society attempts to socialize men in particular to a set of values in opposition. For men there is probably a greater need to overcome the forces of environment and socialization that have until recently encouraged a macho image, a dominator mentality, and a mystique of the machine. In their place TPD encourages freeing oneself from the limiting influences of environment, from lower-level drives, in favor of relationships of partnership. It is refreshing and ultimately satisfying to both sexes, fulfilling women's needs and allaying men's fears.

Interiority. Few psychological theories acknowledge reflection or interiority as a force in human nature. Some may use it as a device for gaining insight; fewer still recognize it as a quality with value in itself, something to be striven for for its own intrinsic worth. TPD sees it not only as a means to an end, but as a quality of higher levels of development. In psychotherapy it is more than the dialogue of client and therapist that works the "cure." The dialogue is the condition, the reflective experience in relationship in which the therapist is the faithful mirror reflecting back the real self of the client so that he or she can see reality, accept or reject it, and decide what should be done about it. It is in those two decisions—acceptance of reality and choice of appropriate action—that the client's interiority comes into play. The best therapy is autopsychotherapy—done by the individual on himself or herself. Not all are capable of this inner dialogue with self. It requires, as we will see later, being both a subject and an object at the same time.

It is anagogic. A quality of TPD that is akin to interiority is its anagogic nature, that is, it describes the ascent to higher places not in a pedestrian use of "higher" as simply a step up, but in the Dantesque sense of the ascent of a spiritual mountain, reminiscent of the great spiritual mystics such as Teresa of Avila and John of the Cross. If the mountain is spiritual, the quest is ultimately self-transcendence toward a oneness with all that is. Laurence Nixon (1990, 1994) has contributed his insights into the interconnectedness of TPD and the experiences of religious mystics.

The Foundational Values of TPD

Values direct our lives; exposing them reveals much about our claims. Values also direct psychologists when they make up theories indicating that some ways of being are higher and better than others. Behind each developmental theory there is a system of values, sometimes only implicit. These values need to be made explicit. Dabrowski was careful to make the foundational values of TPD clear. Figure 5.1 gives a list of personality characteristics the presence of which indicates lower and higher levels of development according to TPD. Although not setting up dichotomies, it shows contrasting values.

Is This an Elitist Theory?

Before going on to explore the levels of development and the dynamisms that shape it, we should explore an objection to TPD that usually centers around "exclusivity" or "elitism." Why is higher development not possible for some people? Is high-level development just for an elite, a kind of exclusive club that most of us can never hope to join? This is a prime question in a democracy and in an age that argues for equal opportunity. Who needs a theory that seems to lure you on to the seemingly impossible?

We have seen already that TPD is not ontogenetic, but evolutionary; that it does not attempt to describe the development common to everyone, but describes the possibilities of human nature. Its evolutionary stance entails the concept of inequality of both genetic and environmental opportunities. Self-determination must always work within these parameters. As such, the theory is realistic. TPD flies in the face of simplistic interpretations that confuse democratic equality of rights with equality of development.

"Lower"	*"Higher"*
Biological—psychophysical facticity	Suprabiological—higher reality
Reactive, unreflective, uninhibited	Conscious, reflective, appropriately inhibited
Adjustment to "what is"	Quest for "What ought to be"
Primitive, biological and instinctive	Idealistic
Heteronomous, socially determined	Autonomous, authentic
Whimsical, narcissistic subjectivity	Objectivity through authentic subjectivity
Reductionism: Human is "nothing but ..."	Human continuous with creation, unique
Victim of lower instincts	Self-conscious and self-controlled
Victim of heredity and environment	Self-determining
Illusion	Authentic self
Limited concern for meaning	Meaning, purpose, ideals
Egocentric	Self-transcending
Rigid	Creative
"Religion" structured for self-protection	Religion, personal, compassionate

Figure 5.1. Value determinants of levels.

The degree of psychological development that actually does occur in an individual's life span is a direct function of what Dabrowski called *developmental potential*. Developmental potential is the original endowment of a person that determines the level of development he or she may reach if the physical and environmental conditions are optimal. The characteristics that define it are the "dynamisms" and "overexcitabilities" that we are about to explore.

Challenges to Positive Disintegration come too from its seeming preoccupation with "higher" levels. It can be described as a "high end" theory. Clearly it does give much attention to the upper reaches of human development. It is unabashedly idealistic in the sense of aiming at higher levels of development, but not in any Pollyannaish sense that says, "You can be whatever you want to be, or as happy as you want to be." It is concerned primarily with what "ought to be because it is better." Basically, the movement from "is" to "ought" calls for a passage: *What is* (Realism), to *what can be* (Imagination), to *what ought to be* (Idealism).

This emphasis on betterness, combined with the limitations imposed by developmental potential, could suggest that this is an elitist theory, just for the gifted and privileged. It could be called elitist in the sense that it charts a course for becoming the best one can be. It is clearly not elitist in the sense that it does not base its criteria on social standing, financial position, or a snobbish intellectual elitism. Instead, it appeals to all to look at their values, choose consciously, and actively aspire to the better. The active desire for something truly better is a quest that transcends social class and education. In this quest the upper and middle classes have advantages: education and the luxury of time and money to explore "personal development." The marginal may be absorbed in the task of simply keeping alive, but this does not preclude the dynamisms of higher development. Developmental potential is personal, not a class thing.

As a physician, Dabrowski identified certain physiological characteristics and reactions related to developmental potential (compare Dabrowski & Piechowski, 1977). His theories came to a large extent from studying the lives of eminent people. The presence or absence of these dynamisms and overexcitabilities is something that psychologists can identify, usually using analysis of written autobiographical statements. The possibility of measuring multilevel development qualitatively and even quantitatively in psychological research is opened up by the definition of these dynamisms and overexcitabilities. His criteria of how they are exhibited physiologically and psychologically have been the basis of the creative work of researchers such as Michael Piechowski and others in developing instruments to measure them. By distinguishing levels of development, by distinguishing and defining which forces (i.e., dynamisms) are active at each level as well as enumerating the channels of communication between the inner self and the outside world, Dabrowski has made it possible for researchers to measure fairly accurately and follow the developmental process of specific individuals. Empirically minded researchers today (Brennan & Piechowski, 1991; Piechowski, 1975, 1978, 1986, 1990, 1991; Piechowski & Tyska, 1982; Lysy & Piechowski, 1983; Miller & Silverman, 1987) are able to measure and describe human development, particularly at its higher levels.

Five Levels of Development and their Dynamisms

The potential developmental passage can be described as five qualitatively different levels of development, each having a distinguishable personality organization. These are not *the* levels of development, a definitive statement of how "real" development comes about for humans. The claim is much humbler than that: no attempt is made to say that this template fits a universal process of human development. Quite the contrary; they describe the development of some, not everyone, and at the higher levels only a few. Piechowski (1975) says, "An individual developmental sequence may cover part of this scale, but none can cover its full extent" (p. 263). The following descriptions outline the levels of development and their interaction with certain dynamisms.

Dabrowski's Levels of Development

Level I, Primary Integration: A Rock, an Island

A stone is a symbol of primary integration. A rock, an island, the primary integrated person is egocentric, unreflective, and quite self-satisfied. Complacency or stuckness is the theme. Level one is characterized by the absence of drives toward development. There may be much motion but very little progress. Instead, the individual is busy with self-serving motives, possessiveness, and in personal relationships conflict, manipulation, superficiality, and insensitivity to others. Lack of reflectiveness, lack of awareness of an inner environment, and awareness of only an external environment mark this level. Although quarrelsomeness and conflicts with external problems may be present, there is an absence of internal conflicts as well as absence of guilt, and of intimate emotional relationships. A person may appear stable and adjusted to "what is," but this apparent adjustment is rigidly maintained and vulnerable to negative disintegration in conditions of stress or even relatively small change. One is narrowly concerned with the self in terms of one's biological functioning. Michael Piechowski (Dabrowski & Piechowski, 1977, p. 20) makes it clear that there are at least two forms of primary integration, one extreme, the other more "normal." The extreme form is exemplified by the psychopath; he has no consideration for others; he tends to exploit, humiliate, and take advantage of others. He can experience temperamental syntony, an undifferentiated feeling of commonality with others engendered by group activities that are more of a gang type. One of the strongest bond-forming activities in his life is aggression against a common enemy. The inevitable fights express a gang camaraderie rather than true emotional relationships. The bond is largely external: race, color, blood relationship, living in the same part of town. One gets the clear image here of black leather jackets being more of a bond than any real relationship. Reality, for the extreme case of primary integration, is looked at in immediate, tangible, sensory terms with no room for any deep appreciation. Moral thinking is on the level of mere avoidance of punishment. An action is moral if you don't get caught doing it.

Traumatic experiences, crises, don't "get to" this kind of person. He or she has little or no sensitivity to experience emotional content or to appreciate the broader dimensions of what is going on immediately before or within him or her. When things go wrong, far from searching for any meaning in the situation, the blame is placed squarely where it belongs—on someone else!

Less dramatic perhaps than the psychopathic personality, yet much more ominous because of their quiet presence in large numbers is the milder form of primary integration described as "normal." Though not totally without feeling, these people have a narrow range of interest, limited thinking, myopic philosophical vision, limited aspirations, and limited affect. They may acquire enough skills to meet the demands of the job market, but they tend to stagnate in a stereotyped role they have adopted for themselves. Problems can be solved by largely physical means such as moving to another house, another city, another job as long as the new does not make any great demands for change. Because problems appear to them to be "out there," their solution to it is also "out there" in a change of environment, a change of friends, a change of job. Primary integrated persons are not feelingless, but the range of their feelings is limited, and the crises that tend to cause the greater upset are not the larger issues of life, and not those involving the well-being of others.

Television has exaggerated and exploited the primitively integrated person for his comic potential. The Homer Simpson-Archie Bunker type is most disturbed when his beer isn't cold, his Twinkies aren't in his lunch pail, or someone takes "his" chair. The death of a friend cannot, it seems, touch as deeply as these immediate and physical issues. If one is touched emotionally, the only resolution is a physical attack.

The level of moral reasoning corresponds most closely to Kohlberg's good boy, good girl and law and order orientations. In both Dabrowski's and Kohlberg's schemata, individuals at these levels follow externally established rules. There is a similarity of this type with the authoritarian personality, governed by stereotypes and social prescriptions, as described by Adorno, Frenkel-Brunswick, Levinson, and Sanford (1950).

Level I, then, is characterized by absence of developmental dynamisms such as appropriate feelings of guilt, reflectiveness, intimate emotional relationships, and absence of internal conflict with an awareness only of the external environment. A level I person may appear stable and adjusted, but this adjustment is rigidly maintained and vulnerable to negative disintegration when stress or change come from that external environment. The film *The Deerhunter* is a fine illustration of level I. Many of its soldier characters are superficial good buddies who remain unchanged by the horrors of Viet Nam.

Level II, Unilevel Disintegration: Pulled in Every Direction

The passage from primary integration to this first level of disintegration is of major proportions. Inner psychic life begins to blossom in a state of turmoil and fragmentation ("I feel confused and shattered"). At this level hesitation, doubt, and ambivalence begin to take over and the person becomes less stable. Moods oscillate; actions vacillate. Inner conflict begins. Sometimes it is a conflict of values. However, without hierarchical (vertical) values, the conflict is merely horizontal, a conflict between equal, competing values. Without a clear sense of what is more worthy of valuing, there are no rules for settling the conflict in terms of what should be. Tolstoy's *Anna Karenina*, paralyzed by her own vacillations, is a classic example of this level.

The rigid organization of level I is broken down, and yet there is no preexisting hierarchical organization to give the individual a sense of direction; hence the risk of developing the most severe forms of psychopathology. Loosened structures tend to come apart under the impact of emotion and stress. Self-insight is still weak, as is the capacity for inner psychic transformation of conflicts. Rather than being transformed into higher levels, tensions must be released or converted. If they are transposed to the body, psychosomatic disorders arise. If they are externalized, they appear as projections, reality distortions, or hallucinations. Guilt feelings do not yet have a creative dynamic, but are passive, founded on lack of self-acceptance that one may trace back to lack of love in childhood. Guilt at this level is not the key to higher levels of moral thinking. Instead, it is debilitating, a dead end. Because from this passive position values are seen as arbitrary, relative, and externally determined, one takes the moral view that what is good is what works (utilitarianism) and that the majority rules in determining morals.

Piechowski says:

> The degree of instability varies in level II and as a result this level has the most multiform structure of all the levels. It encompasses total mental fragmentation as in psychosis and drug-induced states, a middle range of more stereotyped forms of behavior—inferiority toward others, dependency, need to conform, seeking approval and admiration—and at the other extreme partially integrated forms that convey a certain degree of stability, even maturity. Because of the lack of direction, inner organization, incapacity for inner psychic transformation, blindness to a larger sense of order, especially in regard to human experience, and blindness to universal values and their hierarchy, we can justify depicting this type of structure as hav-

ing one plane only; this structure is called unilevel (Dabrowski & Piechowski, 1977, p. 26)

The rumblings of the earthquake that threatens to shatter the monolith of self send the person scurrying back and forth between the old and comfortable and the new and threatening. Separation from myself is the most profound of separations. Now, at level II, some perhaps unconscious sense of the awful proportions of what is being asked may dawn on the person. Anxiety and dread of loss of comfort, of others, of, above all, one's old self-induced ambivalences and ambitendencies: wavering thoughts, wavering actions. At this point I can't let go of the old familiar self. It can be envisioned as annihilation or at least an amputation, but if all goes well it has the potential to be part of the continuing disintegration experience that is to come in levels III and IV.

At the beginnings of this level, I am not yet sufficiently differentiated to integrate this old self as "other"—to objectify it. It is hard to see the old, familiar as "Not me." It is a kind of death experience. Self-concept suffers. I define myself in terms of others' expectations or, worse, in terms of my fluctuating interpretations of others' expectations. I am "a reed shaken by the wind." Relationships typically are excessively emotional, showing up in extreme jealousy or overdependence. Because of the breakdown of the rigid integration of level I, and because there is no preexisting hierarchical organization at this level, there is danger of developing severe psychopathologies such as psychoses, schizophrenia, phobias, alcoholism, and drug addiction. Behavior is disoriented or externally oriented and unstable. Although they may appear sophisticated, designs of thought are often circular. There is no real autonomy, only a lower drive to be independent. A person may fly from fad to fad with no self-evaluation. Rebellion likewise is not based on values or principles, but a blind, directionless opposition to whatever becomes the enemy because it is outside the self and irritates the self. Delinquent behavior is the best example. Level II is chaotic in the sense that there is hardly any structure, and creative in the sense that there may be, somewhere in the chaos, the beginnings of order that can be rallied at level III if the necessary dynamisms are in place.

Level III, Spontaneous Multilevel Disintegration: Evaluating the Self

The self that passes from level II to level III is still unsure, vulnerable, and threatened, yet in its depths incipiently autonomous. A newly discovered and consciously constructed hierarchy of values begins to emerge and take control at this level. One begins to get one's priorities straight. Directions of disintegration are beginning to be set, and real progress can be made after the stagnation and vacillations of the two previous levels. Instead of domination by the external environment—"what is"—behavior begins to occur on the basis of an internally evolving sense of "what should be." With the emergence of a hierarchy of values, behavior is more guided by considerations of moral responsibility. Inner conflict, now more of a struggle to bring one's behavior up to standards, can be described as vertical. Marsh and Colangelo (1983) name Tolstoy as an example of level III.

> Tolstoy's ideal of the simplification of life was a unifying philosophy of his life, but it also led him into constant bickering with himself and his family over the variance between the ideal and their daily lives. His life was fraught with conflict concerning his moral principles and ideals.... Tolstoy's dominant characteristic is disintegration, characterized by inner conflict and discontent with his life in relation to his ideals, existential anxieties and suicidal tendencies. In addition to these conflicts, Tolstoy also evidenced an emerging hierarchy of values, a deepening empathy, awareness of moral responsibility, and self-evaluation. (pp. 219, 223)

Level III is marked by reflection and self-evaluation. A typical statement would be: "There's a part of me that pulls me this way" (St. Paul's "I do not understand my own behaviour; I do not act as I mean to, but do the things I hate," Romans 7:15). Marcus Tullius Cicero's "*Video meliora proboque deteriora sequor*—I see the better but I do the worse.") Idealism and with it existential anxiety may emerge. Because an inner ideal is dawning, a sense of one's shortcomings in the light of "What I should be" may be very strong. This self-scrutiny may be taken for neurosis and even more serious dissociative disorders, maladjustment, and personality disorders. Some schools of psychotherapy will confirm this diagnosis and attempt to "save the patient from this illness." They will attempt a kind of psychological surgery. Here is where Dabrowski's (1972) claim that "Psychoneurosis is not an illness" emerges with an appreciation of the necessity of letting the patient have the pain; the pain is necessary for real growth. Without this appreciation, the truly positive dynamisms of level III may be written off as mere neurosis or some other psychopathology to be removed by "surgical" therapy.

The difference between spontaneous multilevel disintegration and neurosis hangs on the presence or absence of appropriate dynamisms. "Self evaluation, reflection, intense moral conflict, perception of the uniqueness of others and existential anxiety are characteristic" (Piechowski, 1975, p. 262). Outside of a positive developmental framework, such behaviors easily get classified as neurotic. Dabrowski's contention that "Psychoneurosis is not an illness" begins to be most clearly evidenced at this level, for it is the level III person who exhibits symptoms that society (psychologists included) are only too ready to label as neurotic and sick, but that Dabrowski maintains may be the instigators of higher level development.

At this third level the wavering and fluctuations of level II are replaced by the onward thrust of a growing sense of direction. Behavior is guided by an emerging autonomous, emotionally discovered hierarchy of values. The individual no longer merely reacts to "what is" in the outside world, trying to conform to it, but there emerges a sense of "what ought to be"—a sense of what is worthwhile, what is of value. And this emergent hierarchy of values is not just an abstract hierarchy; it is also a hierarchy of aims. In other words, the values, being more than mere velleities, actually influence action, so that the rising clamor of various needs and values and purposes and goals that tore him apart before now converge within the individual according to the ordering of a hierarchy of values that is consciously chosen. The moral conflicts and moral concerns that come to the fore in this period do so in a contest of inner reflectiveness, not outward blaming, of productive guilt and not merely neurotic guilt.

Part of the neurotic burden of this period comes from the heavy realization that one is responsible for oneself. This is a two-edged sword, liberating on the one side because one realizes one is (or can be) free from blind subservience to external determination, but burdening on the other side because now the individual is challenged to find the locus of control within the self. Fear, dread, and anxiety may result, but not as the alternation of fear and short-lived courage (ambitendencies) that marked the former level. Now the neurotic burdens at level III tend to express themselves in existential fears, including the fear of death, and one must work through reflectively the responsibilities of the truly healthy neurotic.

Dynamisms of development at work particularly at this level are (Dabrowski & Piechowski, 1977, p. 87): Astonishment—One is astonished with oneself. At one time I say, "How could I have been afraid?" At another time I rightfully conclude: "That is worth fearing." This dynamism has a distinct intellectual component. It is a reflection on the fact that some of one's own mental qualities and activities catch one by surprise. Disquietude—One's behavior becomes subject to self-awareness, self-criticism, and ultimately to self-control. The egocentric component of one's anxiety is reflected on and replaced by a higher-level anxiety that may paralyze one's development by wallowing in the fear. The allocentric and altruistic anxieties that mark this period also contribute the disquietude that moves one to say, "There are people out there who need me and for whom I can do some good; I am wasting my time and shirking my responsibility by sitting here navel gazing, concentrating on my own fears." This kind of discontent with primitive behaviors in ourselves can lead to transcendence of them and movement toward higher, existential, and transcendent levels of concern. Feelings of inferiority—Feelings of inferiority that previously were directed toward others whom we envied or judged better than ourselves now become directed toward oneself. We begin to see what *we* "ought" to be with our own particular configuration of talents and the opportunities that our time and place give us. We feel inferior now to what we can and should be, rather than merely inferior to others. Feelings of shame and guilt—"neurotic" guilt in this context shakes off its aimlessness and rids itself of its ability to frustrate every worthwhile action. Instead, guilt, remaining an active dynamic in the process, leads us to discover the more altruistic elements in our neurosis, for example, fear for others and the need to help others in their fears and anxieties, in their neurotic conflicts, is much stronger. Dissatisfaction with oneself leads to constant readiness to counteract the pressure of primitive tendencies. It is not the dead-end street of lower levels; it is a motivating dynamic and actively involved in goading us on to what ought to be. Positive maladjustment—*adjustment* and *maladjustment* have been overworked words in the history of psychology. Dabrowski makes some typically refreshing distinctions that throw new light on them. Dabrowski sees social adjustment as the ability to live in harmony with social norms and act successfully in one's society. However, this may amount to mere conformity to social standards that prevail at the time (1970, p. 162). This kind of conforming adjustment is usually considered by many psychologists and educators as a sign of mental health, whereas social maladjustment is for them a clear symptom of mental disturbance.

R.D. Laing, after many years of dealing with emotionally disturbed people, proposed a revolutionary concept of adjustment. Basically, his approach is to say that those symptoms that mental hospitals label as neurotic and psychotic are often only the apt reaction of sensitive people responding appropriately to the society around them which is itself sick. The novel *One Flew Over the Cuckoo's Nest* and the movie that came from it graphically illustrate in incidents rich with humor but tinged with tragedy that happens when a person with brilliance, sensitivity, and imagination is "treated" by lesser human beings who, "well adjusted" as they may be, have become adjusted to a system that is itself sick.

Dabrowski celebrated the positive side (and the pain) of this when he greeted in poetry those rejected ones (these are not the original words, but a personal rendering inspired by Karen Nelson, 1989):

Hail to You Psychoneurotics

Hail to you, psychoneurotics!
For you see sensitivity in the insensitivity of the world
    uncertainty in its certainties
For you are often as conscious of others as of yourself.
For you feel the anxiety of the world, its abysmal narrowness and
unfounded self-assurance.
For your phobia of washing the dirt from your hands,
    for your dread of being locked in the world's limitations;
    for your fear of the absurdity of existence.
For your restraint in holding back what you see in others.
For your awkwardness in dealing with practical things, and for your
practicality in dealing with unknown things,
    for your transcendental realism and lack of everyday realism.
    for your creativity and ecstasy.

For your maladjustment to "what is" and adjustment to "what ought
   to be."
For all your unrealized possibilities.
For being treated instead of curing others,
      for your enabling power squashed by brutal force,
      for that which is prescient, unsaid, infinite in you.
For the loneliness and strangeness of your ways,
      Hail to you!

To help us understand "adjustment" and his attitude toward it, Dabrowski
makes these unique distinctions.

Adjustment

Negative. Conformity to the prevailing norms, customs, and mores without any critical evaluation, or perhaps with the evaluation: "Everybody's
doing it, so it must be all right." It is not autonomous and is basically
inauthentic. It is adjustment to "what is."

Positive. Shaping one's life around a considered hierarchy of values
consciously developed and expressive of the individual's personality ideal:
what he or she would like to be. This is adjustment to "what ought to be."

Maladjustment

Negative. Denial and rejection of social norms, not for the sake of higher
values, but because lower-level primitive urges and pathological structures
are in control. In its extremes negative maladjustment is represented by
psychosis, psychopathy, and criminal activity.

Positive. This is partial adjustment to what is, accompanied by increasing
adjustment to higher levels of development. It is expressed in conflict with
and rejection of standards, patterns, and attitudes in the environment that are
incompatible with one's growing awareness of and loyalty to a higher scale
of values. While being well aware of what is going on in society, what
expectations society puts on me, and what moral force social custom has, I
nevertheless must respond to higher values that do not exist in some social
norms. This can be a lonely and threatened position. But this is the route to
authenticity and is autonomy in its fullest sense of taking into account what
the social environment has to teach, parceling out what is higher from what
is lower and living according to the higher principles.

In summary, level III, spontaneous multilevel disintegration, is a kind of
turning point level where the individual's own forces *begin* to take hold and
begin to direct the disintegrative process toward higher levels. We have
explored in a fair bit of detail some particular dynamisms because they are
the forces that are particularly operative at the third level of development
(see Figure 5.2).

Level IV, Organized Multilevel Disintegration: James' Twice-Born

Conscious forces bringing development into synthesis characterize this level. Now the hierarchical organization of goals and values integrated into an actualization hierarchy blossoms with the nourishment of consciousness and self-direction. This level is characterized by strong inner autonomy similar to that of Maslow's self-actualizing people. These are men and women with a clear sense of universal values deliberately chosen. Their values are not merely personal likes and dislikes, but reflect their appreciation of others and their solidarity with them. A confirmed sense of responsibility leads them to take up tasks for the sake of others. These people are focused on problems outside themselves rather than on self-protection or the enhancement of their own egos. Alert to the needs of their times, they not only see but respond appropriately. Piechowski and Tyska (1982) pointed to Eleanor Roosevelt as an outstanding example of this level. The guiding principle of this level is "What ought to be will be."

Comparisons have been made between this and Maslow's form of personality organization, which he called self-actualization (Piechowski, 1991). Level IV seems to correspond to Maslow's concept of the self-actualizing person, whereas level V parallels Maslow's self-actualized person. The integration that takes place between these levels is not just something personal, but social—the image is that of one who says with full understanding: "Mankind my kind."

There is some overlap of level III and level IV, with level IV being distinguished by a greater degree of consciousness that leads to a directed and self-determined organization of development. The individual knows much more clearly not only what he should be, but arising from this, what he will be. Tensions and conflicts are not as strong as in level III. Autonomy, authenticity, and an enhanced sense of responsibility are the predominant dynamisms of this period. The advancement of this period involves, besides responsibility, the operation of the "lodestar" dynamism—personality ideal. The "ought to be" quality of some of the previous levels, having moved far beyond any "tyranny of the shoulds" as Karen Horney expressed them in her study of the neurotic personality, becomes a "lure," as Whitehead would say, and the strength increases at level IV of this dynamism of the personality ideal. It is an image of the ideal self that is not neurotically unrealistic, nor a mere velleity that one would like to strive for "sometime but not now." Instead, it is an active and powerful dynamism that will play an increasingly important role in the next level: secondary integration. Behavior at level IV tends toward the two different but mutually reinforcing goals of self-perfection and the service of others.

Using the example of Antoine de Saint-Exupéry, author of *The Little Prince*, Dabrowski and Piechowski (1977, Vol. II) demonstrate that the characteristics of level IV correspond to the traits of the self-actualized person as described by Maslow (1950). Dabrowski and Piechowski sum up this level in these words:

> In the overall process of multilevel restructuring, subjection to governance of lower levels yields to the supreme harmony an autonomy of the highest levels. The lower levels are disassembled and are excluded from the structure of secondary integration; with their disappearance, regression to a lower level of functioning is not possible. (1977, p. 29)

Dabrowski's schema of developmental levels begins with integration (primary) and ends with integration (secondary), but what a vast difference between them! Both are characterized by lack of conflict, but the lower-level integration is more like the lack of conflict one would find in a stone. Without sensitivity, without conflict that can "get to" a person there is no disturbance. It is the kind of lack of disturbance Simon and Garfunkel seem to yearn for in their song "I am a Rock, I am an Island."

Level V, Secondary Integration: Past the Pairs of Opposites

We are talking here of an integration vastly different from primary integration. This is a state not of contentedness, but of wholeness, of peace and centeredness. It is not an ultimate plateau, a dreamy haven of oblivious nirvana (as Eastern thought is sometimes interpreted), or static perfection (as some would interpret Western ideas of sainthood). Rather, it is dynamic and still actively seeking. But now the seeking has come full circle or rather full spiral. The "what is" of the lowest levels, replaced by "what ought to be" at more advanced levels, now returns as a new and, for the individual, ultimate "what is." "What is *is* what ought to be."

The story is told of Gandhi that a mother brought her child to him, asking Gandhi to tell the child to not eat so much sugar. Gandhi told the mother to bring the child back in two weeks. When she returned in two weeks, Gandhi simply said to the child, "Stop eating sugar." The mother retorted, "Why didn't you tell him that two weeks ago?" Gandhi replied, "Two weeks ago, I was eating sugar myself." This authentism is one of the hallmarks of secondary integration. But the principal and strongest dynamism of secondary integration is personality ideal. At these highest levels, far from being unrealistic or a mere velleity of what might be, it is consistently realized in the person as a life theme. Personality ideal remains the active, driving, luring force as further integration progresses. Secondary integration is not a static state of perfection. It is itself a moving on.

Secondary integration is discontinuous with the other lower levels. It is so stable that regression to lower levels is not possible even under extreme stress.

Such eminent persons experience psychological equilibrium because they act in a way that is harmonious with internal actualizing principles. A harmonious unity and integration guided by personality ideal flows with universal compassion, love and service to humanity, and the realization of timeless values. Their caring is gentle and not moralistic. Dichotomies dissolve. The words of Joseph Campbell exemplify this kind of thinking:

> The separateness apparent in the world is secondary. Beyond that world of opposites is an unseen, but experienced unity in us all. To-day, the planet is the only proper "in group." When you have come past the pairs of opposites you have reached compassion. (Osbon, 1991, p. 24-25)

Very few have come into this level according to Dabrowski. Christ, perhaps the Buddha, Gandhi, Schweitzer, Dag Hamerskjöld, and a tiny handful of unknown human beings who have realized this high mystical state.

We have seen in this section something of the levels, the stages that psychologists find to describe the upward motion of development. Now we go on to look at what forces drive and guide this development. Dabrowski called them "dynamisms."

Facilitators of Development

Dynamisms: Shapers of Development

Dynamisms is another of those Dabrowskian words with a specialized meaning. Because they are not the common vocabulary of other psychologies, and because Dabrowski has given them specific and original meanings, the dynamisms deserve our careful attention.

Dynamisms are the shaping forces of development. They do this shaping both by empowering inner psychic transformation and by inhibiting lower-level inclinations and behaviors. Dynamisms are defined as "intra-psychic dispositional traits which shape development" (Piechowski, 1977, p. 37). They determine tendencies or predispositions to respond. Kawczak (1970) called dynamisms "psychological compounds which unite intellectual and intuitive insights with affective involvement and commitment" (p. 8). Some dynamisms work at several levels, but each level is characterized by its own constellation of dynamisms. The presence or absence of certain dynamisms is the empirical basis for (a) determining an individual's current level of development, (b) ascertaining the presence of developmental potential, and (c) distinguishing positive from negative disintegration.

Figure 5.2 depicts the dynamisms and shows how they characterize each level of development. The shaded bars indicate the emergence and gradual disappearance of each dynamism. Shaded areas indicate tension in the operation of a dynamism. This tension tends to abate toward higher levels of development with the exception of personality ideal, which increases in significance and power as development advances. Note that at each level of development there is a different constellation of dynamisms. For example,

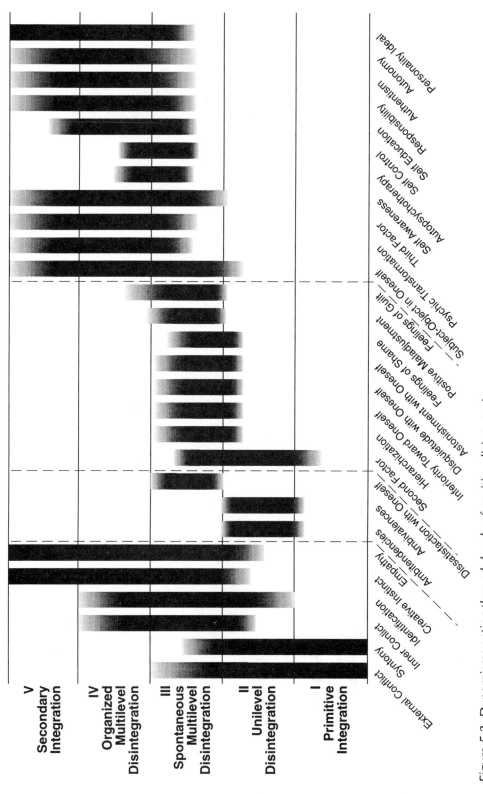

Figure 5.2. Dynamisms acting through levels of positive disintegration.

ambivalences and ambitendencies characterize the unrest of level II, whereas dynamisms such as dissatisfaction with oneself, inferiority toward oneself, and astonishment with oneself together with feelings of guilt and shame mark level III development where the direction toward self-development begins to take hold. At the interface between levels you can see that disappearing dynamisms from the lower level coexist for some time with the emerging dynamisms of the higher level. This emphasizes the point that dynamisms at a higher level are not simply transformations of lower-level dynamisms, but are discontinuous with lower level dynamisms. They are not derived from the transformation of lower-level dynamisms. This illustrates Werner's (1948) developmental principle of differentiation and discontinuity referred to in chapter 4; the new structures emerge not *from* as simply modified extensions, but emerge *next to* the old ones, to *replace* in time the old structures. Dynamisms form the network of the inner psychic milieu, the internal environment in which one lives. Because different dynamisms are active at various levels of development, they form a pattern by their presence, which relates to and is indicative of the individual's level of development. Throughout the process of development, a truly higher dynamism does not dominate, but works with lower-level dynamisms until they cease to be needed. For example, feelings of inferiority toward others lead to more complex and higher feelings of inferiority toward oneself.

We have already discussed some of the dynamisms when examining Dabrowski's levels of development, and it would be superfluous to explore in detail the nature of each dynamism as Dabrowski conceived it because Piechowski (1977, pp. 39ff) has described the dynamisms individually, lucidly, and in the context of their role in the whole developmental process. To get a sense of this rather complex issue, we will especially look at some dynamisms chosen for their relevance to our present themes, first skimming over the lower-level dynamisms before concentrating on those that drive levels III, IV, and V.

Dynamisms of Levels I and II

Because primary integration is rigid and narrow, automatic, unreflected, primitive, instinctual drives predominate rather than productive dynamisms in the strict sense.

External conflict: The individual at this level is well aware of problems "out there" in the world external to him, but these rarely disturb his own set ways as he finds no fault with himself.

Temperamental syntony: an easy, unreflected adaptation to the external environment. It is the group feeling of camaraderie rather easily arrived at in gangs, wars, picket lines, sports (perhaps most of all sports spectators), and drinking buddies.

Ambivalences: Confused feelings of wanting and not wanting, inferiority and superiority, love and hate, that often lead to ambitendencies, self-defeating behavior.

Environmental intrusion: The insensitivity that kept a shield between the world and oneself has cracked. The opinion of others begins to penetrate. "What will people think?" causes one to pause, maybe even leading to feelings of inferiority toward others. Authorities (from parents and church to gossip magazines), whether worthy or not, dictate values.

Identification: Unlike syntony, identification centers not so much on groups as on other persons. It does not at this level flow from a deep appreciation of the other person made possible by empathy. Rather, it is identification with an image, and that identification may come from superficial contacts or even from media hype. The "best" singer is the most popular. The rich and famous become heroes. Emulating the star can be as dogged as following him or her into drugs and suicide.

Creativity begins at this level and will drive development up through the higher levels as it becomes more reflective and complex itself. In the beginning it is impulsive, having little to do with personal growth. One is impressed with the endless variations of the world, but cannot discriminate and evaluate as to relative value. There is fascination with pathology, evil, and the most "way out" experiences such as Satanism. Religion and magic merge.

Dynamisms at Level III

Dynamisms at this level are characterized by spontaneity and lack of organization. These operate in the first phase of multilevel disintegration. They are:

Positive maladjustment. "Adjustment" has become a cliché in psychology and is almost automatically accepted as a good thing. As we have seen, Dabrowski, on the other hand, makes some refreshing distinctions that open up new dimensions of understanding and challenge. The tendency to live in harmony with social norms and to act successfully in society without causing any ripples is lauded. Parents, church, and school encourage conformity because it helps them to get on with their business, and their business most often is preserving the status quo. However, the tendency to live in harmony with social norms may amount to mere unreflected conformity. Although this kind of adjustment is looked upon usually as a sign of mental health, there are times in life when society itself is so sick that conformity amounts to wallowing in social illness. Maladjustment is the only honest answer, and the only healthy one.

Instead of the all-too-facile conclusion that adjustment is "good" and maladjustment is "bad" (which in itself is a conformist conclusion), Dabrowski invites us to make some cardinal distinctions not only between adjustment and maladjustment, but between the negative and positive aspects of each.

The positive maladjustment of higher-level persons comes at a price. This is a lonely and threatened position. (Recall what the Pharisees did to Christ for his nonconformity to their rules, what the Nazis did to Dietrich Bonhoefer, and what police in central America do today to anyone who is "different.") But this is autonomy in its fullest sense of taking into account what the social environment has to teach, parceling out what is lower and what is higher and living according to the higher principles.

This is the root to what Dabrowski calls "authentism"—actually living according to one's hierarchy of values. It involves autonomy: freedom from the lower levels in oneself, and enough confidence in one's developmental past to move onward.

Feelings of shame and guilt. Shame is usually associated with feelings of inferiority toward others, leading to anxiety and urging one to withdraw and hide away. Guilt, on the other hand, strikes a moral tone of having failed in relationships. Guilt is the forerunner of the higher dynamism of responsibility.

Astonishment and disquietude with oneself. The surprise and shock of coming face to face with the reality of oneself and the anxiety that can arise about one's own behavior or even one's sanity can themselves be dynamisms of growth.

Feelings of inferiority toward oneself. When dissatisfaction with self joined by the ability to initiate a hierarchy of values unite with this dynamism, one begins to appreciate the gap between where one is and where one strives to be.

Dissatisfaction with oneself. This dynamism shows itself in anger and frustration not just with the outside world, but with oneself. It is an inchoate distancing, the ability to stand back and evaluate self on the basis of a hierarchy of values.

Dynamisms Predominant at the Highest Levels

Hierarchization. Before one can have a conscious hierarchy of values, one must come to the important realization that different things have different values *in themselves,* and not just because I put value on them. We have here, then, not only the beginnings of valuation, but the beginnings of real value and even moral objectivity.

Personality ideal. This is the dominant dynamism of level IV and the signal dynamism of level V. It is the core of a self-aware, self-chosen, and self-affirmed personality structure. Through its centripetal force the spiral of development is drawn toward a single-mindedness that will have nothing less. Initially perceived intuitively in a broad outline, it becomes later the model for shaping one's personality, the criterion of value. It is defined in meditation, prayer, and contemplation in which the individual perceives gradually the existence of hierarchical design of personality that must go above and beyond the self. This ideal proves to be a lure to what is highest and best. This is mysticism in its purest sense; clearly its domain is the transcendent and its object nothing short of God.

Autonomy. Autonomy makes one open to others, but selectively. Autonomy is freedom from lower-level drives within the self and from the influences of the external environment. This dynamism, coming about through the aegis of personality ideal, far from cutting one off from the influences of the outside world, only makes one sharper in discriminating them; far from compacting one into a self-centered position, it draws one to address the needs of the world.

Authentism, not to be equated with authenticity, brings awareness and expression of one's own emotional, intellectual, and volitional attitudes. It involves insight into self and, moreover, an appreciation of oneself for one's unique, individual qualities. It is a profound appreciation, without pride, of one's own preciousness, one's own unrepeatability. Autonomy and authentism see to it that the individual, freed from lower-level instincts and selectively independent of his or her environment, finds a centeredness, a stillpoint in the self marked by a high degree of unity in one's thinking, emotions, and activity. This is conscious activity in accordance with one's "inner truth" but not cut off from others.

Responsibility lies first and foremost toward one's own personality and its ideal. This is not egocentrism (that has been left far behind). This is care, concern, respect for others and self, realizing that it is through one's best self that this care is realized. The sources of responsibility are the highest level of empathy and love for every human being, and the need to turn this love to action.

Autopsychotherapy and education of oneself. Autopsychotherapy is self-education under conditions of stress in times of crises and neuroses. Conflicts, depressions, and anxieties are handled consciously by the individual. Conscious self-healing exemplifies this process at work. Autopsychotherapy replaces therapy by others when this level is achieved.

Inner psychic transformation is observed in fundamental, deep responses, sometimes sudden and intense, that change the direction of behavior, deepen sensitivity, and bring about a conversion or *metanoia.* One may, in Dabrowski's words, "transcend the biological life cycle" or "transcend one's psychological type." In the first case, somatic determinants connected with age may be replaced by richer, accelerated development. In the second case, transcending one's psychological type may mean balancing the personality by introducing some traits of an opposite type, an extrovert, for example, adopting the best of introversion, a timid person becoming a leader. When this transformation reaches the point of irreversibility, even under stress, the transcendence is true. Dabrowski points to the importance of meditation in achieving these major and stable transformations.

Third Factor (Autonomous factor). Psychology has recognized the influence on personality development of the two classic factors of heredity and environment. Dabrowski invites us to consider a Third Factor. At lower levels of development much of human behavior is unmediated by deliberate choice. TPD says we need not, however, be helpless victims of heredity and environment. We have a hand in our own development, and by that (with the insights of the last decade of this century we might add) in the development of our planet and in the evolution of the human race. One sets apart (as the process of evolution does) in oneself and one's environment those elements that are positive and to be cherished. One rejects inferior demands and selects the better, higher demands. Through this process we develop a consciously chosen hierarchy of values. Subject-object in oneself uncovers these values; third factor decides and selects, while inner psychic transformation puts the decision to work. One accepts responsibility not only for specific choices, but, more than that, one accepts responsibility for the course one's life takes, for the direction of one's development. This is *metanoia*, profound, life-directing conversion in the fullest sense of the word. Responsibility for one's actions is enhanced by responsibility for one's development.

The third factor is a dynamism of conscious choice, self-determination in the long run, by which one distinguishes in self and in environment those elements that are positive and those that are negative. This is the basis for the higher and lower ordering of elements that is the essence of forming hierarchies. That which is lower can be rejected; that which is higher can be sought. One sees, for example, that higher levels of consciousness are what make up the essence of one's humanness, rather than feeling a sense of identity that is limited to one's body.

The third factor is the dynamism of valuation. With it one becomes consciously involved in developing an autonomous hierarchy of values. The third factor judges what subject-object in oneself has uncovered.

Subject-object in oneself. This novel name discloses a fascinating and important dynamism of development. In one swoop it brings a flash of insight into understanding and overcoming a classic philosophical problem: the Cartesian dichotomy between subject and object. Paradox and enigma vie here. Most of us are experts in subjectivity; we know our own experiences. Occasionally we can even manage to experience the other in their subjectivity. But there is, says Dabrowski, something much more than that. The other side of the coin (which few psychologies or philosophies explore) images the person at this level as able to step outside of that subjectivity that comes so easily to the more challenging and difficult task of viewing himself or herself objectively. Like someone looking in a mirror, we can glimpse the self, the subject, as an object to be examined. It may be a passing flash, gone in an instant; it may be a life-changing and enduring insight into self. The sources of this objectivity are in the higher levels of subjectivity. Lonergan (1974) puts this experience, the convergence of subjectivity and objectivity, succinctly: "Objectivity is the fruit of authentic subjectivity" (p. 214). We will get back to this later.

Overexcitabilities

Developmental potential is defined operationally as the sum of the psychic overexcitabilities and the developmental dynamisms present in an individual. It would help in our understanding of developmental potential to examine what Dabrowski means by "psychic overexcitabilities" and "dynamisms," giving some examples of the different kinds he distinguishes.

Types of overexcitability. I still have trouble with the "over" part of this word that Dabrowski has coined. It has the inferential meaning in the English language of "too much" and that is a pejorative meaning. What Dabrowski means is "more than the ordinary"—something that the prefix *super* implies in a positive sense. Perhaps the word *superresponsivity* might carry the intended meaning better. It is more positive and also conveys the double action of reception and response, not only being responsive to stimuli impinging on the person, but strong in like response. Dabrowski's overexcitable people are more than ordinarily sensitive to certain stimuli and, although this is commonly looked upon as a desirable quality in stereos it is often regarded as a nagging problem when we find it in the people around us. Again, perhaps this is one of the recurring paradoxes of TPD along with the notion that disintegration leads to growth; along with the notion that a crisis is an opportunity; along with the notion that psychoneurosis is not an illness comes the idea that to be "overexcitable" is not bad, but potentially productive of great humanness.

Dabrowski's distinction of five kinds of mental functioning is based on his clinical observation of "types of overexcitability." He observed that some children, some adolescents, and some adults consistently overreacted to both external and intrapsychic stimuli. Their overreacting expressed certain dimensions of their personality: (a) psychomotor, (b) sensual, (c) imaginational, (d) intellectual, or (e) emotional. Some individuals seemed to be more sensitive to one kind of stimulus, some to a broad range of stimuli. Some showed sensitivity at lower psychomotor levels, others at higher levels more closely connected with cortical functioning. Dabrowski was thus able to arrange them into a hierarchy rising in the order in which I have listed them above. These overexcitabilities are like two-way channels or radar receptors bringing stimuli into the individual and sensing those stimuli that the individual produces intrapsychically. The openness of these channels and the number of them operating determine the amount of psychic stimuli the individual is receiving. More importantly, the level of the channels that are operative determines the process of dissolution of lower-level activity and organization and growth toward higher levels. Messages from the higher-level channels bring about the dissolution of lower-level responses and open up the possibility of reorganization at a higher level. Less automatic, more voluntary responses that come later in development conflict with earlier, more automatic modes of functioning. Higher-level processes disorganize and inhibit more automatic ones. The disequilibrium these overexcitabilities produce brings on the emergence and organization of higher levels of control.

In brief, psychic overexcitability refers to an especially heightened reaction of some individuals when exposed to certain classes of stimuli. The experiences and responses of such individuals are above average in terms of their intensity, frequency, and duration.

It would serve us well to look at each of these types of overexcitabilities individually, beginning at what I see as the lower end of Dabrowski's ranking.

Psychomotor

Psychomotor overexcitability is a result of an organic excess of energy expressing itself in the neuromuscular system. Emotional tension may come out in psychomotor forms of expression such as restlessness, drumming fingers on a table, rapid talk, or chainsmoking. This overexcitability finds release too in violent games and dances, intense athletic activities, and, perhaps in a sublimated form, in a heavy foot on the gas pedal of a car.

Sensual

Sensual excitability, a function of heightened experiencing of sensory pleasure, shows itself as a need for comfort, fashion, and beauty in a stereotyped sense, varied sexual experiences, and numerous relationships, which may not extend to any depth. Overeating and obsession with food, sex, and physical stimulation are examples of the transfer of emotional tension into sensual forms. Sexuality at this level is appreciated merely as a sensation with little thought given to personal relationships. This is the playboy mentality, demonstrated often as voyeurism in males without emotional involvement and as a sensual exhibitionism in females.

Lest the descriptions of these first two levels seem to be totally pejorative and even moralistic, I think it is good to remember that psychomotor and sensual excitabilities, although low in Dabrowski's hierarchy, do have a legitimate place and are often expressed in the "fun" things of life from water skiing to stroking a cat to liking a velvet painting for its texture. The important thing is that if the appreciation stops there, as with the velvet painting, and no higher intellectual and emotional sensitivities are active, these overexcitabilities remain truncated, as does the individual.

Imaginational

A further rung up the ladder of overexcitabilities is imagination. Imaginational overexcitability in its negative sense manifests itself in dreams, nightmares, mixing of truth and fiction, and fears of the unknown. In a more positive sense imaginational overexcitability shows itself in imagery, metaphor, inventiveness, and vivid visualization. Life may move into a world of fantasy full of magic and rich with poetry. A fictional person with active imaginational overexcitability was Anne of Green Gables.

Lucy Maud Montgomery has in her classic *Anne of Green Gables* created a little human creature who exemplifies all that is best in sensual and imaginational overexcitability. In the following passage, the author contrasts Anne with the unimaginative but kindly Matthew as he brings her in his horse-drawn buggy to Green Gables for the first time:

> The "Avenue" so called by the Newbridge people, was a stretch of road four or five hundred yards long, completely arched over with huge, wide-spreading apple trees, planted years ago by an eccentric old farmer. Overhead was one long canopy of snowy fragrant blooms. Below the boughs the air was full of purple twilight and far ahead a glimpse of painted sunset sky shone like a great rose window at the end of a cathedral aisle.

> Its beauty seemed to strike the child dumb. She leaned back in the buggy, her thin hands clasped before her, her face lifted rapturously to the white splendor above. Even when they had passed out and were driving down the long slope to Newbridge she never moved or spoke. Still with rapt face she gazed afar into the sunset west, with eyes that saw visions trooping splendidly across that glowing background.... Through Newbridge, bustling little village where dogs barked at them and small boys hooted and curious faces peered from the window, they drove, still in silence. When three more miles had dropped away behind them the child had not spoken. She could keep silence, it was evident, as energetically as she could talk.

> "I guess you're feeling pretty tired and hungry," Matthew ventured at last, accounting for her long visitation of dumbness with the only reason he could think of. "But we haven't far to go now—only another mile."

> She came out of her reverie with a deep sigh and looked at him with the dreamy gaze of a soul that had been wondering afar, star-led.

> "Oh Mr. Cuthbert," she whispered, "that place we came through— that white place—what was it?"

> "Well now, you must mean the Avenue," said Matthew after a few moments profound reflection. "It is a kind of pretty place."

> "Pretty?" Oh pretty doesn't seem the right word to use. Nor beautiful either. They don't go far enough. Oh it was wonderful—wonderful. It's the first thing I ever saw that couldn't be improved on by imagination. It just satisfies me here"—she put one hand on her breast—

"it made a queer funny ache and yet it was a pleasant ache. Did you ever have an ache like that, Mr. Cuthbert?"

"Well now, I just can't recollect that I ever had."

"I've had it lots of times—whenever I see anything royally beautiful. But they shouldn't call that place the Avenue. There is no meaning in a name like that. They should call it—let me see—the White Way of Delight. Isn't that a nice imaginative name?" (1968, pp. 19-20)

Perhaps Lucy Maud Montgomery betrays her own emotional and imaginational overexcitability when in *Anne of the Island* (1968, p. 11) she makes these comments on the adolescent Anne, locked in reverie beside a shining brook: "And she was richer in those dreams than in realities; for things seen pass away, but the things that are unseen are eternal."

Intellectual

Intellectual overexcitability is shown in the avid search for knowledge, persistent question asking, the search for a theoretical framework, and the love of logic.

Pierre Teilhard de Chardin, to whom we have referred from time to time, drawing on the resources of his intellectual development, was even in childhood an example of intellectual overexcitability. His mother was cutting his hair one day when he was a child of four or five. To his horror he watched some of his tresses fall into the fireplace and become consumed in the flames. He saw something of himself perishing and, grasping the perishableness of his world, he began to search for things with permanence. First he found pieces of iron, and clung to his collection of iron objects to reassure himself that some things do endure. Then one day he noticed streaks of rust on a farm plow and came to the conclusion that even iron was slowly perishing. His quest for the enduring sent him off in search of rocks in the hills of his native Auvergne countryside. Fortunately for him (and ultimately for us), the rocks around his home were a rich source of quartz and amethyst. He started a collection that was the beginning of a lifelong interest in paleontology. Freud might have had other interpretations of this childish passage in the life of a young boy, but such interpretations fade into foolishness. I see the dynamisms in action here as those of a budding intellectual overexcitability, for they combine the intelligence, curiosity, and intensity of emotional grasp that comprise intellectual overexcitability.

To combine the concepts *intellectual* and *excitability* seems at first look impossible if we are to maintain the classical distinction between cognitive and affective, between intellect and emotion. How can we have an "excited intellect". R.S. Peters (1974), shows the congruence of this idea when, in reacting to Hume's (1978) equating reason with the sort of reason that goes on in logic and mathematics or in science, illustrating a broader view of "reason." Peters points out that there is a cluster of "passions" closely connected with reason without which its operations would be unintelligible. He is referring to "the passion for truth," "abhorrence of the arbitrary," "hatred of inconsistency and irrelevance," "love of clarity and order," and "the determination to look at facts" (p. 329). Both Dabrowski and Peters remind us that, though we have separated them for our own convenience in understanding, intellect and emotion are inseparable companions in real life. To speak of "intellectual overexcitability" is not only possible, but an exciting idea in itself! Pearce (1992, pp. 42ff), explores the threefold human brain: the "Mind of three minds, thought, feeling and action" in his book *Evolution's End*. Mere intellect found in the cortex of the highest brain is not enough. All three work together in the richest of situations, uniting especially feeling with intellect and action to yield something more than mere intellect: full intelligence. Bruno Bettelheim (1960) called it "the informed heart."

Emotional

Emotional overexcitability is a heightened mode of experiencing and re-sponding to emotional relationships. The relationships can be with persons, objects, living things, or even places (remember Anne and her intense relationship with the "White Way of Delight"). From the point of view of Positive Disintegration theory, mere intensity of emotions or great displays of emotions are not enough. There must be a relationship. Piechowski gives an example: When a child is refused a candy, he may throw a temper tantrum to show his anger. Or he may go away sad, thinking he is not loved. In the first place we have only a display of emotion and perhaps an object relation-ship; in the second, a human relationship (1977, pp. 34-35).

Emotional overexcitability may show itself either in direct, positive ex-pression such as enthusiasm or in inhibition such as timidity and shyness. Emotions may center around fears, anxieties, loneliness, depression, feelings of insecurity, or concern with death. They may delve into the past in the form of affective memory ("They're playing our song"). Feelings that are con-nected with interpersonal relationships if they are intense may express themselves in a widespread concern for others (Mother Teresa of Calcutta), or in deep exclusive relationships with only a few or only one person. For some, one of the most profound of emotional relationships will be with God, who for them is a very real person.

Children display emotional overexcitability when an infant looks per-plexed and worried at the sound of another child crying, when the child cries at the sight of a dead animal, when he or she shows compassion for an injured friend, when he or she is moved to be generous and acts accordingly without looking for a reward.

My own son Daniel at the age of three surprised us with his response to a scene in a movie, in which an exasperated father poured milk over the head of one of his children while his brothers and sisters laughed uproariously. Daniel, in a serious mood and stern language, said, "That is not funny—I would get a cloth and wipe the boy's face." Injustice toward a child from an adult was too much for him to accept.

It should be noted in conclusion that each type of overexcitability does not usually exist in isolation from the others; usually there is a dominant form accompanied by others in varying degrees. Overexcitabilities may be absent altogether or present only at the psychomotor or sensual level, but this is the case only when development is limited to primary integration.

The hierarchical ordering in which I have placed the overexcitabilities is significant for the process of development. The two lowest forms—psychomotor and sensual—characterized by restlessness and an extroverted pleasure-seeking, cannot engage psychic processes, nor are they by themselves productive of the reflective attitude and enriching human relationships Dabrowski sees as essential for positive disintegration.

But the story is quite different with the three overexcitabilities at higher levels: imaginational, intellectual, and emotional. They enrich personal development, giving insight into the many levels and dimensions of the world and our relationships with it. They enhance retrospection, introspection, and prospection. With these important channels open and sensitive, there is possible a deeper appreciation of the past, a more vivid appreciation of what is going on within and without a person, and a glimpse (more than passing), of what might be.

Summary

Dabrowski's conception of development stands in sharp contrast to those theories that are based on the principle that humans are motivated by a desire for homeostasis or equilibrium, that the optimum state of well-being is to exist in some sort of quiescent, conflict-free situation where one can be at rest. Instead, it says that life, both from outside the psyche and from intrapsychic dynamics, forces conflicts on individuals that can be disintegrative of lower-level functioning and offer the opportunity of rising to higher levels of development. We have seen that the theory of Positive Disintegration eminently expresses the developmental theme of movement away from egocentrism toward empathy and caring. It also shows a movement through development from external control toward autonomy and authenticity and inner directedness. It demonstrates a movement away from tyrannical forces out of control, from subjection to whim and caprice, toward greater personal choice, directed it is true by what is learned from outside oneself, but guided ultimately by a contemplative, reflective approach toward a personality ideal. Moral differentiation of others is based on the deepest empathy, which is the fruit of insights gained in contemplation.

Intense inner conflict, dissatisfaction with oneself, disintegration of what we *are*, to make room for what we *might be*—these are the themes of Positive Disintegration, which builds on the idea that lower-level functions have to disintegrate when challenged by higher-level functions, then disappear to make room for the higher. This is the process of growth, the dynamic of movement from lower to higher, that has been propounded by psychologists as the driving force behind development.

Our lives have both passive and active phases. The suffering that Dabrowski envisages is not mere passive acceptance of an unhappy lot in life; it is the active grasping of opportunity to really participate in life. TPD says we humans can in a special way respond to this call to be participant in life. Acceptance of suffering may be passive; it may on the other hand (and this is what TPD deep down is saying) be a bold "Yes," not just to this pain, this disintegration, but to the greater soulful pains of all creation continually giving birth. Ultimately it is a "yes" to the God of creation, still in the toil of bringing pattern and ultimately beauty out of chaos. We can choose to side with God as co-workers, co-creators, accepting the challenge to join forces on the side of life. When we take this wider stance we must admit that humans are not consistently Godlike: on the side of life. But, though we may see ourselves as part of a universe that is itself sometimes brutal, and belonging to that portion perhaps most brutal of all, we also recognize that while we live we are gifted with choice. We are responsible agents. We can change things, not just immediate things, but if we reflect on it nothing less than the course of creation. Our principal task is not merely shaping self, not even influencing society, but nothing less than the building of the universe. This calls for daring choices of a justice tempered by compassion. Virtues like care, responsibility, and the ability to identify with others are signposts throughout TPD as goals and measures of higher-level development. Overall, the movement is from egocentrism to a balanced allocentrism that, though caring for others, does not neglect fidelity to oneself.

In the next chapter we will pick out of this broad theory of Positive Disintegration those components that have special relevance to religion and morality. Related readings not already cited in this chapter are: Dabrowski (1964, 1966), Borofski (1981), and Hague (1976, 1988a, 1990a, 1990b, 1993b, 1993c, 1994).

Chapter 6

Positive Disintegration and Religious Development

Positive Disintegration is a general theory of development and, as such, would not be considered a specialized theory of religious development. However, its themes are those of religious development, and the insights it gives are creative, profound, and unique, offering a synthesis that no other theory seems to have either the depth or the breadth to encompass. The source of this can be traced directly to its founder, Kazimierz Dabrowski, who was himself deeply religious with a great respect for God and for his neighbor.

The best way to begin our discussions of the implications of Positive Disintegration for religious development is to approach the topic as Dabrowski himself would, looking at religion as a *multilevel* concept. Dabrowski did this in two ways in the first volume of his *Theory of Levels of Emotional Development* (1977) considering the religious attitude first as an emotional-cognitive function (pp. 142-144), and then going on to consider the levels of religion looked at as a discipline (pp. 215-217). These two major expositions of religion as a multilevel phenomenon are worthy of full repetition here.

The Religious Attitude

Level I. The primitive anthropomorphic conception of forces of "good" and "evil" is based partly on a magical approach and partly on unreflective tendencies of approach and avoidance. One appeals to higher forces primarily to obtain support and protection in the realization of primitive endeavors and satisfaction of biological needs. Success in such undertakings brings about a sense of power and a magic attitude toward oneself such as conviction of possessing superhuman heroic attributes or even of being a demigod. Such attitudes are easily produced by self-suggestion, that one is in favor with the gods because one or another of one's undertakings has succeeded. Such a religious attitude is characteristic of primitive tribes and psychopathic individuals who believe themselves to possess superhuman powers. Outstanding examples are Nero, Ivan the Terrible, Pope Alexander VI, Hitler, Stalin, and Charles Manson.

Level II. Ambivalences and ambitendencies manifested as belief and disbelief, as "spiritualization" of one's approach to a divinity, as periods of fear or disregard of a divinity. Symbolization of personal fears and inner conflicting impulses in the guise of different gods is characteristic here as a personification of human opposites. Or there may be a feeling of an exclusive contact with the divinity symbolized by a ritual of betrothal to a divine personage, often followed by a feeling of letdown or a lack of favor (grace). Also characteristic at this level are periodic attitudes of atheism alternating with search for contact with a deity and its protective power.

Level III. Under the influence of multilevel dynamisms develops a hierarchy of religious values. This is followed by a need to spiritualize and differentiate the conception of divinity. The image and a conception of divinity grow out of one's developmental tendencies and strivings. The concreteness of immanence is linked with the concreteness of transcendence. In religious immanence, one creates an idea of God through one's subjective needs; in transcendence, one sees God independently of one's subjectivity. Concrete transcendental realities correspond with strong emotional realities of a high level of development. Immanence and transcendence may appear as an antimony, yet at the same time they constitute a two-part harmony. In the search for grace, it is experienced as coming from two directions at once: from the subject and from higher reality. Sometimes one observes deviant, more unilevel, forms of devotion to the divinity characterized by artificiality, excessive self-criticism and self-abasement, or spiritual narcissism.

Level IV. With the development of a high level of allocentrism, one observes gradual development of existential attitudes, of delving into the essence of valuing divinity as an embodiment of love, together with a deepening need of faith in the uniqueness of God and his personal attributes. As a result of experiences gained through systematic meditation, contemplation, and the effort at self-perfection, a tendency develops toward making one's subjective religious needs more objective and toward making transcendence a concrete reality. Religious attitude is manifested as a search in transcendence for objective supernatural realms.

Level V. Development of the relationship "I" and "Thou" in the sense of development of absolute religious values of faith, together with all-encompassing empathy and universal love. The search for a transcendental hierarchy in the religious attitude finds expression in authentism and in idealization of personality. Such an attitude develops through an intuitive synthesis of one's personal relationship with the divinity. In this level, religious attitude is marked by clarity and simplicity that is nourished by great depth of religious experience. It also characterized by an effort to make the relation between immanence and transcendence understandable, to make God a concrete experience, to carry on with Him a dialogue in place of one's monologue. Breaks and interruptions may occur in such a dialogue leading to the "dark night of the soul," but the need and the search for the dialogue remain intact and unassailable. The search is calm though intense (pp. 142-144).

Religion

Level I is characterized by primitive naturalism, frequently as a function of self-preservation; fear and "humbleness" before "higher forces," expectation of punishment; primitive symbolization of gods; praising the gods and bribing them with gifts and offerings; brutality and cruelty in making live sacrifices; and instances of deification of oneself.

Level II is characterized by the beginnings of experiencing and adopting an immanent attitude; some degree of respect for divinity; fluctuation of feelings toward gods or toward one god, manifested in fluctuation of atheistic and personalistic attitudes; variable attitudes of fear, self-abasement, and subordination alternating with periods of self-confidence; emotional attitude toward a god of good and a god of evil is not elaborated and is, therefore, inconsistent and unstable. The conceptions of immanence and transcendence are vague because a superficial external attitude toward a god prevails, hence attraction toward religious ceremony and ritual.

Level III. The attitude of respect toward the divine is distinct. There is a gradual hierarchization of values and of divinity; prevalence of monotheism; development of religion based on respect and conscious, freely accepted dependence; immanence combined with a tendency to see transcendence as a concrete possibility; development of inner religion with diminishing needs of external expression, more of inner worship and less of external worship.

Humility that grows out of a sense of personal relationship with God increases, while authoritarian attitudes grow weaker. Religious attitudes and feelings undergo distinct differentiation into many levels due to dissatisfaction with oneself, feelings of inferiority toward oneself, and feelings of shame and guilt. Sincerity develops. Religious attitude based on "what ought to be" rather than on "what is," that is, a growing need to be consistent in one's religious beliefs and one's actions. Objection to a formal and abstract conception of God grows stronger because one's religious attitude becomes experiential, mystical, and also empirical. God is perceived less as a God of power and more as a God of love and justice.

Level IV. Here there is organization of an autonomous hierarchy of religious values; projection of religious ideals and the personality ideal onto other functions and values; the appearance and development of the "instinct of partial death," that is, the aim in striving for self-perfection to destroy all that is undesirable, negative, and an obstacle in development. This can be accomplished through deliberate frustration of one's basic needs. There is a turning away from excessive institutionalism and dogmatism of religious organizations. Distinct action of developmental dynamisms causes separation of higher from the lower religious levels. There is a strong need to feel and realize love in relationship with others; and consistency between religious convictions and one's actions. The balance between an intellectual and an emotional attitude toward God grows stronger because, at this level emotional and intellectual functions begin to operate in unity and harmony. Concrete transcendentalism also increases as does the distinct need for dialogue with God.

Level V. Here there is a fully developed attitude of love stemming from the highest values, which personify divinity and people in their unrepeatable and individual relationships. Active love results from experiences gained in meditation and contemplation. There is total readiness for sacrifice for the sake of others and for one's faith. Union with God is experienced in meditation or in strong intuitive projections, leading to an inner understanding of God, the so-called infused knowledge. The deepest respect and love of God do not obliterate the awareness of one's individuality. This means that the sense of affinity and union with God exist together with preservation of distinct and permanent individual essence. At times, when it becomes difficult to obtain a response from God, one's relationship to Him is built through continuing work of inner perfection and through creating and discovering ever higher values (pp. 215-217).

Religion at its Best, the Best of Human Development

Pierre Teilhard de Chardin, priest, paleontologist, philosopher, theologian, and mystic, saw in his vast perspective on the evolution of the universe a coming together of all things as they emerge from lower to higher. He enunciated this in a principle that loosely expressed says, "All that rises must converge." Teilhard de Chardin (1969a, 1969b, 1973) saw in the rising of the universe from inanimate to animate, from lower forms of life to higher, a coming together of a new integrity, wholeness, and organicity. In doing this he acknowledged two things: that reality is multilevel, with a rising from lower to higher levels; and that at its highest levels, something not found at lower levels, which are marked by disparity and confusion, creation finds a remarkable unanimity, a sharing, a oneness. It is like the voices of a great choral group who have practiced painfully and separately over long weeks; when they come together they discover the miracle that "it all fits" to form one work of art. No one is lost, no one diminished, no one the less because they have become part of the whole; each individual makes his or her contribution; each has value, and the miracle is that "it all fits." It all makes something more than each individual; it all makes something that transcends all individuals. Together they have individually risen to new heights, and in that rising they have converged, and in that converging they have transcended. The whole is something greater than the sum of its parts.

Dabrowski shared and enhanced de Chardin's multilevel image of the universe, and just as these two great men ascended that multilevel staircase of understanding what it is to be human, so too they converged in their thoughts. And it is here that I see the best doorway to understanding the theory of Positive Disintegration as a theory of religious development.

Dabrowski recognized in his own lifetime the remarkable similarity of ideas, values, and goals that the eminent men and women of history had discovered for themselves and taught others. Eminent persons like Christ, Gandhi, Albert Schweitzer, Jean Vanier, and Mother Teresa of Calcutta share ideas and principles not by chance, but because by the rising process of their own personality development, by their high levels of emotional development and sensitivity, they have converged together with one voice, or rather with one song that sings of what is best in being human. And that is where I would like to enter into this thing we call religion—with the idea of "what is best in being human." Paradoxically, it transcends what we typically regard as "merely human" and touches the divine. (By now we are used to finding paradoxes whenever we get to a really important idea.) For it is in religion that the human and the divine touch, like God's strong hand reaching out to give life to Adam's limp hand in the creation scene on the ceiling of the Sistine Chapel.

So at this important point I would like to come back to one of the principal themes of this book: that religion at its best is the best of humanness; that the best humans are truly religious, and it is, therefore, with the highest-level human beings that we will get the clearest, sharpest focus on the picture of religion. And this is fitting, for we have said that religion is best found at the highest levels of human consciousness. Dabrowski's eminent human beings are religious in the sense that their consciousness is profound, their peace is deep and lasting, their perspective on life is vast, and their relationships with the universe, with their fellow man, and with God are real and deeply personal. This is to say that those who have reached the highest of Dabrowski's levels are religious, thoughtful, reflective, prayerful, mystical. I think this is what he is saying, and the examples he uses, like Dag Hammarskjöld, even though they are not always canonized saints and holy men, have all these qualities that make religion an integral part of their being. All that rises must converge.

Positive Disintegration best tells us what is religion when it tells us what is the best religion. We saw in the initial chapters of this book numerous attempts at defining religion that began from the low end of religiosity as neurotic needs, conformity needs, need of reassurance, alleviation of guilt, and so on. We saw that it is true that much of what passes for religion is just that, satisfaction of low-level needs—humans at their dependent or exploitative worst. Regrettably, that is the content of much of the emotional baggage we bring with us when we approach the topic of religion. But what a distorted, negative approach! Dabrowski gives us a new way of understanding the great religious people who exemplify all that is best about religion and who show us something of the process of developing to those religious heights.

By reminding us that religion at its best deals with mystery and, like other things, is a many-leveled reality, and especially by describing from a psychological viewpoint what religion is at its highest levels, Dabrowski has set goals for religious development and thereby some norms for religious education. The kind of person he describes at the upper levels of development bears a remarkable similarity to the higher reaches of human nature described by Maslow and Jung and is very unlike the "religious" person described by Freud. Again there is a remarkable consensus between Dabrowski's higher level individuals and the twice-born described by James. In contrast to the once-born or "healthy-minded" individuals who bear much resemblance to people at Dabrowski's lower levels, the sick soul is searching, agonizing, hungering after truth and justice, dying and being born again in a process of positive disintegration. "The religious attitude is manifested as a search in transcendence for objective supernatural realms" (Dabrowski, 1977, p. 143) at Dabrowski's fourth level of development. There is in Dabrowski's theory a fifth and higher level of development, secondary integration, and in describing this Dabrowski goes beyond James's sick soul and even his twice-born and paints a more realistic picture of the higher levels of religious development. It is a picture more in keeping with the traditional concept of the religious mystic who has found peace and integration with other persons, especially with God as a person, and there "rests" in a union with divinity that is special and ultimately ineffable. The search at this level is "calm though intense" (p. 144).

Jung, as we have said, and not Freud most closely coincides with Dabrowski, for Jungian psychology is basically mystical, and the religious experience is consummatory, probing the depths of what it is to be human and drawing one up to the heights of what humanness can be in the transcendent. For Jung the developmental process is a process toward individuation, a stage beyond mere health when new meaning is sought and one strives to live up to one's potentialities. We see here a similarity with Dabrowski's probing, searching levels, as the individual moves from what is to what ought to be and is guided by the personality ideal as the ultimate expression of one's unique possibilities.

The context of religion has broadened in recent years. We have seen, for example, how Frankl singled out purpose in life as the special need of our time, creating a spiritual setting for a response to the cry for meaning.

It is remarkable that today the search for meaning is not being pursued solely by theologians and ministers of religion, but by scientists who belong to a profession long considered to shun religion in favor of materialism. It is as though, by pushing their research to the outer limits of the material world, they have glimpsed the existence of the spiritual. Einstein did not hesitate to speak of God. In a remarkable and beautiful book (1992), *Belonging to the Universe: Explorations on the Frontiers of Science and Spirituality*, the scientist Fritjof Capra joins with David Stendl-Rast, a theologian, to dialogue (not just argue) about the spiritual dimensions each has found in their studies and reflection. Barlow (1994) entitles her anthology *Evolution Extended: Biological Debates on the Meaning of Life*. A few years ago many would have scoffed at the suggestion that biology has anything to say about life meaning, but Barlow in this landmark volume weaves the words of Julian Huxley, George Gaylord Simpson, Charles Darwin, Gregory Bateson, Karl Popper, Jacques Monod, Theodosius Dobzhansky, and others into a scholarly and reflective tour de force.

On the cutting edge of scientific research are those who study chaos theory (compare Birch, 1991; Briggs & Peat, 1990; Gleick, 1988; Pickover, 1991; Prigogine & Stengers, 1984). "Chaos" has long been the descriptor for total and uncontrolled disorder, but scientists using advanced computer technology have searched into the depths of chaos and found there not only order and pattern, but beauty. There seems to be some order hidden deep in the chaos. Where we looked before for meaning we sometimes found only chance; where we looked for life we found death; where we looked for growth we found disintegration. Chaos theory has given us some scientific hope that though the world may not be just as we would like it to be, there is a grander plan, a moving on toward integration, a great process of reintegration no less real because we have failed to see it.

The theory Dabrowski called Positive Disintegration comes at this question, this mystery, as we saw in the last chapter, from the vantage of psychology. It tells us something of the order that can come from chaos, the meaning, purpose, and spirituality that may emerge from and through disintegration.

The Paradox of Religion: Communal and Solitary

I don't know how much Dabrowski was directly influenced by the philosophy of Whitehead, but it is in Dabrowski and Whitehead that I see the most excellent convergence in their rising together. As we have seen in our introduction to the nature of religion, there are two classical points from which to view religion: one can see it from the aspect of the communal—that religion is a social organization; or one can see it from the aspect of the individual. In his introduction to a revised edition of *Religions, Values and Peak Experiences* (1977), Maslow acknowledges his tendency in the previous edition to downplay the communal aspects of religion in favor of seeing it as an individual experience. Whitehead has been accused of the same overemphasis by those who have latched onto his definition of religion as "what the individual does with his own solitariness," interpreting it out of context. Whitehead's real view is a balanced one. He maintains individuals are constituted by their experience of one another. Whitehead sees solitariness as especially important for certain aspects of religion:

> The great religious conceptions that haunt the imaginations of civilized mankind are scenes of solitariness. Prometheus chained to his

rock, Mahomet brooding in the desert, the meditations of the Buddha, the solitary Man on the Cross. It belongs to the depth of religious spirit to have felt forsaken even by God. (1973, p. 19)

Here Whitehead is emphasizing the aloneness one feels when faced with ultimates, an aloneness that Tennessee Williams expressed so beautifully in his plays and more directly when he said, "We are all prisoners inside our own skin," an aloneness that Christ felt in those hours of profound hesitation in Gethsemane and that he expressed on the cross in the ultimate religious experience of death for others, "My God, my God, why have you forsaken me?" Although this motif of solitariness picks up the theme of James's sick soul, Kohlberg's seventh stage, or Dabrowski's level IV, it does not without its context represent the full view of either Whitehead or Dabrowski. For Whitehead a person is always an individual in community, a self emerging through relationships. Bernard Lonergan too (1973) asserts this theme, emphasizing that the love that is involved in religious experience breaks through the isolation of the individual, causing him or her to act not just for the self, but for others (p. 289). This thrust of developmental movement away from egocentrism to allocentrism is, as we have seen, one of the mainstreams of Positive Disintegration. It helps to make a theory that at first blush is just another secular psychological theory, at its heart essentially a beacon of a spiritual, even a mystical, ascent (Nixon, 1990). Whitehead's philosophy and theology remind us that this relatedness moves beyond the human community to the structure of all the relationships of the individual to the cosmos (1938, p. 164). In this religious context the solitariness of the coming to be of a person is also the condition of that person's freedom and responsible choosing—the Third Factor in Dabrowski's terms. The following quote from Whitehead's *Religion in the Making* (1973) might just as well have appeared in one of Dabrowski's works:

The moment of religious consciousness starts from self-valuation,
but it broadens into the concept of the world as a realm of adjusted
values, mutually intensifying or mutually destructive. (pp. 58-59)

Whitehead and Dabrowski converge too with their emphasis on consciousness. For both the process is one of evolving to higher levels of consciousness so that one may be more participant in the unfolding of oneself and in the building of the universe. The higher the level of consciousness, the more one can choose and fully assent to the values one holds.

With the emphasis on consciousness in both Whitehead and Dabrowski, a larger picture of the process of the universe emerges, especially in Whitehead's writings. Here is an area where the theory of Positive Disintegration can be enriched by putting it in a cosmic context that makes more explicit the grand vision that Dabrowski held. We will see later (in the morality half of this book) how a cosmic perspective and respect for the web of interconnectedness within it makes these ideas not just theoretical, but eminently practical.

As we have seen, Whitehead envisioned levels of consciousness as running through all of the cosmos and not just humanity. We know that atomic particles are "conscious" of each other in the view of some physicists, and it would seem that a stone in some sense is "conscious" of its environs and thereby participant in the process of the universe, even if it is the long process of the Rocky Mountains being slowly eroded and washed down to the sea. But consciousness at the human level has the special quality of choice and freedom to participate in the process, choice of the degree to which one will participate, the level at which one participates, and consequently the amount of value one adds to the enduring nature of God. This is ultimate religion.

We have in this discussion emphasized the high end of religious development, looking at the highest levels of human development because that seemed the best doorway to understanding what religion is all about. This does not mean that the theory of Positive Disintegration neglects the ordinary man or woman who has no real possibilities of reaching the lofty mystical levels of religion. In fact it is one of the beauties of Dabrowski's theory that he takes such pains and goes to such lengths to describe the lower levels of development and the lower levels of structures and functions, religion included. By giving a detailed description of the many levels of religion and the religious attitude, Dabrowski has thoroughly elaborated those aspects of religion that are most real to most people. It is regrettable that, for many, religion is a rationalization for power or an excuse to persecute one's neighbor; it is regrettable that, for many, religion stops at the level of an organization because it promises to overcome loneliness by demanding blind conformity, or that by presenting a set of dogmas or moral rules given by others promises to take away the "threat" of having to choose for oneself. It is regrettable that sometimes this is the reality of religion. But it is a reality that Positive Disintegration presents bluntly and honestly by reminding us that spirituality and religion are not spared from being multileveled. There is a vast variety of ways of being religious; some of them are better than others. On the positive side, TPD is a challenge to individuals to rise to higher levels of religious development themselves; it is a guideline to religious educators of the kind of religious people they want to produce and themselves *become*.

Conclusion

This first section on the psychology of religious development has been long and complex; without adding to its length, perhaps we can sort out some of the threads that run through the knots of its complexity.

You were asked in the beginning to examine the psychological baggage you brought to the whole idea of what religion is. You were asked to suspend any definition and encouraged instead to glance from many perspectives at the multifaceted crystal that religion is. You were initially barraged with ideas about religion, incomplete and undeveloped as they were. Then we explored some of the sources of these ideas: religion as process, religion as a multileveled thing, religion as human beings have experienced it at its highest levels, setting thereby the criteria of what religion might be.

We saw religion as that which gives perspective to life and how faith complements it as the guide to proper perspective and the shared meaning (particularly ultimate meaning) of the community. We saw that today religion and science have converged in their appreciation that there is more beyond the obvious; that there is mystery, but that light is thrown on the mystery of life and death, and ordering principles may be found deep within even what we have called sheer chaos. We have seen that not only religious people, but some physicists, astronomers, biologists, psychologists, and other scientists have come to questions of meaning and purpose in life.

We saw that through it all runs a paradox: that religion, though solitary, is interpersonal, communal, potentially giving meaning to life in a way no mere philosophy does, by having it flow through relationships with other people and ultimately with a deity.

Another paradox illustrated our developmental theme: simultaneous convergence and divergence. We saw divergence within the developmental life cycles as the human person became more and more complex while inwardly converging in a process of integration.

And if the image is one of spirals diverging and converging within themselves, it is also one of individual spirals converging with others. We have seen this exemplified in the remarkable convergence of the scholars whom we have studied; we have seen it in the convergence of science and religion; we have seen it in the convergence of people who have reached the highest levels of development. I conclude this first half with the hope that we, reader and writer, have experienced some measure of this concrescence in ourselves.

Part II

Chapter 7

What is Morality?

When you prevent me from doing anything I want to do, that is persecution, but when I prevent you from doing anything you want to do, that is law, order and morals.
—*George Bernard Shaw*

The aim of education is the knowledge not of facts, but of values.
—*William Inge*

In the first half of this book I have outlined something of what we mean by developmental psychology in general and then gone on to look at the narrower field we call religious development, considering it still from a psychological perspective, but with the help of philosophers, sociologists, anthropologists, and other social scientists. It is now our task to look at what we know of morality from the viewpoint of developmental psychology. Again, we are emphasizing the developmental aspects of moral judgment making, although, as we shall see, there are other psychological approaches to the study of morals.

Moralizing versus Moral Philosophizing

First, though, a note about two major ways of approaching this whole topic of morals. Politics, religion, sports, and sex are popular topics for heated discussions. Almost anyone will argue some point of view. Almost anyone has his or her own opinions, often quite heavily loaded with emotion. The same is true of morals. Mention the fact that you are interested in morality and someone will have a "case" to discuss whether it be to weigh ponderously the pros and cons of nuclear war, or just to cluck their tongues over the latest scandal. Mention of the word *morality* almost automatically leads to a discussion of specific, concrete actions and a debate about whether these actions are "good" or "bad." Mention that you are interested in moral education and people will nod affirmatively and say, "That's good; I hope you can get those young people straightened out." Try to teach a class in moral development and you will find that you must constantly fight the powerful attraction of a class discussion on specifics of "explosive" moral issues ranging from the nuclear bomb to women's necklines. That's why a distinction is important at the very beginning. It is the distinction between *moralizing* and *moral philosophizing*. What we have been talking about so far is moralizing: offering judgments about specific principles, values, and behaviors in a particular setting. The aim of moralizing is both evaluative and educational; usually to pass practical judgments on a moral issue and try to convert someone to our view. It is often marked with considerable fervor.

On the other hand, moral philosophizing is more general, a more rational study (abstract if you wish) of moral concepts, problems, and issues. It includes the analysis of problems in moral philosophy and moral education, for example, what is the role of reason in ethics; should we let our emotions guide us; how should morals be taught (if at all they can be); or are morals only "caught" by example? Moral philosophy seeks to synthesize systematic answers to problems such as "What is good?" and "Why should we be good?"

At first look, moral philosophizing seems much colder, more abstract, and less fun than moralizing. And in many ways that might be true, but morals is eminently a practical science (or art), and a good theory, particularly a theory of morality, is never far from its practical application. And ultimately it is a much more satisfying human experience to work through from the depths of moral philosophy to the practical problems than to start with practical problems and find one has no depth of understanding of principles to give satisfying solutions.

That is why we will be doing more moral philosophizing than getting involved in the specifics of moral cases. Chazan and Soltis (1973) put it well: "Programs in moral education have often been devoid of critical thinking and clarification. The result is that although moral education has been rich in fervor it has often lacked conceptual depth" (p. 5). It is our purpose here to achieve some degree of conceptual depth, without losing the fervor.

What is this Thing Called Morality?

First of all, what is this thing we call morality? What makes it different from arithmetic, geography, baseball, driving a car, or fishing? Or better, what is it that makes it different but still gives morality a special relationship to all these things, in fact a special relationship to all of life? The first step in answering this question is to say that morality is about action and gives a valence, a positive or negative loading, to actions. It evaluates actions, not things. If we ask: "Is the fishing good here in this lake?" we are asking a question, not yet a moral question, but a value question. "Is this lake good for fishing?" It is a value question about an object, the lake. Values, as we have seen, are valence-laden concepts expressing worthwhileness and as such are much broader than moral questions. In other words, only *some* values are moral values. With moral values the valence takes on an aspect of "oughtness" and the value expressed in terms of "good" and "bad" now tells me how I *ought* to behave. The lake may be good for fishing in the sense that it is a desirable place to fish, but it may be a place I ought not to fish because it is on private property and to take fish from it would be a form of stealing. Thus morals are a special kind of values that contain a message of special obligation within them. It looks, then, as if the first logical thing to consider in depth is the idea of values, because values, broader than morality, are inclusive of morality.

What are Values?

It is with considerable trepidation that one approaches the task of "defining" values. The word *value* like the word *religion* is monstrous in the challenges it poses to definition. If centuries of thinking, arguing, and writing have not come up with a satisfactory answer, it is not presumed that we shall get one here. What we can hope for is a clarification of the concept and as clear an explanation as possible of how the term is used in this book, proceeding from there with at least mutual understanding if not agreement.

What Values are Not

First, it is important to say what value is *not*. Value is one of those words that seems so clear at the beginning of a discussion, but when you come to the end of the discussion or the end of a class in values, you find you have been talking about different things. Perhaps one of the most common errors is to confuse values with rules, regulations, laws, customs, mores. This is particularly true of the classroom when what goes as a value discussion actually amounts to a discussion about rules and laws. It is easy to spend much time discussing the relative merits of a school's rules about smoking and even come to a value conclusion pro or con without really getting at the values that underlie such things as school rules, in this case values like care of one's health and concern for other people. It is values such as these that dictate specific rules, and until we get down to the bases of the specific rules, the values they express, we are really only having a rule discussion, and the danger is that values behind them will not be clarified at all.

Not rules. Values are the bases of rules and laws, but are not themselves rules and laws. A value like honesty is not a rule; it is an abstraction from which we interpret certain rules of behavior. Values are generally enduring, relatively unchanging. Rules, on the other hand, are specific, adaptable to the occasion, changing. The key, if the rules are to be good rules, is that they reflect worthwhile values. The word *reflect* is a good one, and the image that comes to mind is that of seismic crews searching for oil on the prairie landscape. Oil is caught in bedrock deep below the surface of the land. It is up on the surface of the earth that all the activity takes place when human beings are searching for oil. How do you on the surface know where to drill to find the oil? What a seismic crew does is send soundings into the depths of the earth and then "listen" or be sensitive to the message that comes back from those soundings. The message back from the bedrock tells them something about its depth and configuration, giving them some rules to guide their decisions about where to drill for oil. The soundings on the bedrock guide their behavior on the surface. So it is between values and rules of behavior. Values are relatively stable concepts of the desirable, broad and general. When we want some specific guidelines, some laws, some norms, we sound out the bedrock of values and interpret our values in specific rules. Values themselves, like bedrock, don't change much over time; it's our interpretation and the order, the hierarchy we put them in, that make the variations.

Because interpretation of what lies below is both fallible and variable according to the circumstances of what is happening on the surface, people make mistakes in making up their rules even though they are presumably sounding out the same bedrock values. Muslims and Christian crusaders have charged at each other across the sands of the Holy Land and slaughtered each other with the same cry: "God wills it." The row on row of crosses in Flanders Fields are all Christian crosses on both sides of the fence that divides the "allies" from the "enemies." Somehow the Christian symbol seemed a suitable marker for the dead on both sides of the war. The Nazis who ran the concentration camps clung to the value "efficiency." In its name they were proud of the ovens of Auschwitz designed to burn bodies more quickly. In the name of certain values, they designed the most atrocious things. Moral mistakes are made not so much because we lack values as that we confuse our priorities, putting inferior values higher than those called for in the situation (Hague, 1993c).

There are gross errors in interpreting values into rules of living, but there are also variations of interpretations from time to time and from place to place that make rules and laws flexible and changeable, although the values they are meant to translate into action remain the same. Take, for example, a value like *modesty*. The 18th- and 19th-century explorers and missionaries who discovered the naked primitive people of Africa sent back to Europe for suitable clothing so that these people might be "modestly" dressed according to European standards. It was clear to them that the European interpretation of modesty was the right one. Interestingly, by contrast, it was not so clear to the Europeans that the "primitive" people had often a much more sensitive interpretation of the value *justice* than did their powerful conquerors. The value modesty is also a good example of how rules change not only from place to place, but from time to time. We smile at the faded photographs of our parents in swimming suits that were considered daring for their time. They would be shocked if they knew how we interpret the value modesty today. Whether the interpretation of people in a particular time or place is an accurate and true interpretation of a value is the point that is up for grabs. The fact of whether something is valuable is up for grabs. The fact that there are values, ideas of what is truly desirable and ultimately humanizing, is beyond discussion. The challenge is to make the rules that truly respond to the values. That is why at the beginning it is so important to know whether we are talking about rules and customs, laws and regulations, and mores or whether we are talking about values.

Morality is not just a system of rules, as Piaget (1932) would have you think. It is a system of values, interpreted as rules of action in specific cases.

Attitudes and beliefs. Because a value is a concept of the desirable, it is a broad term, broader not only than a law or rule, but broader even than a very popular psychological term, *attitude*. An attitude is usually pointed at something specific; we have an attitude toward work, an attitude toward a minority group, but we value industriousness; we value brotherhood and equality. Values transcend specific objects and are expressed in broader, more abstract terms than attitudes. Values must be distinguished from beliefs. Beliefs are ideas we have about the world around us; they may even, like a value, carry a valence, a positive or negative weighting. We may believe, for example, that all should be treated equally. But a belief may stop there at simply believing in this abstract principle without ever acting on it. A belief is something we may publicly affirm, talk about, proclaim, but unlike value it does not necessarily flow into action. A belief may be a purely theoretical expression of a judgment of worthwhileness, but a value if it is to be a value in the full sense must flow into action, must actually influence our way of behaving, not just our mind set or the way we talk. A value is a concept of the desirable that flows into action.

Toward a Definition of Values

We are now ready to "define" value, at least to the extent of clarifying how the term is used here. The definition reads like this. A *value* is a conception of the desirable that actually influences the selection from among various modes, means and ends of action.

The definition can best be understood by breaking it down into its three main parts. A value is:

1. a conception—it is a concept in the intellectual, cognitive sense of the term; not just a passing fancy, a whim, a wisp of emotion, but an understanding in the full cognitive sense of the term.

2. of the desirable—here is where the positive-negative loading of value concepts is acknowledged. Values are not mere abstract or factual concepts like $2 + 2 = 4$. They are, as we have said, concepts to which the understanding attaches a valence, a judgment about the desirability or undesirability of something or some action, including a judgment about the degree of desirability or undesirability. Value judgments are judgments of attractiveness. This is where the affective, the emotional component, comes in. Emotions make value judgments; we feel attracted or repulsed by something. It is the heart that deals with attractiveness, but as Bruno Bettelheim (1960) reminds us, it is the "informed heart" that gives sound guidance—the emotions acting, as Dabrowski says, in equipotential collaboration with the intellect.

We can now see that values are judgments of desirability made by the whole person, not just "cool intellect" or "hot emotion," but the whole warm, living, vital person. In fact the tendency we have to break the person down into two systems, one cognitive the other affective, is one based more on our own conscience than on the biological makeup of the nervous system. We have one nervous system that thinks and feels. We have distinguished thinking and feeling for our own convenience of understanding these two aspects of our mental activity, and the distinction has been so handy and so ingrained in our vocabulary that there is a real temptation to view them as two quite discrete systems, granting them at most some sort of relationship, such as intellect controlling emotion.

Our definition here acknowledges the involvement of the whole person, emphasizing the crucial role of feeling in making value judgments because we are dealing with attractiveness, the domain in which we see emotion especially involved. Our definition, then, has acknowledged two aspects of valuing, cognitive and affective. It goes on to acknowledge the third, the conative: the aspect of striving for, of acting, of actually doing something about that which we find attractive or unattractive. The third part of the definition says "Which actually influences the selection from among various modes means and ends of action"—this is the aspect of value that lifts it above mere ideas, beliefs, attractions, and velleities. A value by this definition moves us to select and actually move toward certain goals by choosing and acting upon the means toward those goals.

3. acted upon. I realize that by saying a value must be something acted upon or it is no value sets rather strict limits on the concept. It goes against the ideas of many value theorists such as Milton Rokeach (1960, 1969), whose research and writings are based on the premise that a value is truly a value if it is expressed as such, even though it is not necessarily acted upon. But the present definition, which is more in keeping with the ideas of Clyde Kluckhohn (1951) and Raths, Harmin, and Simon (1966), is more rigorous. It means that we will find we have fewer values if they are something we must actually live by and not just enunciate. By including this third, conative requirement we elevate value to a higher level, making it more precious and special in our lives and also opening the way to a reminder about valuing and value teaching: the importance of authenticity in not just proclaiming a value but actually living it. We will see more of this later on.

Seven Criteria for a Value

Our working definition of values has delineated three processes of valuing: (a) knowing, (b) prizing and choosing, (c) acting upon. Raths et al. in their influential book *Values and Teaching* (1966) outlined seven criteria for a true value that flow quite naturally from these three processes. Although they have not given explicit attention to the distinction between cognition and affect, these two components are there, for these authors require that values be chosen after thoughtful consideration and with knowledge of the alternatives. Raths et al.'s criteria for a value are the following.

Knowing

1. Choosing freely—Values must be selected freely, without coercion. This involves freedom to know.

2. Knowing and choosing from among alternatives—There must be alternative choices; there can be no choice if there are no alternatives from which to choose. There can be no choice also if the alternatives are not understood, or if we don't know what they are. A child who does not know what the words *chocolate* and *vanilla* mean cannot really choose a chocolate or vanilla ice cream cone. The alternatives might be present, but if we don't understand them, we do not really make a choice.

3. Choosing after knowing and thoughtfully considering the consequences of each alternative.

The understanding of the alternatives described in criterion 2 means understanding not only what they are, but the consequences of choosing them. For something intelligently and meaningfully to guide one's life it must emerge from an understanding, a comparing, and a weighing—a comparing of the valences of each alternative, positive or negative, and if positive to what degree is each positive? This is the important cognitive factor involved in knowing what the alternatives are and collaborating with a sense of weighting each alternative for its relative value.

Choosing

4. Prizing—When we value something it has a positive tone. We cherish it, esteem it, respect it, hold it dear. In other words, we must be happy with our values or they are no values at all. A soldier may choose freely to go to war for his country and be proud of the value he holds dear: the defense of his homeland. He may at the same time choose freely and after thoughtful consideration to do all he can to kill as many of the enemy as he can, but unless he is happy with this choice killing people is not a value for him; it is only a reluctantly chosen means to an end.

5. Affirming—The soldier we have used as an example for criterion 4 must also be willing to affirm his choice publicly. A choice that you will not affirm in public is, according to Raths et al., not a value. We must, they say, be proud of our values.

Acting upon

6. Acting upon choices—According to this way of defining value, a value cannot be something chosen in secret or even just verbally affirmed. It must in fact give direction to our actual living.

7. Repeating—This criterion flows naturally from the last because something that is a value tends to reappear on a number of occasions in the life of a person, giving some sort of direction to that life. We would not think of something that appeared rarely in a life as a value. Values are persistent; they tend to create a pattern. They are the stars by which we steer our lives.

Where Do We Find Value?

Before going on to explore some distinctions we must make in talking about values, an important premise on which this chapter is built needs to be made explicit. Philosophers have long argued about the location of values. Where do they exist? In things or in people? In objects that have value or in persons who hold values? Is value some kind of quality that exists in objects of and by itself, or does it take some sort of valuing entity to recognize and thereby create that value? It is something like the discussion of whether a tree falling in the forest makes a noise if there is no one there to hear it? Of course, the answer all depends on what our definition of value is, but once one makes a choice of one or the other of these approaches—value in the object itself or value in the perceiver—a series of important ramifications follows. It is a watershed decision. It is probably clear by now that our definition of value is on the side of value as a perception and attribution of the valuer, whether the valuer is as lowly as an earthworm that shows a preference for a good, moldy leaf to munch on or a human being who selects a volume of Shakespeare for his or her weekend reading. Both objects are valuable because a valuer has discovered some sort of attractiveness in them.

This premise, though not traditional and contrary to much of ancient Greek philosophy, is much more satisfying psychologically, and it gets us away from the problems inherent in seeing value in *things* awaiting discovery by psyches whose main tool in discovering that value is intellect or pure reason unhindered by passion or feeling. The "value in objects" approach leads to all sorts of problems when we look at that specialized area of values we call morals, for there is the peril of the "naturalistic fallacy," a swaying bridge that attempts to take the moral philosopher across the gap from *is* to *ought*. Morals, as we shall see, are characterized by oughtness, a demand they place on us to follow them. This oughtness, a naturalistic philosopher claims, comes purely from the nature of things. Because things are of a particular nature, they say, we ought to behave in a certain way toward them. But these philosophers have been hard pressed to prove oughtness. Perceiving value in the valuer, or better still in the interaction between the valued and the valuer, puts it in its proper dynamic place where the action of attraction, especially emotional attraction, takes place. Robert Pirsig put it succinctly in his novel *Lila: An Inquiry into Morals* (1991, p. 66): "Between the subject and the object lies the value."

Various Kinds of Values

Some further distinctions must be made when considering the various ways we look at values.

Explicit-Implicit

Values may be explicit or implicit. That is, they may be something we have reflected on and thus brought more fully into consciousness. Hopefully, this consciousness is the end result of any value reflection or value clarification exercise. The opposite are values that we may live by but are not conscious of because we have not reflected on them and consciously affirmed them. The point I am trying to make here is that people do not come into a value education class without values. We all have values from birth in the very broadest sense of the term, where we value comfort over pain, food over hunger, and so on. We go on making "value" choices, preferences for one thing over another, all through a lifetime until we come up against a question of values, perhaps in the form of a crisis or conflict in our lives, perhaps in the form of a dilemma posed by a teacher, and then the choices must be made consciously, not just automatically. Mature, explicit value choices are made with reflection and awareness of what we are doing, as opposed to more automatic choices that are the consequence of decisions made perhaps a long time ago that still implicitly and without reflection affect our actions (Hague, 1976). For example, someone with a nine-to-five job who can't resist pushing the snooze button on his bedside clock "just one more time" for an extra ten minutes of sleep each morning and often comes just a little late to work as a result is implicitly expressing a value: sleep is more important than the value of *punctuality*. Now punctuality may be something he maintains meticulously during the rest of the day, but when it competes with personal comfort, it usually loses out. In other words, he may value both punctuality and comfort, but on reflection he will find that comfort takes a higher place in his hierarchy. And that is one of the main benefits of making this distinction between explicit and implicit values. By bringing values out into explicit conscious expression, it is all the more likely that their importance relative to other values will become clearer; their places in our own personal value hierarchy will be clarified. That is why much of value education is not "teaching" values at all; it is really just bringing values into consciousness and asking whether we want to keep them, and if we do want to keep them what place they will take in relationship to other values. That is why value education to a large extent amounts to building a value hierarchy, not only, as we have seen, of what we express orally or have put down on paper, but what we live by.

Subjective-Objective

This is a distinction that is highly contentious, but extremely important. The question is: Do I see values as something personally chosen based on my own preference for those things and ways of acting that help me to relate to my world of people, things and ideas? Instrumentalists and philosophers in the tradition of John Dewey (1909) would see values as such; not as something stable and universal and a guide to mankind, but as something purely personal and subjective. Dewey in his effort to create citizens for a democracy strove mightily to keep out any kind of indoctrination, any kind of force from the outside that would impose regimentation on value choices. That indoctrination coming from social pressure of institutions such as schools or churches would, according to Dewey, diminish an individual's inalienable right as a citizen in a democracy to choose for himself. John Gardner (quoted in Raths et al., 1966) reflected this idea when he said that "the task of young people is not to stand dreary watch over ancient values but to recreate those values continuously in their own time" (p. 10). Raths et al. followed in the same tradition when they wrote *Values and Teaching,* and it has influenced, as we shall see, the Values Clarification approach ever since. According to this stance values are subjective. Values are of necessity my own choice, not something imposed on me either consciously or unconsciously. What is more, and this is the essence of the subjective approach, I need not answer for my values to any outside criteria. It is enough that I choose them freely from among alternatives, am proud of them, and live by them. This is the essence of the subjectivist view.

Objectivists, on the other hand, maintain that there are enduring, lasting stable criteria that tell us that some values are better than others, that some things are objectively preferable whether or not they are in fact sensed or conceived of as desirable by an individual or a group, that some actions are objectively good or bad. In essence, there are objective criteria for the desirability of certain values over others, and we do have some common ground to appeal to in comparing values, some measuring sticks to see if our values measure up objectively. Objectivists come in a variety of colors and present a whole spectrum of views on what is the origin of value objectivity, starting with dogmatic traditionalists who tell us that values have a supernatural source in God who has revealed them to us clearly and in great and unchanging detail in revelation. The spectrum of value objectivists continues with those who say that value resides in the nature of things, and if only we can logically get at the objective nature of things we will know what is valuable and what is not. At the other end of the value spectrum are those who say we know objectively what is good and bad by pure feeling. If it feels good, it is good and is objectively valuable. If it feels bad, it is bad and we can be just as objectively certain about lack of value because personal pleasure, hedonism, is our guiding norm. We will see more of this later. For now, continuing our introduction, let us go on to another value distinction.

Religious-Human

Another distinction that is frequently made and is really a pseudodistinction (based more on the ways people have come to express themselves than on facts) needs clarification. It is the distinction between "religious" and "human" values often expressed as "merely human" values. It is based on a dichotomy we have imposed on human beings that flows from body-soul distinctions, spiritual-material distinctions, natural-supernatural distinctions. We tend to build a wall between them, the rigid line that says these are two quite separate entities. From this it seems to follow logically for some that if one side is to prosper, the other side must diminish. Like arms of a balance scale, emphasis on one side must mean deemphasis on the other. In this rigid thinking, if the human thrives it is only at the expense of the religious. If the religious prospers it is because the human has in some way diminished. This exclusivity, this competition between the human and the religious, is something we have built into our conception of the world.

It is the heart and essence of this book that the contrary is true. If something is to be truly religious it must be truly humanizing; what is fully human brings man to his fullest heights, which are religious. The two are not in competition; they are one. Religion is not diminished by being human, nor is the human being something less when we find he or she is a religious animal. "The glory of God is man fully alive" (St. Irenaeus), and the glory of a good psychology of values is that religion, proudly flying the flags of the best values, has the greatest potency for humanizing.

Chapter 8

What Does Religion Have to do With Morality?

*To know that what is impenetrable to us really exists, manifesting
itself as the highest wisdom and the most radiant beauty which our
dull faculties can comprehend only in their most primitive
forms—this knowledge, this feeling, is at the center of true
religiousness.*

—*Albert Einstein*

What does religion have to do with morality? For many the answer to this
question is "Everything." Religion is the one source of morality. God is the
source of rightness and wrongness. He knows what is right and wrong and
tells us through his prophets, priests, ministers, and, above all for Christians
and Jews, the Bible. Religion has always included morality and taught moral
laws, promising rewards for those who were good, damnation for those who
were not. Religion seems to have a source of knowledge of right and wrong,
and the moral clout to enforce it. But is the fact that religions have always
taught and enforced morality, and the argument that religious people have a
direct line to the will of God, enough to make this a sufficient proof that
religion *should* be involved in morality? The answer is "No." The theme of
this chapter, however, is not to throw out religion's claim to a place in moral
education, but to place it on firmer ground, ground that is acceptable not
only for logical reasons, but for the psychological reasons that it acknowledges higher levels of development in both religion and morality and sees
the vital link between the two most perfectly accomplished at those higher
levels. The main thrust here is to reinforce religion's place in the moral order,
but not merely from arguments of long tradition or claims of moral authority
to be blindly accepted. To do this we will consider several alternative
answers to the question: What does religion have to do with morality?

Four Answers

1. Everything: Religion is the Authoritative and Punitive Source of Morality

To see religion as the source of morality because it has authority and
threatens punishments harks all too clearly back to the psychology of Freud,
who saw God as a dictatorial, punishing father in the 19th-century Germanic

image. We know from studies done in the primitive moral thinking of children that they do not see goodness and badness as based in any objective order of things or any rules for social living with which their parents also must comply. Instead, they tend to see adults, particularly parents, as above the moral order, in fact as the source of the moral order. It is Mom and Dad who arbitrarily decide what is right and wrong and make rules for children based perhaps on nothing more than their whims. Parents are the source of the moral order just as they are the source of punishment for infringement of that order: "He who bears the rod makes the rules for its use." The very young child has a pragmatic, "keep out of trouble," "try to get rewards" approach to right and wrong. It is an immature approach. Too often it is, as Freud elaborated, carried over into one's relationship with God and continues on through adulthood as an immature conception of religion's involvement with morality.

Even if we do not accept Freud's conception of the Father as a stern, distant, demanding person who gives us our image of God, but, rather, see our God image as coming from remembrances of a warm, loving father figure, the problem remains; one can be fixated on a concept of God who, though warm and accepting, is still an *arbitrary* source of morality. The fact that he is kindly, though it makes the scene more pleasant, may not diminish the childishness of the image nor take away from the danger of an immature rationalization of why God should be involved in morals.

Let me make it clear; the problem is not in the image of God as Father. Christ himself used the imagery in a most mature way and taught us explicitly to call God "Our Father." The problem is in *leaving* the image at a very immature level with all the following difficulties.

1. It keeps a person passive as a child, dependent for worth on the whims and acceptance of others in positions of power. Those others may be God as the individual sees him, or any social or ecclesiastical hierarchy that he perceives to be above him and in control.

2. The element of free choice in morality is diminished. One is not truly free to conform or not to conform to rules that carry with them the unconscious loadings of motives acquired in childhood—including neurotic guilt.

3. Morals seem objective (God-given) but are really subjective (Father-given)—whether the "Father" is parent, family, church, or society in general.

4. Stagnation of moral growth takes place because morality is so deeply ingrained within an infantile personality, one cannot get a deeper, more integrated view of it.

5. If morality is a personal relationship between "me and God" based on personal feelings and a subjective conception of God, one may fail to see other sources of obligation, for example, one's relationship with

one's neighbor. Christ's first commandment "Love God and love your neighbor" often becomes the last, buried deep under subconscious motivations to maintain the childish relationship one has established with God.

6. Immediate recourse to authority often means blind recourse to external rules, not to a personal hierarchy of values and self-chosen rules to live by.

7. When one is convinced of having such a direct connection to God, close-mindedness follows with all the bigotry, narrow-mindedness, and prejudice that religion has been famous for over the centuries.

An additional argument for religion's presence in morality is its involvement in issues of sin and guilt. We have seen in an earlier chapter how religion is a way of handling guilt. Religions have a long tradition of not only causing guilt, but of promising to relieve it not only through a personal conversion of being "born again," but through a ritual absolution. Confession and absolution are built on the assumption that religious authorities, like judicial authorities, are to be involved in moral judgments, serving as channels of forgiveness.

Even closer to the core of the human psyche is the habit, natural or taught, of "turning to God for forgiveness."

2. Nothing: Religion has Nothing to do with Morality

An answer to the question of what religion has to do with morality that is opposite to our first answer "Everything" is the answer "Nothing." For some this is the most authentic solution to the problem. In some cases it is a reaction to the popular theistic view outlined in the previous section. Some see religious people as not being especially moral, and in some cases even less moral than those who claim there is no God; or, if there is one, then they claim that he has no concern with morality. Sometimes this reaction to a morality dominated by an immature kind of religiosity is: "If that's religion, who wants it? It's immature, working on extrinsic rewards and punishment. I think I can be a good person without religion, thank you."

At a more scientific level, some social scientists see religion as useless or even harmful in giving us moral norms. At the most, some social scientists would say that religion is just one more manifestation of social consensus: what people in general believe to be moral. Religious organizations have about as much validity in setting moral direction as any other organization that gives guidelines for behavior by gathering together and expressing people's opinions of what is right and wrong. If utilitarianism is the norm for moral rightness, then if what religion proposes as guides to good living actually do help us to live together better, religion is merely another channel by which we can know society's expectations. The social scientists also come up with evidence that seems to support the popular rejection of religion as something that is not helpful for encouraging good moral behavior and is perhaps even harmful. Research has indicated a positive correlation between religiosity and prejudice, between religiosity and lack of social concern. Rokeach (1960, 1969), for example, has found a positive relationship between orthodoxy of religious beliefs and lack of social concern in the content of Sunday sermons. However, it should be remembered that, as true sociologists, these researchers are often measuring religiosity largely in terms of amount of church attendance, frequency of Bible reading, and so on. These quantitative measures do not always express true religion. Religion is a much more profound concept than can be measured in quantity of church attendance (compare our section on social scientists' definitions of religion).

3. Religion is "Nothing But" Morality

A third way of answering the question: What does religion have to do with morality? is what we might call the "nothing but" approach. This approach says religion and morality are the same thing. Proponents claim that religion is morality, and this approach begins with an interpretation of what religion is in terms closely akin to Tillich's definition of faith as "The state of being ultimately concerned." According to Tillich, whatever your ultimate concern is, that is your religion, whether it be the service of God, making as much money as possible, or having as much personal pleasure as possible. Any ultimate concern is the final goal of living, and even though it might be something as low-level as personal wealth or power, this doesn't make it any less possessive of the person's energies and the ultimate in his life than the place religion holds.

Those who maintain that religion is morality would pride themselves on not stooping to lower-level ultimate concerns. Their concerns are social justice, equality for all, universal brotherhood, and ridding the world of injustice, none of which we can quarrel with as good and highly moral aims. But the proponents of this concept of religion would say that the battle against social problems and the moral crusade or revolution they mount to overcome them is itself the essence of religion. Although often commendable in itself, this view narrows the concept of religion too much.

4. Religion and Morality are Complementary

The fourth and most satisfactory answer to our question is that religion does have much to do with morality because, even though the two may be considered separate entities, they are complementary; they complete each other. But just how do they do this? There's the question.

To strike a balance on this question we can compare two common approaches to the issue of religion's role in teaching morals. We have seen one approach in answer 2: "No need of religion, thank you; I can figure it out for myself." It is true that one may get at ethical truths by some rational process, without resorting to formal religion or revelation. In reality most of us acquire much of our morals from simply observing the lives of good people. The praxis of good people, struggling for right living, is in itself a moral example. The lived experience of good, ordinary people has much to contribute to religious organizations themselves, if they too search for the right way to live and are open to learn. Much of what religions teach about morals comes from the experience of living; even the Ten Commandments were the Hebrews' version of the code of Hamurrabi, a secular set of laws for which the Jewish people claimed divine authority by giving them a theistic source.

Some individuals, on the other hand, mistrust themselves. "Who am I to know moral truth? I need someone in authority to tell me what to do." This is the dependent response. In the past the moral practice of religious people leaned heavily on this dependent approach, replacing the voice of one's own conscience with the voice of authority. We realize today, however, that this approach loses much. It loses (a) the autonomy of the individual and (b) the contribution to moral discernment that individuals make to religions. The teaching of a church should not replace conscience, but *enlighten* it.

The ideal conscience is not childishly dependent, nor is it individualistic, cut off from the experience of the human race over centuries. Conscience is not a matter of deciding by ourselves what is right and wrong. As members of a community we have a rich resource to draw on, a community of experience, reflection, and memory.

Now all this moral wisdom is too vast to be comprehended by individuals, so it comes down to us in articulated form. An ordinary individual is not so intelligent, not so wise, not so exquisitely emotionally attuned that he or she can attain a fine sense or moral "oughtness." (Later, in the chapter on oughtness, we will see how every life is itself a kind of moral perspective.) Thus some who have a broader horizon, a deeper appreciation of the issues and sensitivity to the human condition, are needed to articulate morality. This articulation, this designing of grand principles, this "justice tempered with mercy" is, it seems, the special quality of some people we can identify as "enlightened spiritual teachers."

Enlightened Spiritual Teachers

This is delicate issue. We are edging back toward the idea of authority when we talk about moral teachers. The idea of a moral authority is a touchy one. *Authority* can connote two things: power *over,* to rule and even dominate. We do not want the "thought police" envisioned by George Orwell for 1984. Nor do we want absolute authorities who demand unquestioning conformity. But authority can also mean power *to,* power to guide, to encourage, to draw out, to enlighten, to share wisdom and experience—to teach. Some people's lives have taken the high moral ground marked by authenticity (Hague, 1989, 1993b, 1994). We need this kind of teaching from this kind of authority. To begin with, children need to be taught morals by parents and teachers who have a broader horizon than the egocentric child. We all need men and women who are moral authorities in this sense. We look for it not only in the words they speak and write, but in the lives they live. They do not force; they gently attract. They do not blind; they enlighten. Their province is usually not only the home or even the classroom; it is the world. Fortunately, history has had a regular sprinkling of these men and women, most recently in people like Lincoln, Gandhi, Albert Schweitzer, Eleanor Roosevelt, Archbishop Romero, Martin Luther King, Jean Vanier, and Mother Teresa of Calcutta. These are known and famous moral exemplars, none of them perfect. They are human; there are flaws in their lives, but they stand out as significant moral beacons.

But let us not forget the little known and certainly not famous ordinary people who live by principle and touch our lives gently from nearby. How many of us can look back on a handful of "unfamous" people who, by what they were, taught us quietly what it is to be an authentically moral human being? In a world of warmongers, crooks, and phoney celebrities they stand out as beacons on the way. They have significance for us. We will see more of this idea of "moral significance" in chapter 10. In chapter, 11 on the sources of moral objectivity, we will explore deeper into the psychological depths of these moral teachers great and small. For now, for purposes of tying religion and morality together as complementary, let's look at how religion and morality come together in some eminent people.

This phrase *enlightened spiritual teacher* is an important one, deserving a word-by-word explanation:

1. *Enlightened*—by this I do not mean merely converted, born again, or even the recipient of visions or mystical experiences. By this I mean the person who has reached high levels of consciousness including not only learning but authenticity, autonomy, empathy. In other words, they are highly integrated people—perhaps after the manner Dabrowski described it.

2. *Spiritual*—Why spiritual? Precisely for the reason that is the essence of this book and one of its major themes: that the fully developed human person is of necessity a spiritually developed person. High levels of human development give fuller consciousness, insight into self and others, perspective, wisdom, articulated values, which, as we have seen, are the essence of spirituality including spirituality expressed in institutional religion at higher levels.

3. *Teacher*—Somehow this eminent person must convey his or her insights and perspective to others in terms intellectually understandable, emotionally moving, and intensely motivational. Attempts through the abstractions of philosophy or just more statements of rules most often fail. The great religious teachers have been those who have used the language of poetry, metaphors, and parables to teach. They touch others in their head and heart; they touch others in

their lives. Moreover, these teachers have underlined these words with the lives they have lived, and in some cases with the death they have gone to because of their lives.

Religion and morality, then, come together best and complement each other at the highest levels of human development. Their complementarity comes from the mystical, speculative, contemplative, interior qualities of religion that readily merge with its opposites, the concrete, practical, social, active qualities of morality. Religion has much to do with morality, as these qualities flow from one to the other in individuals at high levels of development, and flow in a religiously moral society, guided by these eminent individuals.

It might seem at first glance that with this fourth answer to the question: What does religion have to do with morality? we are back full circle to our first answer which was "Everything." But our first answer relied heavily on authority; this fourth answer is saying in effect that for the majority of people the source of their moral principles is authority outside of themselves—not a dominating authority, but a teacher who has reached higher levels of development. There are vast differences between answer 4 and answer 1. Answer 1, when we take it in the sense of religion as a theistic institution, rests all its authority on God, who determines the rightness and wrongness of things. It is the task of theologians, priests, ministers, and witch doctors to know the mind of God or the gods and convey this to their disciples. The sources of these rules are found in holy writings, personal revelations, omens, and the traditions of the people. The authority, the source of oughtness, clearly rests somewhere outside the teacher. He usually admits he is merely the conveyor of laws revealed to him by some divine source. Answer 4, that morality flows from human individuals who have reached high levels of development, is no less religious, even though it has a human source, nor need it be any less theistic. The highly developed human being who by that fact is a profoundly religious person may well have a religion that is thoroughly theistic. There usually would be a God in his or her life, and that God would be imaged as a person. It is only reasonable to conclude that the more an individual develops the capacity for deep interpersonal relationships, the more likely he or she is to find an interpersonal relationship with God. Once again our problem is that when we talk about God as a person we begin to have images of the old man in the white robe with the long flowing beard, because that is the person image many of us have been accustomed to, in the Christian tradition at least. Christ told us something about the personhood of God His Father and how to relate to Him. It is no mere accident that the Gospel that gives the highest-level account of that witness, the Gospel of John, is profoundly mystical in its concept of person. John says, by way of introduction: "In the beginning was the Word, and the Word was with God, and the Word was God." God, then, is the "Word" or, later, "God is love." These are dreamy, abstract, mystical words, and at first glance they do not seem to introduce us to a person. But perhaps that conclusion comes only from our limited concept of "person." We need a broader, deeper meaning of person, and that is what our most highly developed human persons have. They help us create our own individual per-sona for God—the mask through which God the mystery enters by word and spirit-breath into our lives.

Chapter 9

Theories of Justification

I could not but feel with a sympathy full of regret all the pain that I saw around me, not only that of men but that of the whole creation. From this community of suffering I have never tried to withdraw myself. It seemed to me a matter of course that we should all take our share of the burden of pain that is upon the world.
—*Albert Schweitzer* (My Life and Thought)

How do we know something is valuable? As we have seen, the concept of value contains within itself the notion of worthwhileness, valence. But how do we know something is worthwhile? More acutely: The concept of *moral* as a subset of value contains within itself the notion of "ought"—a special kind of valence that tells us how we ought or ought not to behave. "Ought-ness" is a special presence within an idea that points a finger of obligation at us. Facts are facts, but moral rules are imperatives to action. That our friend is drowning is a fact that, by itself, we can consider quite speculatively. That we perhaps ought to dive into the river to save him is a moral obligation with practical consequences. The moral philosopher Max Scheler expressed it in these terms:

> a finger pointing toward me from the depths of this value, as if it were whispering "for you." The specific content of this individual value assigns me a unique place in the ethical cosmos and it commands also the performance of actions, deeds and works, all of them crying out "I am for you" and "You are for me." (1927, p. 510)

Two questions arise when we look at the topic of moral obligation. The first is practical and immediate: What are our moral obligations? The second, although less immediate, is still practical. How do we know what our moral obligations are; what means do we use for getting at oughtness? Philosophers, theologians, and social scientists have discussed this question for centuries, and we certainly are not going to solve it here, but perhaps we can get a little closer to the truth; and the best way of doing this is first to review some of the classical theories of justification.

Naturalism

It seems quite logical to assume that if we know the nature of things, then we can logically conclude to how we ought to behave toward them. It has often been argued, for example, that if we had a clear understanding of the nature of man, then it would be clear just how men ought to live. By way of a further example, if we thought of man primarily as a rational animal, then those behaviors that show rationality in its highest degree would be moral. We need only make the logical conclusion. Likewise, if we conclude that man is essentially a social animal, then those things that help him get along well in society are the things that are logically moral. Because he is social, he ought to act in a way that enhances this.

The trouble with naturalism is twofold: first, there is a great deal of difficulty involved in getting to know the "true" nature of things, and still more difficulty in getting people to agree on it, particularly on such a complex thing as human nature. The second trouble with naturalism is summed up in what is called the *naturalistic fallacy*. It revolves around the question of just how one makes the transition from *is* to *ought* in such a logical way; in stressing the nature of things, naturalism makes too tight a connection with the moral conclusions that "follow" from that nature. All too easily, some philosophers (following Hume) note, our words slide from talking about the way things are to the way we must behave toward them; all too easily our concept of the nature of things drifts into conclusions about their goodness or badness. Critics of naturalism point out that the *ought* argument seems to creep in from nowhere and they question its validity. "Each person has life as part of their human nature; therefore, we ought to preserve that life" has an immediate and seemingly logical appeal, and indeed this argument is probably enough for most to induce them to behave properly. However, if we stick with logic alone, the conclusion does not follow. Over and above the argument that *ought* does not proceed logically from *is* are the difficulties referred to earlier in determining the nature of things, and beyond that the difficulties involved in interpreting the moral circumstances. How about the argument: Every rattlesnake has life as part of its nature; therefore, I ought to do everything to preserve the life of this rattlesnake rearing up its head and sticking out its tongue at me?

Naturalism makes every effort possible to preserve the objectivity of moral reasoning; it seeks a firm, objective basis for morality in the "unchanging" nature of things. For example, naturalism is a seemingly firm basis for denouncing war and slavery as exploitations of human beings by other humans, and it maintains that because all humans have the same nature they are to be treated in the same way no matter what their nationality, color, creed, or social status. Naturalism appeals to logic and strives for objectivity; the main thing it neglects, besides its leap from *is* to *ought*, is to take into account the autonomy of the moral actor. We will look at *is* and *ought* again in the next chapter, and at objectivity in chapter 11.

Intuitionism

Intuitionism, on the other hand, does preserve the autonomy of ethics. Intuitionists deny that terms like *good* or *ought* represent qualities of the actual nature of things, and they deny that moral judgments can be inferred from generalizations. These two sweeping denials that seem to knock out both legs from under the naturalistic argument substitute something in their place. The intuitionist argument is that, in the end, the goodness of an activity or the rightness of a principle is a matter of "seeing" or grasping a quality or a relationship. Moral knowledge, then, is grounded on some kind of indubitable and self-evident propositions. Some intuitionists, following Plato, assume that terms like *good* stand for a special property of things that is grasped by a reflective mind. This goodness is not something discernible by the senses, but rather an inner quality that can be intuited only with an inner eye. Another brand of intuitionism maintains that moral principles flow with mathematical precision from the apprehension of basic forms composed of self-evident moral axioms. Certain moral principles could, like mathematical theorems, be logically deduced from these axioms. It was this philosophy, maintaining that certain moral axioms were evident and known intuitively, that formed the thinking behind the American Declaration of Independence, which maintains that such rights as life, liberty, and the pursuit of happiness are self-evident and inalienable rights.

Plato was among the first major philosophers to suggest intuition as the basis for moral knowledge, and, following Socrates, he made an immediate connection between knowledge and action. He took from Socrates the conviction that virtue is knowledge and that no one does what he knows to be evil. According to Socrates, knowing what is good led to doing good. If someone did not do good it could be put down to a defect in his knowledge. It is in this way that contemporary intuitionists explain the connection between the intuitive grasp of moral principles *in theory* and the effect they have on the knower (or intuiter) *in practice.*

Intuitionism, then, if you accept the immediate "seeing" of moral principles by the reflective mind, becomes a complete moral system beginning with sure moral knowledge and leading immediately to moral action. Moreover, it preserves the autonomy of the moral agent in a way that naturalism in its pursuit of objectivity could not. Unhappily, intuitionism seems to many to let go of objectivity. By preserving the individual's autonomy, it introduces the likelihood of arbitrariness. If truth is grasped in the form of nonnatural qualities and relations are seen by an inner eye, immediate problems arise as to various perspectives all those inner eyes may have. Perspectives will certainly vary from person to person and, even more importantly, the ability to intuit and the sensitivity of the intuiter will vary from person to person. Now intuitionists, Plato included, have always stressed that the fullest "seeing" is granted only to reflective people who think detachedly, clearly, and logically. Their intuition is the basis beyond which further reasoning is impossible. This leaves great masses of people without any immediate contact with moral principles because they are not equipped with the reflective disposition, the emotional detachment, and the cool logic required to intuit moral principles. They must then trust in the moral intuitions of an intellectual elite, with all the elite's claims to objectivity based usually on cool reason ultimately going back to nondemonstrable intuitions! The field is open for the "logic" of a few to lead the many astray in an arbitrariness under the guise of clear thinking. We could be back to the authority of an intellectual elite, the kind of moral domination we eschewed in the last chapter.

Emotivism

Contrasted with the intuitionists' claim to moral objectivity by the strength of their intellectual grasp and logical deductions is the *emotive* or voluntaristic school of thought. Emotivists generally make no claim to rational justification of moral principles. In fact they maintain that reason falls apart in the transition from *is* to *ought*. The philosopher Hume concluded that it was emotion that bridged the gap between *is* and *ought*. He argued, "when you pronounce any action or character to be vicious, you mean nothing, but that from the constitution of your nature you have a feeling or sentiment of blame from the contemplation of it" (*A Treatise of Human Nature,* Book III, Part I, Section I). *Good, bad, ought, ought not* are words explained purely in terms of the emotions they arouse. Following this tradition, Max Scheler (1927) has educed an intriguing theory of emotive ethics that stresses moral decision making as a highly personal emotional demand made on the will of the individual. More recently, Robert C. Solomon (1977) has tried to reinstate emotion into various aspects of human life, including moral judgment making. He attempts to answer one of the most acute criticisms of emotivism, that of sheer arbitrariness, by more clearly delineating what the emotions are.

That is perhaps the most telling criticism of emotivist ethics; that it opens the doorway to sheer subjectivity not only because it seems to say "Just let your feelings be your guide," but because it fails to help us understand our feelings. Emotivism certainly preserves the autonomy of morals but, in its popular interpretations without a full understanding of emotions, it seems to relinquish objectivity, putting down reason and replacing it with what has consistently been maintained as the ultimate of subjectivity—feeling. Hume himself did this when he said, "Morals excite passions and produce or prevent actions. Reason of itself is utterly impotent in this particular" (*A Treatise of Human Nature,* Book III, Part I, Section I).

Such a quote out of context does not do justice to Hume's ultimately more balanced view. He associated emotional reaction with the general view of the disinterested spectator who sees individual actions in the context of their suitableness or usefulness to the individual himself or to the society. In classifying moral emotions as "disinterested passions" that arise when one takes this more general view of impartiality, he put into this seemingly "pure" emotivism a cognitive rational core. Hume's emotional moralist was also expected to give reasons that came from his distanced general view if he was to make any claims to objectivity.

In the last analysis, perhaps the emotivist view suffers most when a superficial interpretation is given the word *emotion* when it is seen as something bereft of reason, or solely as something intense, overwhelming, and despotic in the power it has to select and influence the will. As we shall see, emotion belongs in a broader context, sometimes violent it is true, but often quiet, reflective, above all perceptive. A picture begins to emerge of emotion in collaboration with cognition, the two not being as separate as we tend to see them, but often with emotion having just that leading edge that helps it delve into the vitality of things. Emotion is often in the forefront of moral judgments so that it can be said: "The heart has reasons the mind knows nothing of." Or better, "Heart and mind together, hand in hand, can explore depths and soar to heights that alone they would know nothing of." Again, we will develop this further in the next chapters.

Revelation

Some would say that ethics does not belong in the philosophical domain at all, that it is a theological concern. Perhaps the most radical of these views on the sources of rightness or the moral order is the one that states that God is purely and simply the source of moral norms. He doesn't just tell us what is right and wrong through the scriptures and religious teachers. He is the source who decides what is right and wrong and then depends on his messengers to convey the norms of morality to human beings. In this stance God is seen as a medieval king, a dictator who makes things right or wrong by an act of His will. This view is summed up in an early American moralistic verse for children:

God is great.
God is good.
Always do what He thinks you should.

A more moderate revelation approach is to see God and his messengers as interpreters of an objective order of things. God doesn't make it wrong to kill another human; he knows it is wrong and reveals that to us. The Ten Commandments are the reflection by God of the right order of things as He above all knows.

The question of where the source of justification is once we take a religious or theological approach was addressed by Plato in the Euthyphro. There Socrates asks, "Is what is holy holy because the gods approve it, or do they approve it because it is holy?" Thomas Aquinas took the side of the more moderate revelation approach in maintaining certain actions are wrong, not because God disapproves of them, but divinely prohibited because they are wrong in themselves.

If you accept the second approach, that some things are right or wrong in themselves, then the question arises: What need do we have of religion or of God and his revelation? Could we not just get at morality without religion? This is a hotly debated issue. William K. Frankena addresses it clearly in his contribution to Outka and Reeder's collection of essays on the topic entitled *Religion and Morality* (1973). Frankena gives the title "Is morality logically dependent on religion" to his essay (pp. 295ff) and stresses the word *logically,* noting (p. 296) that morality's dependence on religion can be considered as a causal or historical connection, enunciating that religion has over millennia had a de facto say in what mankind has considered to be moral or immoral. Frankena also points out that morality may be motivationally or psychologically dependent on religion. But faced with the immediate question, is there a *logical* connection between religion and morality, Frankena is hard pressed to find any within the boundaries he has set for himself in his understanding of religion. And this is important. Frankena is limiting his argument to a concept of religion taken in the theistic sense: the sense that religion is a system centered on the existence of a special being known as God. He maintains that if we take religion in a much broader sense, as do theologians such as Tillich and Reinhold Niebuhr, as a search for answers to questions of ultimate meaning without necessarily being theistic, then one can conclude that religion does have a logical connection with morality. Religion in this broad sense is in essence a system of values, and indeed a search for ultimate values. But, keeping to his theistic definition of religion, the only plausible logical connection he can see between religion and morality is contained in the proposition that if God is love, then we ought to love. On this important point, Frankena's own words are:

> Suppose again that one has a sincere belief in or convincing experience of God as love and vividly realizes what this means as Bergson's mystics do. Must he not take the "law of love" as his guiding principle in life, and regard it as entirely reasonable that he should do so? (1973, p. 316)

He goes on to say that religious beliefs and experiences do suffice to justify this and perhaps other ethical principles, at least for those who hold them. But he maintains that, though these religious beliefs and experiences are sufficient to support logical moral conclusions, they are not *necessary* for these moral conclusions; one could arrive at them by an entirely nonreligious, logical route.

In the preceding pages we have looked at the problem of the sources of morality, the sources of oughtness, as a philosopher would in the domain that philosophers call axiology, the theory of value. Axiology is concerned with the nature, criteria, and metaphysical status of value. We have merely traced an outline of axiology by considering some of the classical theories of justification that go back to Plato's "Ideas of the Good" and were expressed in Thomas Aquinas's attempt to build on Aristotle's identification of the highest value as having its cause in God as the source of all good. Clearly there is no one philosophical answer to the question: How do we know what is moral? We have seen that religion has, at least historically, had much to do with morality, and because this is a study of religion and morality the connection between the two has been explored in chapter 8. Because it is also a book on the psychological development of religion and morality, we will look at another issue now from a psychological point of view, remembering that psychology has something to say not just about the teaching of morality or moral persuasion and motivation, but about the sources of moral oughtness and moral objectivity.

Chapter 10

In the Full Current of Life: Character

Talent develops in quiet places, character in the full current of human life.

—Johann von Goethe

Sow an act, and you reap a habit. Sow a habit and you reap a character. Sow a character and you reap a destiny.

—Charles Reade

What is character but the determination of incident?
What is incident, but the illustration of character?

—Henry James

I have a dream that my four little children will one day live in a nation where they will not be judged by the color of their skin, but by the content of their character.

—Martin Luther King

In the last chapter I used an old-fashioned and somewhat stodgy term *theories of justification* to get at a basic philosophical question: Where are the wellsprings of morality? Where does ought come from? Philosophers are worried about how easily we can slip from talking about how things are to how they ought to be as though it were just one consistent rational statement. "This country has always been ours, so we ought not let those foreigners in." In our minds we can make a passage from a statement of fact to a statement of obligation without even knowing it. It is called the is-ought problem. In a later chapter (13), which is about models of moral education, we will again come back to character from various angles as we explore several approaches to "character education." In this chapter I would like to take up these themes, exploring them under the developmental, psychological paradigm as *movement* from is to ought.

From *Is* to *Ought*

I am going to stretch a point by putting a philosophers' phrase in a developmental context. As a psychologist, I would like to look at the is-ought question not so much as a philosophical, abstract problem, but as a psychological challenge to trace the course of how a human being in the process of development makes a personal transition from is to ought—from merely seeing things as they are to conceiving how they ought to be, and beyond that to *making* things (self included) what they ought to be. That is the course of full moral development. And that is a brief summary of this chapter.

As we have seen in chapter 7, morality is usually expressed (like the Ten Commandments) as rules or norms of behavior in terms of *should* or *ought*. A certain obligation to behave in a particular way is imposed by such *ought* statements. Philosophers have speculated for centuries on the source of this moral obligation. Why *must* we behave in certain ways? Why are we *obliged* to follow certain rules? One can give quick answers: "Because that makes society work better"; "God wants it that way"; "It keeps you out of trouble with the law"; and so forth. We looked at these issues in the previous chapter. Now we dig in behind all these helpful but not completely satisfactory replies for an answer to the deep-down question: Why be moral? Where do these obligations come from, and why is it imperative that I take them on?

Obligation

Somewhere along the line most of us have accepted some oughts in our lives and made them part of ourselves. As children we learned about the real world, and with it accepted certain obligations: "Don't cross the street alone." How does an individual make this passage from *is* to *ought*, from simply seeing things as they are (and, lacking any sense of obligation, possibly deciding just to leave them that way) to feeling a personal sense of moral obligation—a sense of should or ought?

As we have seen, philosophers have debated the is-ought problem. They have long argued how we get from the *isness* of things (their essence and their existence) to the obligations that go with them. For example, how does driving a car impose certain obligations on me to behave responsibly with it? This is a car; among its many potentials is the possibility to cause death and destruction. I ought not use it for such purposes. The obligation seems so obvious: I don't want to kill anybody. But what if somebody asks "Why not?" To reply "Because it's wrong" begs the question. Morality involves a moving beyond what merely *is* to conceiving how things *ought* to be and behaving accordingly. Morality arises somewhere in that hinterland between is and ought. Morality begins when we cross from is to ought. But we are not necessarily in the moral realm just because we use the word *ought*. It is not, like an international border, "a line drawn in the sand," one step taking you over from is to ought. This struck me one day at a gas station. A talkative gas jockey said, "You ought to wash your car." I heard him use the ought word but I felt no *moral* obligation, in fact no obligation at all; it was simply a good idea; I could take it or leave it. But if the police had stopped me and said, "You ought to slow down!" there would be some obligation. There are, in other words, degrees of obligation.

Ought is a Grey Zone

Consider the following: I ought to put a little more salt on the meat. I ought to tidy up my room. I ought to take my elbows off the table. I ought to take a shower. I ought to stop smoking. I ought to stop my drunken driving. The word *ought* appears in each statement, but the obligation comes from various sources—taste, custom, manners, concern for others, respect for myself, and my own life. The examples range from something that is clearly amoral (taste) to something eminently moral (the preservation of life). On the former we can give or take easily; on the latter we can feel a heavy obligation. How do we move from indifference and ignorance through concern to obligation? We can arrange these steps in order of their increasing moral obligation. The order goes something like this:

Ought in the sense of it would be nice if ... "You ought to wash your car."

Ought in the sense of it is customary or helpful to others—good manners. "Fork on the left, knife on the right."

Ought in the sense of the welfare of others and yourself demands it. "You ought to keep the speed limit!"

There is, I think, another highest sense of ought, but I'm saving it for later in this chapter. Three are enough for now.

The Passage from Is to Ought

If there are degrees or shades of oughtness, then perhaps there is a parallel developmental process of moving from the lowest level of not even being aware of or simply ignoring moral obligation to living a full moral life. The process that involves seeing the possibility of things being different and better would go something like this.

Step 1, *Stuckness,* without an appreciation of the *possibility* of things being different. Children are bundles of imagination and possibility, but some adults are not. Their sense of wonder has withered. Some cannot see or refuse to see even the possibility of change. "It's always been that way." There are no conceivable options. If I believe that I should have a gun always at hand on the truck gunrack, I may not even be able to imagine any other scenario. "Guns are just a part of life; read my bumper sticker. It says, 'Peace is having more guns than the other guy.'" Or "How could things be different? We've *always* done it this way." "Our family always respects its women, but we keep them in their place." "Women are just naturally given to cooking and cleaning; that's their place—at home with the kids." This kind of "realism" if it is to be shaken, calls for:

Step 2, the *creative ability* to *imagine* things different. "I wonder if my wife really does like staying home with the kids all the time; maybe she could have a break ... sometime." One can imagine that there are other ways of doing things. One wonders about alternatives—things as they *could* be. This is not always easy, and it may end in only a dream verging on a wish. But if the *possibility of change* is established, one can move on to:

Step 3, the *desirability* of change. "It would be good if ..." leading on to (in what is usually a big jump):

Step 4, the *necessity* (oughtness) of change in the vision of things as they *should* be. "I ought to take the kids on my days off." This is the basic moral vision that most of us share. Sometimes it stops right there without any action. It ends in a mere velleity. "I ought to stop smoking, but ..." It is not morality because there is no action. But there is in it the possibility of an essential step beyond that makes it incipiently moral.

Step 5, Actually going beyond the hypothetical and *acting* on the moral incentive, maybe even just once—taking care of the kids, for example. But there is a step beyond:

Step 6, The last step is to make the obligation a *consistent theme* in one's life. Some (all too few) realize their moral obligations consistently in their own lives. If one does consistently act on moral obligations, things then actually are what they ought to be. What is *is,* what ought to be—the ideal—is achieved quite *consistently.* The kids are a shared responsibility; gradually more and more responsibilities are shared in a relationship of true partnership. Consistent moral behavior is diffusive. It spreads to those who see it and benefit from it. The children themselves have no difficulty imagining a cooperative life and envisioning a similar future for themselves. The circle of repeating "what we have always done" is broken. A careful respect for one another and for community in all its forms is the lived theme.

Steps 4 and 5 involve a double ought—4 the acceptance of an *ontological* oughtness (Things ought to be different), and 5 the psychological grasping and acceptance of a *personal* obligation to make them so. (I ought to make myself and my world better). Figure 10.1 is a schematic outline of this movement from mere realism to ideals achieved. This schema introduces some ideas (like authentism) that we haven't yet looked at so far in this chapter, but they will come in the following pages.

Before going on, it might be helpful to indicate that this schema parallels Dabrowski's levels in the theory of Positive Disintegration, and to give a note on what I mean by *Horizon of Significance,* which comes from a different and perhaps not well-known source. Horizon of significance is a philosophical term with foundations in existentialism. It is borrowed from Charles Taylor (1989, 1991).

If you were an early explorer like David Thompson in Western Canada, you would spend much of your life traveling across the open prairies where the sky is like a great blue dome above, and the prairie a vast unobstructed circle around you. As you trekked across the open prairie, you would look for features that give you guidance, a sense of direction—a small hill here, a coulee there, maybe even a snowcapped mountain just peeking over the horizon. These features would give you bearings to set the direction of your

Lives lived by:	Horizon of Significance	Predominant Virtues
1. What is ...	Things simply as they are	Range from complacency to threshold of realism
2. What can be— the promise of possibilities	Things as they might be To see what might be	Imagination, wonder, creativity
3. What ought to be— To *have* a perspective	Things *seen* as they should be—moral oughtness	Idealism realized through courage and authenticity
4. What should be actually is—To *be* a perspective	Things (including self) *are* what they should be	Morality of Authentism

Figure 10.1. The movement from is to ought.

journey. They would be significant landmarks on your horizon—especially significant if following them closely was a matter of life or death. One significant landmark we know David Thompson used was Mt. Edith Cavell near Jasper. This outstanding summit with its beautiful Angel Glacier was known in those days as *La Montagne de la Grande Traverse.* Fur traders paddling up the Athabaska River knew that in the shadow of this mountain they must turn into the valley of the Whirlpool River to find a gentle pass over the Great Divide and into the Columbia Basin. The mountain had great significance for their journey.

The analogy with finding one's moral way follows closely. In the parameters of our individual lives many features appear. Some are trivial; following them would indeed be a "Trivial Pursuit." Some may *seem* significant but do not have real significance. Some within our horizon are in themselves significant, the major signposts and passages of life: our beliefs, our attitudes, our home, friends, education, relationships, marriage partner—these are signposts of significance in our ever-changing individual horizon. They signify values, and they mature into our accepted values, becoming when we choose them the stars by which we steer our lives. They not only *are* in our lives, but in some cases signify how for us things *ought* to be. What is significant for us (and hopefully of significance in itself) determines the level of our moral appreciation and whether we let that appreciation actually influence our lives.

Morality, as we have seen, involves a shift from what merely *is* to how things *ought* to be in the full sense of obligation. We have seen above that this requires, most basically, an appreciation by the individual (and society in turn) of the *possibility* of things being different, followed by the *creative ability* to imagine them different. Some people aren't very good at seeing possibilities; they don't see much beyond what is and are content to leave things as they are. But when the possibility of change is established, one can move on to the desirability and even *necessity* (oughtness) of change in the vision of things as they should be. This is the moral vision we can have. Most of us share this vision and abide by it in society.

Authenticity and the High Moral Ground

Some people have not only this common sense of moral oughtness, but are driven to realize it in their own lives, and as much as they can in the realities of life around them. They make this moral sense a theme of their lives. It gives their moral development a direction. At the highest levels of this oughtness, things in this vision *are* what they ought to be. These people are not just idealists in theory, but they shape themselves so that ideals are achieved in their own lives. The real and the ideal are one.

We are edging closer and closer to the word *authenticity* as key to understanding the sense of oughtness at all levels of development, but particularly at its highest levels. It will come in again in the next chapter when we see the role of authenticity in striving for what is generally called an "objective" morality. Some defining of this word would help here: Authenticity can simply be "The state of being what you *seem* to be." The real core of the person corresponds with appearances. If we see authenticity as "living in intimate communion with one's true identity as both a being and a process of becoming" (Gruba-McAllister & Levington 1994, p. 2), the process itself is a step beyond authenticity, for then authentic morality is not a willy-nilly, ad hoc adaptation to the moral problems of life, but a pervasive theme to living. Authenticity leads to what Dabrowski called "authentism"— a life pattern (Hague, 1994).

Integration of the Moral Self

If a strong sense of ought identifies the moral self, the ideal moral self is the self as one *should* be—integral, whole, healthy, having all essential human qualities. The dimensions are intra- and extrapersonal. In chapter 4, we saw how Gordon Allport described the most highly developed people as mature, and we moved on from the word *maturity* to a more contemporary appreciation that men and women at the higher levels of development are more appropriately described as integrated, or better still integrating, because no one is perfect but always in process. Integration is a process, and integrity (or wholeness) is gained in varying degrees. Developmentalists choose to identify these as *levels*. These levels tend to ascend from heteronomy to autonomy, from egocentrism to solidarity with others. There is a call from self-centeredness to self-transcendence in the attraction to a moral ideal self. With the call there is a drivenness that comes not from compulsion or addiction, but from the desire to be my *best* self in the span of the opportunities I have as a unique occasion in space and time. One sees one's life span as one's "moment" in the vast panoply of time. The task is to make the most of this moment by making it most valuable—a contribution to the building of the universe, to bringing a beneficent pattern out of chaos—to participate in

---

Authenticity. To be what one seems to be. General consistency between real self and self concept (or at least between real self and image deliberately projected). Sometimes inconsistent and far from ideal but the person knows, desires and strives for ideals as goals.

Authentism. The enactment of what one believes—a hierarchy of values in action. Action is consistent with self. Consistency with hierarchy of values—ideal realized. The ideal has become the real.

Four characteristics of authentism:

1. Confidence of going the right way toward the realization of one's own personality ideal.

2. Universality of inner growth which means that all aspects of personality are being developed.

3. Awareness of one's uniqueness.

4. Having arrived at a solution of the relation of "I" and "Thou" based on uniqueness and unrepeatability of individual traits, and of a commonality of highly developed qualities (e.g., empathy, compare Dabrowski, 1970, p. 78).

Consistency within the self and consistency of life pattern seem to be the major motifs.

Figure 10.2. Authenticity and authentism.

the creative work of chaos itself. This participation in the story of the universe is the ultimate moral action, penetrating the self, and can pervade a lifetime.

Self-esteem

Self is found in context. The figure of self emerges from ground, from the context of one's life, the horizon of significance. Reflection opens the door to seeing oneself in the context of space and time. One's self-concept and self-esteem are involved in how well one carries through this moral partici-pation. The ground is there in contrast to self. The ground is context, highlighted with value to give significant bearings for a life journey, some-thing against which we measure ourself and evaluate the self. The moral environment is community. If one truly "finds oneself," it is in relationships. We live in a web of interconnectedness that is not just context, but part of the self. The relationships are human but, as we are discovering more and more, include environment taken literally in its ecological sense. I am me only in systems—systems of human relationships, in ecosystems too. In Taylor's (1989) terminology, such a ground is the *Horizon of Significance.* Taylor sums up the self and morality issue, when he says:

> Being a self is inseparable from existing in a space of moral issues, to do with identity and how one ought to be. It is being able to find one's standpoint, being able to occupy, to *be* a perspective in it. (1989, p. 112)

That's a novel and important idea: to *be* a perspective, not just to *have* but to *be* a perspective. It seems to imply an active role in shaping morality not just for ourselves, but in some kind of objectifying context. It is to influence morality as such by what we as humans have to offer to help bring order and design out of chaos. Some individuals (like Gandhi, or Mother Teresa currently) are acknowledged moral perspectives. They are exemplary, moral models. They set the standards by their words and lives lived in authenticity. Yet, in lesser or greater degrees, for good or for bad, we are all perspectives for one another, and if we are self-reflective, perspectives for ourselves. It is our choice. Perhaps moral objectivity is realized only when we are authentic perspectives. Objectivity, as we will see in the next chapter, is, according to Lonergan, the fruit of authentic subjectivity.

The Ethic of Authenticity

Charles Taylor (1988, 1989, 1991) proffers the "Ethic of Authenticity" in his book, *The Malaise of Modernity* (1991). He situates the ethic in the current context of postmodernism.

The ethic of authenticity is, he claims, something relatively new and peculiar to our culture. Other eras have touted social conformity or rationality more. Currently we look for the sources of morality within ourselves more than in law. Intuitive feeling for right and wrong has been placed in competition with traditional ways of making moral decisions based on the consequences of moral behavior, especially those approaches that religion would describe as "divine retribution." The ethic of authenticity insists that the sources of goodness and morality are deep within us. It has its roots in the common conviction that each of us has an original way of being human. Consequently, fidelity to self is important. Being true to myself is being true to my own originality; that is something only I can discover and articulate. However, this credo has been known to lead to narcissism and an individualistic idealism. "I do my thing and you do yours." Paradoxically, this "self-fulfillment" can be self-defeating if it ignores our ties with others or limits itself to narcissistic desires. It can, neglecting traditional wisdom, lead to moral subjectivity in its worst sense. But there are moral signposts that, like highway markers, are valuable for their significance, which is to give clear direction. But, Taylor maintains, there is another significance: There is a special significance in giving shape to one's own life. This we call autonomy. But, even if I get my sense of the significance of my life from it being self-chosen, this depends on an understanding that this must be done in a broader context of responsibility for society. Rather than a narrow individualism, Taylor proposes a healthy autonomy that not only concentrates on individual freedom, but goes beyond to propose models of society. Individualism as a moral principle or ideal must offer some view of how the individual should live with others. Recognizing differences requires a *shared* horizon of significance, If contemporary thinking (including contemporary psychological theories of development) centers fulfillment only on the individual, relationships become purely instrumental, neglecting the demands coming from beyond one's own desires.

Taylor says (1991, p. 73), "The struggle ought not to be *over* authenticity, for or against, but *about* it, defining its proper meaning. We ought to be trying to lift the culture back up, closer to its motivating ideal." And later, "I can find fulfillment in God, or a political cause, or tending the earth. Indeed, the argument above suggests that we will find genuine fulfillment only in something like this, which has significance independent of us or our desires" (p. 82).

I have given considerable attention to Charles Taylor on this point of putting oneself in a moral perspective not only for the intrinsic value of what he says, but because what he has to say clarifies notions of contemporary moral culture and supports values such as autonomy and authenticity. This helps us see the kind of growth possible not just as personal, but as moral development. It helps us to see the danger of fragmentation of individualism; the solution is people forming a common purpose and actually living it out.

Character: To Be a Perspective

In chapter 13 we will look at the renewed interest of moral educators in character education (Lickona, 1991). Here I would like to propose a special meaning for character, linking it to Taylor's idea of *being* a perspective and thereby taking an active role in *creating* morality—not simply accepting rules, not even just acting morally, not simply teaching morality or even exemplifying it, but *creating* morality in the ongoing process of our lives within a universe context.

One day I put a dilemma to my undergraduate class in religious and moral development, concocting a scenario where it would be safe for any one of them to steal an expensive gold watch from a department store. I asked them why they would not steal the watch. Many reasons were given by the students, such as "I still might get caught" or "It's the property of the store." Then one girl said, "I wouldn't steal it because that would not be me." That answer, serene and simple, would not get her points in a Kohlberg-scored dilemma as the other answers would, but it does speak of character and self-respect. Perhaps ultimately we behave morally out of respect for what we are, a perspective even to ourselves. At higher levels than circumscribed by guilt or social obligation, we take on moral obligation out of respect for our own integrity.

Conscience at its core, then, is one's reading of one's own objective worthwhileness. "I wouldn't steal because that isn't me, that is, the 'me' I respect." This is authenticity because it employs an objective reading of self and contrasts that real self with personality ideal, leading to the intention to close the gap between the two.

We have come, then, to the last stage of development of a moral sense—a sense of oughtness to be added to the process outlined at the beginning of this chapter. It is ought in the sense of "It is truly significant not only for one's feelings of self-worth, but for one's objective, real self-worth, because it encompasses not only one's responsibility to society, but one's integrity, wholeness, within relationships that are not mere context, but the very fiber of oneself."

Chapter 11

True Values, Right Action

---

*One cannot conceive of objectivity without subjectivity. Neither can exist without the other nor can they be dichotomized ....
Neither objectivism nor subjectivism, nor yet psychologism is propounded here, but rather subjectivity and objectivity in constant relationship.*

> —*Paulo Freire* (Pedagogy of the Oppressed)

Between the subject and the object lies the value.

> —*Robert Pirsig*

*Objectivity is a matter of seeing just what there is to be seen.
Objectivity is the fruit of authentic subjectivity*

> —*Bernard Lonergan*

We live in a time of an important shift in thinking about morals. In recent times psychology has been concerned with being *objective,* seeing "things as they are." However, we are increasingly aware that the human mind itself has an influence on what we perceive. Some postmodernists would even go so far as to say that there is no objective reality; the only morality is that which we create *subjectively.* The way we think about this issue of objectivity and subjectivity has important implications for how we live. This chapter is an attempt to look at the question in a balanced way.

The Importance of Objectivity

People from all directions and varying persuasions claim that they have a set of values, some of them moral values, that others should adhere to because they are "true," "objective," "the proper" values, and it is evident to them that if only other people would accept their values, the world would be a happier place. There would be more peace, less crime, more justice, or more souls saved. No wonder we are confused; sometimes these so-called objective values are in opposition to each other; frequently they come to us clothed in language that is persuasive yet obscure, language that is grossly manipulative yet subtly elusive. We desperately want to know, when faced with a variety of moral alternatives, which one is the *right* one? In our grasping for moral straws often we seem to get only a handful of water.

This chapter is shaped something like this:

1. It is the whole person, "head and heart," that makes decisions about right and wrong.
2. Feelings are primary in valuing, including moral valuing; when we value we feel attracted to something.
3. It is foolish to make, as some philosophers do, a dichotomy out of subjectivity and objectivity. So-called objectivity is a kind of subjectivity.
4. The question then becomes: What kind of subjectivity produces objectivity?
5. The answer is *authentic* subjectivity.
6. The next question is: What is authentic subjectivity?
7. The last question is: Does all of this really matter?
8. The answer (of course) is: Yes.

Some sociologists such as Durkheim have placed the source of value objectivity in the consensus of society. Social consensus, in Durkheim's view, dictates the norms of behavior. Society is the source of objective values. But society images a confusion of values, and those who try to speak about value run into problems of language. Roberts (1981) points out how the individual can be engulfed by his society:

> Language is paradoxical. On the one hand it represents the medium for the expression of a person's self as an authentic being-in-the world, whereas on the other it represents the medium for engulfment of the person into the background of social conventionality. That is while man has the power of language to create and re-create his symbolic universe, he is at the same time paradoxically subject to the power of the creations of himself and others expressed through language ... while man presupposes the world which he creates and re-creates, he is also presupposed by the world which is created and re-created through the language of himself and others in society. How he acts in response to this dilemma created by language paradox is his expression of his personality, the level at which his self emerges as either authentic or conventional. (p. 78ff)

Some hope for a secure sense of "doing the right thing" by simply conforming to "what everyone's doing." But one who is under the sway of mere conventionality and is not acting authentically is not in touch with a personal core of objective, chosen values (Hague, 1990a, 1990b).

The Role of Affect

Feelings about feelings run high when some academics talk of values, especially moral values. They want to get rid of feelings that seem so out of control so they can be "objective." Yet again, paradoxically, it is feelings that are channels of value. In chapter 7 we saw how morals come from values and values are concepts of the desirable that attract our emotions. Emotions are important in valuing and in moralizing; so let's look first at affect.

People have searched for objective values as something "out there," outside oneself, existing in an objective order of things, and the predominant Western philosophy of how to get to this right order of things dates back to the Greeks and Romans. The answer for them was "Let reason be your guide." Not only did reason have, it seemed, the unerring tool of logic, it was, if properly established in the human psyche, capable of controlling that great enemy of pure reason and the source of all subjectivity, emotions. Traditional philosophy, which we have inherited from the Greeks, has dichotomized intellect and feeling. The claim was that they are opposites; if you have one, you exclude the other. You can't be objective if you are subjective. Psychology has picked up this distinction and put it in terms of cognition and affect and imposed it on descriptions of our psyche, giving the impression that it is made up of two parts, thinking and feeling, not only separate from each other, but in opposition to each other. However, the biological fact of the matter is that our human nervous system is not divided into two discrete systems—cognition and affect, intellect and emotion, thinking and feeling. We have one nervous system, yet for our own convenience in understanding what goes on in it, we have sometimes talked about it as if it were two separate systems. The dichotomy has so worked into the language of psychology that it seems to be a description of reality. We have assigned roles to these two children locked in the closet. Intellect was given the (male, dominant) role of guiding emotion, controlling feeling, lest emotion lead us astray. Psychology has given much greater attention to the cognitive not only because it was supposed to be much closer to "reality," but because it was much easier for behaviorists to measure and more respectable for a scientist to be concerned with than anything as amorphous as emotions (Hague, 1988a). Recently a more inclusive view is beginning to assert itself. One example is that of Joseph Chilton Pearce, author of *The Crack in the Cosmic Egg*. In his later book, *Evolution's End* (1992), Pearce points out that evolution has really given us three major neural systems, developed throughout evolutionary history: the reptilian, which is action-oriented; the old mammalian, which deals primarily with feeling; and the new mammalian, which specializes in thought. The three are designed to act as an integrated unit (pp. 42ff). Pearce distinguishes between *intellect* alone and *intelligence*, which employs all levels of the nervous system.

> Intellect involves the brain while intelligence involves the heart. Intellect may be likened to a "masculine" side of mind perhaps—analytical, logical, linear, inclined to science, technology, the search for external novelty and invention; while intelligence is more a "feminine" side, open to the intuitive and mysterious interior of life, seeking balance, restraint, wisdom, wholeness, and the continuity and well-being of our species and earth.

Each of us, male and female, embody both intellect and intelligence, of course, and the complementary nature of these two polarities is the creative tension between mind and heart, the very spark of life. Disaster befalls us, however, when we develop intellect but not intelligence, as we have done for generations now. The fundamental complementarity then goes awry, and the principle polarity of life falls into petty but deadly struggles between ego positions: personal, social, and eventually global. The dying social body we see today is the outer display of such an inner civil war ... Should intellect win its battle with heart's intelligence, the war will be lost for all of us. We will be just an experiment that failed, evolution's end on a negative note. (pp. xix-xx)

Not only is the partnership model of thinking and feeling more appropriate, but it takes into account the fact that valuing is primarily an affective process. We are drawn to choose a certain value because it is more attractive to us; we *like* it better. Ultimately it is a more holistic approach (Hague, 1988b).

Feelings and emotions help to tell us what is worthwhile, and they can be trusted. The Canadian philosopher-theologian Bernard Lonergan had this conviction; he saw the heart very much a part of moral action. According to Lonergan (1974), "The heart is what's beyond the understanding, experience and judgment of mind on the level of 'is this worthwhile?'" (p. 220). "Without feelings this experience, understanding, judgment is paper-thin. The whole mass and momentum of living is in feeling" (p. 221).

Symbolization and the Use of Language

Values are apprehended and symbolized (usually in language) before a judgment is made as to their worthwhileness. The apprehension and symbolization of value meanings is based on a process called *distanciation*, the increasing differentiation of a symbol situation. To put a fancy word in simple terms, distanciation as a psychological process is something like what you do when you are decorating a Christmas tree; every now and then, after working up close hanging ornaments, you step back to get the whole picture, and see if you like it. Some distance gives a more holistic, objective picture. But note: two things happen; you see the tree better, and you see if you *like* it. You see the tree in relationship to yourself, your own tastes, and ultimately your own values if you go on to reflect a bit. You evaluate, and you evaluate more objectively from a distance. During the Gulf War, Bette Midler came out with a song called "From a Distance." It was all about distanciation (although she probably never heard the word) and putting things in perspective.

Now take the tree decorating model and extend it to viewing your wallpapering efforts, your wanderings through an art gallery, your choice of friends, or even your choice of a spouse; some distance in all these activities makes not only for greater objectivity, but for some insight into oneself as your own subjective self becomes an "object" to be better understood. Gordon Allport, writing about the integrated person (see chapter 4), counted self-objectification as an essential characteristic of the mature person and linked it with a sense of humor. Dabrowski (chapter 5) named an important dynamism of development, "Subject-Object in Oneself." Things start to come together when you step back, distance yourself to get a more objective picture.

Person-object distanciation, as Werner and Kaplan (1963) have stated, represents an increasing differentiation and hierarchic integration of the world of objects and the world of self. In other words, this can be done through symbolic vehicles such as images and words that objectify the outside world to the subject. This is one reason why keeping a personal journal, telling your troubles to a friend, or consulting a therapist works; it helps to objectify the situation, and that leads to insight. Words, and especially symbols, reflect both objective and subjective meaning. From the perspective that the symbolizing process gives—the distanciation—figure emerges from ground, self emerges from environment, yet in relationship to environment. It is the discovery of oneself through symbols. That self is in relationship; the proportions, the meanings of those relationships become clearer. At one and the same time the self is not only subject, but object seen in perspective. At this point the traditional dichotomy between subject and object is transformed. Rather than simply being opposite poles of a continuum, the continuum is in a sense changed from a straight line into a circle with subject and object at the reconvergence of the circle, identified within the self.

We are all naturally specialists about our own subjective states; it is what we know best. (Just listen to some conversations where there is competition for air time to tell one's own story, which seems much more fascinating than someone else's.) The challenge is to step out of subjectivity at times, to step back, to distanciate from oneself, to see oneself as an object. This calls for the kind of self-talk language a person uses when he or she says, "There I go falling back into my old ways again; there's the old selfishness, the old pride, the old egocentrism coming back. I really must do better." Like the self-directing speech of a three-year-old who tells herself aloud that this jigsaw puzzle piece doesn't fit and she must try a better one, the adult uses the symbols of language to direct his or her development. Language and other symbols such as archetypes and myths provide the distance for viewing subject and object in oneself. That is one reason why people keep diaries and journals or do art.

One quality this distanciation gives is the opportunity to transcend the self as individual, to see the identification of self with others. By giving the perspective of relationships, language bridges the gulf between individuals who see themselves as just so many isolated "islands." If I am *related*, then I am *responsible*. New values, new moral imperatives, begin to emerge.

Paradoxically, as I step back in distanciation, I come closer in relation. Not only do I begin to look at myself as object, but I begin to perceive and appreciate more the individuality of others; I can experience in some small way the other self as subject. A new perspective on values emerges. A new objective moral insight is born.

Dabrowski (Dabrowski & Piechowski, 1977) describes a reflective person reaching higher levels of development:

> Thinking appears to me to be one-sided; it has lost somewhere its logical certainty. I am more uncertain and more hesitant, yet at the same time, I find myself richer in my thoughts and feelings. Perhaps loss of certainty in thinking and its closer interdependence with feelings are really tied together with a greater complexity and depth of thinking as a way of knowing.... There was a time when I was sure of the independence of thought. I believed that when one passes the experiential sphere of emotions to the discursive sphere of thought, then the whole of human life is raised to a higher level. Today I know that these were just speculations based on unfounded presuppositions. Events and experiences in my life, especially when I felt isolated, sad, in mental pain, broken down, convinced me that my intellectual interests underwent fundamental changes. My thinking has lost its clearly delineating boundaries of thinking for its own sake. It became an instrument of something higher, something you could call a synthesis of intuition and ideal. Isolated thinking has lost its appeal for me, but such thinking that is geared to "higher functions" gives me at times the feeling of reaching to others, to (the) ideal, and maybe to something even higher, like the reality of transcendental experience. (p. 150)

Again a convergence: here we have an individual saying about his own personal development in terms of Positive Disintegration theory what authors such as Maturana (1978), Capra (1975), and Zukav (1980) were saying years ago about the physical sciences: that there is a movement away from the arrogant "certainties" of Newtonian physics with its trust in intellect and exact measurement to a more transcendent, "mystical" view of the physical world in which the involvement of the subjective observer is acknowledged.

The objective truth is a function largely of the questions we ask, a function of the logic of those questions, it is true, but a function of the imaginational and emotional loading we give to those questions. It is a function of the language and symbols we choose to use, and much of that language, much of that symbolization, goes beyond the bounds of intellect and resides more in the realm of feeling, taking us into the transcendent, which is suprarational and rich with the symbols of emotion. There is much of the subjective in every "objective" judgment. In fact the greatest objectivity is found in the highest levels of subjectivity.

Distanciation and Authentic Subjectivity

The last statement was carefully worded; it did not say, "the greatest objectivity is found in the greatest subjectivity," but in the "highest levels" of subjectivity. Now we are somehow linking objectivity with authenticity. As a person develops, his or her values become more complex, more subtle, more numerous in their nuances of meaning and feeling, yet always more integrated into a hierarchy that becomes clearer with development to higher levels. The movement is away from egocentrism toward autonomy, and above all authenticity. The higher levels of development are levels of clarified relationships with others and with oneself. They are levels in which the distanciation of which we spoke earlier has had full effect. Fineness of feeling characterizes the person as one moves upward to higher levels of development, and it is this emotional sensitivity that guides one in establishing a personal hierarchy of values, a hierarchy that clearly delineates the way things ought to be. What is and what ought to be become clearly differentiated, as we saw in chapter 10. This approach to oughtness avoids the naturalistic fallacy that has bothered philosophy. It sees oughtness as clearly emerging from the sensitivity of individuals at higher levels of development. And it is the higher levels of the individual's development, the autonomy—freedom from the pressures of the crowd, the authenticity—the inner coherence and integrity, the empathy: the fine feeling for others and the ability to put oneself in another's place that create objective value judgments. Lonergan (1974) sums it up in one telling sentence: "Objectivity is the fruit of authentic subjectivity" (p. 214). Reading this line was for me a few years ago an "Aha!" experience. Everything we are talking about in this chapter comes together in these seven words.

Authentic Subjectivity

What do we mean by authentic subjectivity? Stewart (1981) develops the point nicely in his explanation of Lonergan's philosophy:

> Slowly one becomes oneself. It takes time to develop from being a "subject" in a sensitive world of immediacy to a "self" in the adult world of meaning. The process is one of self-creation. One moves from empirical to intellectual consciousness to rational consciousness to rational self-consciousness. (p.175)

Lonergan (1973) states, "Man achieves authenticity in self-transcendence" (p. 104). Stewart's (1981) commentary on this is the following:

> That achievement has to be the result of one's judging and deciding for oneself. It cannot be the result of a secondhand effort. It must be an original creation. Further, the self-transcendence is twofold: intentional and moral ... Beyond judgments of fact there are judgments of value ... Knowledge of value of the moral good ... is one thing, performance quite another ... It is only in performance in the actual pur-

suit of the moral good that one achieves self-transcendence. With decision and choice comes the realization that through these acts one makes oneself either an authentic or an unauthentic subject. One becomes conscious of personal value and personal responsibility. (p. 176)

Stewart (1981) goes on to develop the notion of authentic subjectivity:

Authentic subjectivity means asking questions, questions that take us beyond experience to understanding, beyond understanding to reflection, beyond reflection to judgment, beyond judgment to questions about whether this or that is worthwhile. To ask whether something is worthwhile or not means to ask more than whether it satisfies a sensitive (sensual) appetite, whether it gives pleasure or pain, whether it is good for me as an individual or good for a group, whether it is apparently good. My questions seek to determine whether it is truly good, it is of objective value. When I live by my answers to questions of objective value I effect in myself a moral self-transcendence. I am willing or loving the good. (p. 177)

The developmental passage is clear and straight from moral sensitivity through authenticity to objective morality, not just in theory, but lived. You can see in this description of authentic subjectivity the same person that Dabrowski describes at the higher levels of development: someone who experiences the world and self in it through a wide range of overexcitabilities, not being limited to the sensual and immediate; a person who has moved from the reactive to the proactive, from lack of reflection to reflection, from mere value words to congruent value actions. In Dabrowski's terms, the person at higher levels of development has developed not only a hierarchy of values, but a hierarchy of aims that actually influence his or her behavior in all authenticity.

Distanciation, then, is not a process of cold distancing, but a process of relating authentically to things as they are, then moving on to how they ought to be.

Moral Objectivity

As we saw in chapter 7, we humans have a penchant for dichotomies that put us in a black and white world seemingly filled with opposites like mind-body, soul-body, spirit-flesh, religious-human. It is sometimes difficult to see shades of grey. Among the others, the objectivity-subjectivity dichotomy is particularly relevant to morality. True morality is objective; but making objectivity the opposite of subjectivity has led us to believe that, like an on-off light switch, you can have one or the other but not both; subjectivity, in this view, precludes objectivity and vice versa (Smith, 1988). If you want to be objective, you must eliminate the subjective (usually accomplished, it seems, by blocking out feelings). And this says something about what we have done with this dichotomy; we have twisted from a bipolar, horizontal comparison into a vertical hierarchy, one above the other, one *better* than the other. And because of the way we have understood the two, in our rationalistic tradition we have put objectivity higher because, seemingly more rational, it was held in greater esteem. The dictum is: If you want to make objective moral judgments, those that are realistic and true, not those that are mere fantasy, rationalization, or whimsy, but those that conform to the way things are objectively, then you must surrender your own colored experience in favor of black and white reason.

But it is only a pseudo-dilemma. Even saying that subjectivity and objectivity are opposites is like saying *mother* and *child* are opposites. The mother is not opposite; both she and her child exist side by side in a relationship; she is the source; the child comes from the mother. Objectivity (as we will see) is the child of subjectivity; objectivity comes from subjectivity.

The novel and movie *The Accidental Tourist* (Tyler, 1985) puts living characters in the places of objectivity and subjectivity. Macon is a travel writer who hates to travel and so writes books for people who want to find familiar things (like McDonald's) in strange locales. He visits and reviews cities such as Paris and Rome to find what is American in them. On his trips, as in his life, he carries baggage that not only burdens him with the familiar, but builds walls around him to keep out new experiences. Macon's travel writing is objective; he has been there and describes what is there objectively. His life is disturbed, however, when he meets the manic, histrionic Muriel, who has never been out of the country but has deeply experienced both the good and bad things of life. In the course of the narrative, life experienced subjectively turns out to have something to teach objectivity. Not only is the dichotomy of reason and emotion an unreal distinction, but giving intellect predominance over intelligence is a mistake.

In the last analysis all we have in evaluating is our own subjective experience, but when the aim of subjective experience is objectivity, it cannot be just any old subjectivity. Objectivity comes from a modified subjectivity, a special kind of subjectivity—authentic subjectivity. In the last analysis it is a *subjective* self that knows. But to arrive at conclusions of praxis that truly are moral, mere subjectivity is not enough; it must be authentic.

What do we mean by authentic? In the previous chapter we explored the ethic of authenticity as something beyond acceptance of things as they are by striving for what ought to be. We saw that within a horizon of significance one can get a sense of bearings, a sense of perspective, a sense of what is worthwhile, even a sense of what is *objectively* worthwhile and thus worthy of our attention. This is, I think, what Dabrowski meant by the dynamism of subject-object in oneself (see chapter 5). One can in growing degrees, through the course of development, move beyond infantile egocentrism where, taken up with one's own experience, one has no sense of others' subjectivity and treats them as objects to be used. What Dabrowski proposed was the possibility and desirability of adding the reverse to an adult, authentic repertoire: to comprehend the other as subject and by distanciation the self as object. Following the great classical moralists, Dabrowski called on us to stop living an unreflective life. He turned us rather toward an objective order by urging a reflective separation from ourselves through self-objectification: what we have called distanciation. The Dabrowskian ideal of disengagement requires a reflexive stance. We have to turn inward and become aware of our own activity and of the processes that form us. We have to take charge of constructing our own representation of the world, which otherwise goes on without order; we have to take charge of shaping our character. This can only be carried out in the first person. The theory of Positive Disintegration clearly enunciates that the pursuit of the ideal self is not a regression to individualism with all the narcissism and soft relativism that goes with it. It calls on me to be aware of my activity of thinking or my habits so as to disengage from them and objectify them. The whole picture of myself as objectified nature that this reflexive stance of TPD has made familiar to us becomes available only through what Allport called self-objectification, what Dabrowski called Subject-Object in Oneself, and Charles Taylor calls disengagement. Taylor insists that disengagement (and, I add, *objectivity*) comes not only through imbibing doctrines, but through all the disciplines inseparable from our modern way of life, the disciplines of self-control in the economic, moral, and sexual fields. Again, I think Dabrowski anticipated this with his exhortation to inhibit lower-level drives, replacing them with higher-level aspirations. We saw that there are several steps up from the lowest-level objectivity of simply seeing what *is* to having a perspective (a sense of relative value) on how things *ought* to be. But some human beings do not simply *have* a perspective; they have arrived at a level where one *is* a perspective. The moral ideal and the real are one. To *be* a perspective is realized not only in the sense of being a moral model, but in the fuller, richer sense of actually creating moral objectivity.

I admit that this objectivity thing is not a matter of simple black and white outcomes. We are not all suddenly going to find the truth. Whitehead points out that the process of contemplative perception and symbolization are fallible, particularly in terms of individual differences, as a result of variance in each person's situation as a being in the world. The very process of distanciation creates the danger of error. Two persons may perceive the same object or event in different ways according to the perspective their position gives them. What one person perceives as love another may see as condescending pity. Such variance of viewpoints that, according to Whitehead, is the stuff of creativity is also the source of misunderstanding, argument, and even war and mass destruction. Witness how the two sides in any war have concurrently stockpiled armaments such as nerve gas in the name of "defense," "protection" of their civilian population, and ultimately "world peace."

If the Holy Grail of value objectivity is found primarily at the higher levels of emotional development of a handful of eminent human beings, what is the fate of the rest of us poor mortals still struggling at lower levels?

Teaching Objective Morality

If social consensus is not the source of objectivity, and the lot of great masses of people is to have not reached high levels of authenticity, where is their source of objective values? It is the core of authentic, eminent persons we have talked of earlier, and language is the first vehicle of morality between the few and the masses. But, as we have seen, language is a fallible vehicle in conveying meaning. Perhaps it is for this reason that philosophers are so infrequently listened to and even less often understood. They have in their hands the tools of logic and the vehicle of language with which to convey their logic, the fruit of their highly intellectual activity. The fact that they are not listened to is not the result of the stupidity of the people, but the fact that for the most part they consult only the head and not the heart, and the language they use is almost exclusively the language of the head.

On the other hand, if we look at the great teachers of values and morals, those who have had centuries of influence and whose followers number millions—Moses, Socrates, Christ, Mohammed, Buddha—we find that their language is not only of words, but of symbols that go beyond words. The teachings of the great teachers and prophets are full of stories, metaphors, parables that have deep concrete meaning in their listeners' lives and are emotion-filled. In our attachment to rationality, we have neglected too the language of the mystics and poets whose emotion-filled language, rich in symbolization, conveys meanings inexpressible in words, yet nevertheless real meanings, objective values.

The great moral teachers have, as we saw in chapter 8, spoken in symbols beyond language, in lives lived, in dedication, responsibility, concern for others, hunger for justice, and sometimes the ultimate symbol of giving up their lives for what they teach.

The language of the great moral teachers is powerful even as it lives on after their death, because it is affect laden, because it is enriched with their perspective. Because these morally eminent persons were in contact with their world from the perspective of their own authentic subjectivity, they can convey to us in myriad rich symbols values that are objective in a language rich with the poetry of words and meanings of lives lived. Value objectivity is not something "out there" to be grasped by logic and reason alone, nor by emotion alone. It is something within us, especially those who are most authentic among us. From the depths of their subjectivity, they speak to us in the language of moral objectivity. We in turn need a way of interpreting their words and actions. This is called *hermeneutics.*

Let me illustrate what I mean. A while ago the movie *Romero* circulated around our theaters. It is the story of Archbishop Romero of El Salvador. I found it moving and noticed other people leaving the theater in tears. But even more moving than his final martyrdom for supporting social justice for the poor was the long personal journey he took, from withdrawal into the hierarchical establishment of El Salvador to identifying with the poor and persecuted. It was movement from a rigid, self-conserving structure to one of mutual presence. A potent image that comes away with you from this film is that of the faces of the poor of El Salvador pleading with the bishop to come to their side in the struggle. If ever there was communication of subjectivity it is there. If ever there was a call for a living hermeneutic it was there. If ever there was objectivity of value judgments it was there not only in the event itself, but on the screen and on the faces of the North Americans who watched the conversion unfold and left the theater sharing *objective* values. The story depicted on the screen was that of the hermeneutics of morality in action in Central America; the experience of the people in the theater was the hermeneutics of morality in North America; the recursive loop had doubled.

To *be* a perspective; not just to *have* but to *be* a perspective; to have an active role in shaping morality, and in our present context to influence it, even to create it by what we as humans have to offer to help bring design out of chaos: This is our choice. Few of us will be eminent moral models, but by virtue of our participation in the process, we are called in some way to be perspectives to one another. It is a different view from the traditional objectivistic stance, which is to see value solely "out there," in the object itself, waiting to be discovered by the "objective observer." Instead, the value is not solely in the observer or the observed, but in the interaction between the two. Robert Pirsig put it succinctly in his moral-philosophical novel *Lila* (1991, p. 66) when he said, "Between the subject and the object lies the value." To *have* a perspective may mean simply to take moral values solely as something given: contained entirely in things (naturalism), or to take values second hand in the form of given norms of behavior (conformity). To *be* a perspective is to first go beyond being just a model of morality. To *be* a perspective means to find *oneself* in a horizon of significance, and consequently to transcend that self in a relationship of self to value so that one's values actually provide the guiding norms so naturally, so instinctively, that morality is not something called on inconsistently, but a powerful and consistent life dynamism. This ideal of being a perspective, like a Bach canon, takes up the theme of authenticity. It attracts us to moral consistency, inviting us to play personal variations on the theme. If to be a perspective means something more than simply being a moral model, it is important to see morality not as something someone *has*, but what one *is*. When we talk about consistent habits of virtuous living we name it *character*.

The authentic self is someone who experiences the world and self in it through a wide range of what Dabrowski calls overexcitabilities (compare chapter 5 and Nelson, 1989), not being limited to the sensual and immediate; a person who has moved from the reactive to the proactive, from impulsivity to reflection, from mere value words to congruent value actions and the moral lifestyle we call character. At higher levels authenticity blossoms into authentism, and at the highest levels into a consistent life pattern where what ought to be *is*. High-level objective morality is attained through *authentic* subjectivity.

Conclusion

All we have in our moral quest is our subjectivity, and that is enough. But to arrive at conclusions of praxis that truly are moral, mere subjectivity with all its whims and machinations is not enough; it must be authentic. In the movement from is to ought we must have the perspective of our individual horizon of significance. This is a step up from the lowest-level objectivity of simply seeing what is. It is an upward motion to having a perspective (a sense of relative value) on how things ought to be. But the best human beings do not simply *have* a perspective; they have arrived at a level where one *is* a perspective. The moral ideal and the real are one. To *be* a perspective is realized not only in the sense of being a moral model, but in the fuller, richer sense of actually creating moral objectivity. This is, I think, what Dabrowski meant by the dynamism of Subject-Object in Oneself. He had a remarkable insight when he pointed out that one can, in growing degrees through the course of development, move from obsession with one's own subjective experience, and comprehend the other as subject and the self as object. One can then transcend the self in a union with the seamless whole of creation in which what *is* actually is what *ought* to be.

High standards need strong sources. Weak sources, such as feelings of obligation or guilt or self-satisfaction, are insufficient for strong morals because ultimately they are egoistic. Dabrowski knew this when he imagined his most highly developed people as being beyond mere ego, and instead integral, whole, authentic persons of character.

Sometimes we are transfixed by celebrities as models of what we ought to be. We follow them, dazzled by the glitz. No such scenario was drawn up here. Those who dare to take the high moral ground are often ignored as irrelevant by most of us. But, though they are often shunned as different, those who think, those who feel, those who give birth to morality, those who dance on the stillpoint of the turning earth where subject and object unite, those who attend to the poetry that is life, whose speaking and seeking is of beauty and for transcending value are the most revolutionary and evolutionary among us. They are doorways to another dimension that, if trusted, leads beyond the superficial world of conformity to an authentic morality.

Chapter 12

The Ethics of Aesthetics— The Aesthetics of Ethics

Art is knowing where to draw the line.

—*G. K. Chesterton*

Let us look more at the multilevel approach to values and morals and see its necessary connection with religion. To do this we have to go back to our good friend Whitehead and pick up his sense of the identity of morality with beauty (which Plato before him had expressed) and then return to Dabrowski's theory of Positive Disintegration to see the multilevel development of moral man intertwined with religious man, and attempt to examine what is involved in morality at the various levels of development.

Whitehead's Ethics

Love is the major motif in Whitehead's view of ethics. Whitehead had little use for moralism, especially the coercion it so often uses to enforce authority's rules whether they be human or divine. God is no ruthless moralist, pushing man on. Man is to be lured, not driven. For Whitehead Jesus' teaching of love, empathy, kindness, and a compassionate attitude (the "Galilean vision" he called it) are truer than anything else in respect of man's life and meaning because this is how the process goes at its deepest levels. Whitehead believed in the importance of ethics, but for him the *aesthetic* (in the special, profound sense he intended) is more important.

This special sense of the aesthetic deserves exploration if we hope to appreciate something of Whitehead's moral philosophy. Naturally, Whitehead saw morals as part of the process, and following his inclination saw it in grand terms. Morality is never a private affair done in isolation from others, nor is its only concern the unity of mankind. There is an essential interrelatedness about all nature that transcends the needs of humanity alone. The concern of morality is the process of all reality, and the survival of the universe, not just mankind, is the ultimate concern.

Whitehead (1967) maintained that the aims of a civilized society are a "fineness of feeling" and a "generality of understanding." This is what process is all about. Each individual occasion contributes its fineness of feeling, and the whole achieves a generality of understanding. For Whitehead, the individual and the totality are of equal value. Morality does not choose between the welfare of the individual or of the community. Morality, if it is to be morality, must be synergistic. It must strive toward individual and societal integration in a way that values both the uniqueness of individuality and the harmony of generality.

The prime task of morals is to safeguard experience and continue the process, and some qualities Whitehead enumerated ought to be furthered by process—his five "eternal objects."

Whitehead saw process as the key to the nature of things. "There is," he said, "the one all-embracing fact which is the advancing history of the one Universe" (p. 192). This community of the world that is "the matrix of all begetting, and whose essence is process with retention of connectedness," this community that, according to Whitehead, was first described by Plato is the heart of process philosophy. Whitehead takes a multilevel view of the factors of human life, with the moral element derivative from the other factors of experience. "Thus the primary factors in experience are first the animal passions such as love, sympathy, ferocity, together with analogous appetitions and satisfactions; and second, the more distinctly human experiences of beauty and of intellectual fineness, consciously enjoyed" (p. 11).

It is appropriate that Whitehead in this brief hierarchization of the factors of human life should strike first of all on man's "distinctly human experience of beauty" as most prominently distinctive of man operating at higher levels of development. In *Adventures of Ideas* (1967), Whitehead lists five eternal objects: truth, beauty, adventure, art, and peace. Interestingly, *good* and *right* are not part of the list, the reason being that Whitehead felt that these words were so overworked their meanings had become imprecise. The five objects include in a general way all that man actually finds valuable in process. But Whitehead, coming from a Platonic background, saw truth, beauty, and goodness as inextricably bound up with each other.

Whitehead (1967) defines truth much as Thomas Aquinas did, as the conformation of appearance to reality (p. 241). Because truth is a relationship constituted when the content of two connected facts participate in the same general pattern, there can be many kinds of truth ranging from mathematical truth to the truth of art. Truth is attained primarily through the senses, with the things we perceive providing consistent values. These values are incorporated into the subjective form of the prehending occasion and help form a part of the data out of which new occasions emerge in the process.

At this point Whitehead introduces one of those statements that, taken out of context, could get him into trouble. You can imagine him writing it with an impish gleam in his eye. He says, "It is more important that a proposition be interesting than that it be true" (p. 244). But then he goes on to lure the reader into the truth of what he is saying in this interesting statement: "the energy of operation of a proposition in an occasion of experience is its interest and is its importance. But of course a true proposition is more apt to be interesting than a false one." A true proposition,

Whitehead goes on to say, also has more emotional lure. "But the importance of a proposition lies in its interest." This is itself a fitting proposition for a book entitled *Adventures of Ideas*.

But Whitehead (1967) continues his pursuit of the truth of ideas by pursuing the concept *beauty*. Beauty is the mutual adaptation of the several factors in an occasion of experience (p. 265). Beauty is thus wider and more fundamental than truth; it goes beyond truth because it deals not only with the conformation of appearance to reality, but with the perfection of the subjective forms that are shaped by their interrelation. The adaptations of beauty arise in the pursuit of an aim, and in this pursuit both intensity of feeling and conformity to a common pattern combine for the attainment of harmony. Beauty is "the one aim which by its very nature is self-justifying" (p. 266). Truth is in the service of beauty and the realization of truth becomes in itself an element promoting beauty of feeling.

> Consciousness, with its dim intuitions, welcomes a factor (Truth) so generally on the right side, so habitually necessary. The element of anticipation under the influence of Truth is in a deep sense satisfied, and thus adds a factor to the immediate Harmony. Thus Truth, in itself and apart from special reasons to the contrary becomes self-justifying. It is accompanied by a sense of rightness in the deepest Harmony. (p. 267)

One is reminded here of the characteristics of Dabrowski's high-level persons, particularly those at secondary integration, where the appreciation of beauty, the beauty of feeling, and the search for truth yield harmony.

Whitehead (1967) concludes: "Truth derives this self-justifying power from its services in the promotion of Beauty. Apart from Beauty, Truth is neither good, nor bad" (p. 267), and "The real world is good when it is beautiful" (p. 268). "Art," Whitehead goes on to say (p. 267), is the "purposeful adaptation of Appearance to Reality" and the purpose of art is twofold truth and beauty, so that art has only one end—truthful beauty. "Truth matters because of Beauty" (p. 267).

Consciousness is the factor of experience that makes art possible by strengthening the artificiality of an occasion of experience, and the merit of art lies in its artificiality and finiteness. Art exhibits for consciousness a finite human effort achieving its own perfection within its own limits. A landscape within the limiting parameters of its medium and even its frame communicates from one consciousness to another, "This is what I saw; this is what I felt. It is not the actual trees and the actual river; it is artificial. It is not all of what was there and it is certainly not all of what I experienced, for it is limited by space and time and by my communication. But it is the communication of my humanity to yours through art and our mutual consciousness."

The work of Art is a fragment of nature with the mark on it of a finite creative effort, so that it stands alone, an individual thing detailed from the vague infinity of its background. Thus Art heightens the sense of humanity. It gives an elation of feeling that is supernatural. A sunset is glorious, but it dwarfs humanity and belongs to the general flow of nature. A million sunsets will not spur on men towards civilization. It requires Art to evoke into consciousness the finite perfections which lie ready for human achievement. (pp. 270-271)

The achievement of Art depends on the perfection of humankind as it has been shaped by beauty. But perfection for a process philosopher is not a static concept. Like civilization it must always promote novelty and originality. Whitehead says:

It is a tribute to the strength of the sheer craving for freshness that change, whose justification lies in aim at the distant ideal should be promoted by Art which is the adaptation of immediate Appearance for immediate Beauty. Art neglects the safety of the future for the gain of the present.... Its business is to render the Day of Judgment a success now. The effect of the present on the future is the business of morals. (p. 269)

Art and morals are inseparable, for the inevitable anticipation of the future adds a qualitative element to both art and morals. Whitehead saw in morals a desperate need for that same vital drive and zest that art needed. "Morals consists in the aim at the ideal, and at its lowest it concerns the prevention of relapse to lower levels. Thus stagnation is the deadly foe of morality" (p. 269). Whitehead adds the regret, "Yet in human society the champions of morality are on the whole the fierce opponents of new ideals." Here Whitehead is talking about the book-burners, the condemners, the censors, and not the true champions of morality—those at higher levels of development.

Part of the zestful ongoing process of art (and morals) is what Whitehead calls art's "curative function ... when it reveals in a flash intimate absolute Truth regarding the Nature of Things." This curative function, this revealing of the nature of things, is hindered by "trivial truths of detail.... Such petty conformations place in the foreground the superficialities of sense experience" (p. 272).

I am reminded by this passage how some "art" fails to be great or even good by attention to "superficialities of sense experience." The black velvet paintings we see for sale on street corners are admired for the sensual glow that the velvet takes on when smeared with vivid, metallic colors. Better still, if on the cheek of the large-eyed child the artist has painted a three-dimensional teardrop that is "so real you want to touch it": This detail, this pseudo-reality in art is parallel to the pseudo-realities of sentimentality that so often replace true empathy in the moral domain.

An essential part of the ongoing process is adventure, lest inspiration lead to mere repetition. The process is the actuality and the processes of the past, which in their perishing are themselves energizing as the complex origin of each novel occasion. "The past is the reality at the base of each new actuality. The process is its absorption into a new unity with ideals and with anticipation, by the operation of the creative Eros" (Whitehead, 1967, p. 276). Adventure has harmony as its goal. Our life is dominated by enduring things, individual things experienced as a unity of many occasions. Each individual occasion collects into its unity the shifting qualities of its many occasions. Such enduring individualities "control a wealth of feeling, an amplitude of purpose and a regulative power to subdue into background the residue of things belonging to the immensity of the past" (p. 280). In other words, harmony puts a multitude of individualities into perspective, giving one the dimensions and coming-togetherness of the whole. No individual is lost in the harmony; in fact, in contributing to the whole each detail "receives an access of grandeur from the whole, and yet manifests an individuality claiming attention in its own right" (p. 282). Whitehead goes on to use the example of the cathedral of Chartres where the sculpture and tracery subserve the harmony.

> They lead the eye upward to the vaulting above, and they lead the eye horizontally to the supreme symbolism of the altar. They claim attention by their beauty of detail. Yet they shun attention by guiding the eye to grasp the significance of the whole. (p. 282)

Harmony has the religious quality of putting everything into perspective.

Finally peace, the harmony of harmonies, beckons to go beyond limitations, to transcend the self without, of course, denying the self. Peace is the integration of order and love, the essence of art and morality, bound together as they are by beauty.

Whitehead (1967) should have the last word: "Here by the quality of Peace I am not referring to political relations. I mean a quality of mind steady in its reliance that fine action is treasured in the nature of things" (p. 274).

With this beautiful and profound statement, Whitehead does indeed have the last word, but, as ever in the process, it is a word of transition, a word of *going on*, and it leads us to new insights into the harmony of Whitehead with Dabrowski. If ever there was a psychological theory concerned with "quality of mind" it is Positive Disintegration. If ever there was a theory concerned with "fine feeling" and "fine action" it is Dabrowski's. The two great men, Whitehead and Dabrowski, come together especially in their concept of human being as moralist—how he or she knows morality and how he or she is motivated to pursue it.

Following Whitehead's lead, which we have acknowledged goes back ultimately to Plato, I would like to pursue the topic of moral development in the theory of Positive Disintegration by paralleling the levels of aesthetic development with those of ethical development. I think we will see that Dabrowski is basically expressing process thought.

Dabrowski's Theory

What I am doing here is taking Dabrowski's description of the levels of development of the aesthetic attitude (1977, pp. 144-147) and paralleling them with his levels of development of ethics as a discipline (pp. 217-219), as he doesn't seem to have published any explicit outline of the levels of individual moral development. The parallels are clear, between aesthetic sensitivity and moral sensitivity through the five levels he describes.

Level I

Aesthetics. This is the "bread and circuses" mentality toward art. A distinct preference for loudness and bigness is evident. If a car is big it is beautiful. If a building is "the biggest in the world" it is the best and most beautiful. The *Guinness Book of World Records* becomes a manual of aesthetics. New is equated with beautiful. Beauty is often confused with utility. In art a kind of primitive realism is the criterion of goodness. Does it look exactly like what it is supposed to represent? There is a preference for sense of realism using mass production media as in the landscapes painted by an "artist" in the middle of a shopping mall, each picture just a rearrangement of the standard houses, trees, and mountains found in all the other paintings. Or the "special effects" realism of the black velvet paintings with the exaggerated realism of a sentimental teardrop on a child's cheek. This is a kind of pathological form of art that Whitehead referred to. It takes a low level in Dabrowski's thinking too.

Ethics. In level one, ethics are at a primitive animal level. The law of the jungle prevails. Might equals right, and leaders are followed blindly primarily because of their ability to punish. Blame is passed on to others by the simple explanation, "I was only doing what I was told." One is reminded of Watergate and the Hitler regime where ethical reasoning stopped at the point of thinking that if the President (or Fuehrer) said it was right it must be. It is an egocentric level of moral reasoning, comparable to Kohlberg's punishment avoidance level or, at most, the good boy-good girl orientation. Dabrowski says: "there is a distinct tendency to identify others with oneself, but never to identify oneself with others" (1977, p. 218).

Level II

Aesthetics. Partial sensitivities to color, dance, music, and art begin to appear, but aesthetic experiences are not involved in a search for new and higher levels of experience. In other words, Whitehead's adventure does not yet enter into aesthetics.

Largely, the motto of this level is "art for art's sake," although human experiences begin to act as stimuli for aesthetic experiences, leading to the beginnings of psychological, and not merely realistic, content in art.

Ethics. Profound egocentrism begins to yield to an initial empathy and identification with others, but this is a fluctuating, off-again-on-again affair. Feelings for others in the form of primitive syntony begin to emerge parallel to the emergence of psychological content in appreciation of art. There is little moral reflection, no clear moral principles, and relativism is characteristic of morality. There is no adventure into new personal ways of moral thinking; conformity to the mores of the crowd dictates morality.

Level III

Aesthetics. Disintegration and decay enter into artistic expression, showing fragmentation of faces, features, and bodies. There is an obsession with pathology, perhaps the result of a restless search for truth in art, but a truth that is still subjective and distorted. An understanding and appreciation for the drama of life begins to find its way into the expression of art and into its appreciation. Others and self begin to be involved in this drama. Art becomes the expression of personal, religious, and moral strivings. There are, Dabrowski says, "unharmonized reaches into the depth of human experience" (1977, p. 145). Whether he was influenced by Whitehead to use the theme of harmony not yet achieved to describe this level I do not know, but the convergence with Whitehead is clear. The level III person does not yet have that harmony that Whitehead described as essential for art at its fullest.

One feels the need to comprehend pathology not as a source of fascination, but to understand the role of suffering and illness in development—the *agonia* of the Greek athlete, straining painfully for the goal. The conflict within people and between people that is the source of great drama is appreciated and expressed. A hierarchy of values can now be expressed in art with empathy as one of the highest values. The beginnings of intuition appear, based on a hierarchy of feelings. One is reminded here of the words of Whitehead (1967, p. 271), "Art heightens the sense of humanity. It gives an elation of feeling which is supernatural."

Ethics. Egocentrism decreases with an increase of empathy. This movement away from egocentrism is the result of dynamisms of dissatisfaction with oneself, feelings of inferiority toward oneself—a sense of the lack of harmony and beauty in one's life.

Values are distinguished, lower from higher, and with this hierarchy of values and aims, one is moved into the adventure of ascending toward the higher levels.

Moral principles begin to emerge based on compassion and helpfulness, and founded in a deep, though still partial, identification with others. Intuition takes one to the core of moral problems without trial and error.

Level IV

Aesthetics. "Nothing human is alien to me." Responsiveness to the drama and tragedy of real life gives rise to a need to express them and appreciate them in art. Religious drama and the drama of conflict of values is more appreciated. Identification with others becomes more complete, and the artist toils with his sense of self-identity and identity with his work of art. Art becomes a function of growing calmness and inner peace, concentration, meditation, and contemplation. This is the synthesis, the harmony and the peace that Whitehead describes.

Meditation and contemplation contribute to the growth of intuition. The framework for intuitive appreciation is much broader because it is taken from a wider frame of reference. "Knowledge is easily applied to particular phenomena because perception is multilevel and multidimensional, having its source in the highest level which organizes in an all encompassing and yet precise manner, all the lower levels of reality" (Dabrowski, 1977, p. 152). Appreciation of the "rightness" of a work of art is objectively founded even though criteria cannot be spelled out in a catalogue of detail. It is a largely emotional sense of rightness, based on overexcitabilities. One may wish to use Whitehead's term "fineness of feeling."

Ethics. Understanding, compassion, and helpfulness toward others are active, even when one cannot approve of the principles and conduct of others as conforming to one's own personality ideal. One is attracted to authentic moral systems (those based on conscious individual responsibility) such as Christianity in the form it came from its Founder. Morality becomes a harmonious complex of individuals, each conscious of and contributing his or her own individuality, which is not lost, but enhanced in its contribution to the whole—a high synergy society in which "My good must be your good or it's no good at all." The organism is enhanced, beautified, when each individual is treasured for his or her unique contribution of value to the process. One is again reminded of Whitehead's concept of harmony and the example he used of the Chartres Cathedral.

Level V

Aesthetic-ethical-intuitive. (At this level the three converge.) A high level of empathy is expressed in art that becomes a synthesis of science and philosophy, goodness and wisdom. Beauty dances hand in hand with morality because religion, art, and morality are now united in a harmony that sees them as inseparable. A man like St. Francis of Assisi exemplifies this (Dabrowski, 1977, p. 147). Moral principles are explained on the basis of personality and its ideal. Intuition is given an important role in discriminating levels of reality, and this intuition is in turn based on the personality ideal. Such intuition is contemplative and mystical, and comes from contemplation, even ecstasy. It comes from reaching the absolute "I" and the absolute "Thou" in relationship. In reaching moral principles and in moving one to act morally, importance is given to a highly developed empathy and the ability to treat others as subjective beings. Transcendental moral ideas are given weight and validity. Objectivity of value judgments is achieved in the fine feeling, intuition, harmony, and peace that mark this highest level of development.

The image of this section is one of spirals—interlocking, merging spirals. If, following Teilhard de Chardin, we believe that "all that rises must converge," then we see in the rising of Whitehead and Dabrowski to greater levels of human understanding a remarkable convergence of thought.

1. First they are both concerned very much with man at his best—what man might be. They are idealists in the best sense of the word.

2. But, second, they are realists too and they, each in his own way, see humans at various levels of development, various levels of contributing to value in the process. Each individual is valued for his or her unique contribution to the process, but the contribution of each is in proportion to the developmental potential, especially to the level of consciousness and willing involvement in contributing value to the process of human development.

3. Third, both men valued beauty and the search for truth. To me Dabrowsk, even in his old age, exuded the adventure of which Whitehead wrote. Where other psychologies grow from the cold ground of "objective" experimentation, Dabrowski's grew from the warmth of his own fineness of feeling. Dabrowski's theory, his art, was always sensitive and empathic but never sentimental.

4. A fourth characteristic that unites the two is a concern with the person as member of the community. Each sought to preserve the integrity of the individual as he gave himself to the building of the universe. Whitehead did it with his concept of harmony by which the individual with his self- perfection contributed to the whole without losing himself. Dabrowski did it with his concept of higher-level individuals who combine within themselves autonomy, authenticity, and fidelity to oneself, with altruism, empathy, and involvement in the real world.

It is obvious that the preceding as a theory of moral justification does not fit neatly into any of the classical categories. It is definitely not naturalistic or cognitive, although it does not exclude real contact with things as they are. It is not intuitionism in the Platonic sense, although it leans heavily on the importance of intuition in the broad psychological sense. Although it stresses the role of emotions in moral judgment making, it is not the one-sided emotivism of Hume or Scheler, placing as it does more emphasis on the psychological processes of the whole person. It is a religious approach, but not in the narrowly theistic sense of God as an arbitrary source of morality revealed to us through human sources. The emphasis on individual conscious responsibility for moral judgments and moral behavior is too strong for that simplistic, low-level view of mankind. The question arises: How, then, do we explain the relationship of religion and morality without being simplistic, but without watering down either religion or morality into something so frequently labeled as "merely humanistic?" It is popular in many religious circles to label whatever is not according to the individual's conception of traditional religion as being "mere secular humanism." We have struck this nerve before, and it brings us back to the main theme of this book: that true religion is found in the highest levels of human development; that humanness is not something mere, but glorious in its transcendence and participatory in all that we call God. It remains to explain how all of this comes about. And if ideas are to be adventures, then that is the task we should next set for ourselves.

Religious Experience and Morals

The Canadian theologian Bernard Lonergan and Whitehead are our guides here. Throughout his writing Lonergan tells us that religious experience involves consciousness rather than only knowledge. In dealing with religious experience one is in a realm in which love precedes knowledge, for Lonergan uses the term *religious experience* to refer to an individual's awareness of being in love with transcendent mystery. It is love that first takes hold of our lives and transforms them; from this the knowledge of God emerges. Lonergan (1974) is using the word *conscious* in a special sense. One can be conscious of being in love without restriction and not know it. Once you know the love and know that it is unrestricted, you can infer that it refers to an absolute being—that you have a love relationship with an absolute being, God.

> What finally is religion but complete self-transcendence? It is the love of God poured forth in our hearts by the Holy Spirit that is given to us (Romans, 5:5).... That love is not this or that act of loving, but a radical being-in-love ... a principle that keeps us out of sin, that moves us to prayer and to penance, that can become that ever so quiet yet passionate center of all our living ... it is otherworldly, a being-in-love that occurs in this world but heads beyond it, for no finite object or person can be the object of unqualified, unconditional loving. Such unconditional being-in-love actuates to the full the dynamic potentiality of the human spirit with its unrestricted reach and, as a full actuation, it is fulfillment, deep-set peace, the peace the world cannot give, abiding joy, the joy that remains despite humiliation and failure and privation and pain. (p. 129)

Our themes are reemerging—the discovery in love of a deep relationship, this time with God, bringing with it the harmony and peace that are the fruit of development, finding joy after failure, privation and pain.

Lonergan says that this complete being-in-love, the gift of grace, is the reason of the heart that reason does not know. It is religious experience by which we enter into a subject-to-subject relation with God.

Religious experience is at a level that Lonergan calls Intentional Consciousness—the existential level of evaluation and love. Lonergan can therefore describe religious experience as the transvaluation of all values.

> Like all being in love, as distinct from particular acts of loving, it is a first principle. So far from resulting from our knowledge and choice, it dismantles and abolishes the horizon within which our knowing and choosing went on, and it sets up a new horizon within which the love of God transvalues our values and the eyes of that love transform our knowing. (1974, p. 172)

Kathleen Fischer points out in her article "Religious Experience in Lonergan and Whitehead" (1980, pp. 69-79) that "it is in his emphasis on value and on the extensiveness of love that Lonergan's description of the core religious experience bears most resemblance to Whitehead's." In *Religion in the Making* (1973) Whitehead describes religious experience as the intuition of immediate occasions as failing or succeeding in reference to a relevant ideal: so far as the conformity is incomplete, there is evil in the world. Whitehead takes great pains to make it clear that there is no direct intuition of a definite person or individual, but rather a rightness is intuited in things that the individual may choose to conform to or not. Deity accounts for importance, value, and a sense of worth beyond ourselves. This is the realm of transcendent values. Fischer points out that, just as Lonergan has his grace in the form of being in love in an unqualified way, so does the peace that Whitehead speaks of in *Adventures of Ideas* come as a gift—a grace.

> God is the source both of the values that move individuals and civilizations, and of their movement toward those values. Both life and thought are sustained by a dim apprehension of the beyond. Whenever and however peace comes, it is the result of an intuition into the final beauty of the universe, and a trust in its efficacy beyond the power of reason to discern the details. (p. 73)

Cognitive beliefs as such are not enough for religion or morality. For Lonergan the trivialities of limited love are overcome by religious experience. For Whitehead, peace or the experience of God comes with an enlargement of one's powers, an expansion of consciousness, and the calmness that comes from this harmony. For Dabrowski the love of God found in reflection and prayer leads to the highest levels of empathy and love for mankind. For all three, it is religion as a powerful consciousness that overcomes trivialities, brings figure out of ground, giving that perspective on life and one's relationships with it that is the essence of religious experience. All that rises must converge.

Moral ought is not merely a preference but an obligation to be not only human, not only ourselves but our best selves; this involves self worth because the highest morality is built on self-worth.

Once you use *ought* you are into the *zone* of morality (self worth), but not necessarily its core.

Concentric circles, outermost to core.

Wants and likes.

Ought in sense of "it would be good if ..." "You ought to wash your car."

Ought in sense of it is customary or helpful to others—good manners.

Ought in sense of "It is truly significant not only for your feelings of self-worth, but for your objective, real self-worth, that is, integrity, wholeness of the actor."

Conscience at its core, then, becomes one's own reading of one's objective worthwhileness. "I wouldn't steal because that isn't me, that is, the me I respect." This is authenticity because it employs an objective reading of self and contrasts that real self with personality ideal, leading to the intention to close the gap between the two selves.

The horizon of significance must have at its core for objectivity to be realized, an authentic subjectivity.

This is not objectivity in the sense of value residing in an object or person like a little lead soldier standing rigidly inside them. No, value is something placed on the person or thing by the beholder, and objective value is there in the degree to which the valuer transcends the self to appreciate the goodness of this concrete object, this real action, this person present in the myriad ways persons are present to one another.

Chapter 13
The Ways of Moral Education

Teach us to care.

—T.S. Eliot

We turn our attention now to the practical domain of how moral education is carried out, or, more precisely, how people change their moral ideas and behavior or have them changed by others. I have chosen the word *ways* rather than the more abstract term *theories* or *systems* because we are talking here about the *practical* means in which moral education can be carried out, and we include some "ways" that really could not be considered well-thought-out systems or theories formulated by any explicit school of education. Moral education takes place in many ways, and authors have described unique and sometimes elaborate systems of moral education. But I have chosen some ways that I think represent the mainstreams of moral education. They form a kind of circle, describing in rough outline the development of moral education over time. We begin with Traditional Character Education and end with what I am calling New Character Education. Between are Psychoanalytic, Behavioristic, Values Clarification, Cognitive-Developmental, and Emotional-Rational interpretations. I have approached each from the point of view of philosophy, sociology, psychology, and education. Each is concluded with a discussion of the expected outcome of that way in terms of the kind of person we expect to emerge from the particular method of moral education. This includes, at least implicitly, a certain view of the nature of human beings, and what the "desirable" kind of person is like, bringing us back again to the underlying philosophy of the system or method of moral education. For each of the disciplines, philosophy, sociology, and so on I have posed a summarizing question. It does not, of course, encompass all the questions each discipline asks about moral education, but serves to pinpoint the approach of each discipline.

Shortly we will look at each way in turn. But before that I would like to consider some practical problems that run through all the approaches and impact anyone who tries to do moral education, but particularly teachers in our public schools. The problems range over questions of what people demand of moral educators and how morality is taught to concerns about what political stances teachers may take. We will look too at that nasty word *indoctrination* and some of the presumptions we have about it.

Pressures on Moral Educators

Imagine a roomful of taxpayers instructing a teacher on what she should teach the children in her school. Here are some of the myriad demands (Hague, 1993a):

1. Just make our children *smart* so they can get ahead in the world.

2. Make our children *good* despite the world's values, and, when you're teaching values, remember: Teach our children *good* values.

3. Don't teach our children *your* values; teach them *my* values—the right ones.

4. Don't teach them *any* values at all; teach them how to think, and they will come rationally to the right values on their own.

5. Leave the children alone, and let their intuitive goodness develop independently to choose whatever values they want.

The demands seem to come from all directions. This is challenging and good; it pushes us back to examine our philosophy and beliefs, which is just what we are going to do a few pages ahead.

Indoctrination

Indoctrination has the connotations of a "bad word" in moral education, yet we continue indoctrinating very young children. We tell them with suitable emphasis "No" when they reach for the fire or run into the street, rationalizing our indoctrination by the fact that these learnings are a matter of life and death, too crucial to be left to trial and error. But where do we draw the line on indoctrination, saying on this side it is good, on that side bad? Perhaps Figure 13.1, which distinguishes two senses of the word, will help.

Beware! Figure 13.1 is full of land mines ready to explode if you touch them. For example: How can we concur on what is a matter of "urgency" and "importance?" My "urgency" may be a joke to you. Second, I cannot imagine a religion that doesn't stress that its teachings are essential for life. If my religion taught me that there are a limited number of places in heaven, and they are filling up fast, I would think it "essential" for you to join. There are no neat solutions; but perhaps I have made my point that sometimes we use indoctrination at the same time as we condemn it.

Now, let's go on to looking at the various ways of moral education.

Traditional Character Education

Traditional character education, which is the most ancient of all the ways of moral education, encompasses the traditional approach of teacher and student, master and novice, guru and disciple. In many cases, probably the majority, with the exception of some Eastern approaches in which the master induces the disciple to find enlightenment for himself, this way of moral

The Stereotype

Intention—to make pupils believe regardless of evidence.

Content—debatable religious doctrine or political ideologies.

Method—nonrational teaching methods.

Consequences—a closed mind.

The Possibilities within Indoctrination

Intention—to teach matters of urgency and importance for the well-being of the child and society.

Content—that which is essential for understanding life and actually living it well.

Method—Act as a caregiver, model and mentor in a classroom or home which is itself a moral community.

Consequences—minds and hearts open to the real-life dilemmas of self and others with an appreciation that one is not *compelled* by others, nor, on the contrary, is one *alone* in making moral choices.

Figure 13.1. "Indoctrination": Its connotations, or How indoctrination got its bad reputation even though we parents and teachers do it all the time.

education depends heavily on indoctrination. Tradition (the same tradition they sing about in *Fiddler on the Roof*) passes on the wisdom of one's forefathers to neophytes. Specific rules of behavior and values that have served well in the past are to be passed on, and the task of the teacher is to make sure they are passed on *unchanged*. Following a static world view, the traditionalist thinks it is essential that what was good for centuries before must be good now. One must keep watch over ancient values.

Philosophy: What is Moral?

Philosophy asks the question: What is moral? And the answer is that which we have traditionally done and found to work is moral and good and to be preserved. Society at large, and particularly institutions (mainly religious institutions), have the largest role in determining what is moral and the punishments involved in transgressing these norms. Morality in this system is usually expressed in terms of specific rules and laws of behavior coupled with canonical norms for handling the transgressor. Values may sometimes be fostered directly, but more often are inferred from the rules. When they are taught, values are expressed in terms of specific virtues (Kavelin-Popov, Popov, & Kavelin, 1983; Kilpatrick, 1986) (a "bag of virtues," as Kohlberg calls them) such as honesty, hard work, bravery, cleanliness, purity, loyalty, friendliness, helpfulness: the kind of thing the Boy Scout and Girl Guide system is built on, inculcating specific virtues. The famous Hartshorne and May (1928/30) studies of moral development looked for and, in Kohlberg's eyes, failed to find any reliable role for virtue inculcation in moral education. More recent reviews of Hartshorne and May's research are less critical.

Another physical embodiment of this encouragement of virtue can be found in the stained glass windows of the legislative buildings in Victoria, British Columbia. There one sees the virtues of the Protestant ethic such as industriousness, initiative, and integrity glorified in the windows dedicated to each virtue.

What is moral? What the old reliable institutions of society have "always" told us is moral. In an unchanging world there is certainly no need to change anything, least of all morality! The task is to pass it on unchanged.

Sociology: What is the State of Society?

In our paradigm sociology asks the central question: What is the state of society? From the moral point of view, society's moral norms are like a medieval castle under siege from the forces of change. Traditional values are always under threat and need guarding to preserve good order. This good order can be passed on to future generations if the forces of change are held back. Change is at least suspect if not downright corrupting. The salvation of wayward citizens is to return to traditional values.

Psychology: How do People Change Their Moral Behavior?

What are the psychological dynamics by which one becomes more moral, or, more generally, how does one change one's moral ideas, inclinations, and behavior? The process is largely one of direct teaching of virtues by word of mouth or good example. The direct teaching may include learning to name certain virtues and recognize them. Reward and punishment play a predominant role; in this life they may be in the form of merit points, gold stars, or the esteem of important people like parents, Sunday school teachers, or religious leaders; or the chastisement these same people can hand out whether in the form of physical punishment or feelings of shame, guilt, and rejection. Religion has the extra punishing power and rewarding power of "the next life" with the threat of eternal fires or an "eternal crown of glory."

Association with good people, those who protect and encourage the traditional values, is important. This has the twofold function of shielding the individual from corrupting ideas and encouraging him or her to learn virtue by the good example of others. Good example in turn comes from two sources: those immediately present to the child in the roles of parents, teachers, and so on, and those who are examples from afar: heroes and heroines of virtue, often recognized by a church as saints.

The psychological process of modeling and identification (Bandura & Walters, 1963) is used as a powerful means of affecting moral behavior. Because the traditional indoctrination approach has much to do with the processes of socialization, it shares with the behavioristic approach a strong tendency to use identification with models. But the traditional approach does not openly stress that the model be powerful so much as exemplary, nor is it always important that the model be warm and loving, only exemplary.

Education

How do teachers teach morals? Basically, teachers expound specific virtues, clarifying their meaning of *honesty, loyalty, kindness* by going to examples from the lives of holy people or, to encourage identification, from catechetical stories involving children who practice virtue. Reward and punishment are powerful tools in the hands of the teacher, as is the good example of the teacher's own behavior. Thus teachers are to be selected carefully as models of virtue and as part of the overall concern of this kind of moral education to protect the child from corrupting influences and ideas that would lead him or her away from the accepted norms.

How do students learn morals? The process is largely a passive one. The child's role is not to oppose or argue or even think independently; it is to accept and learn the rules of behavior, memorizing them if necessary, receiving punishment for any infringement of them, and correcting peers when they show weakness.

Outcome: What Kind of Person Results?

What kind of a person do we have as a result of this education? Built on a rigidly structured and unchanging concept of both society and the make-up of the human person, the traditional indoctrination approach is content with a passively accepting person who does not question, but obediently keeps rules and passes them on to others faithfully, thus protecting the unchanging standards of society. This approach does not see the individual as particularly directive of his or her own life, nor does it give a high place to consciousness or individual freedom. Will is not something to be encouraged, but tamed. Feelings are seen largely as motivating forces in the sense that they are used to influence behavior in the form of fear, shame, and guilt. The stress is on intellect: right understanding of what society expects of you and conformity to those expectations. Autonomy and self-direction are not only neglected, but deliberately avoided because they may lead to nonconformity. The individual is not seen as being self-directive or particularly responsible for anything except obediently holding fast to tradition.

Psychoanalytic (Freudian) Tradition—Identification

I have used the word *tradition* here in an effort to encompass the vast variety of psychologies that may be called psychoanalytic. To say that there is one psychoanalytic view of moral education would be a gross oversimplification. We have already seen that some of Freud's immediate disciples such as Jung differed from him greatly, and neo-Freudian psychologists like Erich Fromm and Erik Erikson have played such variations on the psychoanalytic theme that it is impossible to neatly categorize it as an approach to moral education. Perhaps it is best at this moment to look at the psychoanalytic view as a "tradition" traced back to Freud, and to understand the roots of that family tree go back to its founding father, Freud himself.

Philosophy: What is Moral?

In the psychoanalytic or Freudian tradition, morality is defined in terms of the cultural superego, the collective body of experience and tradition maintained in society. This cultural superego has its genesis in the "impressions left behind them by great leading personalities, men of outstanding force of mind, or men in whom some one human tendency has developed in unusual strength and purity" (Freud, 1952a, p. 800). These impressions become the values, the moral expectations, the guidelines for the present Zeitgeist and future evolution of society. Society's standards, moral expectations, and ideals that derive from these societal values are in turn transmitted to the individual members of society by its institutions of authority, and in the case of children by their parents and those who represent parental authority.

Sociology: What is the State of Society?

According to Freud, society serves one primary function: it protects its members from nature—human nature. All men have an innate instinctual predisposition to aggression such that,

> men are not gentle, friendly creatures wishing for love, who simply defend themselves if they are attacked, but ... a powerful measure of desire for aggression has to be reckoned with as a part of their instinctual endowment. (1952a, p. 787)

Society's role, then, is to impose limits and constraints that will regulate human interaction and control the expression of aggression; in sum, protect man from himself. The development of culture that accompanies the establishment of ethical systems, ideal standards, and moral values is intended to curb the instinctual nature of man sufficiently for society or civilization to be possible. Whether this process will be successful remains to be seen. As Freud (1952a) somberly reminds his readers:

> The fateful question of the human species seems to me to be whether and to what extent the cultural process developed in it will succeed in mastering the derangements of communal life caused by the human instinct of aggression and self-destruction. (p. 802)

Yet precisely because society seeks to impose bounds on instinctual predispositions, the future of society hangs in an uneasy balance. The threat of societal collapse looms imminent should the civilizing forces lose their influence even momentarily. By the same token, the very presence of human instincts makes any cultural gain the result of a difficult struggle.

> For the masses are lazy and unintelligent, they have no love for in-
> stinctual renunciation, and they are not to be convinced by argu-
> ment of its inevitability; and the individuals composing them
> support one another in giving free rein to their indiscipline. (1950,
> pp. 3-4)

Not surprisingly, then, order is maintained through coercion, and it is this imposed regulation that accounts for the major problems of society.

Society exerts its moral authority on two levels, the most evident being that of the rules and regulations by which everyday life abides; and the second residing in the psychological responses of shame and guilt that are manifestations of the superego function. These two levels on which societal authority is exercised represent the distinction between, and transition from, external to internal coercion. External authority, the laws and regulations of society, gradually become internalized to form the superego. Because the internalization of societal demands does not eradicate instinctual nature, but rather calls for an ever-increasing "neglect of instinctual realities" (Rieff, 1979, p. 312), man becomes increasingly miserable and inwardly hostile as civilization progresses. The general malaise reaches a point where neurosis develops as a means of dealing with society's continued denial of the instinctual nature of man. As Freud observed,

> It was found that men become neurotic because they cannot toler-
> ate the degree of privation that society imposes on them in virtue of
> its cultural ideas, and it was supposed that a return to greater possi-
> bilities of happiness would ensue if these standards were abolished
> or greatly relaxed. (1952a, p. 777)

As a result of this paradoxical situation, this double bind, Freud pro-nounced that "every individual is virtually an enemy of civilization, though civilization is supposed to be an object of universal human interest" (1950, p. 2). It is the resentment engendered by the unrelenting promotion of culture and cultural ideas at the expense of man's instinctual nature that results in outbreaks of violence, war, and revolution. War becomes a "massive balanc-ing of the psychic budget, bringing ethically bankrupt humans back to living within their means" (Rieff, 1979, p. 313). In conclusion, the price of civiliza-tion and society is neurosis and periodic violence and bloodshed. What is the state of society? Tragic: humans cannot live without civilization, nor can they abide within it; no amount or quality of moral values or standards can ameliorate the situation, only exacerbate it.

Psychology: How do People Change Their Moral Behavior?

Individual moral development is a two-stage process in psychoanalytic thought. The first of these stages belongs to the pre-superego period of life, early childhood; and the second is characterized by the emergence of superego influence on behavior in later childhood. Only with the development of the superego does the child become a moral and social being (Freud, 1950, p. 7).

As described above, the community superego, society's ensemble of moral expectations, rules and regulations, and ideal standards, is transmitted to its individual members through its institutions. Thus the contents of the societal superego are internalized by the individual to constitute the personal superego. Every person becomes a guardian of the community's past, its traditions, and culture.

Parents, and those who share their role in the care and upbringing of children, embody the moral authority of society; they are responsible for transmitting society's expectations to the child. In the early years of a child's life parental dominance and coercion regulate the child's behavior. Gradually, however, these demands are internalized by the child and the personal superego begins to crystallize and function. When the superego assumes the role of external authority and leads the child to live by society's standards, the child is considered to be socialized (Hall & Lindzey, 1954, p. 165).

In demanding conformity to society's demands, the child's newly formed superego perpetuates his parents' superego and its characteristics almost *in toto*:

> It takes over the same content, it becomes the vehicle of tradition and of all the age-long values which have been handed down in this way from generation to generation. (Freud, 1952b, p. 834)

The superego forms in opposition to the ego; it regulates the actions of the ego just as the parents controlled the child early in life (Freud, 1952b, p. 832). Shame and guilt result from the tension between the superego's moral demands and the desires of the ego. The controlling power of guilt arises from two sources: the dread of parental authority and, later, the dread of the superego (Freud, 1952a, p. 793). Because the superego knows the innermost desires and inclinations of the ego, it acts as an even harsher judge than did the parents in early childhood. All the ego's secrets are laid bare before the scrutiny of the superego; the guilty ego stands accused and fit for punishment. The due punishment is administered by the superego through the voice of conscience, which is essentially no more than man's aggressive instinct assumed by the superego and redirected inwardly against the ego. Freud noted,

> The aggressiveness is introjected, *internalized*; in fact, it is sent back where it came from, that is, directed against the ego. It is there taken over by a part of the ego that distinguishes itself from the rest as a superego, and now, in the form of *conscience*, exercises the same propensity to harsh aggressiveness against the ego that the ego would have liked to enjoy against others. The tension between the strict superego and the subordinate ego we call the *sense of guilt*; it manifests itself as the need for punishment. (p. 792)

Freud characterized the superego as the heir to the Oedipus complex (1952b). Indeed, proper superego formation can occur only when the Oedipus complex is adequately resolved and overcome. Briefly, the Oedipus complex represents the child's intense desire to sexually possess one or both parents as love objects. However, fear of parental reprisals induces the child to deny and repress his desire for the love object and the mode of possessing it. But although the child may give up his sexual attachment to one or both parents, through identification he or she can compensate for the loss of the coveted parent. Identification with the desired parent serves to recreate the forsaken love object in the child's ego and restore it to his or her possession.

> If one has lost a love-object or has had to give it up, one often com-
> pensates oneself by identifying oneself with it; one sets it up again
> inside one's ego, so that in this case object-choice regresses, as it
> were, to identification. (p. 833)

Identification with the parents following in the wake of the Oedipal complex is clearly essential to the proper development of the child's superego: for only through identification do the parental values, and the expectations of society they represent, become the moral and cultural property of the child. In other words, only with identification does socialization occur and can moral ideas change.

Education

How do teachers teach morals? In view of the influence of parents and parental figures on the development of the superego in children, it follows that the single most effective way for teachers to transmit society's moral values is to actively model them in their daily interactions with pupils. In this way teachers, who after the parents are the most significant authority figures in a child's life, offer their ideal model to the identification process and the formation of the superego. Demonstrating warmth and acceptance of the child facilitates identification with the teacher. In addition, because identification is dependent on the resolution of the Oedipus complex, it is useful for the teacher to understand the workings of the complex in order to assist the child in dealing with it.

As a man of his time, Freud believed that the answer to many of the world's woes would be furnished through man's rational faculties, morality being no exception. In Freud's view, a new chapter in mankind's moral history will begin to unfold when the instincts, for whose control moral teachings exist, are submitted to the reshaping influence of rational tutelage (Rieff, 1979, p. 313). Society's malaise will diminish as increased emphasis on rationality in education produces

> new generations, who have been brought up in kindness and taught
> to have a high opinion of reason, and who have experienced the

benefits of civilization at an early age, will have a different attitude
to it. (Freud, 1950, p. 4)

Only through reason can profound resentment at the degree of instinctual
privation imposed be disarmed; and this, as one comes to understand and
accept the necessity of instinctual sacrifice for society's sake. On the other
hand, much of the violence in society can be traced as a reaction to
civilization's exaggerated moral aspirations. Society demands of its members
a standard of behavior and moral conformity that is well beyond the capacities of many. Frustrated by this state of affairs, some individuals respond with
aggression. Part of the solution to the dilemma of morality may naturally be
education in the use of reason; the other may necessitate an inevitable
lowering of society's moral expectations (Rieff, 1979, p. 274).

How do students learn morals? From the psychoanalytic perspective the
single most important factor in moral development is the child's social
context and, more specifically, relationship with parents and significant
others. Through modeling and identification, parental and societal values are
incorporated into the child's superego. Whereas before the emergence of the
superego the child was controlled by means of parental coercion, the
superego embodies and perpetuates the parents' authority and regulates the
child's behavior through the use of shame, guilt, and conscience.

In order to learn moral behavior the child must be presented with an ideal
model, usually one or both of the parents, whose values the child will adopt
as part of the identification process following upon the Oedipus complex.
Secondary ideal models—teachers, heroes, and so forth—also have a certain
impact on the child's growing moral character, but in general these models
only supplement the parental influence. The teacher can only hope that the
values presented in the classroom will correspond to those modeled in the
home. If these conditions prevail in a context of warmth and caring, psychoanalytic theory would expect the modeled moral values to become part of
the child's superego.

Outcomes: What Kind of Person Results?

If the process of identification and superego formation is successfully completed, Freudian theory would expect the individual to have integrated and
to be able to demonstrate a socially acceptable level of moral behavior. The
child at this point would be controlled not by fear of parental authority, but
through dread of superego punishment by guilt and conscience. In order to
avoid the unpleasant feelings of shame and guilt, the child must behave
morally, that is, according to society's standards and values.

On the contrary, because the price of moral behavior is the suppression
of fundamental instinctual desires for the sake of community life, the moral
individual often unconsciously harbors deep-seated feelings of resentment
and frustration against the social order that force renunciation of so many

natural satisfactions. Frustration or "discontent" may occasionally exceed one's personal tolerance threshold, resulting in outbreaks of immoral or otherwise antisocial behavior or, again, neurosis and other forms of mental illness. This is how Freud saw the process of moral development in his own society, yet he did not consider this to be the only approach to the origins of morality. Rather, he insisted that education to morality in the future could proceed along two paths: first, a revision of society's moral aspirations, that is, a lowering of the societal standards that would take into consideration the realities of human nature; and, second, the development of rational faculties in the appreciation of society's benefits and the necessity of limiting instinctual drives in the interests of the human community.

The individual resulting from this type of moral education would be what Freud called a "third Adam," a person who is no longer controlled by shame and guilt nor subject to violent aggression of the moral conscience. The morality of this new Adam will be characterized, he says, by rational awareness of human nature and instinctual realities; he will make conscious decisions to forgo personal instinctual satisfaction for the sake of society. Morality, then, will no longer mean an unwilling or unconscious subjugation to external authority made internal, but a rational and conscious choice to endure instinctual privation for the choice to be moral in the community.

Despite all the gloominess, Freud had somewhat noble dreams of what men and women might be given the proper kind of moral education: more rational, more fully conscious, with the principles of morality centered within the person and not coming from some extrinsic, societal source. But still there remained that enmity between society and the individual. Freud saw this antagonism between the individual's instinctive goals and the goals of society as at least a shadowy threat always lurking in the background. His vision does not encompass that harmony between the individual and the collective that Whitehead described as both desirable and possible. Freud missed the religious vision of that peace created by the harmony of individuality and relatedness. Perhaps, ironically, Freud's system fails because it is *not* religious.

Socialization: Behavioristic Approaches

Philosophy: What is Moral?

From the behavioral or social learning perspective, moral education is but one of the many types of education the child receives as a member of society. An individual is said to be socialized when his or her behaviors and attitudes correspond to the standards and attitudes of the parent society, giving him or her the ability to function adequately in the community. As such, one of the major roles of socialization is to effect a practical means of social control. To this end,

> socialization efforts are designed to lead the new member to adhere
> to the norms of the larger society or of the particular group into
> which he is being incorporated and to commit him to its future. The
> group's values are at least to be recognized by him as having legiti-
> macy. (Clausen, 1968, p. 6)

In social learning theory, moral behavior is dependent not on maturational or developmental processes, but on learning and conditioning through
the rewarding of appropriate behaviors and attitudes. This distinction is
extremely important in social learning.

What, then, constitutes morality in social learning theory? Majority consensus, the opinion of the group. Morality and moral behavior refers to the
ensemble of behaviors and attitudes that society in general values as right or
appropriate. Following this definition,

> moral behavior is behavior a social group defines as good or right
> and for which the social group administers sanctions. Moral values
> are beliefs, again shared in a social group, about what is good or
> right. (Maccoby, 1968, p. 229)

Consequently, the moral person is one who demonstrates the greatest number of desirable or "good" behaviors and attitudes. This is a quantitative
approach.

Sociology: What is the State of Society?

Moral values, by virtue of the way society defines them and chooses to abide
by them, are not fixed or immutable, but vary from place to place and time
to time according to the consensus of the majority. In all but the most static,
stable societies moral standards and norms are in a continual state of flux as
interpretations and applications of rules and principles change, are rede-
fined, or are modified by the evolving nature of society (Clausen, 1968, p. 6).
In the process of becoming socialized, the child adopts whatever moral
values prevail in his social context, or he does not and remains either
amoral, immoral, or premoral in his society's view; but it is inconceivable for
him to espouse another system of morality. As Maccoby informs her readers,
"[In social learning theory] there is no provision ... for a new generation to
acquire a set of values systematically *different* from those held by their
parents" (1968, p. 245).

Although its moral standards and values may be in perpetual motion,
society still maintains a remarkable cohesion and exerts its control over the
individual. Given the time span of generations, the majority consensus
regarding particular values may change with attendant effects on community
moral expectations and norms, but as the transmission of values proceeds
from parent to child, the chain of tradition is maintained more or less intact
although individual links may be replaced. With the passing of a number of

generations the chain may come to be composed of more new links than old, and so the process goes on; but the chain of tradition remains.

Psychology: How do People Change Their Moral Behavior?

From the point of view of social learning theory, children learn moral behavior through two primary modes: identification with powerful role models, and reinforcement of appropriate behavior. Identification and modeling here are understood in a more impersonal sense than in the Freudian tradition whose concepts of superego and ego Bandura and Walters consider burdened with "surplus meaning" that tends to overly "personify the controlling forces" (1963, p. 162). In response, social learning theorists seek to demonstrate how moral behavior results not from the identification with and integration of parental superego values, but rather from social training and reinforcing of desired behaviors and attitudes.

As in psychoanalysis, the acquisition of moral behavior also involves both external and internal sanctions that exert control through shame and guilt. However, in social learning these responses do not represent an integration of the parental authority, but rather the activation of a conditioned response. Bandura and Walters write,

> Guilt is mediated by an internal moral agent, which originated and developed from sanctions imposed by the parents or other primary socializing agents, but which is now completely independent of an individual's current social experiences. (1963, p. 163)

Clearly the moral individual has acquired, through conditioning and reinforcement, at least the minimum number of society's behavioral expectations. Parents contribute significantly to the moral formation of a child, but the greatest influence rests with the agent who holds the power of reward and punishment, usually, but not necessarily, the parents. The contents of morality take the form of various rules and ordinances, obedience to which is rewarded and reinforced by the parents, teachers, and society at large. In the process of learning appropriate behavior, the controlling responses of shame and guilt are also conditioned into the child's moral character. Evidently, morality in this view has no link with maturational or developmental processes, but is completely a matter of learned behavioral responses to various stimuli.

Education

How do teachers teach morals? The moral educator, from a social learning perspective, need not undertake any activity appreciably different from that of any other teacher. Social learning theory sees morality as essentially no more than the integration and adequate performance of a set of behaviors defined by society as moral. As with any behavior, what one would call moral behavior is acquired through conditioning. In the course of normal education the teacher rewards the child for displays of socially acceptable, moral behavior in appropriate situations. Thus the principles of moral education follow the same fundamental principles of learning theory in general. As Maccoby explains:

> For social learning theorists, the acquisition of moral behavior and values is not different in any significant way from the acquisition of any other class of behavior. If one wishes to understand the acquisition of morality, one must study the processes which underlie the acquisition of any behavior, that is to say, the processes of learning. (1968, p. 241)

How do students learn morals? Following the above, children learn moral behavior as they do any other type of behavior. They are presented with role models early in life, whose influence tends to persist and is reinforced as part of socialization. In this view children are not active moral agents seeking out their own norms or moral behavior, but passive, almost the classical blank slates on which society engraves its moral expectations. Theoretically, as long as a strong enough reward is present, children will accept whatever example their models hold forth as desirable behavior. Through proper modeling and rewarding, this technique would produce acceptable moral individuals. Nonetheless, in spite of the seeming simplicity and clarity of this approach to moral education, a serious reservation surfaces with Bandura and Walters' observation that learned behavior does not imply performed behavior (Maccoby, 1968, p. 258). In other words, the demonstration of moral behavior in a learned situation does not mean a child will act morally in a real-life situation. Learned principles are not necessarily lived principles.

That moral behavior, although conditioned, does not automatically become fully internalized is a troublesome point in social learning theory. Internalization is problematic on two counts: first, according to theory, behavior is always controlled by external, discriminative stimuli, only sanctions are internalized (Maccoby, 1968, p. 259); second, apparently independent, internally motivated behavior may in reality be behavior for which the subject receives the approval, actual or imagined, of some personally significant but smaller reference group or individual (Bandura & Walters, 1963, p. 164). In sum, internalization of moral behavior is dependent on some sort of external reinforcement of modeled behavior accompanied by internally produced sanctions; this sets up a contradiction in terms of locus of control that does not permit the postulation of a purely autonomous moral agent. As a result, the child learns moral behavior, but remains passively identified with and controlled by the rewarding person.

Outcomes: What Kind of Person Results?

Social learning produces an individual who fulfills the better part of society's expectations, moral or otherwise. Because the child has been conditioned through reward and punishment to display appropriate moral behavior in given situations, his or her continued performance of that behavior remains contingent on consistent reinforcement while the behavior is being learned. Unless the child receives strong counterindications for different moral behavior, his initially learned pattern of responses should continue indefinitely. In the final analysis, the child resulting from the social learning way of moral education does not become an autonomous moral agent, but remains a conformer, passively controlled by others' expectations.

The "moral person" who emerges from social learning theory's approach to moral education is not very appealing. One need not go to the extreme images of Alex in Anthony Burgess's *A Clockwork Orange* to be repelled by the thought of a programmed moral behavior. Conformity, often *blind* conformity, is the theme, and this is hardly moral behavior. Perhaps social learning theory reminds us best just how potent an influence reinforcement, modeling, and identification are in moral education. It tells us how these forces can consciously be used by teachers to shape desirable behavior— whatever "desirable" might happen to be. Even more ominously, social learning theory reminds us of how powerful unconscious forces are in shaping moral behavior, forces of which sometimes neither the subject nor the teachers of morality are aware themselves.

Values Clarification: Subjectivity in Action

In the tradition of John Dewey, three authors, Raths, Harmin, and Simon (1966), have given us an influential book, *Values and Teaching*, which attempts to align value education (moral education included) with the spirit of a democratic society. Their ideas and techniques for "Values Clarification" have throughout almost two decades influenced many popular workshops and set new directions for massive curriculum rebuilding in the schools (Simon, Howe, & Kirschenbaum, 1972).

Like Kohlberg, they arrived on the American scene just in time to meet typical North American needs. First, they encouraged democracy, a sacrosanct political institution; second, they caught the swing of the '60s toward individualism, self-choice, and self-actualization in all the varieties of meanings Maslow's term came to take on; third, they opened the door to values teaching in a society where religion was often barred from the schools by legislation. Values clarification seemed to permit some sort of moral education that avoided the issue of any kind of dogma or moral code and concentrated instead on the individual's own personal arrival at a unique and subjective hierarchy of values. In a pluralistic society making special efforts to avoid all absolutes, they presented a timely alternative that promised to avoid the nemesis of "keeping dreary watch over ancient values," and to move instead into the more exciting fast lane of democratic rugged individualism based on the glories of subjectivity in valuing. The process of valuing was the shared mandated goal; the content of valuing was strictly left to the individual.

Philosophy: What is Moral?

The values clarification approach to moral education starts with the presupposition that values of right and wrong, or *oughtness*, are determined by each individual for oneself. This position offers itself in opposition to traditional thinking that sees moral education as a process of indoctrination whereby the child is taught society's immutable moral values and is expected to assimilate, integrate, and demonstrate them in everyday behavior. Values clarification, on the other hand, takes the position that values, and the moral behavior they motivate, are not unchanging, objective absolutes, but variable personal reactions and responses to real-life situations. Rightness or wrongness in a given situation or context is determined by the individual's unique and personal reflections on the values he or she holds. These personal values are the foundation and guide of one's moral behavior.

Sociology: What is the State of Society?

In values clarification, societal values as objective, consistent, principles do not exist. Although society may hold a particular value or group of values stable over a certain span of time, eventually even these succumb to change and are replaced by different interpretations and applications as customs and traditions change. In society, then, values are in the end no more than the combination, conflicting or agreeing, of the subjectively determined values of the individual members of society. As one perceives life and its contingencies in different ways as personal situations change, so too the values one holds change. Consequently, if values are personal and subjective, making societal values impossible to define objectively and with certainty, there can equally be no objective ethical principles that serve as the foundation of society. The subjective experience of the individual and the values he or she ascribes to it become the base of any values and ethics in the larger society.

Psychology: How do People Change Their Moral Behavior?

Because of their subjective nature, values are seen as the result of one's interaction with and reflection on life's experience. It follows, then, that two individuals with vastly different experiences would necessarily hold significantly different values. Because of these differences in personal experience, individual values and the behaviors they produce can in no way be consistently predicted or normalized.

Nonetheless, Raths et al. propose that although it is impossible to determine the most appropriate values for someone, certain criteria must be met before a value can be defined as such. In ordering these criteria Raths and his associates have presented what they call the "process of valuing" (1966, p.

28), which contains the seven conditions they consider essential to value formation. Each of the seven criteria must be met before one can be said to hold a value. The seven criteria are as follows.

1. Choosing freely. The value must be the product of free choice, no element of coercion may be involved.

2. Choosing from among alternatives. Values are freely chosen and free choice can occur only in the presence of at least one alternative.

3. Choosing after thoughtful consideration of the consequences of each alternative. True values are born of rational and intelligent consideration of alternatives, with an understanding of the implications and consequences of the choice.

4. Prizing and cherishing. One must be happy and proud of one's values, esteem them and hold them dear.

5. Affirming. One is proud of one's values and is not afraid to be associated with them even where public affirmation of values is demanded in spite of the threat of ridicule, etc.

6. Acting on one's choice. Values must give direction to life and effect change in one's life. Values must translate into action.

7. Repeating. Values are persistent and recur throughout one's lifetime. Values tend to initiate patterns of response to experience. (pp. 28-29)

Only when an individual has fulfilled all these criteria does he or she possess values in the proper sense of the word. Once one's values have been clarified or brought to conscious awareness and have been assessed according to the above seven criteria, their impact on moral behavior is direct and significant. Moral ideas change as the values underlying them are more fully recognized and understood, accepted, or rejected.

Although values clarification was intended for the examination of a broad range of values ("Do I value stamp collecting, picnics in the park, popular music?"), it was also intended for and used in clarifying moral values. Using this technique, individuals would change their moral values through a consciousness-enhancing process. This involved a new awareness of what the individual professed to be his values, examination of them under the seven criteria, and acceptance or rejection of them into a personal hierarchy of values. The situation that aroused these value questions could be a real value crisis in one's own life or a contrived value conflict produced by a trained workshop leader or teacher in a classroom.

Education

How do teachers teach morals? Raths et al. (1966) have provided a variety of strategies for using values clarification in the classroom. Many of these value clarifying strategies stem from a person-centered tradition; that is, the emphasis is always on what the student is thinking, expressing, and feeling. One of the principal techniques advocated by Raths and associates is the clarifying response, which is the teacher's way of

> responding to a student that results in his considering what he has chosen, what he prizes, and/or what he is doing. It stimulates him to clarify his thinking and behavior and thus to clarify his values; it encourages him to think about them. (p. 51)

In employing the clarifying response the teacher must avoid all moralizing or criticizing, any suggestion of being judgmental. The purpose of the response is only to induce students to reflect more deeply on their statement, their position, in order to make their values more evident. The clarifying responses themselves must be open-ended so as to convey no expectation on the teacher's part of a specific reply or value statement from the student. Raths et al. present some 30 clarifying responses to be used in teacher-student conversations. Many of these lead the student to consider one of the seven criteria for valuing in formulating a response: "Is this something you prize?" or "Did you consider any alternatives?" or again, "Was that something that you yourself selected or chose?" (p. 57).

Another important classroom strategy for values clarification is the values clarifying discussion. In this type of discussion the teacher leads a group of students to express their beliefs and attitudes, their values, on various topics or dilemmas. In directing students through the values clarifying discussion the teacher

1. endeavors to examine alternatives and consequences in issues,
2. does not tell them, directly or indirectly, what is "right" for all persons and for all times,
3. is candid about his or her own values but insists that they not be blindly adopted by others,
4. sometimes limits behavior that one considers ill advised but never limits the right to believe or the right to behave differently in other circumstances,
5. points to the importance of the individual making his own choices and considering the implications for his own life. (p. 115)

At the end of the discussion the teacher asks for a summary of what value positions have been taken. Role-playing, the contrived incident, the value continuum, and other similar values clarification strategies may also serve as grist for the value clarifying discussion mill. Regardless of which particular strategy is used, the teacher maintains value neutrality and affirms the students' choice of values.

How do students learn morals? Properly used values clarifying techniques, Raths et al. maintain, will get students actively involved in the process of choosing, affirming, and acting on their own values, and this in turn will extend into the realm of moral behavior. Implicit here is the theory that students learn morals by first becoming aware of the values they hold, and through the values clarification process becoming actively committed to those values or to others they have alternatively selected. Morality is based on a sound understanding of, and commitment to, personal values. Arriving at that understanding and commitment is the goal of values clarification.

Outcomes: What Kind of Person Results?

Ideally, the values clarification approach to moral education produces an individual who knows what his or her values are, why she or he holds them, and who is not afraid to act on them. As a result of applying the seven criteria of valuing one has learned a process by which one can identify one's values in any given situation, through any experience, and at any time in life. Therefore, moral judgments and behavior should pose no problem to this person. Values clarification will have made this person an autonomous moral agent whose actions are consistent with his or her beliefs, attitudes, and, ultimately, his or her values.

There is no need to critique values clarification extensively here. Many others, including Kathleen Gow (1980) in her popular work *Yes, Virginia, There is Right and Wrong*, have extensively criticized the subjectivistic approach to morals and have tried to lead the way back to a more conservative ethic of right and wrong, with its emphasis on clear definition of moral content in teaching and on the importance of preserving and passing on moral standards to succeeding generations.

However, Raths et al. (1966) have made their contributions to moral education, among them the emphasis on consciousness. To remind us that we all have values and live by them whether we know it or not, and to prod us to reflect on those values, be conscious of what they are, and make deliberate choices of whether we want to keep those values and live by them is a valuable service. This prodding creates the possibility of creating a personal hierarchy of values and hierarchy of aims, creative of genuine multilevel moral development. Second, Raths et al. have presented us with a definition of value more rigorous than some other authors would demand. To say that a value is not a value unless it is lived, unless it flows into action and sets some theme for one's life is a radical departure from some other concepts of value (e.g., Rokeach's, 1960, 1969) that require only that a value be professed. One could argue on purely speculative grounds the relative merits of each definition of value, but to maintain that the proof of a value is in the action is akin to the grandmotherly wisdom that "the proof of the pudding is in the eating." The stress on consciousness and the need for a hierarchy of values also to be a hierarchy of aims are two valuable elements of the values clarification heritage.

Cognitive-Developmental Approaches: Kohlberg and Others

The name Lawrence Kohlberg has, at least in North American circles, become almost synonymous with moral education. Like the values clarification movement, Kohlberg's cognitive-development theory came along at a time when it met society's needs for a system of moral education that eschewed the "bag of virtues" approach and sought instead to teach individuals how to think well on moral issues. Again, content yielded to process, and this fit in well with the American political and educational landscape of the time (Kuhmerker, 1991).

Philosophy: What is Moral?

In cognitive-developmental theory, morality is determined by each individual as a function of his or her own cognitive and rational capacities, at whatever level they may be operating. Thus, in the stage/level perspective offered in the cognitive-developmental approach, each member of society is morally sophisticated only to the highest level of moral reasoning that he or she can understand and appreciate. From this perspective, therefore, it is not possible to present a blanket statement of what society holds as moral, for that varies with individuals; rather, it can at most be determined that the majority of society gravitates and functions at some particular level of moral reasoning, usually termed *conventional*, and that society's moral expectations reflect either the level of the majority or some higher stage.

In spite of the difficulty in defining absolutes of morality, Kohlberg (1968, 1974, 1977, 1981) outlines some of the philosophical considerations that go into the formation of a moral statement or judgment. For Kohlberg, "moral judgments tend to be universal, inclusive, consistent, and based on objective, impersonal, or ideal grounds" (p. 490). That is, all judgments that qualify as moral judgments per se would do so regardless of who makes the statement, where and when he makes it. The universality, objectivity, and consistency of the statement is of fundamental importance.

In his earlier writings Kohlberg is more concerned with the structure of moral reasoning than with its content. The entire focus of the cognitive-developmental point of view dwells on the evolution of moral reasoning, how the conceptual structure expands and is modified to deal with new and ever more complex moral situations. With this emphasis on the development of the cognitive processes, it is possible in Kohlberg's view to assign worth to a moral judgment without considering its content; what counts is the process by which the judgment is arrived at.

More recently, however, Kohlberg and his colleagues have developed a set of 12 norms that refer to the specific content of moral reasoning, norms that represent the central values of any social system (Arbuthnot & Braeden, 1981, p. 68). With this set of norms it is possible to evaluate both the structure of moral judgments and the value of the moral content they contain.

As a person proceeds through the various levels of moral reasoning, his or her moral judgments increasingly reflect the concept of justice, which applies universally and objectively to all individuals in all situations. As Kohlberg explains:

> It is also evident that moral development in terms of these stages is a progressive movement toward basing moral judgment on concepts of justice. To base a moral duty on a concept of justice is to base that duty on the right of an individual; to judge an act wrong is to judge it as violating such a right. (1968, p. 490)

By "right" Kohlberg intends the equality and reciprocity that each member of society expects to enjoy in his interactions with the state and other individuals. A higher level moral judgment, therefore, upholds and promotes this expectation objectively and impartially. In the cognitive-developmental paradigm, then, morality is defined in terms of cognitive level or stages of moral reasoning based on the principle of justice. This concept of justice assures the fundamental right or expectation of individuals in relation to each other and to society. A moral judgment is a cognitive judgment, a choice of action that fulfills the right of the individual to the extent possible, or more properly, conceivable at one's given stage of moral reasoning.

Sociology: What is the State of Society?

The cognitive-developmental view on the relation between society and morality lies somewhere between the theories of socialization and the cultural relativism of moral values, and utilitarianism, which deems an act right that affords the greatest good for the greatest number (Kohlberg, 1968). Kohlberg points out that, in reality, moral judgments in all cultures embody features of both socialization and utilitarian perspectives. The extremes of socialization theory and utilitarianism are not incompatible opposites, but merely two points along a developmental continuum. Socialization represents the earliest stage of moral development, whereas moral judgment based on utilitarian principles represents a higher level of moral reasoning.

> Moral judgment and emotion based on respect for custom, authority, and the group are seen as one phase or stage in the moral development of the individual rather than as the total definition of the essential characteristics of morality it was for Durkheim. Judgment of right and wrong in terms of the individual's consideration of social-welfare consequences, universal principles, and justice is seen as a later phase of development. (p. 487)

Consequently, cognitive-developmental theory holds that individuals pass through a series of moral stages characterized by the development of increasingly complex cognitive structures whose focus shifts progressively from specific to general, universal principles, moral statements, and judgments. In this context, then, moral development is directly linked to cognitive development.

In society one can observe a number of stages or levels of cognitive development; similarly, varying levels of moral development can be found. Individuals, organizations, and institutions may, according to Kohlberg, be found at three levels of moral development—Pre-Conventional, Conventional, and Post-Conventional—indicating a process from egocentric, self-serving moral reasoning, through social conformity, to principled moral thinking at a high level of abstraction and generalization. Just as the majority of society gravitates around a certain level of cognitive development, so too in morality society tends to cluster on, and function by, the standards and norms of a particular level of moral reasoning. This, of course, does not mean that the moral judgments made by individuals at the same level of moral development represent the same set of moral values; rather, what is common between them is the process and structure of the moral reasoning behind them. As was emphasized earlier, what is important in moral judgments is the structure, the principles involved, not the actual content of the judgment. In other words, from the cognitive-developmental point of view society's norms, rules, and mores may change over time, but the principles behind them and the processes by which moral judgments or choices are made remain stable.

Psychology: How do People Change Their Moral Behavior?

In the cognitive-developmental model, people change their moral ideas through the maturation and development of cognitive process. This may occur naturally as a result of development, or it may be induced by being exposed, or rather confronted, by the challenges of higher-level moral reasoning. In this view moral advance is definitely based on cognition rather than emotional or learned responses.

In the presence of higher-level moral reasoning processes, the lower-level individual experiences cognitive dissonance, an unpleasant mental state that demands resolution. When faced with this type of cognitive disequilibrium, one can follow either of two routes, assuming one is aware of the discrepancy between one's thinking and that of the more adequate higher level. One can ignore the tension, or can attempt to understand the structure and processes involved in the higher level pattern of moral reasoning. In the latter case, maintains Kohlberg, an understanding of the more advanced level of moral reasoning usually leads to dissatisfaction with that of the lower level. This discontent with one's own mode of thinking and the awareness of its shortcomings are often sufficient to promote a shift to the next higher stage of moral reasoning. As one progresses through the sequence of stages, one's moral reasoning becomes more abstract and grounded in principles, most notably justice. As a result, each successive stage is necessarily more generalizable and universal.

In summary, individuals change their moral ideas (and Kohlberg maintains, against criticism, their moral behavior too) as a result of cognitive development. This may come about through normal maturation and development, or it may be occasioned by exposure to higher levels of moral reasoning. The basic theoretical position behind the cognitive-developmental approach is that for most individuals, cognitive dissonance is an unpleasant state of disequilibrium that seeks resolution. In theory this resolution should represent achievement of a higher stage in the sequence of moral reasoning.

Education

How do teachers teach morals? In Kohlberg's approach to moral education teachers teach not morals, but moral reasoning. The aim is to elevate each student to the highest possible stage of moral thinking, to the most universal and principled level of moral reflection. To this end Kohlberg supplies a variety of moral dilemmas that are used in the classroom to spark debate and discussion. Each dilemma is carefully constructed to include the following qualities.

1. It presents conflicting claims that superficially appear to be plausible and reasonable.
2. It focuses on the particular level of moral reasoning shared by the majority of the students in the group.
3. It involves some life experience that is meaningful for the students.
4. The facts of the moral issue are clearly defined and determined so that the focus centers on the moral issue itself.
5. It includes questions that force students to think more deeply on the moral issue or issues presented.

Many of Kohlberg's dilemmas such as Heinz and the druggist are well known, but Joe and the summer camp is another standard example:

Joe is a 14-year-old boy who wanted to go to camp very much. His father promised him he could go if he saved up the money for it himself. So Joe worked hard at his paper route and saved up the $40 it cost to go to camp and a little more besides. But just before camp was going to start, his father changed his mind. Some of his friends decided to go on a special fishing trip, and he (Joe's father) was short of the money it would cost. So he told Joe to give him the money saved from the paper route. Joe didn't want to give up going to camp, so he thinks of refusing to give his father the money.

To be most effective the moral dilemma should be integrated into the general educational program and not restricted to only one particular classroom setting. The force of the dilemmas comes from their evident relation to real-life situations. Any school subject that deals with life concerns is an appropriate background for Kohlberg's moral dilemmas.

After the dilemma has been presented the teacher invites discussion by posing some provocative and stimulating questions. Effective discussion questions are of six major types.

1. *Perception* questions check whether students understand what has been said.

2. *Participation* questions get one student to respond to another's argument.

3. *Clarifying* questions call on students to explain the meaning or significance of their statements, e.g., "What do you mean by honesty?"

4. *Role-switch* questions ask a student to put him/herself in the place of different characters in the dilemma.

5. *Universal-consequences* questions ask, in effect, what would happen if everyone behaved or thought in one certain way.

6. *Seeking-reason* questions ask Why? Probe for reasoning or justification.

How do students learn morals? As a result of the dilemma discussion, conflicts may be set up in students' minds that render past moral assumptions inadequate and consequently inappropriate. Through the active cognitive exercise of giving justifiable and defensible reasons for moral choices, students are exposed to higher-level moral reasoning that may resolve the cognitive discomfort they experience. Students learn morality as their cognitive moral reasoning abilities develop as a result of maturation, or as they adopt the patterns of what Kohlberg calls higher-stage moral thinking.

Outcomes: What Kind of Person Results?

If Kohlberg's cognitive-developmental approach to moral education has been successful, the outcome should be an individual who functions at a higher level of moral reasoning than that demonstrated at the outset. Kohlberg's moral dilemmas should have awakened a new awareness in students of the inadequacy of their habitual mode of moral reasoning. As they cannot tolerate such inadequacy the students will have adopted the next highest level above their own.

Higher-stage moral reasoning is not automatically followed by matching moral behavior. Ordinarily, one can observe similar behaviors often stemming from different levels of moral reasoning. This difficulty, compounded with the fact that individuals at varying stages of moral development tend to make different behavior choices or moral responses in the same situations, leads the cognitive-developmental theorist to concentrate primarily on the quality or level of the moral reasoning process and not the content or behaviors deriving from it. In the end one should wonder at this; is not the ultimate aim of moral education none other than moral behavior?

That Kohlberg has such a huge influence on moral education is a mark of his own personal genius. His philosophy, based on Piaget and Rawls, was carefully developed in the beginning, and though much flawed according to his ardent critics such as Peters (1969, 1974), it formed one of the best-thought-through moral philosophies of modern times. His research, again much criticized (compare Kurtines & Grief, 1974; and others), was at least research, making it outstanding among many moral education theories that often rested on untried purely speculative foundations.

As I have said, Kohlberg answered to the needs of his time. He also happened to produce a technique of moral education that caught the interest of educators and the imagination of entrepreneurs. His neat six stages of moral reasoning (later reduced to five) were handy for amateur psychologists to use to categorize people and thus acquire an air of "understanding their level of moral development." These stages, plus the dilemma technique of moral education, spawned the creation of many new dilemmas and teaching aids. This made the theory eminently suitable to inspire the production of books and kits that promised quick understanding and the ability to accurately score responses to dilemmas. With this ready information for the teacher appeared a profusion of teaching aids offering ready-made shortcuts to unprepared teachers suddenly required to become moral educators. That the cognitive-developmental approach became superficial and gimmicky was indicative of the seeming simplicity of the concepts, stages, and techniques, and indicative too of the crying need teachers had for some sort of help in performing educational tasks they were not prepared for either philosophically or methodologically.

A "Kohlberg Bandwagon" did develop, but the horde of followers who rushed to get on should not blind us to the genuine contribution Kohlberg made to principled moral education, and ultimately to religious education.

Emotional-Rational Approaches: Love in Action

While philosophers and psychologists in North America were busy creating moral education systems that could be used in schools where religion and doctrinal tradition were forbidden, scholars in Great Britain were faced with a task quite opposite in many respects. For many years England was a comparatively monolithic society with the Church of England as the established church and the education system rather well defined along elitist lines that favored the conservation of tradition. Religion was an established and compulsory part of the curriculum. With changing times educators were faced with the task of presenting religious education to a pluralistic society. To many scholars the answer to the question of how to present religious education was to develop something much more akin to moral education, adapting it to meet varying needs, varying demands, and varying interpretations. Thus for, in a sense, opposite reasons from their counterparts in the United States who were forbidden to teach religion, moral educators in Great Britain set out to meet the legal requirements for compulsory religious education by devising approaches to moral education that would work in a pluralistic society.

Among these many scholars were John Wilson of Oxford University who attempted a rational approach to moral education, and Peter McPhail of Cambridge who developed an emotional-rational theory. At this point we will pursue the McPhail approach, partly because it is more holistic and because McPhail and his associates created concrete techniques and teaching materials for moral education.

Philosophy: What is Moral?

Peter McPhail, in his emotional-rational approach to moral education developed for the British Schools Council, seeks above all to help students create for themselves a moral lifestyle. For McPhail, a moral lifestyle incorporates certain qualities that are not essentially different from traditional moral values. What is different is the motivation behind the demonstration of these values in moral choices and judgments and the means by which such values are acquired or taught. In the following discussion it should become evident what differentiates McPhail's model of moral education from the traditional authoritarian approach as well as the other models considered previously.

Some of the qualities of moral behavior as defined by McPhail are: care, affection, tolerance, understanding, compassion, sensitivity, concern, and respect. These are not a "bag of virtues" as in the traditional view, that is, imposed from the outside on the individual, but prerequisite elements or values that must be brought forth from the child and consolidated into the framework of his or her personality. In this view, McPhail would maintain that true moral behavior must emerge from within the child as a function of personality, as a total emotional and rational response to a situation.

The context for integrating and manifesting these moral qualities is a lifestyle based on care and consideration for others and self (Kupchenko, 1981, p. 107). McPhail reduces this type of lifestyle to its essential, "love in action" (McPhail, Middleton, & Ingram, 1978). In this light, morality is any mode of behavior, attitudes, or responses that translate into love in action.

> Our aim is not to develop a theory of moral behavior, nor to increase children's capacity to argue morally, nor to improve their ability to say good things. It is the practice of doing good things, of actually taking another's needs, feelings and interests into consideration as well as one's own, which concerns us first and foremost. Our purpose is to help children not only to know what "love in action" is, but also to act in love, in affection—to act warmly and caringly. (p. 5)

As the designation *emotional-rational* suggests, McPhail understands morality, or better, the process of being moral, in terms of both emotion and reason. In his program, McPhail places the primary emphasis on the emotional component of morality because he considers the motivational power of emotion or affect to be greater than that of reason alone. This is not an attempt on his part to deny the role of reason in making moral choices and judgments, but he reminds his reader that a moral judgment based merely on rational principles is not in itself a necessary and sufficient cause for moral behavior, and that behavior is his objective.

> Our concern is the practical one that people shall express in action their concern for others' needs, feelings and interests. We know that, whatever moral principles or procedures people advocate, and whatever stage of moral reasoning they may lay claim to, in the final analysis, to act morally, everyone has to be concerned with (and sensitive to) real-life situations. (McPhail et al., 1978, p. 3)

In summary, morality as defined by McPhail in the emotional-rational approach to moral education is a practical, concrete style of life that incorporates and demonstrates love in action at all levels of interpersonal relationships from self to family to the community, society, and the world at large.

Sociology: What is the State of Society?

Any discussion of society in the context of McPhail's emotional-rational model of moral education must begin with what he terms "the fundamental need ... to get on with others, to love and be loved" (McPhail, Ungoed-Thomas, & Chapman, 1972, p. 3). That is, the basic human need is relationship, man is an interactive creature; he creates his world through interaction with his environment, and he creates himself and others through human relationships (Kupchenko, 1981, p. 107). The state of society at any one time reflects the state of individuals' relationships in that society, the degree to which their fundamental need is, or is not, being met. McPhail's concept of morality, love in action, is ultimately the individual's striving to fulfill this fundamental need to "get on with others, to love and be loved."

The qualities of moral behavior—care, affection, tolerance, and so forth—are the lasting human values in society that make life full and complete. It is these essential factors that constitute the building blocks of relationships, and these, as in McPhail's concept of morality, must be manifested in action through the everyday living of a considerate lifestyle. As a result of such "moral" living, a richer society, a better world will be created, a world in which "individuals' needs, interests and feelings were taken more into consideration and where man showed greater care and responsibility for the rest of creation as well as himself" (McPhail et al., 1972, p. 4).

Indeed, the challenge of this vision in society lies in how one balances consideration for others without denying one's own needs (McPhail et al., 1978, p. 6). This challenge McPhail addresses with his emphasis on the role of both emotion and reason in the process of making moral choices. Although rationality in moral judgments is significant and necessary, the primary influence is provided by emotions, if only they can be clearly felt and listened to. Our better emotions, which are by nature altruistic, are not always accessible and operating in moral choices. Without their guiding influence one cannot always act or choose morally in accordance with those values that make life satisfying and complete. The McPhail approach attempts to establish or restore the missing connection between emotion and reason in society by means of the various exercises and dilemmas set up in the classroom. How the use of such techniques results in moral awakening or change will be treated in the following section.

Psychology: How do People Change Their Moral Behavior?

In the McPhail paradigm the key to a morality that is based on human interaction is ultimately communication. A "morality of communication" underlies all morality and, consequently, any sound attempt at moral education (1972, p. 62). The quality of person-to-person interaction McPhail envisions is based on Buber's "I-Thou" relationship. For such a relationship to exist four communication abilities are required:

1. *Reception ability,* meaning the ability to be, and remain, "switched on" to the right wave length, to listen, to look, to receive the messages sent out by others.

2. *Interpretative ability,* meaning the ability to interpret accurately the message that another person is sending, what he really means, what he really wants.

3. Response ability, meaning the ability to decide on and adopt appropriate reactions—to meet another's needs. It involves decision making, evaluation, the use of reason as psychological know how.

4. Message ability, meaning the ability to translate appropriate reactions into clearly transmitted unambivalent messages. (p. 63)

Personal morality as a function of relationships can begin to change only as individuals begin to acquire these abilities necessary for a morality of communication. As their quality of communication develops, people's moral ideas may begin to change as they:

1. improve their ability to recognize their own and others' needs, interests, and feelings;

2. improve their ability to interpret accurately the messages, both verbal and non-verbal, that other persons are sending;

3. improve their ability to predict the possible and probable consequences of actions;

4. improve their ability to see things from another's point of view;

5. develop a strong sense of identity and see themselves as people who have a contribution to make in their community;

6. identify the various legal and social rules of our society;

7. identify the various expectations and pressures put on them by society;

8. learn to choose, to decide in a particular situation, what they will do so long as it is consistent with the needs, interests, and feelings of others as well as their own. (Kupchenko, 1981, pp. 108-109)

Education

How do teachers teach morals? In McPhail's emotional-rational model teachers do not *teach* morality per se, but rather use various methods and techniques to help students know and experience love in action. Each of these teaching methods is to be used in small groups ranging from four to ten students. McPhail outlines six teaching strategies that may be used with moral education materials in any number of classroom settings and with different ages of children.

1. *Expressive and communicational activities:* Can be used alone or in groups, and can involve speaking; writing prose, poetry and plays; modelling, photography, etc. The intent is to motivate greater honesty and innovation in solving problems.

2. *Discussion:* To use when the subject is of immediate interest to the students and good participation can be generated.

3. *Drama:* Very effective with children who would otherwise be hesitant to participate in role-play or simulation. Following a script can effectively facilitate the perception of who one really is vis-à-vis the role being played.

4. *Role-play:* Assigned roles based on children's situations can greatly increase their understanding of how they tend to behave in real-life contexts.

5. *Simulation:* An unscripted and unprepared playing out of a situation in which individuals literally "do their own thing"an ideal approach because it can be tailored to be relevant to individuals and involve the students totally.

6. *Real-life involvement:* Both a method and an end in itself. Helping people is the best practice for helping people. The true test of "love in action. (Kupchencko, 1981, p. 110)

The teacher can use any of the above six teaching strategies deemed appropriate. However, McPhail suggests that they are best employed progressively as each represents a closer step to the actual concrete practice of morality. However the teacher decides to deal with the learning situation, he or she "must take a modeling role, demonstrating care and consideration for each student" (p. 115). The classroom climate should be one of warmth and acceptance where all the students feel comfortable and secure. As McPhail is wont to say, morality is not "taught but caught" (McPhail et al., 1972, p. 4).

As part of the School Councils Project, McPhail and his associates (1972) have devised the *Lifeline* program for use in the classroom. The materials included in the accompanying kit consist primarily of situations, moral dilemmas that proceed from the extremely personal to the less personal, the community at large, the country, the world. *Lifeline* initially challenges students on three fronts: "Sensitivity," "Consequences," and "Points of View" (p. 1).

McPhail explains the rationale behind the threefold approach of the *Lifeline* moral education materials kit:

"Sensitivity" is designed to improve pupils' ability to recognize their own and others' needs, interests and feelings and to help them understand why people behave as they do. "Consequences" puts the emphasis on improving boys' and girls' ability to predict the possible and probable consequences of actions. "Points of view" involves learning to choose what to do in conflict or disagreement situations after first considering one's own needs and then those of the other person involved. The three approaches together prepare adolescent boys and girls to act considerately towards other people because they are able to take the role of the other, to put themselves in other people's shoes. (McPhail et al., 1972, p. 100)

In addition to the three types of materials described above, the program contains two more components, the "Proving the rule" and "What would you have done?" series. The former transfers the moral judgment or choice developed in the first section of *Lifeline* to its application in relationships in small groups and communities. The aim in this series is for students to

develop a strong sense of identity and see themselves as people who have a contribution to make in their community, without at the same time telling them what kind of adults they ought to be or what system of values and beliefs they ought to have. (p. 112)

The final section of the *Lifeline* program, the "What would you have done?" series, presents factually based incidents occurring in different cultural settings around the world. Here students are led to consider the effects of differing cultural, social, and economic conditions on people's behavior (p. 134). The objective is to encourage students to develop a "sense of compassion, independence of mind, or of autonomy, and a willingness to act upon one's beliefs" (p. 138).

McPhail prescribes no set methodology for dealing with these various education materials, apart from the six general teaching strategies described above; teachers should use their own creativity in finding ways to integrate the *Lifeline* program in the classroom.

How do students learn morals? In the emotional-rational approach to moral education, students must assume an active learning role. In addition to acquiring knowledge about the community's standards, rules, and other moral and legal expectations, they must explore their own personal feelings, needs, and responses to situations in which moral choices are required. They must be able to take on the perspective of others, to walk in others' shoes as well as in their own. This objective is promoted by working through, confronting students with various moral dilemmas and situations, either of their own invention or those McPhail provides.

The process of learning morals is, however, incomplete if the newly developed or discovered awareness of emotions, personal values, and rational judgments is not actively expressed and actualized in terms of concrete actions, moral response. Morality in this approach is definitely not a purely intellectual game of moral stages and levels, a theoretical and noncommittal affair; it concerns active doing, the actual practice of morality.

Outcome: What Kind of Person Results?

McPhail's emotional-rational approach to moral education should produce a balanced individual, sensitive, emotionally developed, who uses both emotion and reason in responding morally in any variety of situations. In choosing love in action he is considerate and sensitive to both his needs and the needs of others; he is profoundly influenced by the interrelation he knows he shares with all of humanity. Above all, the person coming from an emotional-rational education is a doer who lives and practices his values and his morality.

1. McPhail's is a practical, action-oriented approach, not merely an improvement in the level of abstract reasoning.

2. It is holistic, taking into account the whole person, cognitive and affective, with an emphasis on the powerful role of emotions in making value judgments. It is an ethic of care and responsibility.

3. It seeks to refine and develop fineness of feeling. It moves toward higher levels of emotional and instinctive functioning. In some ways it is, like other theories, based on the concept that development comes from disequilibrium created through moral crisis. But the crisis is one of the whole person, not just of the intellect, more in the line of positive disintegration of lower-level functions to make way for higher-level functions.

4. It is replete with content, and not just a style change. It is not afraid to espouse certain virtues, taking at the same time deliberate steps to define them clearly. It is objectivistic.

5. It recognizes the power of identification and modeling, as do the Freudians and social learning theorists, without, however, leading us to the anomalies and limitations of these theories.

6. The theme *love in action* flows naturally from process thinking, in fact precisely from the ideas of Whitehead himself.

7. If perhaps *love in action* is a term too ephemeral for the positivistic scientists to get hold of and research as systematically as they would like, it is nevertheless a moral response to the real experiences of life lived and moral education taught.

Crossroads in Moral Education Today: Demands and Alternatives

Today, when renewed interest and renewed passion for moral uprightness mark some in our society, anyone setting out on the difficult, challenging task of actually doing moral education is beset by voices calling in all directions that theirs is *the* way to go. I think that today moral educators stand at a crossroad where the voice of ultraconservatism is especially strident, calling us to follow that direction in the name of a way of thinking that has become particularly popular in recent times—a way of thinking that has been forced on us by economic necessity and by the inevitable swing of the moral education pendulum that is seen to have reached new extremes of permissiveness, subjectivity, and substitution of form for content. It is time, many say in an atmosphere of "back to the basics" education, to get back to law and order in moral education. For many the call for a new moral order means a rather simplistic and rabid return to a rather ruthless indoctrination, a type of indoctrination that outdoes the traditional character education we have looked at as the first of our ways of moral education. For many it is the obvious solution to our social ills. For those who reflect, this archconservative approach to moral education is no solution, but on the contrary an entrenchment of those very forces that create moral weakness and immaturity.

For these reasons I would like to examine, using the same format we have used in exploring the "classical ways," this contemporary alternative that one may feel pressured to follow. I call it an alternative because I will subsequently contrast it with another approach available to us today that builds on the major themes we have explored in this book, an approach that I am calling Multilevel Moral Development. But first let us look at the reactionary approach.

Reactionary Archconservativism

Philosophy: What is Moral?

The philosophical grounds of this approach are quite shallow. It looks back with golden memories to what we remember or at least imagine we had in the past. What is moral is what we "always" believed and good people lived by, but which we have recently lost somehow. The "good days" and the "old ways" were comforting and reassuring. A man knew where he stood with his fellow man and, above all, with God. The rules for salvation, though strict, were clear-cut. The line between the good and the bad was distinct. Above all, authority was respected, and no ordinary man had to shoulder the burden of choice. Respect for authority whether it was the Bible, the church, the government, or parents clearly delineated righteousness.

Sociology: What is the State of Society?

Society, by contrast with the pristine goodness we once had, is in chaos today. Disorder prevails. Traditional values are ignored, as is evident from the way people live and make their own decisions. Above all, respect for authority has gone. The answer is a prompt reestablishment of strong authorities that will enforce law and order so that the common good can prevail. Clear rules strongly enforced with clear-cut and even extreme penalties, including the death sentence, are necessary. A man has a clear right to protect his private property with his gun.

Psychology: How do People Change Their Moral Behavior?

Psychology is suspect. It operates at a level that is "merely human" and not God-given. Control is important. If clear enunciation of rules and laws doesn't control behavior, reward and punishment must be used. The extreme importance of what is taught may call for extreme punishment. Those who do not conform must be ostracized. Good behavior is measured in the degree to which it conforms to the dictates of authority.

Education

How do teachers teach morals? Teachers must clearly enunciate moral principles that children must follow. They must convince students of the necessity of following them by citing authorities. The authorities may be secular or religious. Religion is a strong ally to the moral educator, because religion contains a set of clear-cut moral norms and carries with it sanctions that have eternal punishments or rewards.

Youngsters must be shielded from contact with vice or at least have its evil consequences pointed out to them before they can be tempted by it. It is dangerous to expose them to situations where they must decide for themselves. There is really no great need to educate them in making choices because authorities and rules will always be there to guide them; more important that they commit the rules to memory, and be trained to follow them. Because what is taught is so clear, unchanging, essential for law and order and for salvation, and so well backed up by authority, traditional indoctrination is called for.

How do students learn morals? The key to good behavior is respect for authority. Above all the student must learn respect. Much of what needs to be known can be committed to memory. Conformity will confirm.

Outcomes: What Kind of Person Results?

The child who comes through this education system can follow one of two main routes: (a) that of a passive person who blindly keeps rules without questioning the authority that imposes them, or (b) that of a rebel against authority, rejecting all kinds of external authority, yet at the same time at a loss to find any guidelines within himself or herself and unfamiliar with personal choice.

I have painted a bleak and probably somewhat simplistic picture of the archconservative approach. Yet I would hesitate to call it unrealistic. Perhaps the picture is all too real, presenting the graphics of the siege mentality that drives many to this extreme approach to moral education.

The alternatives, contemporary character education and positive disintegration (which I have modified and developed into a system of moral education), are ultimately a more attractive solution because of their inherent ability to develop all that is best in human beings. I present these approaches now, using the same chart format that outlined the other ways of moral education.

New Character Education

I mentioned at the beginning of this chapter that we would come full circle, starting with the ancient tradition of character education and coming back to it in new forms that meet the needs of our times and yet preserve the basic values and tenets that have served well in the past.

Philosophy

Aristotle defined good character as the life of right conduct, in relation to others and to oneself. Character is a psychological system of virtues identified by religious traditions, literature, wise people, and people with good, plain common sense. The concept of virtue is therefore not to be scorned. It represents something beyond ad hoc solutions to moral dilemmas, and highlights instead a consistent way not only of *acting*, but of *being*. Besides moral rules given by society, there are virtues in the person, habits of good behavior that reflect something more than mere conformity; more even than consistent moral reasoning. Virtues like honesty, patience, loyalty, and perseverance are strengths (the Latin word *virtus* means strength), and just as physical strength is built through exercise, so moral strength is built through practice. With habit comes relative ease; morality becomes more natural with practice because it becomes part of one's self-concept. Virtues reflect a sense of self-consistency and worthwhileness. There is for each person a "horizon of significance" (Taylor, 1988, 1989, 1991) where what is meaningful can be assessed for its real significance, both subjective and objective. Values given high place give moral direction. Certain highly developed people whose actions flow from their high values can be used as models of morality.

Some philosophers who stress character and the importance of virtue are: Alasdair MacIntyre (1984, 1988), Stanley Hauerwas (1985), and Gilbert Meilander (1984).

The person is to be understood holistically, not as either rational or emotional. Intelligence involves recruitment of the whole person. Moral behavior is behavior of the *whole* person.

Sociology

Values are relatively consistent across cultures and are passed on by evolving moral traditions, usually in the form of explicit rules of behavior or in virtues named, explained, and encouraged. Enduring values are thus passed on. However, values can be neglected or distorted in society. An era of value relativity and confusion has in our time led to anarchy, crime, and immorality. Materialistic, self-pleasing values are chosen in an attempt to fill feelings of emptiness. Even the shallow optimism that once substituted for real hope has given way to pessimism, depression, and a cry for meaning sometimes not heard even by the one who cries.

Psychology

How do we live morally? We live morally by examining and choosing our values consciously; by developing habits of good behavior intimately connected with self-image, especially self-worth. Habits are learned modes of behavior acquired by practice and reinforced with self-esteem. This discovery of self involves positioning oneself in a context (a life story) that explores one's roots in a heritage from the past and looks forward to the possibilities of a moral future.

How do we change moral behavior? We change moral behavior principally by the practice of virtues: the strength of good habits that tie moral behavior with self-concept and feelings of self-consistency.

Education

Virtues can be taught directly by naming and describing, or encouraged by reward and punishment (especially in very young children), or by emulation of models. They can be learned also by being attracted as a person (not just cognitively) to a whole range of virtues (not just justice) to behavior that combines self-respect with compassion for others. Values can and should be taught in schools. Values should be modeled in schools. Above all, virtues should be not just be talked about, but practiced.

Most effective in school settings are concrete, realistic moral dilemmas relevant to the life of students. These may involve current moral dilemmas or powerful, full-blooded moral dilemmas of literature, drama, and films. They should lead beyond speculation to action.

The acknowledged major proponent of character education from a practical perspective is Thomas Lickona. In two popular paperback books (1985, 1992) he has presented the down-to-earth practice of character education in the home *(Raising Good Children)* and in the schools *(Educating for Character)*. In the latter (pp. 20-22), he sums up the case for values education this way:

1. There is a clear and urgent need.

2. Transmitting values is and always has been the work of civilization.

3. The school's role as moral educator becomes even more vital at a time when millions of children get little moral teaching from their parents and when value-centered influences such as church or temple are also absent from their lives.

4. There is common ethical ground even in our value-conflicted society.

5. Democracies have a special need for moral education, because democracy is government by the people themselves.

6. There is no such thing as a value-free education.

7. The great questions facing both the individual person and the human race are moral questions.

8. There is broad-based, growing support for values education in schools.

9. An unabashed commitment to moral education is essential if we are to attract and keep good teachers.

10. Values education is a doable job.

Kaplan (1991, pp. 530-531) gives a brief, interesting, and probably accurate summary of how morality might be taught in the future. Looking at the present too, he suggests a practical approach to moral education, using Kevin Ryan's "Five E's." They follow from the ideas we have looked at here, and could be implemented in today's classroom (see Figure 13.2).

Outcome

A Person of Character

Character has been defined as "Personality evaluated." When you are asked for a character reference, your prospective employer wants to know not only about your previous jobs, but how well you *behaved* in them, or better still how you *generally* behave from a moral point of view. Are you *habitually* industrious, honest, conscientious, kind?—all virtues, that is, habitual ways of acting in a good way. It is this persistent, good action coming from internal strength that is character. The values that one has may come from tradition,

---

Example—Teachers and parents are themselves role models; models from history and literature can teach values and morals by example. The power of narrative.

Explanation—Character Education does not neglect reason. If rules are to be enforced, students deserve to know the reasons behind them.

Exhortation—Young people need encouragement to risk change and to persevere in a new moral direction.

Environment—The classroom and the school must themselves be environments where the individual and the community can together work out their ways of being moral.

Experience—If values are the foundations of action, and if morality is not just something to be discussed hypothetically ("What do I think?") but actually lived ("What kind of a person am I?" "How do I *usually* act?"), then the richest value and moral education will provide opportunities not just to talk, but to be and to act.

Figure 13.2. The "Five E's" of moral education.

but they are self-chosen; they are tied up in one's self-concept and self-respect to the degree that they are not automatic, but habitual—an authentic morality—proactive and even creative of morals. Moral is not something you *have,* but *are.*

Multilevel Moral Education

This section goes on to describe a way of moral education closely akin to the new character education, but set in the broader developmental foundation of Dabrowski's ideas of Positive Disintegration.

At the beginning of this chapter on the ways of moral education you found a line from T.S. Eliot's *Ash Wednesday.* I repeat it now in its context.

Suffer us not to mock ourselves with falsehood
Teach us to care and not to care
Teach us to sit still
Even among these rocks.

These words are especially significant here for they round out our theme and illumine it with words of beauty that are themselves a prayer for illumination. They touch on the theme that the eminent British moral philosopher R.S. Peters (1969) came to see as the ultimate question of moral education: How do children come to care? That is the question we come face-to-face with as we conclude this study. Moral education is too important and too delicate a task for teachers to confound with falsehood, when if we listen we can hear our students demand: "Teach us to care." It is their need, calling for our response.

Interestingly, perhaps in response, the psychology of moral development and education seems to be turning in a new direction at the present time.

Perhaps Carol Gilligan (1982; Gilligan, Ward, & Taylor, 1988; Johnston, 1988) from a woman's perspective has provided one of the strongest incentives for this change in direction by distinguishing an ethic of responsibility and care from an ethic of principles, rules, and justice. The ethic of principles has long held sway in studies of moral education. Presently, the ethic of care is taking the place it should rightly have as a legitimate approach to morality. Kohlberg, one of the most cognitive of cognitivists, has recently (Kohlberg & Candee, 1984) accepted the legitimate role of "intuition," "heart," and "conscience" to generate a judgment of responsibility. Nel Noddings (1984) has gone a step further and tended to identify caring with a feminine approach to ethics and moral education, pointing out the elements of openness and relatedness that are intrinsic to real caring. One danger at the present time is to be caught by the human penchant to dichotomize, calling one ethic masculine, the other feminine; calling one an ethic of the head, the other an ethic of the heart. That could take us back to the cognitive-affective dichotomy that has plagued psychology and led us to think in terms of rather simplistic dualities. That is why there is needed at the moment a theory and a mode of moral education that is truly holistic. While avoiding the demands of reactionary archconservatism, the teacher must not fall into the trap of oversimplification. Whitehead (1925) said, "Seek simplicity, and distrust it."

What we need now, then, is a way of moral education based on a comprehensive philosophy, a holistic psychology, and practical in its implications. It must be a way of expressing the ethic of caring by incorporating two principles adapted from R.S. Peters (1974) that pervade such an ethic:

1. To be rational is to care about truth.

2. To be whole is to care about persons and things and to have found oneself in the perspective of relationships (p. 295).

The approach I am proposing to meet our common and current need is one I am calling Multilevel Moral Education. First, that title acknowledges that, at its foundation, it rests on Dabrowski's theory of Positive Disintegration with its core theme of multilevelness. Second, the title hints that it goes beyond Dabrowski's theory, incorporating the contributions of the theologians, philosophers, and psychologists we have reviewed, together with whatever is unique to the present work.

Philosophy: What is Moral?

The multilevel view speaks to this basic philosophical question by first asserting that an objective morality is possible, desirable, and in fact necessary. This objectivity is not "absolute" in the sense of being handed down from some divine source by a process of traditional revelation, to be passed on by traditional indoctrination. On the other hand, the multilevel approach avoids the chaos and moral anarchy of utter subjectivity that leaves morals equally in the hands of everyone as though all were equally capable of understanding and caring. The answer it presents is that morality is *determined* by (and not just *discovered* by) reflection on the part of individuals. These individuals are to be found at various levels of development. All individuals in a sense have some say in what will be considered moral. The extent and effect of that say is in proportion to the individual's power; the moral objectivity of that say is in proportion to the individual's level of development. The level of development of each individual is a function of developmental potential, which in turn is a function of those aspects of the person that Dabrowski has labeled overexcitabilities. We can see these as special sensitivities, two-way channels, open to receiving stimuli that are emotional, intellectual, imaginational, sensual, and psychomotor, and open to acting on the world in the same five modes. Positive Disintegration theory reminds us of the primacy of emotional development, but without opposing this to cognitive development. Instead, returning to the diamond metaphor with which we began this book, we can, looking from various perspectives, describe the person as a spectrum of functions, a spectrum of ways by which one may be sensitive to a situation and act on the world outside. These sensitivities are ways in which the individual interacts with his world. Dabrowski described five colors in his spectrum; others may discover a different variety of hues. What is important is that we have a holistic image of the one who makes moral choices, thereby grasping the varieties of perspectives that one might have. Certainly the greater the diversity, the greater the possibility of integration. The greater the sensitivity to beauty, the greater the possibility of creating moral beauty. Morality is beauty with all the harmony and peace integral to it.

Given that everyone is not equally open to the appreciation of beauty, moral beauty included, and given that only some as a result will reach higher levels of development, it follows that the moral judgments of some will be more objective than those of others, because objectivity is the fruit of *authentic* subjectivity, and not of subjectivity in itself. Those at higher, more authentic levels of development make objective moral judgments. This is illustrated in the remarkable convergence of the moral principles of eminent persons who have graced human history. It is the high level of authentic development of great moral leaders (who are often religious leaders) that creates objective morality.

It is the task of each human being to work out what is moral, not just for oneself, but in response to objective moral standards. Initially, and if one becomes fixed at lower levels of development, these values and moral norms must come from authority outside oneself. But advancement through levels of development creates the possibility of, and even demands, greater and greater inner-directedness and answering to personal ideals, which to the extent they are objective correspond with the values, norms, and ideals of a healthy society. Each individual is in some sense, then, responsible for determining what is moral. Each is an occasion in the process of the moral development of the cosmos, contributing to it in proportion to his or her own level of consciousness and development.

Sociology: What is the State of Society?

Society is itself a multilevel situation in which individuals can be found at all levels, some stagnated at primary integration, some in motion through the levels by the process of positive disintegration. The numbers who have reached higher levels of development is by necessity (like Maslow's "growing tip" of the human race) very small, because these levels require rare combinations of many dynamisms of the developmental potential. Various interpretations of what is moral can be expected, then, from the different levels of development in society, ranging all the way from the indifferent and pathological with no sense of rightness and wrongness (psychopaths and sociopaths) to the highest levels of moral sensitivity and moral action.

In the individuals who make up society, moral values exist in a hierarchy. By actualizing these values in society, individuals make a real contribution to the building of society, and indeed the universe. Individuals can, if they so choose, add value to the world and contribute to society's development through their own inner development. This inner development, if it is full, flows into social action. Each person is an "occasion" (Whitehead) in the process of building the universe and contributes value to that universe in proportion to the level of consciousness attained and according to the positive assent to the demands or lures given by one's time and place in the creative process. One's place in society, one's time in history, united with the unique inner dynamisms of the individual, coincide to create a never-before, never-to-be-repeated opportunity to contribute beauty and value to the process. The likelihood of making this contribution and the richness of it are in direct proportion to the level of consciousness of the individual. With consciousness so crucial in making the nexus between individual value and societal value, religion in its sense of fullest consciousness (and not merely institutional membership or adherence to creeds) is a vital part of society. It is society operating at its highest levels. Without religion, society is incomplete and lacking in higher level moral direction.

Psychology: How do People Change Their Moral Behavior?

How do people change their moral behavior? The psychological questions of moral education are answered by the theory of Positive Disintegration in this way: because society itself is composed of people at various levels of development, moral education must keep in mind that moral decision making abilities vary from individual to individual. Some are at higher levels than others. Thus a simplistic "democratic" view does not apply to reality. Not all people have the same ability to make moral decisions, and thus a total trust that all individuals should be their own subjective guide is unwarranted and unrealistic. Persons at lower levels of development (and this does not mean children just because they are younger) need explicit moral teaching, guidelines, and rules intelligently interpreted to them. All individuals need some sort of crisis situation in which they will be forced to question their values and encouraged to move on to a hierarchical organization of their values and to seeking higher-level values. The famous moral dilemma approach is one means of doing this, but with emphasis on its ability to touch and arouse fineness of feeling. Above all, every person needs the incentive and guidance to convert a hierarchy of values into a hierarchy of aims, to act on one's values.

Beauty of landscape, music, architecture, and art will help; but even in the ugliest of situations one can nourish morality if it is filled with the beauty of persons who can lure the emotions to greater sensitivity, moving one to create moral beauty in one's own life.

Not only does the multilevelness proposed by the theory of Positive Disintegration remind us that not all persons are at the same level of development, it reminds us of the role of psychology to induce movement upward through these levels. Gradually, dissatisfaction with one's world, with society, can lead to dissatisfaction with oneself and inner conflicts. Feelings of inferiority toward others can be transformed into feelings of inferiority toward oneself and a clear moral sense of what one *ought* to be as opposed to what one *is*. Ultimately, the goal is to be guided by a personal ideal, based on a hierarchy of values and a hierarchy of aims. Intrapsychic development is combined with interpsychic development, and the individual, increasingly aware of his or her relationships with society, may find himself or herself maladjusted to what *is* in society, perceiving principles beyond the common norms and feeling obliged to live by them. In the case of the more highly developed individuals this takes the form of positive maladjustment, which, though it may go against the grain of many who accept social norms unquestioningly, will be ultimately more humanizing of the whole social milieu. Movement through the levels is painful and agonizing, the pain coming both from inner conflicts and conflicts with a society that is not ready for the higher-level principles of morality that are proposed and lived by those who rise to higher levels of development. The New Testament is full of accounts of Christ's conflicts with the Pharisees who represented the religious establishment of His time. Over and over again He breaks their low-level rules of morality, appealing to a higher moral principle. For example, when He cures a man on the Sabbath and the Pharisees object that this constitutes work, which is forbidden, He teaches them the higher principle of love of neighbor and care for human welfare. Finally, the sufferings of continual conflict with the establishment lead to the ultimate agony of crucifixion and death at the hands of those He chided for their moral narrowness. Internal agony and external conflict are the price and at the same time the source of moral growth.

A practical danger lurks in Dabrowski's concept of positive maladjustment. It is the temptation to label too easily one's own maladjustment as positive, to see it as growthful when it is merely obstreperous; to see it as reflecting higher-level principles when really it is only an expression of lower-level primitive needs. But this is a problem of individuals and not of the theory. Dabrowski is most hesitant in labeling maladjustment as positive unless it is accompanied by signs of other dynamisms of higher levels. Positive maladjustment, far from being a kind of license to follow one's subjective whims, is, rather, an idea that puts heavy demands on the individual to be authentic. "Objectivity is the fruit of the most authentic subjectivity."

Education

How do teachers teach morals? By its very nature Positive Disintegration theory evokes a more holistic answer to this question than any approach to moral education that emphasizes technique or philosophy alone. Positive Disintegration is a theory comprehensive of human development. Its scope is broad, taking us beyond philosophy alone or mere techniques. It also has a personal aspect, a lure drawing the reader to apply the theory to self. It is not a speculative study of others as specimens of development, but the kind of theory that inevitably forces reflection on oneself and quietly demands self-evaluation. That is why, in answering the question, How do teachers teach morals? we cannot slip immediately into techniques, bypassing the teacher; rather, we must look first at what is demanded of the teacher.

An old philosophical adage says: *Nemo potest dare quod non habet* (No one can give what they do not have). A teacher cannot give something he or she does not already possess, whether it be an idea, a motivation, an inspiration, a determination, a love, or a goal. This does not mean that students are limited by the level of development their teachers have attained and cannot go beyond. History is full of students who have gone beyond their masters. But this is transcendence and sometimes development "in spite of" and the student goes on because of his or her own developmental potential. The point I am trying to make comes back to that important word *consciousness*. Teachers are effective in moral education in direct proportion to their consciousness of the real values they hold. Unless the teacher is reflective on his or her values, value education and moral education will be a haphazard affair with the hidden curriculum (or rather the unknown curriculum) often more potent than the values that appear in the lesson plan. This reflectiveness, this awareness, this consciousness is especially needed in a system of moral education that does not take an extreme moral indoctrination approach, nor the opposite view that the teacher must pretend to be morally neutral. This approach requires that the teacher take a moral position. Teachers can't be expected to have worked out a firm position on every moral dilemma (capital punishment, abortion, genetic manipulation), but the modeling they can present in these specific moral problems is recourse to values, their values, and how they are trying to work through their values to find practical solutions to the moral problems that confront them. It is real-life modeling of the agony of moral decision making, much more powerful than trite recitation of rules from tradition or authority.

Thus the starting point for the teacher is self-consciousness in the sense of being conscious of the values one holds and conscious of the values one subsequently transmits. Positive Disintegration theory with its emphasis on hierarchy of values brings out the idea that a value educator does not so much give values to her students as help them to rearrange the values they have into a better hierarchy. Everyone has values; they may not be conscious of them; but they have them right from infancy (when the newborn values pleasure more than pain) to the person who has reached Dabrowski's fifth level, who has a complex, intricately hierarchized elaboration of values. Values education works in the process between these two extremes, asking the students to reflect on their values, know what they are in full consciousness, and then challenging them to rearrange these values in a hierarchy ultimately more humanizing to themselves and the world around them.

How do students learn morals? In the section on how teachers teach morals I have said little about techniques, emphasizing instead the personal demands placed on the moral educator; techniques will become clearer as we see them flowing from their true source: the needs of the developing person who is to be taught.

In looking at the ways of moral education, although we have not restricted education to a formal school setting, including also family and religious settings, we have tended to see our scholars as bright faces grouped rather homogeneously in the typical classroom according to age. This homogenous grouping makes things rather neat for any theory of moral education that presumes most people of the same age are going through the same phase of development. But Positive Disintegration theory does not tie stage to age; it throws the emphasis on *individual* level of development, the way each person experiences morality in his or her life. All too neat oversimplifications will not do; the task is more challenging than that. Instead of following age-related presumptions about the level Johnny is at, or even test data on his stage of moral reasoning from the way he answered some speculative moral dilemmas, the teacher is challenged to look for those dynamisms that indicate his developmental potential, the presence, even though germinal, of those dynamisms that, as we have seen, constitute the caring person: emotional, intellectual, imaginational excitability; empathy, the ability to get outside childish egocentrism and see things from another's point of view.

Morality is not a science the child learns, but an art he lives. Moral learning goes beyond words to action. Values must be lived to be real values; and values will be taught and learned by being lived. That is why the beauty of goodness is not just something to be admired and commented on at a distance like a landscape, but something to be involved with. Education is a process, as we have seen in Lonergan's philosophy, that leads from experience through understanding and judging to deciding: actually setting directions in one's life. If one *really* cares, one *must* act. That is why the teacher who is a moral educator ensures that there is an action component in it all. Complete moral education flows into compassion and service to others.

If an educational model is to be true to the principles of Positive Disintegration, it must express that moral growth comes about through disintegration of lower-level functioning and replacement with higher-level dynamisms. We have talked about higher-level feelings and how the "informed heart" guides the individual to better, more objective moral judgments. But merely to state that encouragement of higher levels of emotional sensitivity is essential to moral development is not enough. It can be the kind of pronouncement a professor of educational psychology might make from his ivory tower because it seems he doesn't have to get involved with "real kids." It becomes meaningful in terms of practical implications for the teacher, including the religion, social studies, and English teacher, when we get down to what is more basic and more real with the children we have in schools. Most teachers in reality are faced with many students at the level of primitive integration. Many students must begin to be truly moral by learning how to experience authentic feeling. It seems strange to talk about experiencing real emotion. We live in a world full of intense emotion. The trouble is that it comes often in packaged containers neatly tailored to fill the gaps between commercials on television. So much of what we "experience" doesn't really involve us. No wonder, then, that adults can watch a real-life murder in our cities and not even lift a telephone to call the police because they don't want to get involved. Positive Disintegration challenges this noninvolvement by encouraging real participation, by not protecting the child from the experiences of real life and from feeling the appropriate emotions—fear, disappointment, sorrow, loneliness, confusion—all part of the human condition, all part of being able to feel for others too, to identify with them, to know their hurts, and to be moved to act morally to prevent those hurts. It is the task of moral education to replace apathy with a caring that asks earnestly: What would be most humanizing in this particular situation? This is the justice to which we are exhorted not just to reason, but to "hunger and thirst after."

Positive Disintegration theory says that one comes to experience this passionate sense of justice and act on it by the process of disintegration through crises. It is classical developmental theory, as we have seen in chapter 4, to say that growth comes about through crises. If any theory centers on this theme and presents the teacher with the challenge of using crisis in moral education, it is the theory of Positive Disintegration. The moral educator should not only allow but promote emotional and moral crises in students.

Intense emotional experiences need not be a catastrophe for the child, but under caring circumstances an opportunity for growth, a "eucatastrophe," as Tolkien (1975) calls it when talking about the emotional power of fairy tales.

> The consolation of fairy stories, the joy of the happy ending ... or more correctly of the good catastrophe, the sudden, joyous "turn" ... this joy is not essentially escapist or fugitive. In its fairy tale—or other world—setting it is a sudden and miraculous grace.... It is the mark of a fairy story of the higher or more complete kind that, however fantastic or terrible the adventure, it can give to child or man that hears it, when the "turn" comes, a catch of breath, a beat and lifting of the heart, near to (or indeed accompanied by) tears as keen as that given by any form of literary art. (p. 68)

An example of a fairy story that presents this "turn" as a moral dilemma is *The Little Mermaid*, in which the dramatic climax is a clash of life and death, a conflict of self-interest and care for others. The little mermaid, victim of the contrivances of the forces of evil, is faced with the dilemma of choosing her own life and all she is familiar with or the life of the prince whom she loves. She stands over the sleeping prince, the knife poised in her hands. It is a dramatic, absorbing moment of real moral conflict when children can be challenged to choose with head and heart by putting themselves in the place of the little mermaid.

Perhaps a note of reality should be included here. The potency of this moral dilemma first struck me while reading this fairly tale at bedtime to my daughter Carolyn, who was then five years old. I stopped at the dramatic moment and asked her what she would do if she were the mermaid. New directions in moral education, it seemed to me, were hanging on her reply. Perhaps it was the lateness of the hour. Perhaps the complexity of the dilemma was too much for a little head. Perhaps it was Dad overeager for an answer. Her reply after very little thought: "Oh Daddy, forget about your question, just get on with the story and see how it turns out."

Individual failures aside, art, especially literature, has a power to draw the child and the adolescent into intense feelings and emotional involvement. *Billy Budd* by Herman Melville is a complexity of moral dilemmas, with emotional intensity enough to draw in adolescents to identify at least with the gentle sailor, if not with the captain who condemns him to death. Which adult who has seen the film *Sophie's Choice* can forget the terrifying scene on the station platform, with the concentration camp trains panting in the background, when the German soldier presents Sophie with the "choice" of having one or neither of her children live? The nightmare of having "chosen" one of her children to die haunts Sophie in a lifetime full of pseudo-choices. This is existentialism expressed in a most concrete and dramatic mode—the kind of stuff to draw forth reflection on the choices one makes (or imagines making) in one's own life.

These are three examples, geared to levels of development that illustrate the potency of great literature to induce positive disintegration. There are many others, some of which have been collected by moral educators and made available in booklets, kits, and tapes. We have already examined the dilemma situations McPhail published in his *Lifeline* series. These have the happy quality of being real-life dilemmas close to the day-to-day experience of the students they are aimed at. The experienced moral educator will soon come to realize that, a step beyond all the literary, all the published moral dilemmas are the real-life dilemmas students carry within them. Converting these into experiences of *positive* disintegration is a deep challenge not only to the teacher's techniques or knowledge of theory, but to the teacher's own self.

We have seen in our study that goodness and beauty walk hand in hand. Beauty must be there if people are to be good. If it is through sensitivity and fineness of feeling that one rises to higher moral levels, then moral education cannot neglect beauty. Art is there to remind us of how others respond to things as they are; art education is integral to moral education. But art is there too, in lives lived to remind us of how one may in harmony and peace respond to their place and time in the process. The beauty of lives lived is there, not just as a source of moral injunctions, but as a lure drawing forth sensitivity and fineness of feeling.

Outcomes: What Kind of Person Results?

Certainly it would be unrealistic to think that multilevel moral education is going to raise every student to Dabrowski's higher levels, but it is realistic to think that this kind of moral education can draw out the best of the developmental potential to the degree that it is there in each individual. In the beginning, the young child (or the adult at lower levels) may simply go through the motions of moral behavior, simply conforming before he or she can grasp the point, the principles behind behavior, and assent to them. Education and the therapy that goes with it from the Dabrowskian point of view help develop the overexcitabilities and the dynamisms that Dabrowski described and hierarchized. At a minimum, moral education would challenge the tight lower-level structures the individual has been enmeshed in, and it is reasonable to expect that a teacher or parent can from most students draw forth the ability to role take, to empathize, to reason better, and, above all, be somewhat more sensitive to moral beauty.

Persons who come forth from this way of moral education will be at various levels of development. Minimally, they will have been exposed to some moral standards that have objective validity. Hopefully, they will have been lured on beyond mere conformity toward the ideal of making conscious moral choices for themselves, accepting responsibility for them, and converting them, beyond abstract principles, into life lived. If beauty has brought forth sensitivity and fineness of feeling leading to autonomy, then education ultimately becomes self-education, therapy ultimately becomes autopsychotherapy, for the dynamisms are within oneself.

This morality will be objective, to a degree depending on the individual's level, but sensitive to the possibilities that may come from human experience; it will be rational and caring, thoughtful and reflective, yet practical and active. In a word, it will be the most authentic level of subjectivity the individual is capable of. Ultimately, the kind of person who results is a spiritual, perhaps religious, person holding a sense of perspective and shared meaning carried over into practical outcomes, participant in the universal process—a generous contributor to the lasting value of the cosmos.

One last comment (which will of course be loaded with my own prejudices): I see a deep kinship between character education and multilevel moral education in the sense that the theory of Positive Disintegration can give a profound foundation to character education and stretch it to new heights of moral development. At the same time, character education can contribute to TPD its practical insights. The relationship is synergistic.

This is a long and complicated chapter, and if it is to be any help to you in choosing what position *you* will take, it deserves some further narrowing into main themes to guide you in your choices. Figure 13.3 is a guide I have built on what Hall (1979) called "hard-line and soft-line" approaches to moral education to assist your choice of a path somewhere between the two extremes.

Two Extremes on a Spectrum

Hard-Line	Soft-Line
Return to traditional moral standards	Encourages self-awareness
Not only values but rules	Interpersonal relationships
	Creative expression
Morals in terms of absolutes	Value-free
Usually expressed in some holy book	Standards are up to the individual to "clarify" for self
Unchanging	Morality is determined by the situation

Problems

Incompatible with public education iin a free society	Inadequate for public moral pluralistic education since it fails to take a stand
Encourages conformity	Leaves individual in a social vacuum in the absence of guidance and help from others
Calls for blind indoctrination	Values, instead of being transmitted, must be self-generated in a social vacuum
	Laissez-faire attitude actually contributes to the moral crisis of our time
	Denies the fact that there are some things to be learned in moral education
	Teaches *about* values instead of teaching values
Rigid so-called objectivity	Total relativism

Both extreme approaches are unacceptable

The middle way: A creative tension

Merits of hard-line approach	Merits of soft-line approach
Tradition	Freedom of choice
Agreement on major values	Autonomy
	Adaptability to solving new moral crises that will arise

Informed decision-making based on:

1. Learning moral traditions
2. Appreciating others' moral perspectives
3. Appreciating the degree of moral consensus in society
4. Personal reflection encouraged
5. Consciousness (awareness) of one's own values and how they affect actions
6. Empathy developed through real-life social involvement
7. Compassion to temper justice

leading to: "Better" decisions

1. More informed
2. "Rational"
3. Emotional
4. Empathic—Capable of identification with another
5. Holistic in two senses: individual and social

Figure 13.3. "Hard-line" and "soft-line" approaches to moral education.

Chapter 14

Toward a Moral Spirituality for our Time

Humanity has reached the biological point where it must either lose all belief in the universe or quite resolutely worship it. This is where we must look for the origin of the present crisis in morality.... Henceforth the world will only kneel before the organic centre of its evolution.

—*Teilhard de Chardin*

I have two enemies in all the world,
Two twins, inseparably fused:
The hunger of the hungry and the fullness of the full.

—*Marina Tsvetaewa*

Religion Today

Religion is not just something "nice" to have. It is at its best challenging; it demands that you be the best kind of human being you can be. Throughout this book we have seen many ways of being religious. Some are noble, elevating relationships with God and fellow humans; love permeates them; they lead to both holiness and wholeness. We have seen too some strange behaviors masquerading as religion. They stretch the limits of credulity. Some of these more aberrant "religions" are easily spotted and avoided.

Between the two extremes is a grey and sometimes muddy zone where the route is slippery and the danger disguised. A religion that lets you center on yourself, that lets you settle down into complacency or sit comfortably, confident that all is secure and nothing more is asked of you is seductively dangerous. A religion that attempts with simple answers to address complex questions of the meaning and purpose of life would be not just childish, but deceitful, promising what it could not give, restricting the growth of its devotees. Yet that is what so many "religions" pledge in the age of the quick fix. Even some mainline religions settle for less. The whole thing becomes, in this scenario, a game of Trivial Pursuit.

Yet the thrust of this book has been not to reject religion, but to explore it at its best as the expression of that spirit-breath that has its origins close to the human heart. Our search here is for a healthy, holistic religious experience, an opportunity to grow in love of God and neighbor and self, knowing all the time that if it really is "the pearl of great price," it will cost.

Spirituality for our Time

This chapter is entitled "Toward a Moral Spirituality *for our Time.*" Periods of history present their own unique crises, and with them their own unique opportunities. Our time is calling for a renewed spirituality, but not just one that repeats what has been done before simply because it *was* done before. Both individually and socially we have insights now into our place in the grand story of creation that we did not have before. An adult understanding demands an adult response. We must, even at the cost of crisis, grasp the moment or we will miss its opportunities.

New understanding brings new images. We now have a sense of God's immanence that sees God not *above* the heavens but *in* the heavens, not controlling from afar but present in a tree, in an insect, in a human person. The call for a new spirituality reflects too our social concerns. It is not enough, not in fact even genuine, to be a navel-gazing, "spiritual" person absorbed in self. Spirituality involves self-exploration and development, but as it reaches fullness it stretches beyond a childish dependency on God-there-for-me, moving out instead to relationships of care for others, for our earth, and for the universe, which in turn brings our minds back to God. The theme playing through this chapter is to say: Any worthwhile religion or spirituality must lead to action in the real world. It should move us to action; it should tell us how to live. That is the moral dimension of spirituality.

It begins in mystery. Religions do not *solve* the great mysteries of life and death, pain and suffering, justice and injustice. But if they are strong and thoughtful, and mindful of more than their own preservation, they do give us some way to handle these mysteries: to live through them and to *act* through them, even to grow through them; not just to speculate theologically or revel in our personal "salvation," but to follow through with moral action. In a word, a religion may not answer the question "Why?" But it should give some response to the question, "How—How should I act?" That is the action dimension. That is the moral dimension.

We explored in a previous chapter the question: What does religion have to do with morality? There we centered on religion in both its institutional and personal frames. Here we look more at something broader in context than the usual understanding of religion; we look at spirituality. We saw that religion in its institutional sense is one way of expressing that deeper and broader spiritual dimension for which we yearn. To understand a spirituality for our time we must first dig deep into this human yearning.

The Unheard Cry

The need runs deep and sometimes silent. Feeling a kind of vacuum in their lives, some rummage for an unknown something to fill it. Frankl (1969) described this as the "Unheard Cry for Meaning." He proposed that lack of meaning or the failure to search for meaning is the "Collective neurosis of our time."

T.S. Eliot illustrated this emptiness in *The Cocktail Party,* when he had one of its characters, Celia Copplestone, say:

> It's not the feeling of anything I've ever *done* which I might get
> away from, or of anything in me that I could get rid of—but of empti-
> ness, of failure towards someone or something outside of myself;
> and I feel I must ... *atone.* Is that the word? Can you treat a patient
> for such a state of mind?

That many today find an emptiness in themselves and try to fill it with things or with other people treated as things is a critique brought against this last decade of the 20th century. Some social commentators such as Philip Cushman (1990) describe the psychological predicament of our times as that of the "Empty Self." Today, he says, people experience

> a significant absence of community, tradition and shared meaning.
> It is as though humans have striven for autonomy for centuries, and
> now, having attained it in large measure, they discover it is empty.
> Humans in North American society consequently yearn to acquire
> and consume as an unconscious way of compensating for what has
> been lost. (p. 600)

Many today do not hesitate to name what has been lost. It is the fulfill-ment of the whole person, and that person has both spiritual and moral dimensions. The call of our times is for a spirituality of lasting values that will meet our particular needs. So the search begins. Often the search is a kind of blindman's buff. Finding a spirituality for ourselves is a challenge to choose among divergent paths. For some, the search is just a "turn-on," a fad, another novelty. For those not caught in the rabid and titillating, the search may begin as a dim longing that has no name. Some "go back to nature" with the dream of discovering again what is primal, basic, and significant. Some seem to know exactly what they are looking for. They fill the churches, synagogues, mosques, and temples, the weekend workshops, and the class-rooms with the hope of finding a kind of larger perspective on life. For some the search for a spirituality takes them to a particular religion, and happily many find spirituality there; others, either because of their needs or because the desiccated institution has little but clichés to offer, fall back on their own interior resources.

Below the surface is a value issue. Even more deeply and inevitably, because this self-interest is a feeling of self-valuation, it is an issue of self-worth. The Victorian restricted self has given way to the empty self, seeking to be soothed and made cohesive by being "filled up" with food, consumer products, and celebrities. Whatever the explanation of the experts, men and women today find themselves in a whirlwind of change, and from that comes the questions: Who am I? What can I be? What possibilities are open to me? and for some, What *should* I be? How should I act as a moral person in this particular world? It is a spiritual crisis and a moral dilemma of vast proportions. The temptation is to turn in on oneself. Narcissism is enticing. We of the last decade of the 20th century have been accused of too much self-centeredness. We have each constructed, we are told, a tower of individualism to shut out the threats to ourselves that seem to lurk in the darkness. But the solution is not individual defense, individual development, but the rediscovery of something lost. We will find if we venture forth that the mist that descended in this dark night of the soul has created in the dawn a shimmering fabric both delicate and strong—the web of interconnected-ness.

The Web of Interconnectedness

Vaclav Havel, president of the Czech Republic, who successfully combines the disparate roles of poet and politician, in a July 4, 1994 speech in Philadelphia, pointed to what is missing:

> the awareness of our being anchored in the Earth and the universe,
> the awareness that we are not here alone, nor for ourselves alone,
> but that we are part of higher, mysterious entities against whom it is
> advisable not to blaspheme. This forgotten awareness is encoded in
> all religions. All cultures anticipate it in various forms. It is one of
> the things that form the basis of man's understanding of himself, of
> his place in the world, and ultimately of the world as such.

As we go through the process of development (beginning sometimes even in early childhood) we find inklings in ourselves of a depth and a height that seems an important part of our humanness. Later, in mature life, many a person realizes that, perhaps through years of running after many things that never satisfied, it was all along the need for something more than the material that was quietly calling to them. This has been standard fare for peoples of the wealthy nations. But our time calls for an awareness broader than traditional family values, an awareness of our interconnectedness in global terms. The seeking, the finding, and the living of the spiritual dimensions of the self must be done today in a global web of interconnectedness. For those who look to our Earth and beyond, the setting is cosmic.

A Cosmic Setting

Spirituality calls for a cosmic setting. But this is more than a fascination with technology and space. Its dimensions begin deep in the self, but spread beyond self to see self in transcendent terms. Not that we can comprehend it all, nor even pretend to do so. Like a fly clinging to the ceiling of the Sistine Chapel, we are in the presence of a great and beautiful design of cosmic proportions, but we have only limited vision and dim appreciation. But the cosmos never lets up; it is always there, daring us to step back for a global perspective, to see the big picture. There is always more beyond. But seeing the big picture does not mean losing oneself in the vast scene. Find your soul and you will find yourself in the picture.

> *I am memory alive*
> > *not just a name*
> *but an intricate part*
> *of this web of motion,*
> *meaning: earth, sky, stars circling*
> *my heart*
> > *centrifugal*
>
> > > > Joy Harjo

Religion as lived, if it is to play its role and realize its potential, must flow from a spirituality that is not egocentric or individualistic. If it is to be relevant for our times and for all times, it must be whole and vibrant with a sense of interconnectedness. The electronic superhighways of the Internet are impressive; worldwide we humans can communicate as we never have before. But this electronic "neural network" is dwarfed by a new sense of how we humans are connected in our shared consciousness. For us humans, it all began with consciousness.

Consciousness

If we were incapable of self reflection, chance and necessity would rule; our actions would be predetermined. Mihaly Csikszentmihalyi (1994) points out that evolution has given humans another vital option—self-determination:

> But evolution has introduced a buffer between determining forces
> and human action. Like a clutch in an engine, consciousness en-
> ables those who use it to disengage themselves occasionally from
> the pressure of relentless drives so as to make their own decisions.
> The achievement of self-determining consciousness, which humans
> alone seem to have achieved on this planet is by no means an un-
> mixed blessing. It accounts not only or the self-denying courage of
> Gandhi and Martin Luther King, but also for the "unnatural" crav-
> ings of the Marquis de Sade, or the insatiable ambition of Stalin. (p.
> 15)

Consciousness is a tendency to see oneself as the narrator of one's life story, poised at the intersection of several possible narratives still in progress, capable of learning from the past to direct the present, and (even more exciting) able to choose the directions of the future not only for oneself but for others. Consciousness can focus fixedly on oneself and never get beyond narcissism, a fascination with what one *seems* to be. (Narcissus mistook the *reflection* of himself in the water for his *real* self.) But if consciousness finds the *real* self it finds that that self exists only in relationships. There are other people in my story. I am not isolated. This interconnectedness extends beyond persons to things, and in the still larger perspective to the earth and ultimately to the universe (Teilhard de Chardin, 1969a, 1969b).

A social, an ecological, a cosmic context enriches our appreciation of interconnectedness. All falls into perspective. The hubris of seeing human beings as some sort of culmination of creation has been modulated by recent events. We have been reminded by Chernobyl, toxic waste, acid rain, and depleted ozone that we are not the be all and end all. Creation is not for us; we are for creation. We do not sit at the top of a hierarchy, dominating all else; instead, we are interconnected, our very existence dependent on the delicate tensions of this web. The moral task, then, is to be in right relationship to all that is, including oneself.

This is deep ecology, not just a fad to be dropped once the novelty is gone and not just to be written off as New Age. This is the larger narrative of consciousness: the world view, the story of the universe. When we tell the full story we have a piece of good news to relate: "I am part of it! This *now* that I have is part of a timeless story. It is *my* story. And, most remarkable, I can influence that story, enrich that process, perhaps only in a small but no less real way." I have voice and vote. I am called to participate in the story of the universe. Brian Swimme (1988) holds out hope for humanity only if we tell the story of the universe:

> I suggest that when the artists of the cosmic story arrive, our monoindustrial assault and suicide will end and the new beginnings of the earth will be at hand. Our situation is similar to that of the early Christians. They had nothing—nothing but a profound revelatory experience. They did nothing—nothing but wander about telling a new story. And yet the Western world entered a transformation from which it has never recovered.

So too with our moment. We have nothing compared with the massive accumulation of hate, fear, and arrogance that the intercontinental ballistic missiles, the third world debt, and the chemical toxins represent. But we are in the midst of a revelatory experience of the universe that must be compared in its magnitude with those of the great religious revelations. And we need only wander about telling this new story to ignite a transformation of humanity.

From two scholars, Brian Swimme and Thomas Berry (who happen to be poets too), comes this scientific description of our potential to contribute to the ongoing course of the universe:

> What we choose to energize will persist and what we choose not to energize will perish. Dreams refer to the unborn, to the darkly felt inclinations toward a new world, a not-yet world. The future as not-yet works in the present by making a bid for a quantum of energy necessary for its fresh and novel embodiment. (1992, p. 56)

Images of God

The call to contribute in our time to the building of the universe comes in many voices. God speaks to us through many and varied masks. Not all of us hear the same voice or see the same image. Some follow the traditional teachings of a religion and image God as a Father, a Rock of Ages, a Shepherd, a King, or a moral bookkeeper. Others, coming from a stance less engaged in images of persons, see God in the complexity of the cosmos, sometimes described as chaos. Chaos used to mean utter, hopeless confusion. Only a dominating, powerful God could impose his order on it. This is the God of Genesis depicted on the ceiling of the Sistine chapel, all-powerful, strong, stretching out his hand over a chaotic world and locking it into a reliable order. But more recently, with the help of computers and some thoughtful reflection, researchers (Prigogine and others) have found a certain order coming out of chaos. Order comes not *despite* chaos, but *out* of it in a certain systematic way. It was always there, but we were too blind to see it. What is more, this is no stodgy order like little tin soldiers standing in rows; it is the order of harmony as we have it in music, of gracefulness as we have it in dance, of beauty as we have it in nature.

Alexander Pope in the 18th century, with a spiritual insight well ahead of science, put it this way in *An Essay on Man.*

All Nature is but art, unknown to thee
All chance, direction which thou canst not see.
All discord, harmony not understood;
All partial evil, universal good.

Because we could not previously see it, we presumed order was not there, but *Strange Attractors* have now been scientifically detected at work in what appear to be hopelessly chaotic situations. The presence there is of a purposeful though unseen power at work in a meaningful process moving toward order, pattern, and beauty. It would be a mistake just because of the complexity of it all to deny the presence of an order too vast and too subtle to be readily seen by mere mortals. The order seems to be coming from within chaos itself. Paul Rapp (*Omni*, February 1990) goes a giant step forward and puts his view succinctly: "I don't see the simple patterns underlying nature's complexity as evidence of God. I believe that is God. To behold a strange attractor spinning on its own music is a wondrous, spiritual event." From his scientific vantage point, Rapp experiences God as present in creation, not outside controlling it.

Sallie McFague, in her book, *Models of God* (1987, p. x), focuses on what she sees as the essence of Christianity when she says: "Christian Faith is most basically a claim that the universe is neither indifferent nor malevolent, but that there is a power (and a personal power at that) which is on the side of life and fulfillment." The power of healing is strong in the universe. If one reflects on what goes on in the world, one sees much strife, pain, even catastrophes. We call them, ironically, washing our hands of guilt, acts of God. But if one looks even more deeply for what goes on beneath, one sees a healing force, a benevolent, renewing, vital, purposeful drive that vitalizes all and drives the process. Gerard Manley Hopkins put it in his poetic way:

> The world is charged with the grandeur of God.
> It will flame out like shining from shook foil.

Traditionally, we name the voice that calls us to actualize this spiritual dimension of ourselves *God*, and the satisfying culmination that ensues from it we call *union with God*. Just how we carry out this spiritual process of union depends on how we construe God. For some, God is what is outside of the immediate, outside the immanent, the natural. This view images God as the great exception to all we know in this life: a divine Person who, unlike us mere mortals, is everlasting, all-knowing, all-powerful—someone well outside of our human realm, worthy of our worship and open to our prayers. Many institutionalized religions, including Christianity, have emphasized a chasm between creation and its creator. In this theological scenario, God stands apart, interested in and directive of the universe, but distinct and transcendent. Religion has traditionally stepped in with its theology, promising to tell us something about this ultimately unknowable, transcendent God and how He is to be approached.

That last sentence rather unobtrusively introduced a small but significant pronoun, *He*. In this context it is a heavily loaded two-letter word. It tells us two things about God: "He" is a *person* who has *male characteristics*. Psychologically this is important, because then we are persuaded through our years of learning and development not only to treat God as a person, but as a male person. We have already seen Freud's interpretation of God the Father. If the emphasis is on transcendence, it tends to put God at a distance. We have said that the goal of spirituality is union with God. But this union can be difficult if this God is distant and is imaged in the likeness of the men and fathers we have known in life. We have seen a little of this difficulty, particularly for women, of imaging God solely in male terms, but for now let us explore two spiritualities, one struggling to burst from these limitations; another seeming never to have had them until "Discoverers" in the name of God imposed dogmas on them.

Women's Spirituality

This last decade of the 20th century has heard at least one clear call to a renewed spirituality. This call has come to a large extent from women, seeking a spirituality in their own voice (Carol Gilligan, 1982, *In a Different Voice;* and Nel Noddings, 1989, *Women and Evil*). Anderson and Hopkins, in their book *The Feminine Face of God* (1992), have vividly illustrated by interviewing many women how they generally work out their own spirituality over the course of development, and frequently in the face of male dominance. Sometimes it is institutions, including, regrettably, religious institutions with their fear of and bias against women that block the way to a personal spirituality. Sometimes religion is a help in finding the spiritual self; sometimes it is a hindrance. Anderson and Hopkins (p. 121) put it well when they say, "I already know I am a child of God. The question is how can I be an *adult* of God." It is a matter of full human development.

To discover a need for liberation we need not go to the barrios of Latin America. Domination and exploitation not marked by revolutions and bloody uprisings can and do go on in the streets and homes of North America. Riane Eisler (1987) has pointed out that our societies discriminate against certain groups and treat them as inferior. This is obvious with the way Afro-Americans have been treated. What is not so obvious and yet real is the sometimes harsh, sometimes subtle ways women are treated throughout the world. Eisler (1987) tells us that we do not live in a society cooperative between men and women. We live, rather, in a male-dominated society, far from the partnership she advocates. The possibility and desirability of partnership between men and women was achieved, she concludes from her studies, by the Minoan people of ancient Crete. Men and women there shared equally in government. Commerce was attuned to peace; cities were built as pleasant places to live, and human skills were employed in making things of beauty and not instruments of war. However, invaders put an end to this humane way of life by conquering, dominating, and imposing demands that, among other things, put women in an inferior position, thus ending a beautiful but brief period of male-female partnership. The glorious exception that once was Crete stands out as a promise of possibilities in an otherwise bleak contemporary landscape of domination of one sex over the other. Eisler insists that the current goal must not be to swing from patriarchy to matriarchy, but to substitute true partnership for any kind of domination. The current feminist movement at its best has this goal in mind.

If the old theology saw God as male, and sometimes as a dominating father figure, the adult way of growing spiritually is not simply by switching to calling God "She," or taking up goddess worship as a fad. That can be as infantile and manipulative as simply trading a male name for a female one to put on our image of God without changing the image itself. Realizing we make the masks through which God speaks, why can we not make feminine masks attributing to God what women know of their experience: a harmony with the cycles of God's universe—the power to give life and nurture it—birth and loving care. Is not this a strong way to glorify the creator, to attribute to God the ability to understand and share the full human experience of both sexes? It is not so much that we need to glorify the feminine as we need to stress those values in both genders that have the power to give life. If St. Irenaeus were alive today, I am sure he would want us to understand his original statement to say, "The glory of God is man *and woman* fully alive."

With the current attention on female spirituality it is natural that some men may feel left out, even diminished. But if the goal of development is not

domination but partnership, men are equally called to grow as spiri͟
adults, exploring their own particular experiences of being a man, of imaging
God, and creating a relationship with God as real and as valid as any other.

Marcia Falk, quoted by Anderson and Hopkins (1992, p. 121), reminds us
that the ultimate goal for both sexes is not power *over*, but power *to:*

> We've been stuck in a childhood relationship with a parental God
> figure, but we can't afford to be there anymore. Far from being arro-
> gant, what this means is taking responsibility, so that we can really,
> deeply celebrate divinity. Which is a better gift to your parent? To
> fulfill your own life and care for the lives around you ... or to remain
> in constant dependency?

Native Spirituality

Not all religions emphasize the distant view of God as primarily *other than*.
God is not the great exception to all we know on earth. God is their best
exemplification. The only gulf that exists between God and mankind is a
respectful distance, not alien territory but space for communication. We
have been described by Rollo May (1991, p. 37) as a goods-rich, symbols-
blind, and consequently meaning-poor society. But there are some societies,
frequently goods-poor, that are awake to symbols in their deep and meaning-
full spirituality.

Some religious traditions, North American native spirituality for one, find
God in natural things—the sun, the wind, the rain, the passage of the
seasons. God is immanent, very close, present in all that is. It is not coincidental or merely faddish that non-Native people have come to take a great
interest in Native spirituality. Native spirituality speaks to something deep
(and perhaps crushed) in the "Whiteman's" soul. It tells us that perhaps the
distant God brooding over the universe does not meet our needs as well as a
God immanent in all that we know and vitally active in the process of the
universe, and in us.

In a remarkable example of concrescence (Whitehead's idea of all experience being brought into unity) Native North Americans developed a cosmic spirituality long before the advent of the white man, and without his
scientific contrivances. Aboriginal people, instead, were close to the natural
world around them and sensitive to its rhythms, its complexity, its benevo-
lence, and its supernatural dimensions. This is beautifully illustrated by a
prayer of the British Columbia Kwakiutl woman:

Prayer to the Sockeye Salmon

Welcome, O Supernatural One. O Swimmer,
who returns every year in this world
that we may live rightly, that we may be well.
I offer you, Swimmer, my heart's deep gratitude.

> ⌐u will come again,
> ᴀr we will meet again in this life,
> II see that nothing evil will befall me.
> ᴛural One, O Swimmer,
> do to you what you came here for me to do.

In a few simple words she expresses a deep appreciation not only of the supernatural dimensions of all that is, but of our interrelatedness and ulti-mately the cycles of life and death

Our discussion has slipped (not by chance) from chaos as the potential source of order, pattern, and beauty (Pickover, 1990) to goodness and morality springing from these sources. This is a giant but not unwarranted leap. A compelling theme of Whitehead's philosophy is that beauty is important to all human activity. Beauty is not disposable; it is essential for goodness. If, as Whitehead proposes, the terms *good* and *right* are too nebulous for our use, then a comprehensible morality stems from aesthetics: Chaos—Order—Pattern—Beauty—Goodness. We have looked at the rela-tionship of ethics and aesthetics in a previous chapter. Enough for now to recall a single line from Whitehead's *Adventures of Ideas* (1967, p, 267), "Truth matters because of beauty."

A Moral Spirituality

We have come, through the mountain pathways of development of the self, to something called *spirituality*. Our approach has been a climb from lower to higher, from the unsatisfactory to the ideal, from egocentrism to an ecosystemic, holistic way of being and acting. Spirituality traditionally strives for "holiness" and that word, even in its root origins, means whole-ness, integrity; everything is there that should be there. Health, wholeness, and spirituality or religiousness have sometimes been looked on as mutually exclusive opposites; if you have one, you can't have the other. "What is good for the body can't be good for the soul." It is an interesting dichotomy we have created from one Old English root word *hāl,* combining *wholeness* and *holiness*. Somehow we have taken one word and not only given it two meanings, but we have set these meanings in opposition to each other. What twists of history of psychology and theology have caused us not only to separate these meanings, but somehow make them mutually exclusive? If human beings are, as we have contended, spiritual or religious by nature, then to live a spiritual life must be as natural as breathing. Spirituality is, quite simply, "How I cope *fully* with life," which includes both a view-point—a perspective on life; and a way of living—actually experiencing life in its fullest measure. Spirituality is the sense and practice of transcendence. Not only do we sense the transcendent within ourselves and others; we follow it through in the practice of care, responsibility, and respect. Spiritu-ality, like religion at its best, is an intensely moral endeavor.

Broccolo (1990) distinguishes two ways of approaching spirituality, the *ideal* and the *real*. His distinction, I think, is good, but it needs some clarification. A spirituality of the ideal, he says, is deductive; it takes the values of our heritage and says, "These are what I have to live up to." It matches personal behavior with outside criteria, with *shoulds*. The spirituality of the real, on the other hand, begins with an acknowledgment of reality rather than an ideal concept. It then moves to discernment by asking, "What is the movement of the Spirit within my reality?" This demands openness to conversion, bringing us back not just to conformity to expectations, but to the objective ideal via the route of exploring personal possibilities. We saw something of this in chapter 10.

Broccolo admits that probably no one exists in one spirituality or the other. We combine them. But it strikes me that some further, finer distinctions need to be made, lest idealism be mistaken for unquestioning heteronomy and lack of realism. So far I have described the approach of this book as *idealistic*. When I say that it is idealistic, I mean it is intentional in striving for what is *best*—best objectively and best for me, according to my capacities, or developmental potential in Dabrowski's terms. We all operate within certain limitations; to know them is *realistic*; to strive to reach the outward boundaries or the highest levels within these limitations is *idealistic*. It is perhaps harder to be realistic than idealistic in Broccolo's sense. That kind of pseudo-idealistic spirituality means clinging to tradition, learning what the rules are, and adhering to them, sometimes under the compulsion of a neurotic "tyranny of the shoulds"; always with some kind of fear. Being realistic may mean settling for things as they are. The sense in which I use *idealistic* here is the sense of going beyond mere facticity (things as they *are*), and searching for things as they *can* and *should* be. The theory of Positive Disintegration exemplifies this. The existentialists warn us of the chasm between mere facticity and possibility, and they call for the courage to risk making the leap. If anything this courage is "metarealism."

Compassion

This realism is ecosystemic. It is not, as we have seen, "me-centered" but "me in place," in context, in relationship to others and to the cosmos. On the action side, spirituality leads to compassion or, as Matthew Fox (1990) points out, *is* compassion. "Compassion is not about ascetic detachments or abstract contemplation, but is passionate and caring," he says (p. 21). Compassion is not anti-intellectual, but seeks to know and understand and share consciously in the inner connectedness of all things. Thomas Merton, in the talk he gave two hours before his death, said: "The whole idea of compassion is based on a keen awareness of the interdependence of all these living beings, which are all part of one another and all involved in one another" (Fox, 1990, p. 24).

Our basic theme has been that a religious or spiritual dimension is intrinsic to human nature and must be addressed in the course of personal development if one is to be whole. The motion of spiritual development, as with other aspects of development, is from egocentrism to ecosystemic relationships with persons and with the environment. For spirituality, this movement may best be expressed in terms of a developing compassion. This is eminently represented in our time on a large social scale by liberation theology. I take it as an outstanding and well-documented example of a current moral response to "the hunger of the hungry." It is compassion in action.

Liberation Theology

One of the impending contexts of our time, crying out for compassionate involvement, is the lot of the poor, the marginal in society. Liberation theology addresses this problem and in doing so creates a realistic spirituality with high ideals. Liberation theology asks: What is the "real" world in which we find ourselves? It discovers a world full of injustices; the rich and the poor, the exploiters and the masses of the exploited, the kingpins and the marginal, the full and the hungry.

The poet, Marina Tsvetaewa, expressed the anguish of compassion in the lines cited at the beginning of this chapter; they bear repetition here:

I have two enemies in all the world,
Two twins, inseparably fused:
The hunger of the hungry and the fullness of the full.

Gustavo Gutierrez (1973, 1985, 1987) is the founder, theologian, and leader of liberation theology. He summed up the moral imperative when he said,

If I am hungry I have a physical problem.
If you are hungry I have a moral problem.

He has focused his life around trying to solve such moral problems compassionately. Gutierrez (1973) attempts to construct a realistic spirituality when he asks, "What is the relationship between salvation and the process of liberation of man throughout history? Or, more precisely, what is the meaning of the struggle against an unjust society and the creation of a new man in the light of the Word?" (p. 149). By posing these questions Gutierrez realizes he is attempting to define salvation, a concept central to religion and the source of much confusion. The zealot's question, "Are you saved?" gets a quick "Yes" from some religious people. Others will reply (at least internally), "I'm not sure, but I'm working at it."

Salvation is a watershed concept; it is the "Great Divide" over which other key theological ideas separate and go their own ways. Is salvation something individual we strive for in this life in order to "reap our reward in the next?" Or is it something communal involving working in the here and now for the full liberation of body, mind, and spirit? Is salvation even something we *can* work for or merit, or is it a gift of God? Is salvation equivalent to the reward of eternal bliss "for me" because I am personally immortal? Or is my salvation found in making some contribution to creation that God will cherish after the brief occasion of my life is spent? The list of dogmas intersected and interpreted by our understanding of salvation goes on and on. It is a key concept by which we enter our discussion of liberation theology as a spirituality (Schipani, 1988).

Gutierrez (1973) approaches the topic using two terms that have been central to our discussion of psychological development: quantity and quality. He passes quickly from the old quantitative and extensive problem of how many shall be saved to the qualitative and intensive approach. He says:

> Salvation is not something other-worldly, in regard to which the pre-
> sent world is merely a test. Salvation—the communion of men with
> God and the communion of men among themselves—is something
> which embraces all human reality, transforms it, and leads it to full-
> ness in Christ.... This fulfillment embraces every aspect of humanity:
> body and spirit, individual and society, person and cosmos, time
> and eternity.... Sin is not only an impediment to salvation in the af-
> terlife. Insofar as it constitutes a break with God, sin is a historical re-
> ality, it is a breach of communion of men with each other, it is a
> turning in of man on himself which manifests itself in a multifaceted
> withdrawal from others. And because sin is a personal and social in-
> trahistorical reality, a part of the daily events of human life, it is also,
> and above all, an obstacle to life's reaching the fullness we call sal-
> vation. (pp. 151-152)

Hoping Amid the Night

Gutierrez's theological reflections on the Book of Job (1987) focus on how one can talk about God, about a God of justice, when faced with the sufferings of the innocent. Like Job, he does not try to solve the mystery or explain it away, but to live in the depths of it. Gutierrez explores the idea of God from a theological perspective that complements the concept of the God of chaos. He says:

> What is it that Job understood? That justice does not reign in the
> world God has created? No. The truth that he has grasped and has
> lifted him to the level of contemplation is that justice alone does not
> have the final say about how we are to speak of God. Only when
> we have come to realize that God's love is freely bestowed do we
> enter fully and definitively into the presence of the God of faith....
> God's love, like all true love, operates in a world not of cause and
> effect but of freedom and gratuitousness. That is how persons suc-
> cessfully encounter one another in a complete and unconditional
> way: without payment of any kind of charges and without externally

imposed obligations that pressure them into meeting the expectations of others.... Job came to see that he must transcend his individual experience ... that his situation was not exceptional but was
shared by the poor of this world. This new awareness in turn
showed him that solidarity with the poor was required by his faith in
God who has a special love for the disinherited, the exploited, the
marginal, the nobodies of human history.

God is a benevolent presence that leads amid darkness and pain, a
guiding hand that inspires confidence. Not all ignorance is dispelled, but the
route is clearly marked. The signals of transcendence are there. Luis Espinal,
a priest murdered in Bolivia, wrote these beautiful and profound words:

Train us, Lord, to fling ourselves upon the impossible, for behind the
impossible is your grace and your presence; we cannot fall into emptiness. The future is an enigma, our road is covered by mist, but we
want to go on giving ourselves, because you continue hoping amid
the night and weeping tears through a thousand human eyes.
(Gutierrez, 1987, pp. 91-92)

Liberation theology as a praxis-centered methodological process of critical reflection owes much to the work and thought of Paulo Freire (1988) in
his struggle for justice, freedom, and peace in Latin America. Freire centered
on the human potential for freedom and creativity in the midst of cultural
and political-economic oppression. He aimed at finding and implementing
liberating options in human interaction and transforming the structures of
society through "conscientization." This is a process of cultural action in
which men and women are awakened to their sociocultural reality, move
beyond the alienations and constraints to which they may have become
accustomed, and affirm themselves as conscious subjects and co-creators of
their future. Conscientization implies a critical insertion into history—an
awareness not only of our place, passively, but of our role, actively, in
determining history. Because of his emphasis on the transformation flowing
from conscientization, Paulo Freire became a leading influence on philosophy and radical pedagogy. This kind of compassion is a spirituality of meat,
not milk; of adults, not children; of love, not masochism; of justice, not
philanthropy. It requires maturity, a big heart, a willingness to risk, and
imagination.

Weeping Tears through a Thousand Human Eyes

The visionary yet eminently practical spirituality of liberation theology
makes it an example of a spirituality akin to the theory of Positive Disintegration that takes us into a broader ecosystemic view of human development.

TPD is not mere narcissistic personalism (self-development solely for
one's own sake), but a movement into self with sufficient depth that the more
the true and full self is found, the more the self in the context of interrelated-

ness is found. This is paradox again: really finding oneself means finding other people and our earth in relationship. I am I only in relationships. Sometimes this relationship is one of need, as in the poor and oppressed who have neither bread nor power, as liberation theology has brought out. Sometimes the need is with those who have the material but are empty of the spiritual—the people of the First World. In both circumstances the call is for compassion, not mere sentiment, pity, philanthropy, or charity, but compassion in all its richness, which is equivalent to solidarity with other humans, other living things, and with our planet. The ecosystemic understanding on which TPD can be based leads ultimately to founded hope. It calls for the development of a full human person, and this means a person with a full spirituality. This spirituality is in turn developmental; it rises through levels. The primary, self-centered levels are initial movements or stages of spiritual searching, a cry for meaning so silent that the crier does not hear it. It may come out in a variety of forms, all of which are primitive, and which compassion moves beyond toward a higher level of dialectical living that is resonant with pain; and not just one's own pain, but the pain of others. At its most profound level, TPD flows into a healing of that pain.

Sometimes the healing is done by taking the pain away, as the medical profession and some therapies attempt to do. This is can be a work of mercy. Frequently, though, the pain cannot be taken away. Sometimes taking the pain away is not possible; sometimes taking the pain away is not desirable. The pain must do its healing, nourishing work. We deprive ourselves and others of possibilities with trite and too prompt "solutions." The disintegration can be positive, Dabrowski says. Making it so is the task not only of psychology, but of spirituality in the partnership their common concerns engender.

One of the less obvious themes of TPD is its power of conscientization. Conscientization in liberation theology leads a person from becoming a passive object of history toward being an active subject. This is resonant with Dabrowski's significant dynamism of Subject-Object in Oneself whereby persons are capable of experiencing not only their own subjectivity, but the subjectivity of others, and can transcend their natural awareness of their own subjective experience to see themselves objectively, in a certain historical context that gives background, meaning, perspective, and direction to their lives. It is a sense of place.

Conscientization also makes life more complicated. It demands resistance to the norms of a dominant society because one is not satisfied with what is, but must strive for what ought to be. This sets one on the road of conflict, of positive maladjustment, incorporating all the authenticity and fine discriminations called for, so that rebellion, now more than mere self-indulgence, is realized in the pursuit of some objective oughts. These are qualities that the lives of people at the advanced Dabrowskian developmental levels illustrate. Individuals whose maladjustment is positive combine a sensitivity to individual cases—the suffering person—with an appreciation of the larger context—the unjust structure by which society actually supports such suffering. This spirituality says that evil must be attacked from both sides: the realm of individual consciences and the area of structures. Most frequently the oppressed need to have the structures lifted off them. Sometimes the oppressors themselves must be liberated from the structures.

"Levels" of Self-Development

We return now to Positive Disintegration to see what is relevant to the moral spirituality we seek. What we look for is not on the surface. It is more like a vein running dark and deep in the depths. Although the theory of Positive Disintegration does not deliberately set itself up as a spiritual psychology, its basic tenets about the positive role of suffering and breakdown and its encouragement to fill the basic human need for meaning and pursue what is higher and better makes it akin to classical spirituality (compare Nixon, 1990, 1994). In constructing his psychological theory, Dabrowski has given a way for us to work out a moral spirituality for our times.

Self-development, often envisioned as a journey, lends itself to topographical interpretations. Developmentalists have a penchant for moving through levels. Like Dante in his *Purgatorio,* the soul wends its way upward through trials and tribulations toward some "higher" state of being. At least implicit in the metaphorical "higher" is the moral "better," but this is not always clear in other theories. If not outrightly condemned, the concepts *ought* and *should* most often lie abandoned in the shadows of Limbo. The field of morality is swampy ground for some developmental psychologists. But out front in TPD and central to its theme of valuation are concepts of *better, ought, should,* and *ideal.*

I would like to present in the following an interpretation (albeit personal) of TPD that I think remains faithful to the theory as such, yet pulls out of it the concepts most relevant to our present themes.

The process of self-actualization, if it is a journey, is an ascent through levels of self-discovery. It starts often from the rather inert base of merely "being myself," accepting myself as I am without exploring what could be. At this lowest level, inklings of what could be better are unheard or turned back to avoid discomfort and disturbance. Although perhaps demanding much of others, this sense of self-satisfaction puts no further demands on me beyond perhaps an urge toward "finding myself" in the most simplistic way.

The initiatory plunge toward self-development often begins with conflict, at first outside oneself with things or other people, but gradually turning inward in the form of ambivalences and doubts about self-worth when self is compared with others. This may find expression in feelings of inferiority toward others. The struggle that ensues is in terms of self-acceptance and, later, self-direction. The predominance of this one-down stage of development is evident in the themes of the popular self-help literature dealing with low self-esteem. The alternative, "pulling my own strings," at its worst materializes as domination; at its best as a healthy assertiveness.

If development goes on, there can be a giant leap from low self-esteem to awareness of the idea of "my best self"—a sense of ideal. Feelings of inferiority toward others mature into feelings of inferiority toward *oneself:* feeling oneself inferior to what one ought to be. With this comes a sense of valuing, creating a consciously chosen hierarchy of values. This attraction to an idealized self, to be authentic, must be accompanied by a commitment to the realization of the best self and willingness to work at it. Usually this is accompanied by a committed sense of obligation, which is not burdensome because it matches one's values—the actualization of highest values based on the criteria for what is ideal. The criteria are not only personal, but social and environmental. If we dwell in a web of interconnectedness, and spirituality leads to compassion or even *is* compassion, then the ultimate goal of development it envisions is not mere self-actualization, but an active concern and care for others and for our earth.

This is a task of literally universal proportions. It entails not merely survival of the individual; not only survival of my community; not only survival of mankind. Survival of the universe is a human, cosmic, ethical, ultimate concern as it is God's. These "ultimates" seem to me to be eminently worthy of our concern. These are the real moral proportions of that religious word *salvation*.

I conclude this book with a figure of levels of spirituality (Figure 14.1). It illustrates that there is no one monolithic thing called spirituality that, like knights of the holy grail, we may all search for and discover so that we might possess it. No two people will take the same route in their journey; no two will realize the same spirituality in their lives. It would be a mistake to say we are all pursuing the same goal by identical routes. To emphasize this I have outlined *spirituality* for what it is: a multileveled concept, rich with complexity but discernible by levels. I am using Dabrowski's criteria for levels of development, weaving in too some of the major motifs of this book. To illustrate the anagogic theme of rising through levels, they go upward from the bottom of the page. Unlike Erikson's stages of development, this is not a description of an ontogenetic process that most can expect to cover a lifetime. Rather, it is a description of possibilities, some of which at the highest levels have been achieved by only a few human beings. For those of us at lower levels the higher challenges us because "higher" in this case is better.

Themes run through the levels of spirituality:

- a sense that, though often unrecognized, spirituality is called forth in all of us;
- this call is a quiet voice often drowned out by a noisy world;
- a search for meaning and purpose in life is central;
- a mature spirituality of moral action is urgently demanded;

Levels of Spirituality

5 Full participation in the "seamless whole" of all that is

Transcends the threat to self-identity that comes from acknowledging oneness with all that is. Oneness with God. Wholeness. Integration, not in the sense of "completed" and "perfect," but still in process.

No compromises or false substitutes. What ought to be actually is. *Is* and *ought* are one.

Whole authenticity. Objective morality because "Objectivity is the fruit of authentic subjectivity."

Peace that surpasses all understanding.

4 A radical, perturbing awareness of one's spirituality

William James's twice-born or sick soul. *Agonia,* that is, pain like that of a runner in a race, accepted as a consequence of striving for moral ideals.

Well aware of the demands made by our spiritual nature.

Perturbed by the injustice and lack of harmony in the world.

Keen sense of sin both individually and socially.

Religion at this level excels in its perspectivistic role in finding meaning.

Values are affirmed and an attempt made to actually live them.

Social consciousness is world consciousness.

True self-actualization in solidarity of self with all that is. Ecosystemic.

Salvation through world consciousness—spirituality is awareness of one's moral role in creation and a "yes" to it.

3 Simple, unperturbed awareness

Sees oneself as spiritual, but in a simplistic, egocentric frame.

Inattention to which questions truly merit ultimate concern.

Questions of meaning, if they arise, are answered by authority.

Child-like, passive virtues are encouraged. Not autonomy.

"Providence" takes care of all without our effort.

Religion is valued primarily for its comforting function.

Little tolerance of ambiguity.

Meditation = "waiting for signs." Prayer is an attempt to manipulate God.

Romantic spirituality. "God is there for me." "Jesus and I."

Social awareness and sensitivity to social justice not strong.

Self-actualization in its narrow, individualistic sense.

The once-born, healthy person described by William James.

2 Superficial awareness of one's spiritual dimensions

But basically egocentric and hedonistic,

"achieved" mechanically by drugs, or

"religious-mystical "turn-ons"—spirituality as a toy

exploited for sensationalism.

Not much different from magic—confusion of spirituality with the occult.

1 Unreflected existence

Spiritual by nature as a human being. A need for meaning, but no active awareness of it.

Relationships are egocentric and exploitative. "I-it" relationships in Buber's terms. ˙

Figure 14.1.

- personal reflection and inwardness open up the possibility of spirituality;
- the soul is drawn to higher levels, though the process may mean pain;
- because all is process, even the highest level described is not static perfection, but continuing process toward wholeness.

There is no one way of being spiritual. Once we see spirituality as multileveled, new possibilities are opened up for the evolution of our own unique spirituality. A personal evolution, because of our interconnectedness, is part of a larger evolution. We all live our own lives, but if we are participant we live something fuller, contributing to that larger story. Men, women, children, products that we are of cosmic evolution, can ourselves progress to higher levels, not without pain, but also not without joy.

In previous chapters we explored the realization that religion, morality, and spirituality can be a personal search for dimensions of the self that one knows to be transcendent, but because they are deep within the person, they are at the same time immanent. It is a matter of living fully in the immediate, but transcending what is restricted for an appreciation of the larger picture of one's own life toward the "more beyond." It is, then, a cosmic vision, the proportions and beauties of which are limited only by the vision of the beholder.

It is a paradox and mystery that when we find the transcendent written across the cosmos in all its awesomeness and glory we find it is immanent—within us—written on our hearts. It is an epiphany of oneness with the seamless whole of all that is.

Reprise

Apart from the religious vision, human life is a flash of occasional enjoyments, lighting up a mass of pain and misery, a bagatelle of transient experience.
        —*A.N. Whitehead* (Science and the Modern World)

This quotation may seem like a negative note on which to end a book on spiritual development. But we are used by now, when coming to something important, to find it a paradox. For here Whitehead has picked up a thread that we have found running through both religious and moral development. Religion is what one does with one's solitariness. We have seen that our time in the process of an evolving world calls us to participate consciously in forwarding that process.

Religion is that solitary quest for meaning that we share as best we can with those around us and ultimately with our God. When this solitary quest becomes a quest for moral beauty, one is struck by the transitoriness of it all. Everything we know in this world is an occasion that is born, flourishes, and then must perish. Every moral motivation, every high moral principle that we come to must, if we are dealing with true ultimates, come under the scrutiny of that ultimate moral question: Why be moral? Why try to live a life of moral caring when few of the people around seem to care in their day-to-day life and yet appear to enjoy an undisturbed existence? Why try to contribute to the building of a world that seems to be bent on its own destruction, which we must taste now and then in the catastrophes that nature herself produces, and that mankind now has the power to produce? Why try to communicate with a God who never answers as we would like him to do? How can you love a life that makes burdensome moral demands on you without offering the consolation of telling you the world is moral and just. Where is the order and sense, if any, and where do I fit in?

Life becomes fulfilled in creative work, human love, suffering, and social reconstruction, as one realizes that life itself was never promised as a purely rational process; birth, life, and death are processes beyond reason. Salvation, in the sense we have used it here—its root meaning of health, wholeness—comes only if we step back from life and see it as a whole. The full experience and acceptance of life, which usually involves the postulation of a supernatural other—God—can be had only if we see this life whole. To see life whole is to love and accept life because it is to see ourselves as necessarily part of it. It is a matter of getting perspective on life, and that is the function of religion. Whitehead's shift from *goodness* to *beauty* is a new perspective discovering morality in the harmony, unity, and proportion of beauty. It is religious in its dimensions, and happiness is its by-product. This experience of happiness is not destroyed, but enhanced by the awareness of the transitoriness of it all. The beauty of art, and above all the beauty of nature, is the beauty, like religion, of one eternal system in itself, not merely one view or another of it. Beauty as a function of religious awe puts things into perspective.

I once sat with a friend watching the sun set over a lake. The sun had not yet turned a radiant red, but the white path of light between us and the sun made the restless water sparkle. My friend remarked, "The water is sparkling like diamonds." Why then was the lake not as "valuable" as a field of diamonds? If it sparkled like diamonds, why did it not have their value? We knew we could not rush out and collect the "diamonds"; we would find only glistening water slipping through our fingers. The water had taken on a transitory beauty; but diamonds, we are promised, "are forever," and that is why they are coveted. It is, then, the permanence, or at least the promise of permanence, that makes diamonds "valuable." But even diamonds are not really forever. Like our lives, they are occasions in the process, and the task of the person in the religious search for value and goodness and what is truly worthy of our quest is to cherish now the beauty of the brief, dancing light on the shifting water in the vast perspective on the whole scene that is the gift of religion experienced.

> *We shall not cease from exploration*
> *And the end of all our exploring*
> *Will be to arrive where we started*
> *And know the place for the first time.*
>
> —*T.S. Eliot*

References

Adorno, T.W., Frenkel-Brunswik, E., Levinson, D.J., & Sanford, R.N. (1950). *The authoritarian personality*. New York: Harper & Row.

Allport, G.W. (1955). *Becoming; basic considerations for a psychology of personality*. New Haven, CT: Yale University Press.

Allport, G.W. (1958). *The nature of prejudice*. Garden City, NY: Doubleday Anchor.

Allport, G.W. (1960). *The individual and his religion*. New York: Macmillan.

Allport, G.W. (1961). *Pattern and growth in personality*. New York: Holt, Rinehart & Winston.

Anderson, S.R., & Hopkins, P. (1992). *The feminine face of God: The unfolding of the sacred in women*. New York: Bantam Books.

Arbuthnot, J.B., & Braeden, J. (1981). *Teaching moral reasoning: Theory and practice*. New York: Harper & Row.

Argyle, M., & Beit-Hallahmi, B. (1975). *The social psychology of religion*. Boston: Routledge & Kegan Paul.

Armstrong, K. (1993). *A history of God*. New York: Knopf.

Asch, S.E. (1958). Effects of group pressure upon modifications and distortions of judgment. In E. Maccoby, T. Newcomb, & E. Hartley, (Eds.), *Readings in social psychology (3rd ed.)*. New York: Holt, Rinehart & Winston.

Bandura, A., & Walters, R.H. (1963). *Social learning and personality development*. New York: Holt, Rinehart & Winston.

Barlow, C. (1994). *Evolution extended: Biological debates on the meaning of life*. Cambridge MA: MIT Press.

Batson, C.D., Schoenade, P., & Ventis, W.L. (1993).*Religion and the individual*. New York: Oxford University Press.

Berger, P. (1970). *A rumor of angels*. Garden City, NY: Doubleday.

Berry, T. (1990). *The dream of the earth*. San Francisco, CA: Sierra Club.

Bettelheim, B. (1960). *The informed heart*. Glencoe IL: Free Press.

Birch, C. (1991). Chance, purpose and the order of nature. in C. Birch, W. Eakin, & J. McDaniel, *Liberating life: Contemporary approaches to ecological theology*. Maryknoll, NY: Orbis.

Borofsky, G. (1981). A brief overview of the theory of positive disintegration. In N.J. Duda (Ed.), *Theory of positive distintegration: Proceedings of the Third International Conference*. Miami, FL: Xerox.

Brennan, T.P., & Piechowski, M.M. (1991). A developmental framework for self actualization: Evidence from case studies. *Journal of Humanistic Psychology, 31*(3), 43-64.

Broccolo, G. (1990). *Vital spiritualities*. Notre Dame, IN: Ave Maria Press.

Briggs, J., & Peat, F. (1990). *Turbulent mirror*. New York: Harper & Row.

Campbell, J. (1968). *The hero with a thousand faces*. Princeton, NJ: Princeton University Press.

Campbell, J. (1988). *The inner reaches of outer space*. New York: Harper & Row.

Capra, F. (1975). *The Tao of physics*. Berkeley: Shambhala.

Capra, F., & Stendl-Rast, D. (1992). *Belonging to the Universe: Explorations on the frontiers of science and spirituality*. New York: Harper Collins.

Chazan, B., & Soltis, J. (Eds.). (1973). *Moral education*. New York: Teachers College Press.

Clausen, J.A. (Ed.). (1968). *Socialization and society*. Boston: Little, Brown.

Cousins, E.W. (Ed.). ( ). *Process theology*. New York: Newman.

Csikszentmihalyi, M. (1994). *The evolving self: A psychology for the third millenium*. New York: Harper-Perennial.

Cushman, P. (1990). Why the self is empty. *American Psychologist, 45*(5), 599-611.

Dabrowski, J. (1993). *Ontologic joy*. Unpublished doctoral dissertation, University of Alberta.

Dabrowski, K. (1964). *Positive disintegration*. Boston: Little, Brown.

Dabrowski, K. (1966). The theory of positive disintegration. *International Journal of Psychiatry, 2*, 275-482.

Dabrowski, K. (1967). *Personality-shaping through positive disintegration*. London: Grey.

Dabrowski, K. (1970). *Mental growth through positive disintegration*. London: Gryf.

Dabrowski, K. (1972). *Psychoneurosis is not an illness*. London: Gryf.

Dabrowski, K. (1973). *The dynamics of concepts*. London: Gryf.

Dabrowski, K., & Piechowski, M. (1977). *Theory of levels of emotional development* (2 vols.). Oceanside, NY: Dabor.

Dabrowski, K., Kawczak, A., & Piechowski, M. (1970). *Mental growth through positive disintegration*. London: Gryf.

Delisle, T.J. (1976). *Psycho-historical interpretations of sexuality within the Christian tradition*. Unpublished doctoral dissertation, University of Alberta.

Dewey, J. (1909). *Moral principles in education*. Boston: Houghton Mifflin.

Douziech, R. (1981). *Guilt as a moral sentiment*. Unpublished doctoral dissertation, University of Alberta.

Droege, T. (1972). A developmental view of faith. *Journal of Religion and Health, 11*(4), 313-328.

Duda, N.J. (Ed.). (1981). *Theory of positive disintegration: Proceedings of the Third International Conference*. Miami: Xerox.

Durkheim, E. (1915). *The elementary forms of religious life*. London: Allen and Unwin.

Eisler, R.T. (1987). *The chalice and the blade: Our history, our future*. Cambridge, MA: Harper and Row.

Eliot, G. (1986). *Middlemarch*. Oxford: Clarendon Press.

Eliot, T.S. (1958). *Collected poems 1909-1935*. London: Faber & Faber.

Erikson, E.H. (1959). *Young man Luther*. London: Faber & Faber.

Erikson, E.H. (1963). *Childhood and society*. New York: Norton.

Erikson, E.H. (1964). *Insight and responsibility*. New York: Norton.

Evans, R. (1967). *Dialogue with Erik Erikson*. New York: Dutton.

Ewen, R. (1980). *An introduction to theories of personality*. London: Academic Press.

Festinger, L. (1957). *A theory of cognitive dissonance*. Stanford, CA: Stanford University Press.

Festinger, L., Riecken, H.W., & Schacter, S. (1956). *When prophecy fails*. Minneapolis, MN: University of Minnesota Press.

Fischer, K. (1980). Religious experience in Lonergan and Whitehead. *Religious Studies, 16*, 69-79.

Flugel, J.C. (1945). *Man, morals, and society*. London: Duckworth.

Fowler, J. (1979). *Life maps*. Waco, TX: Word Books.

Fowler, J. (1981). *Stages of faith: The psychology of human development and the quest for meaning*. San Francisco, CA: Harper & Row.

Fowler, J. (1984). *Becoming adult, becoming Christian*. San Francisco, CA: Harper & Row.

Fowler, J. (1986). Faith and the structuring of meaning. In C. Dykstra & S. Parks (Eds.), *Faith development and Fowler*. Birmingham, AL: Religious Education Press.

Fox, M. (1990). *A spirituality named compassion*. San Francisco, CA: Harper & Row.

Frankena, W.K. (1973). Is morality logically dependent on religion? In G. Outka & J. Reeder (Eds.), *Religion and morality*. New York: Doubleday.

Frankl, V. (1959). *Man's search for meaning: An introduction to logotherapy*. New York: Simon & Schuster.

Frankl, V. (1965). *The doctor and the soul: From psychotherapy to logotherapy*. New York: Knopf.

Frankl, V. (1967). *Psychotherapy and existentialism: Selected papers on logotherapy*. New York: Simon & Schuster.

Frankl, V. (1969). *The will to meaning: Foundations and applications of logotherapy*. New York: World Publishing.

Frankl, V. (1978). *The unheard cry for meaning*. New York: Simon & Schuster.

Frazer, J. (1911). *The golden bough*. London: Macmillan.

Freire, P. (1988). *Pedagogy of the oppressed* (M. Bergman Ramos, Trans.). New York: Continuum.

Freud, S. (1928). *The future of an illusion*. London: Hogarth Press.

Freud, S. (1950). *Totem and taboo*. New York: Norton.

Freud, S. (1952a). Civilization and its discontents. In *The major works of Sigmund Freud, Great books of the Western World, 54*. Chicago, IL: Encyclopedia Britannica.

Freud, S. (1952b). New introductory lectures on psychoanalysis. In *The major works of Sigmund Freud, Great books of the Western World, 54*. Chicago: Encyclopedia Britannica.

Fromm, E. (1956). *Art of loving*. New York: Harper.

Gilligan, C. (1982). *In a different voice*. Cambridge, MA: Harvard University Press.

Gilligan, C., Ward, J., & Taylor, J. (Eds.). (1988). *Mapping the moral domain*. Cambridge, MA: Harvard University Press.

Gleick, J. (1988). *Chaos: making a new science*. New York: Penguin Books.

Glock, C.Y. (1964). The role of deprivation in the origin and evolution of religious groups. In R. Lee & M. Marty (Eds.), *Religion and social context*. New York: Oxford University Press.

Glock, C.Y., & Stark, R. (1965). *Religion and society in tension*. Chicago: Rand McNally.

Goode, E. (1966). Social class and church participation. *American Journal of Sociology, 72*, 102-111.

Gordis, R. (1974). *The Song of Songs and Lamentations: Study, modern translation, and commentary*. New York: KTAV.

Gould, S. (1989). *Wonderful life: The Burgess shale and the nature of history*. New York: Norton.

Gow, K. (1980). *Yes, Virginia, there is right and wrong*. Toronto, ON: Wiley.

Groome, T. (1980). *Christian religious education*. New York: Harper.

Gruba-McAllister, F., & Levington, C. (1994). Authenticity as open existence. *Advanced Deelopment, 6*, 1-10.

Gutierrez, G. (1973). *A theology of liberation*. Maryknoll, NY: Orbis.

Gutierrez, G. (1985). *We drink from our own wells*. Maryknoll, NY: Orbis.

Gutierrez, G. (1987). *On Job: God talk and the suffering of the innocent*. Maryknoll, NY: Orbis.

Hague, R. (1978). *Meaning in life and religious commitment of Catholic high school students*. Unpublished master's thesis, University of Alberta.

Hague, W.J. (1976). Positive disintegration and moral education. *Journal of Moral Education, 5*, 231-240.

Hague, W.J. (1986). *New perspectives on religious and moral development*. Edmonton, AB: Publication Services, University of Alberta.

Hague, W.J. (1988a). Moral objectivity: Toward a new understanding of intuition. In W.L. Baker, Mos, & H. Stam (Eds.), *Recent trends in theoretical psychology*. New York: Springer-Verlag.

Hague, W.J. (1988b). Toward a holistic psychology of valuing. *Counseling and Values, 33*, 32-46.

Hague, W.J. (1989). "State of the art" moral development: Moral development in the post-Kohlbergian age. *Advanced Development, 1*, 15-26.

Hague, W.J. (1990a). Attaining objective values through development of higher level dynamisms. In B. Holyst (Ed.), *Mental healh in a changing world* (pp. 112-125). Warsaw: Polish Society of Mental Health.

Hague, W.J. (1990b). Shared values for shared life meaning—The transcendent dimensions of the global village. In B. Holyst (Ed.), *Mental healh in a changing world* (pp. 27-38). Warsaw: Polish Society of Mental Health.

Hague, W.J. (1991). Kohlberg's legacy—More than ideas. *Alberta Journal of Educational Research, XXXVII*, 277-294.

Hague, W.J. (1993a). Teaching values in Canadian schools. In L. Stewin & S. McCann (Eds.), *Contemporary issues in education: A Canadian mosaic* (2nd ed., pp. 241-251). Toronto, ON: Longman.

Hague, W.J. (1993b). The power to give life: Religious and moral growth through chaos. *Panorama: International Journal of Comparative Religious Education and Values, 5*(2), 96-130.

Hague, W.J. (1993c). Toward a systemic explanation of valuing. *Counseling and Values, 38*, 29-41.

Hague, W.J. (1994). Authentic morality: The route to high moral ground. *Advanced Development, 6*, 11-26.

Hall, C., & Lindzey, G. (1954). Psychoanalytic theory and its applications in the social sciences. In G. Lindzey (Ed.), *Handbook of social psychology*. Cambridge, MA: Addison-Wesley.

Hall, R. (1979). *Moral education, A handbook for teachers*. Minneapolis, MN: Winston Press.

Hammarskjöld, D. (1964). *Markings*. London: Faber & Faber.

Hartshorne, H., & May, M.A. (1928/30). *Studies in the nature of character, Vol. 1: Studies in deceit; Vol. 2: Studies in service and self-control; Vol. 3, Studies in organization of character*. New York: Macmillan.

Hauerwas, S. (1981). *A community of character*. Notre Dame, IN: University of Notre Dame Press.

Hauerwas, S. (1985). *Character and the Christian life*. San Antonio, TX: Trinity University Press.

Hawking, S. (1988). *A brief history of time*. New York: Bantam.

Heidegger, M. (1962). *Being and time*. New York: Harper & Row.

Horney, K. (1950). *Neurosis and human growth*. London: Routledge & Kegan Paul.

Hume, D. (1978). *A treatise of human nature. Book III, Part I, Sec. I*. Oxford: Clarendon Press.

Jacobi, J. (1970). *C.G. Jung: psychological reflections; A new anthology of his writings*. Princeton, NJ: Princeton University Press.

James, W. (1958). *Varieties of religious experience*. New York: New American Library.

Janz, G. (1983). *Life, death and religious attitudes: An existential perspective*. Unpublished master's thesis, University of Alberta.

Jaspers, K. (1962). *Socrates, Buddha, Confucius, Jesus*. New York: Harcourt Brace.

Jaynes, J. (1976). *The origin of consciousness in the breakdown of the bicameral mind*. Boston, MA: Houghton Mifflin.

Johnston, D.K. (1988). Adolescents' solutions to dilemmas in fables: Two moral orientations, two problem-solving strategies. In C. Gilligan, J. Ward, & J. Taylor (Eds.), *Mapping the moral domain*. Cambridge, MA: Harvard University Press.

Jung, C.G. (1928). *Man and his symbols*. London: Aldus Books.

Jung, C.G. (1938). *Psychology and religion*. New Haven, CT: Yale University Press.

Jung, C.G. (1966). *The practice of psychotherapy*. London: Routledge & Kegan Paul.

Kaplan, P. (1991). *A child's odyssey*. St. Paul, MN: West.

Kavelin-Popov, L., Popov, D., & Kavelin, J. (1983). *Virtues guide*. Ganges, BC: Wellspring.

Kawczak, A. (1970). The methodological structure of the theory of positive disintegration. In K. Dabrowski, A. Kawczak, & M.M. Piechowski, *Mental growth through positive disintegration*. London: Gryf.

Kilpatrick, W. (1986). Moral character, story-telling and virtue. In R. Knowles & G. McLean (Eds.), *Psychological foundations of moral education and character development*. New York: University Press of America.

Kluckhohn, C. (1951). Values and value orientations in the theory of action. In T. Parsons & E. Shils (Eds.), *Toward a general theory of action*. Cambridge, MA: Harvard University Press.

Kohlberg, L. (1968). Moral development. *Encyclopedia of the Social Sciences, 10* (pp. 483-494). New York: Macmillan.

Kohlberg, L. (1974). Education, moral development and faith. *Journal of Moral Education, 4*, 5-16.

Kohlberg, L. (1977). The implications of moral stages for adult education. *Religious Education*, 183-201.

Kohlberg, L. (1981). *Philosophy of moral development*. San Francisco, CA: Harper & Row.

Kohlberg, L., & Candee, D. (1984). The relationship of moral judgment to moral action. In W. Kurtines & J. Gewirtz (Eds.), *Morality, moral behavior and moral development*. New York: Wiley.

Kupchenko, I.M. (1981). *The development of a values materials analysis system*. Unpublished master's thesis, University of Alberta.

Kuhmerker, L. (1991). *The Kohlberg legacy for the helping professions*. Birmingham, AL: Religious Education Press.

Kurtines, W., & Grief, E. (1974). The development of moral thought: Review and evaluation of Kohlberg's approach. *Psychological Bulletin, 18,* 453-470.

Kurtz, E., & K. Ketcham (1994). *The spirituality of imperfection.* New York: Bantam.

Kushner, H. (1981). *When bad things happen to good people.* New York: Schocken.

Langer, S. (1951). *Philosophy in a new key.* New York: New American Library.

Laurence, M. (1966). *A jest of God.* Toronto: McClelland & Stewart.

Lerner, M. (1980). *The belief in a just world.* New York: Plenum.

Lickona, T. (1985). *Raising good children.* New York: Bantam

Lickona, T. (1991). *Educating for character.* New York: Herder & Herder.

Lonergan, B.J. (1974). *A second collection.* Philadelphia, PA: Westminster.

Lonergan, B.J. (1978). *Insight, a study of human understanding.* New York: Harper & Row.

Lysy, K.Z., & Piechowski, M.M. (1983). Personal growth: An empirical study using Jungian and Dabrowskian measures. *Genetic Psychology Monographs, 108,* 267-320.

Maccoby, E.E. (1968). The development of moral values and behaviors in childhood. In J. Clausen (Ed.), *Socialization and society.* Boston: Little, Brown.

MacIntyre, A. (1984). *After virtue.* Notre Dame, IN: University of Notre Dame Press.

MacIntyre, A. (1988). *Whose justice? Which rationality?* Notre Dame, IN: University of Notre Dame Press.

Marsh, C., & Colangelo, N. (1983). The application of Dabrowski's concept of multilevelness to Allport's concept of unity. *Counseling and Values, 27*(4), 213-228.

Maslow, A.H. (1954). *Motivation and personality.* New York: Harper.

Maslow, A.H. (Ed.). (1959). *New knowledge in human values.* New York: Harper & Brothers.

Maslow, A.H. (1962). *Toward a psychology of being.* Princeton, NJ: Van Nostrand.

Maslow, A.H. (1966). *The psychology of science.* New York: Harper & Row.

Maslow, A.H. (1967). A theory of metamotivation: The biological rooting of the value life. *Journal of Humanistic Psychology, 7,* 93-127.

Maslow, A.H. (1971). *The farther reaches of human nature.* New York: Viking.

Maslow, A.H. (1973). Self-actualizing people: A study of psychological health. In R.L. Lowry (Ed.), *Dominance, self-esteem, self-actualization: Germinal papers of A.H. Maslow.* Monterey, CA: Brookes/Cole.

Maslow, A.H. (1977). *Religion, values and peak experiences.* New York: Penguin.

Maturana, H. (1978). Biology of language: The epistemology of reality. In G. Miller (Ed.), *Psychology and biology of language and thought.* New York, Academic Press.

May, R. (1953). *Man's search for himself.* New York: New American Library.

May, R. (1991). *The cry for myth.* New York: Norton.

McFague, S. (1982). *Metaphorical theology: Models of God in religious language.* Philadelphia, PA: Fortress Press.

McFague, S. (1987). *Models of God: Theology for an ecological, nuclear age.* Philadelphia: Fortress Press.

McPhail, P. (1972). *In other people's shoes: Teacher's guide.* London: Longman.

McPhail, P. (1982). *Social and moral education.* Oxford, UK: Basil Blackwell.

McPhail, P., Middleton, D., & Ingram, D. (1978). *Startline: Moral education in the middle years.* London: Longman.

McPhail, P., Ungoed-Thomas, J., & Chapman, H. (1972). *Lifeline: Moral education in the secondary school.* London: Longman.

Meilander, G. (1984). *The theory and practice of virtue.* Notre Dame, IN: University of Notre Dame Press.

Michener, J.A. (1966). *The source.* New York: Fawcett Crest.

Miller, N.B., & Silverman, L.K. (1987). Levels of personality development. *Roeper Review, 9*(4), 221-225.

Montgomery, L.M. (1968). *Anne of Green Gables.* Toronto: McGraw-Hill Ryerson.

Montgomery, L.M. (1968). *Anne of the Island.* Toronto: McGraw-Hill Ryerson.

Moore, M.E.M. (1991). *Teaching from the heart: Theology and educational method.* Minneapolis, MN: Fortress Press.

Moore, T. (1992). *Care of the soul: A guide for cultivating depth and sacredness in everyday life.* New York: Harper Collins.

Nelson, K.C. (1989). Dabrowski's theory of positive disintegration. *Advanced Development, 1,* 1-14.

Nixon, L. (1990). *The mystical struggle: A psychological analysis.* Unpublished doctoral dissertation, Concordia University.

Nixon, L. (1994).Multilevel disintegration in the lives of religious mystics. *Advanced Development, 6,* 57-74.

Noddings, N. (1984). *Caring: A feminine approach to ethics and moral education.* Berkeley, CA: University of California Press.

Noddings, N. (1989).*Women and evil.* Berkeley, CA: University of California Press.

Noddings, N. (1993). *Educating for intelligent belief or unbelief.* New York: Teachers' College Press.

Osbon, D. (Ed.). (1991). *A Joseph Campbell companion.* New York: Norton.

Ostow, M., & Sharfstein, B. (1954). *The need to believe.* New York: International Universities Press.

Outka, G., & Reeder, J. (Eds.). (1973). *Religion and morality.* New York: Anchor.

Pearce, J. (1992). *Evolution's end.* San Francisco, CA: Harper.

Peters, R.S. (1969). *Ethics and education.* London: Allen and Unwin.

Peters, R.S. (1974). *Psychology and ethical development.* London: Allen and Unwin.

Piaget, J. (1932). *The construction of reality in the child.* New York: Basic Books.

Piaget, J. (1967). *Language and thought of the child.* New York: Meridian Books.

Pickover, C. (1990). *Computers, pattern, chaos and beauty.* New York: St. Martin's Press.

Piechowski, M. (1975). A theoretical and empirical approach to the study of development. *Genetic Psychology Monographs, 92,* 231-297. Provincetown, MA: Journal Press.

Piechowski, M. (1977). In K. Dabrowski & M. Piechowski (Eds.), *Theory of levels of emotional development.* Oceanside, NY: Dabor.

Piechowski, M.M. (1978). Self-Actualization as a developmental structure: A profile of Antoine de Saint-Exupéry. *Genetic Psychology Monographs, 97,* 181-242.

Piechowski, M. (1982, October). *Inner growth and transformation in the life of Eleanor Roosevelt.* Paper presented at the Eleanor Roosevelt Centennial Conference, Vassar College, Poughkeepsie, NY.

Piechowski, M.M. (1990). The heart of Leta S. Hollingworth. *Roeper Review,* 12.

Piechowski, M.M. (1991, May). *Giftedness for all seasons: Inner peace in time of war.* Paper presented at Henry B. and Jocelyn Wallace National Research Symposium on Talent Development, University of Iowa, Iowa City.

Piechowski, M.M., & Tyska, C. (1982). Self-actualization profile of Eleanor Roosevelt, a presumed nontranscender. *Genetic Psychology Monographs, 105,* 95-153.

Pirsig, R. (1991). *Lila: An inquiry into morals.* New York: Bantam.

Pittenger, W.N. (1981). *Catholic faith in a process perspective.* Maryknoll, NY: Orbis.

Price, L. (1954). *Dialogues of Alfred North Whitehead.* Boston, MA: Little, Brown.

Prigogine, L., & Stengers, I. (1984). *Order out of nature: Man's new dialogue with nature.* New York: Bantam Books.

Raths, L., Harmin, M., & Simon, S. (1966). *Values and teaching.* Columbus, OH: Merrill.

Reik, T. (1951). *Dogma and compulsion.* New York: International Universities Press.

Rieff, P. (1979). *Freud: The mind of the moralist.* Chicago, IL: University of Chicago Press.

Roberts, C. (1981). *Language and the emergence of self.* Unpublished doctoral dissertation, University of Alberta.

Rokeach, M. (1960). *The open and closed mind.* New York: Basic Books.

Rokeach, M. (1969). Value systems in religion. *Review of Religious Research, 11,* 3-23.

Ryan, K., & McLean, G. (1987). (Eds.). *Character development in schools and beyond.* New York: Praeger.

de Saint-Exupéry, A. (1946). *The little prince.* Paris: Librairie Gallimard.

Sartre, J.-P. (1965). Questions about the meaning of life. *Religious Studies, 1,* 125-140.

Scheler, M. (1927). *Der formalismus in der Ethik und die Material wertethik* (3rd ed.). Halle: Niemeyer.

Schipani, D. (1988). *Religious education encounters liberation theology.* Birmingham, AL: Religious Education Press.

Simon, S., Howe, L., & Kirschenbaum, H. (1972). *Values clarification.* New York: Hart.

Smith, B. (1988). *Contingencies of value.* Cambridge MA: Harvard University Press.

Solomon, R. (1977). *The passions.* Garden City, NY: Doubleday.

Spinks, S. (1963). *Psychology and religion.* London: Methuen.

Spiro, M.E., & D'Andrade, R.G. (1958). A crosscultural study of some supernatural beliefs. *American Anthropologist, 60,* 456-66.

Stewart, I. (1990). *Does God play dice? The new mathematics of chaos.* New York: Penguin.

Stewart, I., & Golubitsky, M. (1993). *Fearful symmetry.* New York: Penguin.

Stewart, W.A. (1981). *Introduction to philosophy, or Lonergan for beginners.* Halifax, NS: St. Mary's University.

Swimme, B. (1988). The cosmic creation story. In D. Griffin (Ed.), *The reenchantment of science.* New York: SUNY Press.

Swimme, B., & Berry, T. (1992). *The universe story.* San Francisco, CA: Harper.

Taylor, C. (1988). The moral topography of the self. In B. Messer, A. Sass, & R. Woolfolk (Eds.), *Hermeneutics and psychological theory.* New Brunswick, NJ: Rutgers University Press.

Taylor, C. (1989). *Sources of the self: The making of the modern identity.* Cambridge, MA: Harvard University Press.

Taylor, C. (1991). *The malaise of modernity.* Concord ON: Anansi Press.

Teilhard de Chardin, P. (1969a). *Building the earth, and the psychological conditions of human unification.* New York: Avon.

Teilhard de Chardin, P. (1969b). *How I believe.* New York: Harper & Row.

Teilhard de Chardin, P. (1973). *Man's place in nature.* New York: Harper & Row.

Tennessen, H. (1966). Happiness is for the pigs. Philosophy versus psychotherapy. *Journal of Existentialism, 7,* 181-214.

Thompson, F. (1922). *Hound of heaven.* New York: Dodd, Mead.

Tillich, P. (1958). *Dynamics of faith.* New York: Harper & Row.

Tillich, P. (1967). *The courage to be.* London: Fontana.

Tillich, P. (1974). *Morality and beyond.* London: Fontana.

Tolkien, J.R.R. (1975). *Tree and leaf.* London: Unwin.

Tyler, A. (1985). *The accidental tourist.* New York: Knopf.

Underhill, E. (1961). *Mysticism.* New York: Dutton.

Von Franz, M-L. (1978). Process of individuation. In C. Jung, M.-L. Von Franz, J.L. Henderson, J. Jacobi, & A. Jaffe (Eds.), *Man and his symbols.* New York: Dell.

Weckowicz, T.E. (1988). Kazimierz Dabrowski's theory of positive disintegration and the American humanistic psychology. *Counseling and Values, 32,* 124-134.

Weisinger, H. (1953). *Tragedy and the paradox of the fortunate fall.* Lansing, MI: Michigan State College Press.

Werner, H. (1948). *Comparative psychology of mental development.* New York: International Universities Press.

Werner, H., & Kaplan, B. (1963). *Symbol formation.* New York: Wiley.

Whitehead, A.N. (1925). *Science and the modern world.* Cambridge, MA: Cambridge University Press.

Whitehead, A.N. (1938). *Modes of thought.* Cambridge, MA: Cambridge University Press.

Whitehead, A.N. (1950). *Aims of education and other essays.* London: Benn.

Whitehead, A.N. (1955). *The concept of nature.* Cambridge, MA: Cambridge University Press.

Whitehead, A.N. (1967). *Adventures of ideas.* New York: Free Press.

Whitehead, A.N. (1973). *Religion in the making.* New York: Meridan.

Wilber, K. (1993). *Grace and grit.* Boston, MA: Shambhala.

Yalom, I.D. (1980). *Existential therapy.* New York: Basic Books.

Zukav, G. (1980). *The dancing Wu-Li masters.* New York: Bantam.

Index